Church and State in Scotland

The interaction of faith and the community is a fundamental of modern society. The first country to adopt Presbyterianism in its national church, Scotland adopted a system of church government, which is now in world-wide use. This book examines the development and current state of Scots law. Drawing on previous material as well as discussing current topical issues, this book makes some comparisons between Scotland and other legal and religious jurisdictions.

The study first considers the Church of Scotland, its 'Disruption' and statutorily recognised reconstitution and then the position of other denominations before assessing the interaction of religion and law and the impact of Human Rights and various discrimination laws within this distinctive Presbyterian country.

This unique book will be of interest to both students and lecturers in constitutional and civil law, as well as historians and ecclesiastics.

Francis Lyall, now Emeritus Professor of Public Law at the University of Aberdeen, was involved in the Church of Scotland, as a church elder, a member of the Presbytery of Aberdeen, several times a commissioner to the General Assembly of the Church of Scotland, and as a three-term member of its Panel on Doctrine. He was a member of the Evangelical Alliance Commission on Faith and Nation (published 2006). In 1993 he held, as Visiting Professor, the Willem E Oncelin Chair of Canon Law in the Faculty of Canon Law, of the University of Leuven (Louvain). He has published many religion-relevant books and articles.

ICLARS Series on Law and Religion
Series Editors: Silvio Ferrari
University of Milan, Italy, Russell Sandberg, Cardiff University, UK
Pieter Coertzen
University of Stellenbosch, South Africa
and
W. Cole Durham, Jr.
*Brigham Young University, USA, and Tahir Mahmood,
Amity International University, India*

The *ICLARS Series on Law and Religion* is a new series designed to provide a forum for the rapidly expanding field of research in law and religion. The series is published in association with the International Consortium for Law and Religion Studies, an international network of scholars and experts of law and religion founded in 2007 with the aim of providing a place where information, data and opinions can easily be exchanged among members and made available to the broader scientific community. The series aims to become a primary source for students and scholars while presenting authors with a valuable means to reach a wide and growing readership.

Other titles in this series:

Religion and Equality
*Edited by W. Cole Durham, Jr. and Donlu Thayer,
Brigham Young University, USA*

Religion as Empowerment
*Edited by Kyriaki Topidi and Lauren Fielder,
both at University of Lucerne, Switzerland*

Church and State in Scotland
Developing law

Francis Lyall

LONDON AND NEW YORK

First published 2016
by Routledge
2 Park Square, Milton Park, Abingdon, Oxon OX14 4RN

and by Routledge
711 Third Avenue, New York, NY 10017

Routledge is an imprint of the Taylor & Francis Group, an informa business

© 2016 Francis Lyall

The right of Francis Lyall to be identified as author of this work has been asserted by him in accordance with sections 77 and 78 of the Copyright, Designs and Patents Act 1988.

All rights reserved. No part of this book may be reprinted or reproduced or utilised in any form or by any electronic, mechanical, or other means, now known or hereafter invented, including photocopying and recording, or in any information storage or retrieval system, without permission in writing from the publishers.

Trademark notice: Product or corporate names may be trademarks or registered trademarks, and are used only for identification and explanation without intent to infringe.

British Library Cataloguing in Publication Data
A catalogue record for this book is available from the British Library

Library of Congress Cataloging in Publication Data
Lyall, Francis, author.
  Church and state in Scotland : developing law / by Francis Lyall.
    pages cm. – (ICLARS series on law and religion)
  Includes bibliographical references and index.
 ISBN 978-1-4094-5064-1 (hardback) – ISBN 978-1-4094-5065-8 (ebook) – ISBN 978-1-4724-0661-3 (epub) 1. Church and state–Scotland.
2. Church of Scotland. I. Title.
  KDC958.L93 2016
  342.41108'52–dc23
  2015035563

ISBN: 978-1-4094-5064-1 (hbk)
ISBN: 978-1-315-57201-7 (ebk)

Typeset in Times New Roman
by Apex CoVantage, LLC

For the grandchildren:
Samuel James, Rachel Alice, Abigail Heather and Susanna Grace

Contents

	Preface	viii
	Abbreviations and other matters	x
1	Introduction	1
2	1560–1843 Reformation to Disruption	4
3	1843–1929 Disruption to union	22
4	The Church of Scotland today	69
5	Outside establishment	100
6	Education	134
7	Personal relationships	158
8	Other interactions of religion and law	178
9	Conclusion	225
	Index	229

Preface

The academic study of church and state has developed considerably since I first ventured into it. Sociology, history and politics have all taken an interest as, of course, have ecclesiastics.[1] For those intrigued by Public Law, the interaction of religious belief and civic rights and duties can fascinate. These pages consider its outworking in the law of Scotland, the original home of applied Presbyterianism. They are the product of an interest that began when I was a student and was fostered by many years of involvement in the machineries of the Church of Scotland. A doctoral dissertation of 1972 led to a book in 1980.[2] Older history remains, but much has changed during the last half-century. I apologise that for reasons of space, by and large I have not sought to cross-refer to different arrangements in other parts of the UK or elsewhere.[3]

After a general introduction, Chapters 2–4 consider the Church of Scotland, dominant for so many years, though disrupted in the nineteenth century by a collision between it and the civil authorities. Chapter 5 covers the developing position and legal recognition of other denominations that came into being as unincorporated associations. The text then turns to other interactions of church and state, Chapter 6 dealing with education and Chapter 7 with personal relationships. The 12 sections of Chapter 8 form a rag-bag of other areas where religion and law can collide, the new emphasis on 'human rights' being not unproductive of difficulties. Chapter 9 is a brief concluding summary.

Faith in many forms remains present in Scotland. Historically Christian churches, denominations and other groupings were its manifestation in Scotland. Other religions now also find a place. However the religious foundations of the law general that permits these

---

1 Many studies: cf. S. Bruce, *Scottish Gods: Religion in Modern Scotland, 1900–2012* (Edinburgh: Edinburgh UP, 2014); T.M. Devine, *The Scottish Nation: 1700–2007* (London: Penguin Books, 2006) and his *Scotland's Shame: Bigotry and Sectarianism in Modern Scotland* (Edinburgh: Mainstream, 2000); M.A. Maclean, *The Crown Rights of the Redeemer* (Edinburgh: St Andrew Press, 2009); S. Ferrari and R. Cristofori, eds, *Law and Religion in the 21st Century: Relations between States and Religious Communities* (Farnham: Ashgate, 2010).
2 F. Lyall, *Of Presbyters and Kings: Church and State in the Law of Scotland* (Aberdeen: Aberdeen UP, 1980). Cf. my inaugural lecture 'Religion and Law', 1976 Jur. Rev. 58–69.
3 For a succinct treatment of the UK see M. Hill, R. Sandberg and N. Doe, *Religion and Law in the United Kingdom* (Alphen aan den Rijn, Wolters Kluwer, 2011).

developments are increasingly well-buried. That may be a danger. Neglect of foundations can cause collapse. I hope that some of the archaeology in later pages will aid an appreciation of how we have gotten to where we now are.

Electronic access has facilitated both research and what Eric Morrison, my old maths master, used to call 'just plain search'. Most of the legislative and governmental materials cited can now be found on the Internet, and many older texts are available as print-on-demand. Cases can be found through official sources, Westlaw and Lexis.

These pages reflect my understanding as at the end of 2014, although account has been taken of some later developments. The mistakes and misunderstandings are mine own. I would thank many for their help over the years, particularly the late Colin Maclean who extracted the first church and state book from me, and Alison Kirk of Ashgate for her support. There are others, but some wish anonymity so I name none. That said, I am hugely grateful for the forbearance of my wife, who has put up with much use of the computer and the grumpiness of authorship. Thanks, Heather.

Francis Lyall
Aberdeen, Scotland, UK.

Abbreviations and other matters

Acts of the Pre-Union Scottish Parliament are cited with their chapter numbers, including to the 12mo ed. when available.

Where appropriate the short titles assigned by the Statute Law Revision (Scotland) Act 1964, Sched. 2 have been used.

Argyll I, II and III	Reports of the Education Commission (Scotland), Chairman, The Duke of Argyll. First Report: Evidence. 1865 [PP 3483 and 3858]; Second Report: Elementary Schools. 1867 [PP 3845] with Reports of Assistant Commissioners [3845 – I to IV]; Third Report: Burgh and Middle Class Schools, 1867–68 [PP 4011]
asp	Act of the Scottish Parliament (from 1999), cited by year and number.
Bettenson	H.J. Bettenson, *Documents of the Christian Church*, 2d ed. (London: Oxford UP, 1963).
Black I	W.G. Black, *Parochial Ecclesiastical Law* (Edinburgh: Blackwood, 1888, 1891, 1901, 1926). Citation is to 2d ed.
Black II	W.G. Black, *Parochial Law of Scotland other than Ecclesiastical* (Edinburgh: Blackwood, 1893).
Bryce, I, II and Retro	J. Bryce, *Ten Years of the Church of Scotland, from 1833 to 1843, with a Historical Retrospect from 1560*, 2 vols (Edinburgh: Blackwood, 1850). The Retrospect is separately paged in Vol. I.
Buchanan I and II	R. Buchanan, *The Ten Years' Conflict: being a History of the Disruption of the Church of Scotland*, 2 vols, new ed. (Glasgow: Blackie, 1856).
Bulloch I, II and III	A.L. Drummond and J. Bulloch, *The Scottish Church 1688–1843* (1973); *The Church in Victorian Scotland, 1843–1874* (1975); *The Church in Late*

Victorian Scotland, 1874–1900 (1975) (all Edinburgh: St Andrew Press).

BUK — *The Booke of the Universal Kirk of Scotland, Acts and Proceedings of the General Assembly of the Kirk of Scotland*, T. Thomson, ed., 3 vols (Edinburgh: Bannatyne and Maitland Clubs, 1839–45).

Burleigh — J.H.S. Burleigh, *A Church History of Scotland* (London: Oxford UP, 1960).

Cockburn, Journals I and II — H. Cockburn, *Journal of Henry Cockburn, 1831–1854*, 2 vols (Edinburgh: Edmonston and Douglas, 1874).

Cockburn, Memorials — H. Cockburn, *Memorials of his Time* (Edinburgh: A&C Black, 1856).

Cox — J.T. Cox, *Practice and Procedure in the Church of Scotland*, 6th ed. D.F.M. Macdonald (Edinburgh: Church of Scotland 1976).

Craik — H. Craik, *The State in its Relation to Education* (London: Macmillan, 1896).

Durham Report — *The Fourth R*, 1970. The Report of the Commission on Religious Education in Schools appointed by the Church of England, 1967.

Duncan — J.M. Duncan, *A Treatise on the Parochial Ecclesiastical Law of Scotland* (Edinburgh: Bell and Bradfute, 1864, 1869).

Dunlop — A.M. Dunlop, *Parochial Law* (Edinburgh: Blackwood, 1830, 1835, 1841). Citation is from 2d ed.

Ehler — S.Z. Ehler and J.B. Morrall, *Church and State through the Centuries: A Collection of Historic Documents with Commentaries* (London: Burns and Oates, 1954).

Enchiridion Symbolorum — H. Denzinger and A. Schönmetzer, *Enchiridion Symbolorum Definitionun et Declarationum de Rebus Fidei et Morum*, 23rd ed. (Friburg: Herder); citation is to paragraph.

Erskine — John Erskine of Carnock, *An Institute of the Laws of Scotland* (1754) 8th ed., J.B. Nicolson, 2 vols (Edinburgh: Bell and Bradfute, 1871). Cited by Book, Title and Paragraph.

Figgis I — J.N. Figgis, *Churches in the Modern State* (London: Longmans Green, 1913).

Figgis II — J.N. Figgis, *The Divine Right of Kings*, 2d ed. (Cambridge: Cambridge UP, 1914; New York: Harper and Row, 1965).

Figgis III — J.N. Figgis, *The Political Aspects of St. Augustine's City of God* (London: Longmans Green, 1921; Gloucester, Mass.: Smith, 1963).

First Book — *The First Book of Discipline*, J.K. Cameron, ed. (Edinburgh: St Andrew Press, 1972).

Fleming I — J.R. Fleming, *A History of the Church in Scotland, 1843–1874* (Edinburgh: T&T Clark, 1927).

Fleming II	J.R. Fleming, *A History of the Church in Scotland, 1875–1929* (Edinburgh: T&T Clark, 1933).
GA	General Assembly of the Church of Scotland.
GA Act	Act of the General Assembly of the Church of Scotland (cited by year and number).
GA Reports	Reports to the General Assembly of the Church of Scotland, published annually by the Church (cited by year).
Innes I and **II**	A.T. Innes, *The Law of Creeds in Scotland*, I (Edinburgh: Blackwood, 1867); II (Edinburgh: Blackwood, 1904).
Kidd	B.J. Kidd, *Documents of the Continental Reformation* (Oxford: Oxford UP, 1911, 1933).
Knox, History	W.C. Dickinson, ed., *John Knox's History of the Reformation in Scotland*, 2 vols. (London: Nelson, 1949).
Lethendy Report	C.G. Robertson, *Report of the Proceedings in the Court of Session in the Lethendy Case* (Edinburgh: Blackwood, 1839).
Millar Report	Moral and religious education in Scottish schools, report of a committee appointed by the Secretary of State for Scotland, chairman M. Millar (Edinburgh: HMSO, 1972).
Morison or **Mor.**	W.M. Morison, *The Decisions of the Court of Session in the form of a Dictionary, to 1808*, 21 vols, Edinburgh, 1811–16.
Murphy	J. Murphy, *Church, State and Schools in Britain, 1800–1971* (London: Routledge & Kegan Paul, 1972).
RSCHS	*Records of the Scottish Church History Society*, 1921–.
Robertson, Auchterarder I and **II**	C.G. Robertson, Report of the Court of Session proceedings in the Auchterarder Case, 2 vols. (Edinburgh: Black, 1838).
Rodger	Alan, Lord Rodger of Earlsferry, *The Courts, the Church and the Constitution: Aspects of the Disruption of 1843* (Edinburgh: Edinburgh UP, 2008).
SBSH	W.C. Dickinson, G. Donaldson and I.A. Milne, eds, *Source Book of Scottish History*, 3 vols (London: Nelson, 1958–61).
Scotland I and II	J. Scotland, *The History of Scottish Education*, 2 vols (London: Univ. London Press, 1969).
Second Book	*The Second Book of Discipline*, J. Kirk, ed. (Edinburgh: St Andrew Press, 1980).
Sjölinder	R. Sjölinder, *Presbyterian Reunion in Scotland, 1007–1921*, trans. E.J. Sharpe, 1962 Acta Universitas Upsalensis Studia Historico-Ecclasastica Upsalensie No. 4.

SSC	*Statutes of the Scottish Church, 1225–1559* (D. Patrick, ed., Scottish History Society, Vol. 54, 1907).
SSFCS	*The Subordinate Standards and Other Authoritative Documents of the Free Church of Scotland* (Edinburgh: Free Church of Scotland, 1955).
Stair	James Dalrymple, Viscount Stair, *Institutions of the Law of Scotland* (1693), 5th ed., 2 vols, J.R. More ed. (with More's Notes (Edinburgh: Bell and Bradfute, 1832); D.M. Walker, ed. (Glasgow: Glasgow and Edinburgh UP, 1981). Cited by Book, Title and Paragraph.
Stewarton Report	*W. Cuninghame, Mutual Cases, record and appendix in causa W. Cuninghame and others, Heritors of Stewarton v. Presbytery of Irvine*, 3 parts (Edinburgh: Presbytery of Irvine, 1842).

1   Introduction

In 1603 the Presbyterian Protestant James VI of Scotland, well-tutored by George Buchanan,[1] succeeded Elizabeth I of England to become James I of England and as such the Head of the Church of England. However the 'Union of the Crowns' was a personal union only, Scotland remaining a separate entity with its own legislature until the Union of the Parliaments of Scotland and England in 1707. That union was what it was presented as: a union of two parliaments, Parliament at Westminster becoming the legislature for the United Kingdom of Great Britain. Three hundred and ninety-one years later the Scottish Parliament was revived and a Scottish Executive established by the Scotland Act 1998. Legislative competence in specified matters is reserved to the Westminster Parliament, but all else is devolved to the Parliament at Holyrood.[2] Unlike Westminster the Scottish Parliament is unicameral and does much of its work through a committee system. It is composed of 129 Members of the Scottish Parliament (MSPs), 73 elected by individual constituencies on a first-past-the post system and 56 for eight larger additional member regions by proportional representation from party electoral lists.

In the 1707 union the two countries were not assimilated. The Scottish legal system, its law and judicial arrangements continued, albeit that desirable changes in Scots law requiring

---

1   Buchanan (1506–82) was the author of *The Art and Science of Government among the Scots: De Iure Regni Apud Scotos*, D.S. McNeil, trans. (Glasgow: Maclellan, 1963): *A Dialogue on the Law of Kingship among the Scots*, R.A. Mason and M.S. Smith, eds. (Aldershot: Ashgate, 2004). Buchanan thought the monarch should be a God-fearing Protestant, and that the monarchy had limitations: unlike the later concept of the 'Divine Right of Kings'. Michel de Montaigne was another of Buchanan's pupils. D. Macmillan, *George Buchanan: A Biography* (London: Simpkin, Marshall, 1906).
2   Reserved matters include foreign affairs, defence and human rights: Scotland Act 1998, ss. 29–30 and Sched. 5 as amended by the Scotland Act 2012. Some restricted matters are noted *infra* elsewhere. The original Scottish Executive was renamed the Scottish Government by s. 12(2)(a) of the Scotland Act 2012. Further amendment is expected following upon negotiations following upon the referendum on Scottish independence of 2014. See *The Smith Commission: Report of the Smith Commission for Further Devolution of Powers to the Scottish Parliament, 27 November 2014* (Edinburgh, 2014) (https://www.smith-commission.scot) and the UK Government White Paper *United Kingdom: An enduring settlement*, January 2015, Cm 8990.

2 Introduction

primary legislation often had to wait before securing a place on the Westminster timetable.³ Matters religious were excluded from the negotiations of the 1707 Union, the presbyterian polity of the Church of Scotland being affirmed by the Protestant Religion and Presbyterian Church Act, 1706 c. 6, and inserted into the 1707 Treaty with England.

Presbyterian government is Scotland's gift to the ecclesiastical community.⁴ Its conciliar structure is democratic, and (to the regret of some) unencumbered by sacerdotal elements.⁵ It affords a role for the informed individual believer's understanding of the Gospel as expressed in whichever Protestant Confession(s) that is/are authoritative within each presbyterian denomination.⁶ Unlike Episcopal systems it needs no permanent authority vested in individuals (bishops), and yet the decisions of its courts provide a continuing centre. Where there is considered to be need for a change in doctrine, worship, discipline or governance, the Barrier Act 1697 requires the affirmative vote of a majority of presbyteries before the General Assembly enacts the appropriate legislation.

When two authorities, the secular and the ecclesiastical, vie for the obedience of the citizen and the latter claims to have eternal effect, there is always a potential for disagreement, which *in extremis* may result in conflict. Within the Christian tradition Augustine spoke of the 'Two Cities'.⁷ History has seen many theoretical solutions imperfectly applied including erastianism,⁸ clericalism (occasionally disparagingly labelled caesaropapism)⁹ and total separation.¹⁰ At present the accepted pattern in Scotland is cooperation, but the norms of our society continue to mutate. As in other countries there can therefore be no finality to the relationships between the state authorities and the individuals and associations of believers who owe allegiance to another authority.

Social expectations and the informal constraints of accepted behaviour have weakened. Being an 'elder of the Kirk' has lost its cachet. Some say that secularism has eroded faith. I disagree. What has happened is that an unacknowledged but long drift from formal religion has been revealed. Doctrinal diversity has produced indifference. Rightly or wrongly, traditional ecclesiastical authority has eroded as office-holders have continued in office (and salary) while apparently no longer believing in the formal doctrines of the denominations

---

3   Thus the Succession (Scotland) Act 1964, a much-needed major revision of the law, was drafted in the early 1930s.
4   Cf. N. Doe, *Christian Law: Contemporary Principles* (Cambridge: Cambridge UP, 2013).
5   G.D. Henderson, *Presbyterianism* (Aberdeen: Aberdeen UP, 1954); J. Kennedy, *Presbyterian Authority and Discipline* (Edinburgh: St Andrew Press, 1960). See also Cox 7–11; J.L. Weatherhead, *The Constitution and Laws of the Church of Scotland* (Edinburgh: Church of Scotland, 1997)(a slim summary); A. Herron, *A Guide to the General Assembly of the Church of Scotland* (Edinburgh: St Andrew Press, 2012), his *A Guide to the Presbytery* (Edinburgh: St Andrew Press, 1983) and his *A Guide to Congregational Affairs* (Edinburgh: St Andrew Press, 1976). W. Mair (1830–1920) produced many editions of a *Digest* of Church of Scotland practice and procedure which included relevant civil law cases. Mair was replaced by the six editions of Cox (1935–76) which contains many historical documents relevant to the union of 1929.
6   The theological knowledge or understanding of many elders may now be defective, or even absent.
7   The *City of God* (many eds) was written between AD 412 and 426. On the sources of its concepts see E. Gilson's Introduction to the Fathers of the Church, Inc. translation of 1950; L.S. Mazzolani, *The Idea of the City in Roman Thought* (trans. S. O'Donnell) (London: Hollis and Carter, 1970), 242 ff.
8   T. Erastus (R.W. Lee, ed.), *Theses Touching Excommunication* (Edinburgh, 1844, Whitefish MO, Kessinger, 2010). Cf. J.N. Figgis, *The Divine Right of Kings*, 2d ed. (Cambridge: Cambridge UP, 1914; New York, Harper and Row, 1965), 'Erastus and Erastianism', 293 ff.
9   Had it been implemented *The First Book of Discipline* of 1560 would have approached this position.
10 Given the number of court cases involving the First Amendment to the US Constitution it would be ludicrous to classify the US as an example.

that give them their role. In a sense this is good. Superficialities vanish. Faith is tested when expressing it penalises and compliance with its outward forms is no longer a passport to respectability. In the modern state, secularism can be a useful adjunct to tolerance. There is a danger that secularism may be abused should militant secularists seek to denigrate and stifle the religious impulse of others. Nonetheless, in a democratic society secularism remains useful as providing a neutral environment within which diverse manifestations of religion can be practised within the bounds of reasonable public order. From the religious point of view, the end result is not determined by the civil arrangements.

2   1560–1843 Reformation to Disruption

Pre-Reformation Scotland

The history of pre-Christian Scotland is obscure. Christianity came to Scotland with such as Ninian and Columba and developed into what is often spoken of as Celtic Christianity.[1] However, the ultimate effect of the Synod of Whitby of 664 AD was to install the authority of Roman Catholicism.[2]

Pre-Reformation Scotland was poor, with significant differences between its parts. Economically the Lowlands and coastal districts were better off than the Highlands. Major seaports could engage in trade and fishing. The burghs and their hinterlands operated a money economy, while rural areas depended on subsistence farming and barter. Agriculture did not improve until the fifteenth century, when a fuller introduction of feudal landholding introduced the relationship of feudal superior and vassal more widely than previously known, with a consequent stratification of society.[3]

In pre-Reformation Scotland, the links between church and state were considerable. The allocation of a defined territorial area for spiritual purposes begins with the responsibilities of bishops early in history, but the further subdivision of that territory into parishes in which particular priests had a responsibility for bringing the ordinances of religion also made sense.[4] Exactly when parishes came to Scotland is unknown, but obviously once the Roman Catholic version of Christianity was dominant that Church's parish structure was effective. Many modern Church of Scotland parishes can be traced back well before the Reformation,

---

1   I. Macdonald, ed., *Saint Ninian* (Edinburgh: Floris Books, 1993); J. Gregory, ed., *The Life of Columba* (Dublin: Wolfhound, 1999); P. Brown, *The Rise of Western Christianity: Triumph and Diversity* (Oxford: Blackwell, 2003); D.E. Meek, *The Quest for Celtic Christianity* (Edinburgh: Handsel Press, 2000); J.P. Mackey, *An Introduction to Celtic Christianity* (Edinburgh: T&T Clark, 1989).
2   B. Ward, *A True Easter: The Synod of Whitby, 664 AD* (Oxford: SLG Press, 2007); P. Wormald (S. Baxter, ed.), *The Times of Bede* (Malden, MA: Blackwell, 2006).
3   J. Wormald, *Court, Kirk and Community: Scotland 1470–1625* (Edinburgh: Edinburgh UP, 1981), 3–72.
4   In its origin the word 'parish' has no necessary ecclesiastical connotations: *para* = near, *oikos* = house: *paroikia* = a neighbourhood.

particularly in rural areas.[5] By the time of the Scottish Reformation all Scotland had, at least on paper, been divided into parishes each with a minimum of one church building, the inhabitants of each area being allocated to that parish and church, and given responsibility for the upkeep. The constitution of a parish for 'spiritual purposes' also brought considerations beyond prayer and church services. The Catholic Church accepted responsibility for education and for welfare, albeit the discharge of that responsibility was erratic.[6] This caused disquiet, not to say dissension, exacerbated by the fact that the Church owned anything up to one half of the land, and one half of that belonged to the monasteries.[7]

The Reformation in Scotland

The Reformation is often spoken of as if it was accomplished swiftly. It was not. There are, of course, the climactic events of the anti-Catholic statutes of 1560 and the adoption of the Scots Confession, but the harbingers of the Reformation are to be found decades before Luther's Ninety-five Theses,[8] and the political, economic and theological struggles of the Reformation went on for decades thereafter. Indeed, notwithstanding ecumenism, it could be argued that the Reformation and the Counter-Reformation are not yet done. More conservatively, the Reformation in Scotland arguably starts soon after the ideas of Luther came to the Kingdom in the early sixteenth century, but did not find substantial completion until the end of that century with the commitment to Presbyterianism.

That said, the Reformation of 1560 is an appropriate point to mark.[9] Previous history is only marginally relevant. The statutes of the Scottish Reformation do in places imply that there was a Church of God in Scotland under Roman Catholicism, but the statutory repudiation of the beliefs and the external manifestations of Catholicism was such that it is of little value for us to delve into the detail of prior history. What was done after 1560 elaborates and builds upon the events of that time, making them a major watershed.

A variety of elements resulted in the Scottish Reformation. Political and economic factors as well as religious, and the exact balance between them at any given time and in the motives of any given participant, may be a matter of dispute.[10] The principal facts were that the Roman Catholic Church in Scotland was wealthy and often corrupt. It was a major

---

5 *Origines Parochiales Scotiae*, 2 vols (Glasgow: Bannatyne Club, 1851); I.B. Cowan, 'The Development of the Parochial System in Medieval Scotland', 40 Scot. Hist. Rev. 43–55; I.B. Cowan, *The Parishes of Medieval Scotland*, 1967, 93 Scottish Record Society.
6 J. Durkan, 'Care of the Poor: Pre-Reformation Hospitals', in D. McRoberts, ed., *Essays on the Scottish Reformation, 1513–1625* (*Innes Review*) (Glasgow: Burns, 1962), 116–28; J. Durkan, 'Education in the Century of the Reformation', at 145–68; D. McKay, 'Parish Life in Scotland, 1500–1560', at 85–115; J. Wormald (*supra* n. 3), 75–94; M. Dilworth, *Scottish Monasteries in the Late Middle Ages* (Edinburgh: Edinburgh UP, 1995), 57–74.
7 I.F. Grant, *The Societal and Economic Development of Scotland before 1603* (Edinburgh: Oliver and Boyd, 1930). Dilworth, *supra* n. 6, at 57, expresses some caution as to Grant's figures.
8 Kidd, Doc. no. 11. Many internet sources.
9 I.B. Cowan, *The Scottish Reformation: Church and Society in Sixteenth Century Scotland* (London: Weidenfeld and Nicolson, 1982); G. Donaldson, *The Scottish Reformation* (Cambridge: Cambridge UP, 1960); W.C. Dickinson, *Scotland: From the Earliest Times to 1603*, 3rd ed. rev. A.A.M. Duncan (Oxford: Oxford UP, 1977); G.S. Pryde, *Scotland: From 1603 to the Present Day* (London: Nelson, 1962).
10 Donaldson, *supra* n. 9, 74, suggest that, notwithstanding the statutes of 1560, the Scottish Reformation was essentially moderate and gradual. For what may be a more detached consideration see J.W. Cairns, 'Historical Introduction', in K. Reid and R. Zimmerman, *A History of Private Law in Scotland* (Oxford: Oxford UP, 2000), Vol. 1, *Introduction and Property*, 14–184. See also Cowan, *supra* n. 9; McRoberts *supra* n. 6;

landholder. By a variety of devices in the late fifteenth and early sixteenth centuries the Crown had obtained what amounted to the right to present (in effect to appoint) nominees to major church positions. Most of the abbeys and priories were in the hands of relatives of the nobility who were often without interest in the spiritual functions of their offices,[11] and the personal lives of many were a common scandal.[12] Protestant doctrines were preached in the kingdom from soon after Luther had begun his work on the Continent, and the Catholic Church in Scotland was beginning to seek to reform itself.[13] The General Statutes of the Provincial Council of the Prelates and Clergy of the Realm of Scotland, held in 1549, 1551–52 and 1558–59 show disquiet and move towards the redress of error and wrongs,[14] but matters had gone too far. For decades, not to say centuries, Scottish scholars had been studying and teaching on the Continent,[15] and some had imbibed the new wine of the Reformation and brought it home.[16] Indeed, some Catholic priests were themselves preaching the new doctrine, and were later to pass over into the ministry of the new Church. Since England was often considered an enemy, and France a friend, Scottish scholars had for years gone to study on the Continent. Indeed there were Scottish 'nations' in the Universities of Paris and Orleans. But some of the ecclesiastical reaction to the new (or old[17]) ideas was fierce. Patrick Hamilton, a young preacher, was burned as a heretic in St Andrews in 1528 by James, Cardinal Beaton. Eighteen years later the similar martyring of George Wishart in 1546 by David, Cardinal Beaton (nephew of the earlier), added to the zeal of his friends and followers. Three months after the Wishart execution Beaton was assassinated in his own castle in St Andrews, and the castle was seized by Protestant forces. After a siege by the French troops of Mary of Guise, the Queen Mother and Regent during Mary, Queen of Scots' minority, the Protestants, including John Knox who had joined them and been called to be their minister, were transported to French prisons and galleys. All this raised the temperature and made a more fundamental struggle inevitable.[18]

While these events were religious in origin, by involving the French Alliance they introduced a political factor, and a tendency emerged for those opposed to that Alliance to side with the Reformers. Some also supported the Reformers because they were keen to seize the lands held by the Roman Catholic Church. But it would be unfair to imply that the basis of the Scottish Reformation was not primarily religious. However, at this time, although Protestant doctrines

---

D.M. Walker, *A Legal History of Scotland*, Vol. III, *The Sixteenth Century* (Edinburgh: Green, 1995), particularly for its sources, and Ch. 9 'The Church', 248–319.

11 Various 'commendators' of such property appear in cases reported in Morison, title 'Kirk Patrimony'.
12 Sir David Lindsay *Ane Satyre of the Thrie Estaits* (1602) (R. Lyall, ed.) (Edinburgh: Canongate, 1989). Cf. the version by M.P. McDairmid and R. Kemp (London: Heinemann, 1967). W.C. Dickinson 'Introduction' to Knox's *History* reviews much of the material. See also Kidd, Doc. nos 334 and 341. Cf. S.S.C. and II S.B.S.H., 98–116.
13 Thus Hamilton's 'Catechism' of 1552, Kidd, Doc. no. 342. Cf. Statutes of the Provincial Council, 1549, S.S.C., 84–134; Statutes of the General Provincial Council, 1551, ibid. 138–48, and Statutes of the General Provincial Council 1558–9, ibid., particularly 163–90.
14 Cf. Donaldson, *supra* n. 9, 1–28, 'Kirks and Kirkmen Unreformed'.
15 John Duns Scotus (c. 1266–1308) was an important Scholastic theologian.
16 The Act 1525 c. 4 prohibited the import of Lutheran books: Kidd, Doc. no. 335. The Act 1551 c. 26 (c.27 12mo) required that printers print no book or other material unless publication was licensed by the Church.
17 It is an error, and a misleading one, to categorise the Protestant movement simply as 'protest', though one can see how that etymology can be constructed. Rather the concept is of *pro-testatio* – a call for a return to the earlier position, to the original doctrine of the church. Only later did questions of polity arise.
18 Knox History (Book I) I, 60–97.

were being more and more widely preached by Catholic priests as well as by men from the Continent, there was no defined body that could be considered to be the Church of Scotland.

Historically the roots of the institutional Church of Scotland might be traced back to the First Covenant of December 1557 in which various ministers and a group of nobles, 'the Lords of the Congregation', bound themselves to maintain, nourish and defend the whole congregation of Christ against the attacks of the 'congregation of Satan' which they expressly renounced.[19] Notwithstanding the language of the First Covenant, it did at first appear that the desired reformation of religion might be obtained within a system of tolerance, but this hope vanished following a riot in Perth in 1559. The Lords of the Congregation took up arms to defend themselves, and naturally the Crown sought to suppress the insurrection. Elizabeth of England intervened to support the rebels, and Mary of Guise having died, the Crown forces, which were mainly French, sought peace. A Treaty of Edinburgh provided for the mutual withdrawal of French and English forces.[20] Under Concessions attached to the Treaty, Queen Mary was to take no reprisals against her rebellious subjects, and the Convention of Estates was appointed to meet in August 1560 to name commissioners to go to France and discuss the religious questions that lay at the root of the rebellion.

The Scots Parliament met in August 1560, but without having been summoned by the Crown and without its normal balance of composition.[21] Although under the Concessions the Parliament was to appoint the commissioners to discuss the religious question with the Crown, Parliament was petitioned to abolish popery. This it was willing to do, and by the Papal Jurisdiction Act 1560 c. 2, abolished the jurisdiction of the Pope in Scotland. The Act 1560 c. 3 abolished idolatry, and the Act 1560 c. 4 proscribed the Mass. Being unwilling simply to leave a vacuum, the Estates asked a small committee of ministers to prepare a statement of the new belief. With John Knox as chairman the committee produced a draft of what came to be known as the Scots Confession in four days.[22] This was adopted by Parliament by the Confession of Faith Ratification Act 1560 c. 1, the Confession being:

> The Confession of Faith professed and believed by the Protestants within the realm of Scotland, published by them in Scotland, and by the Estates thereof ratified and approved as wholesome and sound doctrine, grounded upon the infallible truth of God's Word.

Certain things are notable about this formula. First, the Confession does not bear to be enacted by the civil authority for the Church. It is the Confession published by the Protestants in Scotland, and *ratified and approved* by Parliament. The civil authority does not act: it approves a statement formulated outside of itself. Second, the Confession is not at this stage the Confession of the Church of Scotland. Nor is it adopted or put forward by authority of that church. It is the Confession of the Protestants in Scotland, and no institutional church

---

19 Kidd, Doc. no. 344. A trigger for the First Covenant was a fear that Mary, Queen of Scots, was to marry Francis, the Dauphin of France, thus potentially strengthening Roman Catholic power in Scotland. The marriage took place in 1558, and Francis became King of France in 1559. However, he died in 1560 and Mary returned to Scotland.
20 Kidd, Doc. no. 347. II SBSH 180–184 includes the 'Concessions to the Scots' attached to the Treaty.
21 These points, together with Mary's failure to assent to the Acts led to the ratifying legislation of 1567, *infra*. n. 35.
22 See Knox History, I, 337–9 (Book II); G.D. Henderson, ed., and J. Bulloch, trans., *The Scots Confession 1560* (Edinburgh: St Andrew Press, 1960); Knox History, App. VI (printed in the original *in gremio* of Book III).

is referred to. Finally, the Confession is not a Confession: it is stated to be wholesome and sound doctrine grounded on the truth of God's Word.[23]

It is noticeable that Act 1560 c. 1, the first enactment dealing with the church, does not contain any detail on the relationship of the church and the state. Indeed, reflecting its theological origins the Confession does not contain either a concept of the church or of the state in their modern aspect. The church is seen in its theological aspect as the company of believers, though it is recognised that there may be 'filthy synagogues', and the 'false Kirk' is dealt with.[24] The civil magistrate is stated to have a proper sphere, including the duty of maintaining true religion and suppressing all idolatry and superstition.[25] But all this is without defining the institution with which the civil authority has relations. The church is simply the congregation of believers. It may therefore be questioned whether the Church of Scotland existed at this stage, or was thought of as The Church in Scotland.[26] The further question therefore emerges, whether the Church of Scotland is the origin of its creed and doctrines, or whether the creed and doctrines are the origin of that church.

Unfortunately the 1560 Parliament was unwilling to go beyond these steps, and there was no settlement of ecclesiastical polity, nor any attempt to deal with the colossal question of the endowments of the displaced Roman Catholic Church. The Privy Council had charged six men, John Douglas, John Winram, John Row, John Spottiswoode, John Willock and John Knox, to draw up a constitution for the church. The Committee speedily reported to the Council, laying a version of what was to become the *First Book of Discipline* before it on 20 May 1560, with a revision submitted to Parliament in 1560 and 1561, but was never approved by it. The *First Book of Discipline*[27] formulated a system of church government based on modified episcopacy. It envisaged a Christian commonwealth in which the church and state would cooperate, the church being responsible for the welfare of the people, while the civil authority would govern. The church would deal with such matters as education[28] and poor relief[29] in addition to its more obvious functions of preaching and discipline. But in order to carry out the schemes, Knox and his friends considered that it would be necessary for the new Protestant church to be given the endowment of the Roman Catholic Church as a patrimony.[30] This was not acceptable to the Lords. Some of them had seized church estates or were to do so,[31] some had relatives in positions of authority over estates and some (including the Crown

---

23 Innes I, 12–17; Innes II, 10–15.
24 Scots Confession, *supra* n. 22, Arts XVI and XVIII.
25 Scots Confession, *supra* n. 22, Art. XXIV.
26 In 1963 the Confession of Faith Ratification Act c. 1 and the Papal Jurisdiction Act c. 2, both of 1560, were among the 'spent, obsolete and unnecessary' enactments proposed to be swept away by a Statute Law Revision (Scotland) Bill. Following protest both were dropped from the final form of the legislation. They remain part of the statute law of Scotland.
27 Commonly called 'First' to distinguish it from Melville's *Book* of 1578 (*infra* n. 44). The *First Book of Discipline*: Knox History, App. VIII. (In the original it is placed at the end of Book III). J.K. Cameron, ed., *The First Book of Discipline* (Edinburgh: St Andrew Press, 1972), at 3–14, reviews what is known of its drafting and revision.
28 See *infra* Chapter 6 'Education'.
29 See *infra* following n. 52. Poor relief was later entrusted to the Church's administration. See A.M. Dunlop, *Parochial Law* (Edinburgh: Blackwood, 1830, 1835, 1841) and Poor Laws of Scotland (Edinburgh: Blackwood, 1825, 1828, 1854); W.G. Black, *Parochial Law other than Ecclesiastical* (Edinburgh: Blackwood, 1893).
30 See *The First Book of Discipline*, Introduction to the Fifth Head, and the Sixth Head 'Of the Rents and Patrimony of the Kirk'.
31 See *infra* n. 41.

itself) received considerable income from ecclesiastical estates.[32] In retrospect the *Book's* failure to receive the approval of Parliament was inevitable. The financial and economic upheaval consequent upon such a redistribution of the economic assets of the country would have been tremendous, eminently desirable though the ends were. But the endowments were left virtually intact, and the polity of the old church was largely undisturbed, though its priests were effectively prohibited by the Reformation statutes from preaching Roman doctrine. Provision for the sustenance of the ministers of the Reformed faith was limited to giving them the right to receive the 'thirds of benefices' as a temporary measure.[33]

The failure of the state to deal with the endowments of the Catholic Church, and of the church itself to organise itself properly albeit without state approval, produced a curious situation. In some ways the old church continued with its estates and revenues, but forbidden to preach and celebrate its sacraments, while the new church struggled to establish its polity with insufficient resources. Thus effectively two churches were in existence in Scotland and matters so continued for some years. The Reformers seem to have considered that there was little point in pressing the take-over of the institutional church, and there was force in this view, especially since the Catholic Church was closely allied to the Crown through the presence of Queen Mary. Her abdication in 1567 changed matters.[34] The regent on behalf of the infant James VI, the Earl of Moray, was a Protestant. The Acts of the 1567 Parliament repealed Acts in support of the Papacy (c. 4), and ratified the abolition of the papal jurisdiction (c. 3) and of the Mass (c. 5).[35] The Confession of Faith was once more engrossed in the register of Parliament. But now steps were taken to establish the reformed church in law.

The Church Act, 1567 c. 6, 'Anent the trew and haly Kirk and of thame declarit not to be of the same' gave legal establishment to the Church of Scotland. Defectively printed in 1567, but re-enacted with due explanation in 1579 as c. 6 of that year, it provides:

> . . . Oure souerane lord with auise [advice] of his thrie estaities . . . hes declarit and declaris the ministeris of the blissed euangel of Jesus chryst quhome god of his mercie hes now raisit vp amang us [raised up amongst us] Or heirefter sall [shall] raise aggreing with thame that now levis [live] in doctrine and administratioun of the sacramentis And the people of this realme that professis Jesus christ as he is now offerit in his evangell and do communicat with the haly sacramentis as in the reformit kirkis of this realme ar publictlie administrat according to the confession of the fayth To be the only trew and haly kirk of Jesus christ within this realme.

The Church of Scotland was thus legally defined and given place as an institution of the realm. The statute 1567/1579 c. 6 defines the standards, and hence the doctrinal identity, of the Church, doing so in terms of its known teaching and the Scots Confession of 1560.[36] But though

---

32 Various 'commendators' of such property appear in cases reported in Morison, title 'Kirk Patrimony'.
33 Donaldson, *supra* n. 10, 69–70; Knox History, App. IX; II SBSH, 192–3. 'Thirds of benefices' was a tax originally payable to the Crown. The Act had to be reinforced in 1566 (II SBSH, 197) and was replaced by the Act 1567 c.7, *infra* n. 37.
34 George Buchanan, *The Art and Science of Government among the Scots: De Iure Regni Apud Scotos*, D.S. McNeil, trans. (Glasgow: Maclellan, 1963), or as *A Dialogue on the Law of Kingship among the Scots*, R.A. Mason and M.S. Smith, eds (Aldershot: Ashgate, 2004) was written in part to justify Mary's forced abdication, although the work was not published until 1579. The Abdication document is at II SBSH, 200–203.
35 Reference point, n. 21.
36 Scots Confession, *supra* n. 22.

the church was defined in terms of its existing standards, and was declared to be the true church, the Act went beyond a mere acknowledgement of the church. Through striking at other beliefs, which by implication were not 'true', the terms of the Act 1567 c. 6 establish the Church as the only church recognised by law in the kingdom.

The next step was the settlement of the jurisdiction of the Church. The Church Jurisdiction Act 1567 c. 12, narrated that the Crown:

> declarit and grantit iurisdictioun to the said Kirk quhilk [which] consistis and standis in preicheing of the trew word of Jesus Christ correctioun of maneris and administratioun of haly Sacramentis . . .

and went on to declare that:

> . . . thair is na uther face of Kirk nor uther face of Religion than is presentlie be the fauour of God establischeit within this Realme And that thair be na uther iurisdictioun ecclesiasticall acknawlegeit within this Realme uther than quhilk [which] is and salbe [shall be] within the same Kirk or that quhilk [which] flowis thairfra concerning the premissis . . .

This was not entirely satisfactory to the Church, but no remedy was forthcoming. The terms of the Act do not make it clear whether the state was recognising that jurisdiction which the Church had undoubtedly been exercising from 1560, or whether the 'grantit' additional to the declaration involved a conferral of power by the state. It was interpreted in the latter sense during the Disruption cases, conforming to the then prevalent legal theory, but this may have been wrong. However it is interpreted, the Act is nonetheless fundamental to the position of the Church as having legal jurisdiction within Scotland.

The Coronation Oath Act 1567 c.8 was the third Act connected with the establishing of the Church, requiring all future monarchs to swear to protect the true Church as established, and to root out all those opposed to its teaching. This was more of political than legal interest, though as we shall see his failure to meet the obligation provided the first complaint of the Claim of Right against James VII and II.

These three Acts represent the establishment of the Protestant Church in Scotland. They may be viewed as recognising the existing Church, or they may be interpreted as constituting the conditions of the establishment of the Church, and conferring, and therefore limiting, its powers. That ambiguity was to be productive of much strife in the future. It is, however, noticeable that the statutes do not attempt in any way to deal with the form of government of the Church. In fact for the next 25 years the Church was without a defined polity, and moved from quasi-episcopacy to quasi-presbyterianism and back depending upon a variety of factors.

The endowment of the Church was another topic not dealt with in 1567. The Act 1567 c. 7 now formally provided benefices for the maintenance of ministers, but only as a temporary measure:[37] '. . . ay and quhill [until] the Kirk come to the full possessioun of their proper patrimonie, quhilk [which] is the teindes . . .',[38] thus enforcing the previous provisions made

---

37 Reference point, *supra* n. 33.
38 Teinds was a tax of one-tenth (a tithe) of the agricultural produce of a parish, payable for the maintenance of the local minister, the upkeep of church property and for the relief of the poor of the parish. When introduced,

by the Privy Council. But curiously in view of the ascendancy of the Church in 1567 and in later years, the civil authority was unwilling to give statutory effect to the provisions of *The First Book of Discipline* as to the maintenance of ministers. Steps were taken not so much to disendow the Roman Catholic Church as slowly to take over its benefices. Thus the Act 1567 c. 10 provided for the patronage of benefices to remain in the hands of the existing patrons, but for the reformed Church, through its superintendents, to be the judge of the qualifications of a presentee to a parish ministry. Intended to result in a gradual placement of reformed ministers as the Catholic benefices fell vacant, this remedy was further extended by the Concordat of Leith of 1572,[39] under which episcopal sees falling vacant were to be filled by Crown appointment, subject to examination of the qualifications of the presentee by the Church. The system was open to abuse, and was used by the Crown to establish its control of the Church since the bishop's oath of office recognised the Royal supremacy in matters religious.[40] But nothing was done to recover properties which had already passed under secular control, nor to deal with the property of abbeys and monasteries, institutions that had not been taken over by the Kirk. Thus, in North-east Scotland, the Abbey of Deer was seized by the then Earl Marischal. That his son George was later, in 1593, to found a university,[41] partly financed from the funds of the Abbey of Deer, does not fully expiate the transfer of that wealth from the ecclesiastical realm to the secular.[42] In any event, the gradual removal of church property into secular hands continued, the Crown itself taking care to benefit. The Act 1587 c. 8 (c. 29 12mo) on the 'Annexation of the Temporalities of benefices to the Croun' dealt with lands which had not yet passed into secular hands. It preserved for the life of existing beneficiaries the tithes, tacks [leases] and so on, but otherwise allowed the Crown to deal with that property. The Act 1592 c. 13 (c.121 12mo) provided that transfers to secular hands after the 1587 Act were valid only if to Lords of Parliament, and the Act 1592 c. 44 (c. 131 12mo) required the compilation of lists of rents and so on of church properties so that the 1587 Annexation Act could be properly implemented. Steps were thereafter taken to see that property or income there-from was not further diverted.[43]

In 1572 the Act 1572 c. 3 enacted testing legislation, requiring ministers to subscribe the Scots Confession as their faith so 'that the adversaries of Christ's Evangell sall [shall] not injoy the Patrimonie of the Kirk'. This made possible the deposition of ministers who refused to conform to the propositions of the Scots Confession, and was partially effective.

---

a special court dealt with their administration. A.A. Cormack, *Teinds and Agriculture: An Historical Survey* (London: Oxford UP, 1930); N. Elliot, *Teinds or Tithes, and Procedure in the Court of Teinds in Scotland* (Edinburgh: Blackwood, 1893); N. Elliot, *The Erection of Parishes Quoad Sacra and the Feuing of Glebes under Authority of the Court of Teinds* (Edinburgh: Blackwood, 1879); J. Connell, *A Treatise on the Law of Scotland Respecting Tithes* (Edinburgh: Hill & Constable, 1815); J. Connell, *A Treatise on the Law of Scotland Respecting Tithes, and the Stipends of the Parochial Clergy*, 2nd ed., 2 vols (Edinburgh: Hill & Constable, 1830); W. Buchanan, *Treatise on the Law of Scotland on the Subject of Teinds or Tithes* (Edinburgh: Bell & Bradfute, 1862). Cf. A.J.H. Gibson, *Stipend in the Church of Scotland* (Edinburgh: Blackwood, 1961). Tithes were abolished under the Church of Scotland (Property and Endowments) Act 1925 as part of the remodelling of the Kirk. See Chapter 3.

39 BUK I, 207; J. Kirk, *Patterns of Reform: Continuity and Change in the Reformation Kirk* (Edinburgh: T&T Clark, 1989); Kirk, *infra* n. 44, 18ff.
40 III SBSH, 12; BUK I, 220.
41 In 1860 under the Universities (Scotland) Act 1858, George's Marischal College was united with King's College, the University founded in 1495 in Old Aberdeen, to form the present University of Aberdeen.
42 G.D. Henderson, *The Founding of Marischal College, Aberdeen* (Aberdeen: Aberdeen UP, 1947).
43 See generally Walker, *supra* n. 10, 770–772, 'The erection of Church lands into secular lordships'.

It was also used by the Crown once more to exact a recognition of the Royal supremacy. The total effect of the Acts of 1567 and 1572 was gradually to convert the benefices to the use of the protestant Church. However, the legislation only dealt with benefices occupied by ministers. Nothing was done to recover benefices that had been put under secular control, or to deal with institutions such as the monasteries and abbeys which had not been taken over by the Kirk.

When Andrew Melville returned to Scotland from Geneva in 1574 he found that the episcopal system then in force was being used by the Crown to control the Church, and by the nobility to continue to divert Church funds into their coffers. Further, despite the legislation, the ordinary ministers were subject to grave financial limitations as the laws as to their maintenance, such as they were, were not being properly administered. To meet this situation Melville formulated *The Second Book of Discipline*,[44] which was approved by the General Assembly of the Church in 1578. This work was crucial in the development of the Church of Scotland, containing as it does the basic elements of Presbyterianism.[45]

The *Second Book* condemned episcopacy on the grounds of its possible abuse, and set out clearly and cogently the presbyterian doctrine of the parity of ministers, and the normal presbyterian form of conciliar church government. It stated rather than argued the independence of the Church from civil authority, the powers and authority of the Church being derived from God. It also argued that the Church had both right and duty to instruct the civil authority in matters of conscience and religion, and indeed the right to tell the civil arm how to exercise its own particular authority in accordance with the Word of God.[46] This threatened theocracy, and, not surprisingly, was avoided and indeed attacked by the Crown as being subversive of its own authority and powers.

It should not be thought that the Reformers were entirely taken up with abstract theological propositions. Catechetical instruction was important.[47] So was the availability of reading material, provided that it was suitable. The Reformers carried over into their practice the control of printing and the prior censorship of materials to be published that had previously been instituted at the behest of the Roman Catholic Church.[48] Heretical books were not to be printed, and any imported into the Kingdom were to be confiscated.[49] The Act 1587 c. 2 (c. 23 12mo) provided for the punishment of adversaries of the 'true religion', and of any who should seek to persuade others to decline from the profession of the true religion. It also prohibited the circulation of books or letters arguing against the reformed Faith, and this was reinforced by the Act 1587 c. 4 (c. 25 12mo) on the trafficking in or importation of 'erroneous' books.

While Scotland fell well short of some twentieth and twenty-first century parallels, the Reformed Kirk took its responsibility for morality with increasing seriousness over the next

---

44 J. Kirk, ed., *The Second Book of Discipline* (Edinburgh: St Andrew Press, 1980). BUK II, 488 ff; III SBSH 22–31. On the antecedents and tenor of the *Book* see Kirk's 'Introduction', 1–157. It was Melville who told James VI that despite being king he was only 'God's silly vassal'.

45 G.D. Henderson, *Presbyterianism* (Aberdeen: Aberdeen UP, 1954); J. Kennedy, *Presbyterian Authority and Discipline* (Edinburgh: St Andrew Press, 1960).

46 See the First Chapter of the *Second Book* on the Two Kingdoms.

47 D. Shaw, *The General Assemblies of the Church of Scotland, 1560–1660* (Edinburgh: St Andrew Press, 1964), 200–202.

48 Shaw, *supra* n. 47, 'Censorship and the Control over Presses and Books', 220–30.

49 Shaw, *supra* n. 47, 220. Intriguingly the Reformed Kirk operated the Act 1551, c. 26 (c. 27 12mo) – a pre-Reformation statute – for these purposes.

decades.⁵⁰ It was not for nothing that the Church Jurisdiction Act 1567 c. 12 noted the Kirk's duty as to the 'correctioun of maneris'. Immediate supervision was through the parish, the minister and kirk session, albeit that it was more than a generation before every parish had a kirk session.⁵¹ Then we find the Act 1592 c. 140, 'against unlawful conditions in contracts', proscribing usury.

Formally, welfare had been a concern of the pre-Reformation church, although implementation seems to have been sporadic.⁵² After the Reformation, parishes continued in measure to care for their sick. However, the control and operation of the hospitals never formally passed to the Kirk, and seems to have become a responsibility of the Crown. The Act 1579 c. 17 (c. 74 12mo) was a major attempt to deal with such questions. The Lord Chancellor was instructed to review the foundation documents of all hospitals with a view to returning them to their original purpose of serving the 'aged, impotent and pure [poor]'.⁵³ To cope with economic relief, the poor were instructed to return to their parishes of their birth or of their ordinary residence of at least seven years, where they would be entered on a Register. Thereafter assistance to individuals in both burgh and landward parishes was to be provided by a tax levied on all inhabitants of the parish, without exception. The Act also dealt with allocating recipients to their appropriate parishes and for transfer between them, severe punishment being meted out on those who refused to obey directions. There is little direct evidence how well this system worked, but the Act 1592 c. 159⁵⁴ anent the hospital in Edinburgh may show how such matters were dealt with.⁵⁵ Later this duty, at least in landward parishes, was passed to the local Kirk Session, and a substantial body of law developed dealing with the administration of Poor Relief.⁵⁶

After the question of poor relief, the Act 1579 c. 17 (c.74 12mo) dealt with 'strang and idle beggaris' and 'vagabondis'. These were to be deterred by stocks and irons, the possibility of a whipping and by having their ears pierced by a hot iron. 'Ordinary' beggars might ply their trade only within the parish of their residence.⁵⁷ Particular other kinds of itinerant beggars were made the subject of further provision. Those who used subtle, crafty and unlawful games such as juggling or fast-and-loose and the like were to be punished.⁵⁸ Gypsies, the 'idle peopill calling themselves *Aegyptians*, or any uther, that feinzes (feigns)

---

50 Cf. C. Kennedy, 'Criminal law and religion in post-reformation Scotland', 2012 Edin. L.R. 178; Cowan, *supra* n. 9, 182–205.
51 *Selections from the Records of the Kirk Session, Presbytery and Synod of Aberdeen*, Spalding Club, Aberdeen, 1846; J. Kirk, ed., *Stirling Presbytery Records, 1581–1587* (Edinburgh: Scot. Hist. Soc., 1981); A. Edgar, *Old Church life in Scotland: Lectures on Kirk Session and Presbytery Records* (Paisley: Gardner, First Series, 1885; Second Series, 1886).
52 See *supra* n. 6.
53 In fairness I note that a similar inspection for the same purpose had been instructed pre-Reformation by the Act 1424 c. 2 (c. 27 12mo).
54 Not printed in Record edition as not being a public and general statute.
55 Shaw, *supra* n. 47, 'The Hospitals', 203–5.
56 On the subsequent Poor Law, see A. Dunlop, *Poor Laws of Scotland* (Edinburgh: Blackwood, 1825, 1828, 1854); R.P. Lamond, *The Scottish Poor Laws* (Glasgow: Hodge, 1870, 1892). In later Victorian times the administration of Poor Relief became a governmental function through Parochial Boards, the parish remaining the appropriate district for the administrative purposes, though the matter had been removed from Kirk Sessions.
57 In the fifteenth century the principle was established that someone might be licensed to beg within the local authority area, if otherwise unable to find work: Act 1424 c. 25 12mo (not in Record edn).
58 Fast and loose was an analogue of the Gordian knot. Cf. F. Lyall, 'The Case of the Cumberland Whale: or "Fast and Loose"', 1999 *Aberdeen Univ. Rev.* 13–28, *ad fin*.

them to have knawledge of Charming, Prophecie, or uthers abused sciences, quairby they perswade the peopill that they can tell their weirdes, deathes and fortunes, and sik uther phantasticall imaginations' were also to be dealt with. So indeed were all minstrels, singers and storytellers who were not in the special service of Lords or burghs. Intriguingly, vagabond scholars of the Universities of St Andrews, Aberdeen and Glasgow, not licensed by their University to take alms, were to be fined, as were seamen who neglected their calling. While in modern terms there may be a social justification for these provisions, nonetheless standing behind it was the Pauline exhortation to work for one's own keep (II Thess. 3: 10), and the Biblical admonition against trafficking with spirits (Exod. 22: 18; cf. I Sam. 28). In any event the Act 1592 c. 69 (c. 149 12mo) instructed the civil authorities in the rest of Scotland to put the 1574 and similar Acts into force in their areas as Edinburgh was doing, and the Act 1597 c. 39 (c. 272 12mo) extended the power to enforce to kirk sessions in landward areas (that is, outside the burghs).

Correlative to the relief of the poor and the ill, concern was shown over undue or conspicuous consumption. Sumptuary laws, as legislation on such matters is known, were common throughout Europe in the fifteenth and sixteenth centuries, as matters of class distinction, morality and the preservation of guild monopolies. Scotland was no different,[59] but it is interesting to find such questions still of concern to the post-Reformation arbiters of propriety, though perhaps their motives were slightly different.[60] Thus the first part of the Act 1581 c. 18 (c. 113 12mo), 'Against the excess of costly clothing', set out a scale of income and status appropriate for particular styles of dress, and similar regulation was repeated in other admonitions.[61]

In the realm of spiritual welfare, Sunday was important and the Scottish Sunday was to become (in)famous. The views of the Roman Catholic Church and that of the Reformers coincided, but after the Reformation there was increased legislative activity. Down to the 1707 Union of the Parliaments a series of statutes dealt with Sunday observance, but the very need for that stream of legislation may indicate that it tended to fail. Public censure by the Kirk Session rather than penal law may have been more effective.[62] However, one long-lasting effect of the attitudes of the Reformers and their successors was that for many legal purposes Sunday was to be a '*dies non*'.[63]

Sexual morality was another matter of concern. The Fornication Act 1567 c. 14,[64] and the three against adultery, 1551 c. 12, 1563 c. 10 (which permitted the death penalty for notour adultery) and 1581 c. 7, remained on the statute book until the Statute Law Revision (Scotland) Act 1906. Parts of the Incest Act 1567 c. 15, incorporating Leviticus 18, remained

---

59 Cf. the Acts 1429 cc. 8, 9 and 10 (c.118 12mo): 'Anent the persones that sall weare claithes of Silke and Furringes' (sc. fur trimmings), and Act 1457 c.13 (c.70 12mo), 'Of coastly clothing'.

60 On the 'Sumptuary laws' see J. Irvine Smith and I. MacDonald, 'Criminal Law', in *An Introduction to Scottish Legal History* (Edinburgh: Stair Society, Vol. 20, Edinburgh,), 1958, 280–301 at 288 – these laws went beyond matters of dress to menu; Walker, *supra* n. 10, 'Restraint of dress', 649.

61 For example, the Act 1587 c.16 (c.36 12mo) required members of the Estates (that is, Members of Parliament) to be modest in their dress, the penalty for any breach being exclusion from Parliament House.

62 Walker, *supra* n. 10, 649–50.

63 See Chapter 8, '7. Sunday Observance'. The bulk of the Sunday Observance Acts were held to have fallen into desuetude in their criminal aspect in *Brown* v *Magistrates of Edinburgh*, 1931 SLT 456. Most of the remaining Sunday Acts were eliminated by the Statute Law Revision (Scotland) Act, 1964.

64 Said by Erskine (2nd ed. 1785) IV.4.52, to have been held to be in desuetude in *Donaldson*, 8th July 1768. Desuetude requires a contrary practice (!?).

longer.⁶⁵ The Parricide Act 1594 c. 30 (c. 224 12mo) is still with us. On that line, the later Act anent Cursing and Beating of Parents, 1661 c. 215 imposed the death penalty for that offence, unless the child was furious (sc. insane), thus enacting Deut. 21: 18–21.⁶⁶

*

It is unnecessary here to go into the detail of the history of the struggles between the church and the state, and between episcopacy and presbyterianism of the next years. James VI sought to control the Church since it was the major alternative power within the kingdom, but political reasons forced him to accept many of the Church's demands. Thus in 1579 the Church Act c. 6 re-enacted the establishment of the Protestant Church, affirming that the 'only trew and haly Kirk of Jesus Christ within this realme' was composed of those who professed the Scots Confession. The Church Jurisdiction Act 1579 c. 7 re-stated the jurisdiction of the Church. In 1581 the King and his household subscribed the Negative Confession,⁶⁷ denying all doctrines contrary to those of the Scots Confession. Despite all this, the Black Acts of 1584 sought to re-impose episcopacy, and placed all authority, including ecclesiastical authority under the Crown. But by 1590 the Presbyterian party was once more in the ascendant.

The General Assembly Act 1592 c. 8, sometimes referred to as 'The Great Charter of the Church', is the statutory foundation of the presbyterian character of the Church of Scotland. It ratified and approved the previous Acts regarding the Protestant religion (though not the Black Acts of 1584), and the form of church governance by the General Assembly, Synods, Presbyteries and Kirk Sessions. These had power and jurisdiction in matters ecclesiastical.⁶⁸ The Act repeated statements from Chapter VII of *The Second Book of Discipline* and gave foundation to what is still in law the present established Church. But, though this Act was of great importance in settling the polity of the Church for it was to be grafted in to the constitution of the United Kingdom at the Union of 1707, by a variety of astute moves James was able to diminish its practical importance. Thus the Act expressly preserved patronage, a device which could be used by the civil authority. Again the calling of General Assemblies was left as a matter for the Crown, and James used this power to call Assemblies at a variety of venues less under Presbyterian control than Edinburgh. In short, in the space of a few years James was able to secure the re-creation of bishops, and through their agency was able to control the Church,⁶⁹ but only after his accession to the English throne in 1603.

The next century saw a struggle between church and state and between rival theories of church government, which need not detain us. For a time episcopacy was enforced and there were the famous struggles of the Covenanters.⁷⁰ The 'Divine Right of Kings' propagated by

---

65 The Incest Act 1567 was repealed and replaced by the Incest and Related Offences (Scotland) Act 1986.
66 D. Hume, *Commentaries on the Law of Scotland Respecting Crimes*, 4th ed. (Edinburgh: Bell & Bradfute, 1844; rep. Law Soc. Scot., 1986) I, 318–9. The Act was repealed by the Statute Law Revision (Scotland) Act 1964.
67 BUK III, 515; III SBSH, 32–5; G. Donaldson, ed., *Scottish Historical Documents* (Edinburgh: Scot. Acad. Press, 1970), 150; J.D. Douglas, *Light in the North* (London: Paternoster Press, 1964) App. I. 'The Negative Confession was the basis of the National Covenant of 1638, and the Solemn League and Covenant of 1644'.
68 Synods were abolished as from 1 January 1993 by GA Act V, 1992.
69 III SBSH, 54–61. Cf. the *Basilikon Doron* (many eds) which James addressed to his first 'dearest son and natural successor', Henry, who died aged 18 in 1612. Charles I, Henry's brother, ought to have read his father's advice. Maybe he did. Had he heeded it history might be different.
70 D. Stevenson, ed., *The Government of Scotland under the Covenanters, 1637–1651* (Edinburgh: Scot. Hist. Soc., ser. 4, Vol. 18); his *The Scottish Revolution, 1637–1644: the Triumph of the Covenanters* (Newton

the later Stuarts at least in part on erastian theories was met by Rutherford's *Lex, Rex* arguing that the law is king, not the will of an autocrat, and that sovereignty inheres in the people the monarch being subject to it.[71] Based upon Covenanting principles, this called for the end of any form of episcopacy and a general revision of the constitutional structure, a revision which the people had the right to require in the face of abuses.

In the middle of this period saw one of the most important developments in Scottish church history. During the struggles between the English Parliament and Charles I the Westminster Parliament resolved on the reformation of the liturgy, discipline and government of the English Church. A Westminster Assembly was convened, to which the Church of Scotland sent eight Commissioners in an advisory capacity.[72] The Assembly hoped to produce a settlement of religion that would secure the 'Godly Commonwealth', a Puritan (and for Scotland a presbyterian) Church throughout the United Kingdom. The enterprise failed. Nonetheless the Assembly drew up the *Form of Church Government*, the *Directory of Public Worship* and *The Longer* and *The Shorter Catechism*. The central result was the *Westminster Confession of Faith*, the main part of the hoped for uniformity of religion in Britain, which was adopted in 1646.[73] The Confession is a much more careful and precise document than the Scots Confession of 1560. It purports to contain the sum and substance of reformed doctrine, rather than being the belief of a group of Protestants in one country, and in most points it fairly reflects the theology of its day. In 1647 the General Assembly of the Church of Scotland – with minor modification, explanations and reservations – adopted it as the Confession of the Church,[74] and two years later required all ministers and elders to further its teaching. On 7 February 1649 the Scots Parliament approved and ratified the Confession and Catechisms. However, following the restoration of the monarchy with Charles II in 1660, the legislation of that Parliament was struck down by the Recissory Act, 1661 c. 46.[75]

Under Charles II episcopacy was restored, and persecution began again to crush the presbyterianism of the Covenants. In 1669 the Act c. 2, an Act of Supremacy, asserted the Royal supremacy over all persons and in ecclesiastical matters. The Test Act of 1681 c. 6 once more asserted the Royal supremacy and required the renunciation of the National Covenant

---

Abbot: David & Charles, 1973); his *Revolution and Counter-Revolution in Scotland* (London: Royal Hist. Soc., 1977); I.B. Cowan, *The Scottish Covenanters, 1660–88* (London: Gollancz, 1976); J. Buckroyd, *Church and State in Scotland, 1660–1681* (Edinburgh: John Donald, 1980); J.D. Douglas, *supra* n. 67.

71 S. Rutherford, *Lex, Rex or The Law and the Prince; A Dispute for the Just Prerogative of King and People, 1644* (London: Maxwell, 1644; Harrisonburg, VA: Sprinkle Publications, 1980).

72 121 ministers and 30 laymen (20 from the House of Lords, 10 from the House of Commons) were appointed by the English Parliament. The Scottish Commissioners had no vote. They were Alexander Henderson, Robert Douglas and George Gillespie of Edinburgh, Samuel Rutherford of St Andrews and Robert Baillie of Glasgow (ministers), the Earl of Cassilis, John, Lord Maitland (later Duke of Lauderdale) and Sir Archibald Johnston of Wariston (ruling elders) and were accompanied by three scribes, Henry Robrough, Adoniram Byfield and John Wallis.

73 C.B. van Dixhoom, D.F. Wright, M.A. Garcia, J.A. Halcomb and I. Jones, eds, *The Minutes and Papers of the Westminster Assembly, 1643–1653* (Oxford: Oxford UP, 2012), The 1163 sessions of the Assembly 1643–49, were not always well attended. Three further sessions were held before the Assembly concluded in 1652. See also R.S. Paul, *The Assembly of the Lord: Politics and Religion in the Westminster Assembly and the 'Grand Debate'* (Edinburgh: T&T Clark, 1985);

74 GA Act 1647, August 27. Sess. 23; SSFCS xxvii–xxviii. Important modifications related to the claim of the Crown to call Assemblies of the Church stressing the right of the Kirk itself to meet irrespective of the will of the Civil Magistrate, and other points relating to their relations.

75 Act anent the Catechisms, Confession of Faith and the Ratification thereof: Chas. 1, Parl. 2, Sess. 2, Act 16.

1560–1843 Reformation to Disruption

and the Solemn League and Covenant by all persons in positions of public trust.[76] In all this the Westminster Confession was not mentioned.[77] However, following the 1688 Revolution and the flight of James VII and II the re-settlement of church affairs gave the Westminster Confession the position that it held for many years thereafter. The Revolution itself was a mainly English affair, but in Scotland the consequent legislation was used once more to guard the Scottish Church against episcopacy, the instrument through which the Crown had sought to subject the Church to itself, and to re-enact legislation establishing Presbyterian Protestantism as the form of church government in the realm. More particularly it was sought to secure that never again would the civil authority have power lawfully to repeat the severities of the suppression of the Covenanters.

The first section of the Claim of Right, 1689 c. 28,[78] narrates that James VII had forfeited the throne on the conveniently hitherto forgotten ground that he:

> Being a profest papist did assume the Regall power and acted as King without ever takeing the oath required by law wherby the King at his access [accession] to the government is obliged to swear To maintain the protestant religion and to rule the people according to the laudble [laudable] lawes . . .[79]

More importantly he did:

> By the advyce of wicked and evill Counsellers Invade the fundamentall Constitution of this Kingdome And altered it from a legall limited monarchy to ane Arbitary Despotick power and in a public proclamation asserted ane absolute power to cass [quash] annull and dissable all the lawes particularly arrainging the lawes Establishing the protestant Religion and to the violation of the lawes and liberties of the Kingdome.

For these and other specified reasons the Estates of the Kingdom of Scotland found and declared that:

> . . . he hath forfaulted [forfeited] the right to the Croune and the throne is become vacant.

The throne was therefore offered to William and Mary in the confidence that they would more properly carry out the duties of monarchy.

Although the first parliament of the new reign abolished prelacy by the Act 1689 c. 4, it was not until the next year that a series of Acts dealt with major questions of the government of the church. Act 1690 c. 1 repealed the Act of Supremacy, 1669 c. 2. Act 1690 c. 2

---

76 James, Lord Stair, one of the institutional writers of Scots Law, was active in the debates on the Test Act, and secured that it set the Scots Confession as the standard of Protestantism. This made the Test self-contradictory since the Scots Confession placed the Church in an independent position while the Test asserted Royal Supremacy. See A.J.G. Mackay, *Memoir of Sir James Dalrymple, First Viscount Stair* (Edinburgh: Edmonston and Douglas, 1873), 144–7.
77 See Innes I, 68; II, 39, noting that the insertion of the Scots Confession into the Test Act was made easy because it had fallen into general oblivion after the introduction of the Westminster Confession.
78 Technically this was an Act of a Convention of Estates rather than of a Parliament cf. the Acts of 1560.
79 A reference to the Coronation Oath Act 1567 c. 8.

re-instated in their parishes all the ministers who had been dispossessed during the previous troubles because of their adherence to Covenanting principles, and the Act 1690 c. 53 provided for the abolition of patronages by their being bought out. However, the key of the Revolution Settlement in relation to church and state in Scotland is the Confession of Faith Ratification Act 1690 c. 7, an Act 'Ratifying the Confession of Faith and settling Presbyterian Church Government'.

As in the Act 1560 c. 1 and the Scots Confession, the Act 1690 c. 7 deals with a settlement of religion that is described as true, as Protestant and as according to the truth of God's Word, but it adds that this religion is secured 'as it hath of a long time been professed within this land', which, in view of history, was rather sweeping. The 1690 Act once more ratified the Presbyterian government of the church, and all the laws against Popery and papists were revived and perpetually confirmed. So were the laws for the maintenance of the true Reformed Protestant religion and of the Church of Christ. Further, the Westminster Confession of Faith subjoined to the Act was approved as the Confession of the Church of Scotland.[80] The Presbyterian form of church government was once more given the statutory approval which it had obtained in 1592, and the Church was enjoined to 'try and purge out all Insufficient, negligent, scandalous and erroneous Ministers'.

There were problems with the 1690 Act. For example while it enacted the Westminster Confession, it did so without the reservations and explanatory notes of the 1647 General Assembly. This had the effect *inter alia* of allowing the Crown alone to call Assemblies – a defect which was not put right until 1927.[81] That admitted, the 1690 Act stands as the second foundation of the Church of Scotland. Nonetheless, other questions arose and had to be settled. An important one was whether the Confession of Faith had to be subscribed by ministers as their Confession, since a Confession need not be a standard of belief. William intervened to aid the former episcopalian ministers who wished to join the Church, and then, the Church delaying, Parliament passed the Ministers Act 1693 c. 38, 'An Act for Setling the Quiet and Peace of the Church'. This required ministers to subscribe the Confession and to submit to the Presbyterian form of government.[82] It also required observance of uniformity of worship 'as the samen are at present performed and allowed' in the Church or would in the future be declared by authority of the Church. In the short term this was a useful intervention, but it raised fears, later justified, that it implied that under law the church establishment might be more subject to the will and legislation of the civil power than Andrew Melville would have welcomed.

*

A projected Union between the Parliaments of England and Scotland was the next major step in the relations of church and state in Scotland. In the last years of William's reign, notwithstanding the abolition of prelacy in 1689 and its condemnation in the Confession of Faith Ratification Act 1690, William had attempted to secure control over the Church by

---

80 Innes I, 71–2, II, 42–3, notes that the adoption of the Confession differs from that of the adoption of the Protestant religion. The Scots Confession was ratified in 1560 as the Confession of the members of Parliament. The 1690 Act ratifies the Reformed faith, and binds the state to maintain the Confession. A distinction is therefore present between the state and its members and the Church and its members. This could be argued to be the beginning of modern concepts of church and state the Scottish legal system.

81 S. Mechie, *The Office of Lord High Commissioner* (Edinburgh: St Andrew Press, 1957), 51–2.

82 This was not changed as a matter of law until the Churches (Scotland) Act 1905, whose major purpose was the solving of the consequences of the Free Church case of 1904. See *infra* Chapter 5.

swinging the Church back to episcopacy.[83] As a result and because of previous history, in the Union negotiations the Scots intended that the Presbyterian polity of the Church should not be affected in any way. This was secured in two ways. First, the Act 1705 c. 50 appointing the Scottish Commissioners for the negotiations concluded with the provision:

> That the said commissioners shall not treat of, or concerning, any alteration of the worship, discipline, and government of the Church of this kingdom as now by law established.

Religion was thus removed from the negotiating table and did not form part of the discussion. Second, Parliament passed the Protestant Religion and Presbyterian Church Act, 1706 c. 6, the Act of Security,[84] and appointed it to be inserted into any legislation that might enact a Treaty of Union with England:

> And that the [Act] shall be therein expressly Declared to be a fundamental and essential condition of the said Treaty or Union in all time comeing.

The Act 1706 c. 6 narrated its predecessors, and, considering that it was necessary that 'the true Protestant religion as presently professed' should be 'effectually and unalterably' secured, it stated that the Queen:

> with the advice and consent of the said Estates of Parliament, Doth hereby Establish and confirm the said true Protestant Religion and Worship Discipline and Government of the Church to continue without any alteration to the people in this land in all succeeding generations . . .[85]

To that end the Confession of Faith Ratification Act 1690 c. 7, together with relative Acts, were once again all ratified and confirmed by the 1706 Act. The Presbyterian form of Church government and discipline were thus secured. Other lesser provisions were added as to subscription of the Confession by professors, the continuance of the universities and colleges of the realm and the forbiddance of the imposition of oaths contrary to the established religion. The Act concluded by providing that future sovereigns should on accession take an oath to preserve inviolable the settlement of the Protestant religion and Presbyterian church government made by this legislation.

As required, the Act of Security was inserted in the Union with England Act 1707 c. 7, and also appears in s. 2 of the Union with Scotland Act 1706, its English counterpart. The Union became effective on 1 May 1707, and the new Parliament began its life.

It soon appeared that the security of the Church of Scotland was not as effective as had been thought, and weaker in respect of state interference than had been intended. In particular, in *Greenshields* v *Magistrates of Edinburgh* (1710) Rob. App. 12, a successful appeal was made from the Scottish courts to the House of Lords, in itself an arguable breach of the

---

83 For this reason Acts 1700 c. 2 and 1702 c. 3 are Acts of Security for the Church.
84 England provided similarly: The Maintenance of the Church of England Act 1706, 6 Anne c. 8.
85 One effect of this language was that the provisions of the Ministers Act 1693 c. 38, allowing for the development of worship as the Church might prescribe, vanished. See text above following n. 82. The worship of the Church was made unalterable.

Union agreements.[86] An Episcopalian, Greenshields had been ordained in 1690 in England just after the abolition of Episcopacy in Scotland. In 1710 he opened a place of worship in Edinburgh, but the Edinburgh magistrates threatened to imprison him if he did not close it down. The Presbytery of Edinburgh, responsible for preaching within its area, had found him not qualified to minister within their bounds, and the magistrates were attempting to sanction their finding. The Court of Session refused to disturb their decision of the magistrates, so Greenshields took his case successfully to London.

The *Greenshields* decision ran contrary to the tenor of the protections of Presbyterianism enshrined in the Union agreements as they were understood by the Presbyterians. The Scottish Episcopalians Act, 1711, c. 12,[87] took this undermining further. Affording toleration to those in Scotland of the Episcopalian persuasion, it caused much offence to the presbyterian Church of Scotland.[88] Again by the Yule Vacance Act, 1711, the Westminster Parliament repealed the Scots Act 1690 c. 22, which forbad the Scottish courts to abstain from sitting on Christmas Day and some other English holidays.[89] This was also considered as an attack on Presbyterianism. Finally, the Church Patronage (Scotland) Act, 1711, re-established patronage in the Kirk. This was to produce the strife and difficulty and eventually in 1843 the disruption of the Kirk, as discussed in the next chapter. Suffice it here to note that these Acts showed the Union Parliament not unwilling to legislate in matters which the Scottish Church considered to lie within its province.[90] However, the basis of such legislation was already there, for the Acts of the Revolution Settlement, and even those of 100 years previously, had seen the civil authority legislating for the Church. Whatever the original position, even were it true that the church had been recognised and not created by the state, there were sufficient instances to make it arguable that the state had the right so to legislate.

A modern argument might be that the General Assembly Act 1592, the Confession of Faith Ratification Act 1690, the Protestant Church and Presbyterian Church Act 1706 and all the others had merely recognised an already existing and self-existent and self-regulating community separate from the state that did not require civil sanction for the validity of its institutions and decisions. But in the then prevalent political requirements of monolithic authority, such a theory was not one that might be listened to. The theory of the single sovereign from whom all power is drawn, expressed in Hobbes' *Leviathan*,[91] and later in the legal theory of John Austin,[92] was in the ascendant. Church history of the next years shows

---

86 The Agreements had prohibited appeals from the Court of Session to 'Westminster Hall', but the House of Lords, which did not sit in Westminster Hall, decided it had jurisdiction to hear the appeal.

87 The Act is sometimes cited as 1712. It was actually passed in 1712, and became effective then. However, until the Acts of Parliament (Commencement) Act 1793 (33 Geo. 3, c. 13) Acts were deemed to come into force from the beginning of the parliamentary term in which they were passed. 1711 is therefore legally correct.

88 The Act gave a toleration to Episcopalians in Scotland, not mirrored by an equivalent toleration of Presbyterians in England.

89 A.V. Dicey and R.S. Rait, *Thoughts on Union between England and Scotland* (London: Macmillan, 1920), 282–3.

90 Senior church dignitaries presented a Memorial to Parliament protesting the 1711 Acts. This Memorial was later held to be 'the deed and mind of the Church' by the General Assembly: GA Act II, 1715, and regularly thereafter throughout the eighteenth century. Buchanan I, 127–31; Innes I, 119.

91 Thomas Hobbes, *Leviathan or The Matter, Forme and Power of a Common Wealth Ecclesiasticall and Civil* (1651), many eds.

92 J. Austin, *The Province of Jurisprudence Determined, 1832* (many eds). His *Lectures in Jurisprudence* were published posthumously by his widow along with a second edition of the *Province* in 1862. The best edition of the *Lectures* is R. Campbell, 5th ed. (London: John Murray, 1885). Cf. J. Bentham, *The Limits of Jurisprudence Defined*, C.W. Everett, ed. (New York: Columbia UP, 1945).

it developing through the Scottish church under the influence of Moderatism, and spread through the institution of patronage. Increasingly the Kirk was seen as subject to the laws of the state, and possessing no more freedom than that which might be directly spelled out of the civil legislation. The Disruption of the Church in 1843 was the direct result of the collision of a theory of the monolithic state with the idea of the independent Church, that earlier had to a degree been expressed in Andrew Melville's *Second Book of Discipline*.

In the meantime other Christian churches came into being.[93] As Chapter 5 shows, at first the law did not recognise their existence, but they did spread. Sometimes they stemmed from dissatisfaction with the organisation of the Kirk, sometimes through objection to doctrine.[94] The Cameronians, descendants of the Covenanters, 'came out' of the Kirk, opposing the 1690 provisions as departing from covenanting principle.[95] There were other Seceders.[96] In 1733 a group headed by Ebenezer Erskine left the Kirk over the question of who had the right to nominate a minister to a charge when the patron had not acted timeously. They formed an Associate Presbytery. Another, the Relief Church, began in 1761. Founded by Thomas Gillespie and others, it was originally named the 'Presbytery of Relief'. Gillespie had been deposed by the General Assembly for refusing to take part in the induction of a minister who had been presented by the patron to the parish of Inverkeithing but whose settlement had been opposed by the congregation. The Relief Church provided 'relief' from patronage.[97] Such groups were to merge and split, in particular over the question of the Burgess Oath and as to elements of the Westminster Confession. However, most coalesced to form the United Secession church in 1820, which, with other traditions, fused into the United Presbyterian Church in 1847. In 1901 that denomination was to join with the Free Church of Scotland, itself to be birthed by the Disruption of the Kirk in 1843, to form the United Free Church of Scotland. The bulk of that Church was to rejoin a new re-constituted Church of Scotland in 1929.

---

93 See Chapter 5 for a more extended survey.
94 Cf. D. Lachman, *The Marrow Controversy* (Edinburgh: Rutherford House, 1988); E. Fisher, *The Marrow of Modern Divinity* (Fearn: Christian Focus, 2009).
95 Cf. http://website.lineone.net/~davghalgh/churchhistorytext.html#cameronians. See also Chapter 5, n. 13 ff. They formed the Reformed Presbyterian Church, the bulk of which joined the Free Church after it came into being in 1843.
96 J. M'Kerrow, *History of the Secession Church* (Edinburgh: Fullarton, 1847); A. Thomson, *Historical Sketch of the Origin of the Secession Church* (Edinburgh: Fullarton, 1848).
97 G. Struthers, *The History of the Rise, Progress and Principles of the Relief Church* (Glasgow: Fullarton, 1843). Cf. *Annals of the General Assembly of the Church of Scotland from the Origin of the Relief in 1752 to the Rejection of the Overture on Schism in 1766* (Edinburgh: Johnstone, 1840).

3   1843–1929 Disruption to union

The Disruption

The period 1834–43 that ends with the Disruption of the Church of Scotland is generally referred to as 'The Ten Years' Conflict'.[1] During it the state and the Church of Scotland collided. The opinions uttered by both the civil and ecclesiastical courts, and the inaction of government, helped form the present law. The civil courts held the Church limited by the statute law of the realm. Government refused remedy or redress. One section of the Church therefore, unable or unwilling to accept what it considered to be an erastian position, seceded to form the Free Church of Scotland. When in the early years of the twentieth century there were moves to reunite, the constitution of the 'new' Church of Scotland had therefore to provide for a new church-state relationship. Here we are concerned with the injury, not the subsequent repair work.

The core of the dispute was the old question of supremacy and control, with an added element from the contemporary movement towards popular government which had produced electoral reform in the Reform Act and the Representation (Scotland) Act, both of 1832.

---

1 The principal contemporary authorities are: R. Buchanan, *The Ten Years' Conflict: Being a History of the Disruption of the Church of Scotland*, 2 vols (Glasgow: Blackie, 1856). J. Bryce, *Ten Years of the Church of Scotland, from 1833 to 1843, with a Historical Retrospect from 1560*, 2 vols (Edinburgh: Blackwood, 1850). Both are partisan. Buchanan is Evangelical, Bryce, Moderate. See also T. Brown, *Annals of the Disruption* (Edinburgh: MacNiven & Wallace, 1883, 1884, 1886, 1892, 1893).

Modern accounts are: G.D. Henderson, *Heritage: A Study of the Disruption* (Edinburgh: Oliver & Boyd, 1943); A.L. Drummond and J. Bulloch, *The Scottish Church, 1688–1843: The Age of the Moderates* (Edinburgh: St Andrew Press, 1973); Alan, Lord Rodger, *The Courts, the Church and the Constitution: Aspects of the Disruption of 1843* (Edinburgh: Edinburgh UP, 2008); G.I.T. Machin, *Politics and the Churches in Great Britain* (Oxford: Clarendon Press, 1977), 112–47; G.I.T. Machin, 'The Disruption and British Politics' (1972), 51 Scot. Hist. Rev. 20; S.J. Brown, 'The Ten Years Conflict and the Disruption of 1843', in S.J. Brown and M Fry, eds, *Scotland in the Age of the Disruption* (Edinburgh: 1993), 1–27; D. Paton, *The Clergy and the Clearances: The Church and the Highland Crisis, 1790–1850* (Edinburgh: John Donald, 2006), 143–73. A fictional depiction based on North-East Scotland is W.A. Alexander, *Johnny Gibb of Gushetneuk* (Aberdeen: Walker, 1871) many eds (some acquaintance with the Doric recommended, though some eds include a glossary).

The occasion of the dispute was the legislative action of the General Assembly of the Church of Scotland in 1834 which passed, first, the Veto Act, affecting the operation of civil statute law relating to the appointment of a minister – the question of patronage – and, second, the Chapel Act, which affected the civil law on membership of the courts of the Church, and their operation.

The disputants were the Evangelicals and the Moderates, and, brought in by the latter, the civil courts. Government and Parliament then became involved. The parties should not, however, be considered as separate contenders. Many were active in a variety of guises. Some in the courts, government and Parliament were not members of the Church of Scotland, and arguably their lack of knowledge or familiarity with the Kirk, and in some cases their adherence to other forms of church government, contributed to the problem rather than its solution. The classification as Evangelical or Moderate is only approximate. Though many of the ministerial leaders were Tories, for example Thomas Chalmers who was to lead the Disruption,[2] the Evangelicals tended to be liberal in politics. They laid stress on individual conversion, were 'enthusiastic' and sought to free the Church from the 'deadening fetters' of 'worldly institutions'. It is difficult to define 'Moderatism' save as being 'moderate', and in being generally opposed to the wildness and ungentlemanly enthusiasm of Evangelicalism. In professed doctrine, most Moderates were as theologically orthodox as the Evangelicals.[3] However, the depth of their doctrinal commitment may be doubted. They were rationalist, devoting only part of their time, talents and energies to their work.[4] Satisfactory performance of their tasks comprised in 'administering the ordinances of religion' – an almost ceremonial approach with little apparent depth of care for their parishioners as fellow human beings[5] – and they were 'moderate' in their zeal. In politics they were aligned with the Tories. These attitudes, opposed in their view of the ministerial function, and in the extent of their desire to see doctrine mould personality and behaviour, collided over the Veto and Chapel Acts.

---

2   H. Watt, *Thomas Chalmers and the Disruption* (Edinburgh: Nelson, 1943); S.J. Brown, *Thomas Chalmers and the Godly Commonwealth* (Oxford: Oxford UP, 1982); A.C. Cheyne, ed., *The Practical and the Pious: Essays on Thomas Chalmers (1780–1847)* (Edinburgh: St Andrew Press, 1985); W. Hanna, *Memoirs of Thos. Chalmers*, 4 vols (Edinburgh: Constable, 1849–54).

3   Drummond, *supra* n. 1; G.B. Robertson, *Spiritual Awakening in the North-East of Scotland and the Disruption of the Church in 1843*, unpublished doctoral dissertation, University of Aberdeen, 1971.

4   Chalmers was originally a Moderate, and lectured in Chemistry in the University of St Andrews while holding his first charge in Fife. His interest in science can be seen in his *Discourses on the Christian Revelation Viewed in Connection with the Modern Astronomy* (Glasgow: John Smith, 1817), which includes consideration of life on other worlds. See *supra* nn. 1 and 2. The Rev. R. Stirling of Kilmarnock invented the 'Stirling Engine' in 1816, which has many modern applications (R. Sier, *Reverend Robert Stirling D.D: A Biography of the Inventor of the Heat Economiser and Stirling Cycle Engine* (Chelmsford: Mair, 1995)); the Rev. A.J. Forsyth of Belhelvie, Aberdeenshire, invented the percussion cap in 1807, a major development for the British Army (see his entry in the Dictionary of National Biography).

5   I.D.L. Clark, 'From Protest to Reaction: The Moderate Regime in the Church of Scotland, 1752–1805', in N.T. Phillipson and R. Mitchison, eds, *Scotland in the Age of Improvement* (Edinburgh: Edinburgh UP, 1970), 200–224. See also Buchanan I, 144–51; Cockburn II, 289–91; Bulloch I, sv. 'Moderates', but esp. 45–81.

I. The Veto and Chapel Acts 1834

The Veto Act[6]

The Veto Act tackled patronage in the Church. Patronage is the right to present someone to be the minister of a particular charge. It went beyond mere nomination, and meant that, unless the individual was so incompetent that Presbytery could not with any vestige of good faith induct him to that parish, the nominee of the patron would be settled as its minister.

Patronage was present in civil law before the Reformation, and a body of law had built up over the years.[7] Usually the right to present to a benefice was vested in the owner of property in the parish, but this was not necessarily the case. Someone who had erected or endowed a church, or his successors, might hold the patronage to that church. More rarely, where a congregation itself came together to build a church, the right to choose a minister might be vested in its members, and exercised by their free election.[8] Patronage was a right of property, inherited, sold or purchased like any other property right. Being civil in its nature, though of obvious religious consequence, it was some time before steps were taken to deal with it.

Patronage was attacked over the years for its many obvious defects. The selection of a minister for a parish might be in the hands of someone out of touch with parochial opinion, and without interest in the welfare of the congregation. The patron might not be capable of assessing the merits of possible appointees and the qualities required for ministry in that particular charge. Though in general the system seems to have worked through informal consultations, its results could be unfortunate.[9] As a matter of law, no formal place or standing was given to the views of members of the congregation. They might comment, but not decide.[10] There was the safeguard that a Presbytery might thereafter refuse to induct a presentee on grounds of qualification,[11] but this was very unlikely, and in practice ineffective.

Presentation to a charge had important financial and other benefits, giving the presentee legal right to the produce of the glebe,[12] the stipend,[13] and whatever other emoluments went with the post.[14] Although both the *First* and *Second Book of Discipline* frowned upon

---

6 Reference point, *infra* n. 48.
7 A.M. Dunlop, *Parochial Law* (Edinburgh: Blackwood, 1830, 1835, 1841), 174–308, and *The Law of Patronage and Settlement of Parochial Ministers* (Edinburgh: Blackwood, 1833); Erskine I.10–20; Stair II.8.27–35, More's Notes cxlii. Patronage was a matter of civil law and therefore amenable to the jurisdiction of the civil courts – see cases cited in these sources, and *infra* n. 53.
8 This was often the case in chapels of ease, whose ministers' membership of Presbytery gave rise to the Chapel Act discussed below.
9 Buchanan I, 151–61; Sir George MacKenzie, *Observations on the Acts of Parliament made by James I–Charles II* (Edinburgh: Anderson, 1687), Observation on Act 1592 c.121 (c.13 Record ed.). Cf. John Galt, *Annals of the Parish*, 1st ed. 1821 (many eds).
10 Under paras 3–4 of the section on 'The Rules of Examination' in the section 'Of the Ordination of Ministers' in *The Form of Church Government*, agreed in 1644 by the Westminster Assembly, and approved by the General Assembly Sess.16, 10 February 1645, parishioners could bring forward 'exceptions' against a person proposed for settlement as their minister. The nominee was required to be present in the parish for at least three days. On each he was to preach and meet parishioners informally. How often this was complied with is uncertain.
11 Erskine 1.5.16.
12 The glebe was an area of land, which the minister might farm or rent out.
13 Stipend was the basic salary paid to the minister. See Chapter 2 at n. 38.
14 Erskine I.5.13; Stair II.8.35; Dunlop, 180.

patronage, it was not swept away until the Act 1649 c. 39.[15] That Act was, however, struck down by the Recissory Act 1661 c. 46 which, as part of the 1660 Restoration, annulled all the Acts of the 1649 Parliament.

In 1690 opportunity again arose to consider patronage as part of the church and state settlement. The clauses regarding patronage were expressly exempted from the Confession of Faith Ratification Act 1690 c. 7 and on 19 July the Patronage Act 1690 c. 53 abolished patronages subject to the payment of compensation to former patrons.[16]

That position as to patronage in the constitution, worship and discipline of the Church whose protection was built in to the negotiations for the Union, the Treaty itself and the Union legislation as described at the end of the last chapter. However, the protection proved ineffective at least as to patronage. In a major infringement of the terms of the Union the Church Patronage (Scotland) Act, 1711, re-established patronage. This, along with the Scottish Episcopalians Act, also of 1711, was the subject of a Memorial of Protest presented to Parliament, since they showed the protective devices of the Union not to be as fundamental and inviolable as had been intended. This protest was repeated annually throughout the eighteenth century, but to no effect. Part of the Memorial stated that: 'by the act restoring the power of presentation to patrons the legally established constitution of this church was altered in a very important point'.[17] That was underlined as difficulties emerged, most notably where the patron was unwilling or unable to present to a charge. Church attempts to solve these problems were not particularly successful, and in part gave rise to the secessions of 1733 and 1752.[18] It is not too much to say as Lord Macaulay did:

> The British legislature violated the Articles of Union and made a change in the constitution of the Church of Scotland. From that change has flowed almost all the dissent now existing in Scotland. . . . Year after year the General Assembly protested against the violation but in vain; and from the act of 1712 undoubtedly flowed every secession and schism that has taken place in the Church of Scotland.[19]

Further dissatisfaction with patronage came from outside the Church. The rise of the evangelical movement throughout Britain in the latter half of the eighteenth and the first half of the nineteenth century is associated with the Wesleys, Whitfield, Robert Raikes and the Sunday Schools, with the creation of the Church Missionary Society, the Society for the

---

15 The *First Book of Discipline* states at Head 4.1.2: '. . . it appertaineth to the people and every several congregation to elect their minister'. The *Second Book of Discipline* states at c.3.4, '[Election to office] is . . . the chusing out of a person or personnes maist abill [able] to the office that vaikes [falls vacant] be the judgement of the eldership [sc. the Presbytery] and consent of the congregation to whom the person or personnes beis [is] appointed'. Both Books therefore indicated a role for the consent of the congregation in the appointment and settlement of a minister. See also n. 10 *supra*. However the Act 1567 c. 7 reserved the right of lay patronage. That Act is quoted Buchanan I, 103 and in *Kinnoull v Presbytery of Auchterarder* (1838) 16 S. 661 at 674 (the First Auchterarder case).
16 Only a few patronages had been bought out by the time the 1690 Act was repealed in 1711; First Auchterarder case (1838) 16 S. 661 at 680–681.
17 GA Act IX, 1715; Buchanan I, 121–31; Innes I, 119.
18 Buchanan I, 151–7; Burleigh, 280–285. See also narration in the First Auchterarder case (1838) 16 S. 661 at 682–6. For these secessions see Chapter 5 at n. 13ff.
19 Macaulay, *Speeches* (London: Longmans Green, 1866), II, 301; Innes I, 120; II, 60; cf. Bulloch I, 259–60. He dates the Act as 1712 but technically an Act was back-dated to the start of the regnal year in which it was passed so 1711 is accurate in law.

Propagation of Christian Knowledge and with the 'Clapham Sect' including Wilberforce and other social reformers. The movement spread into Scotland, particularly through the Haldanes,[20] and, having first been productive of independent congregations, began to permeate the established Church. As part of the normal (normative?) evangelical attitudes, patronage was criticised as incompatible with Christian freedom and responsibility. Indeed, most evangelicals were vehemently opposed to patronage, although, perhaps curiously, Thomas Chalmers was originally open-minded on the matter.[21]

The so-called Voluntary controversy strengthened opposition to patronage. An initial effect of the evangelical revival had been the creation of independent congregations. For them the Church of Christ should not be financed or beholden in any way to the state. Strict separation of church and state was the watchword and they attacked the established church for its subservience to the civil law as to patronage. Naturally, as in so many theological disputes, the most acrimonious debate was between the Voluntaries and the evangelicals within the Kirk, that is, between those who were otherwise closest in doctrine. While the evangelicals were willing to argue for a principle of establishment, they were not willing to defend the concept of state-created patronage. There were two lines of attack. First, the theological concept of the Church espoused by the Voluntaries required separation. Patronage was an evidence of the shackling of the Kirk to worldly institutions. Spiritual independence and the gospel privileges of the church had been sacrificed for financial gain. Second, and more practically, was the construction and maintenance of church property. Increasingly the established Church needed new churches to cope with a growing population particularly in the towns and cities, but the state was unwilling to make available any finance for the purpose. The burden necessarily therefore fell on the 'heritors', property owners in a parish who by law were required to defray the costs of the construction and maintenance of the established Kirk's buildings. Heritors who were not members of the established Kirk and opposed to the state connection did not see why they should be so burdened.

As he stated in 1826 and re-stated in 1838 in a series of public lectures which attracted much attention, Chalmers came to the view that the establishment of the Church of Scotland was not attended by the demerits with which it was usually taxed. For him the Assemblies and Presbyteries of the Kirk were capable in law of doing anything they thought right.[22] Following him, evangelicals asserted the power of the Kirk to govern its own affairs. To curb lay patronage by Act of Assembly without the intervention of Parliament would demonstrate that omni-competence.

Means were found in the concept and procedure for the 'call' of a minister to a parish which at least in theory came from the congregation and expressed its will. The 'call' had been introduced prior to the re-establishment of patronage in 1711, and had been retained despite its inconsistency with the right of patronage.[23]

---

20 Robert and James Haldane were influential Scottish Evangelicals in the early nineteenth century. A. Haldane, *The Lives of Robert Haldane of Airthrey and of his Brother James Alexander Haldane* (Edinburgh: Kennedy, 1856).
21 Bryce, Retro. 221–56; Buchanan I, 113–89; Bulloch I, 180–219; Burleigh, 309–33.
22 T. Chalmers, *Lectures on the Establishment and Extension of National Churches, Delivered in London April 25th – May 12th 1838* (Glasgow: Collins, 1838); Hanna (*supra* n. 2), IV, 45; Bryce I, 12; Buchanan I, 314–8. His declaration later came to be directly challenged by the Moderate wing of the Church and by the civil courts, but it does clearly indicate the mind of the evangelical wing of the Church at the time.
23 Buchanan I, 198–210. The operation of the call at this time is explained in the First Auchterarder case (1838) 16 S. 685–6.

Eleven overtures to the 1832 General Assembly proposed restoring the importance of the call of a minister to a parish. Members of the congregation ought to be given a greater say in the nomination and appointment of the person who was to minister the Word of God to them, and this could be achieved through a revivification of 'the call'. However, Principal MacFarlane of Glasgow University suggested that it was unnecessary and inexpedient to entertain the proposed measures at that time.[24] The matter was not proceeded with. In 1833 the General Assembly received 65 overtures on 'the call' and a motion: 'to appoint a committee to prepare the best measures for preventing the induction of a presentee should a majority of the people dissent with or without reasons' was lost by only 12 votes.[25] In response the Moderate majority carried a Declaratory Act which permitted 'objections of whatever nature against the presentee or against the settlement taking place' to be made by 'the heads of families in full and regular communion with the church'. The Presbytery was to be bound to investigate. Should it find the objections valid, the presentee was to be rejected as not qualified.[26]

Though it was never the subject of judicial decision, in the light of later court cases it is arguable that the 1833 Declaratory Act went as far as possible under the then ecclesiastical system and the civil law of patronage. Bryce, a staunch Moderate, thought it went to the very limit since it allowed objection not only to the life, literature and doctrine of the presentee, but to matters beyond.[27] But the 1833 Declaratory Act proved forlorn and the next year was to vanish.

In 1834 Evangelicals were the majority in the Assembly and carried their view into the law of the Kirk by GA Act XII, 1834, which has gone down into history as the Veto Act.[28] It declared it to be a fundamental law of the Church of Scotland that no minister should be intruded on a congregation contrary to the will of the people. Presbyteries considering a call to a vacant pastoral charge were to reject a presentation if a majority of the male heads of families, being members of the congregation, disapproved. No reasons had to be given for disapproval, nor was Presbytery to consider the merits. So long as each disapprover was prepared to declare that he was actuated by no malicious or factious motives, and to swear that he was moved solely by a conscious regard to the spiritual interests of himself and of the congregation, the settlement should not proceed.

The Veto Act can be (and was) criticised. It is vaguely framed, perhaps regrettably vaguely. People may 'disapprove' of the call, though inconsistently the call is the free gift of the people. Disapproval implies a test of qualification though the test of qualification was

---

24 Buchanan I, 210–228.
25 Acts of Assembly 1833, 45–6. Buchanan I, 210–238. Cockburn, Journals I, 44–5, notes that the minority contained a majority of ministers and suggests that had this motion been successful it would have deprived the anti-patronage movement of much of its strength. The defeat of the motion was therefore rather a defeat of the Moderates.
26 GA 1833, XLVI; Bryce I, 15.
27 Bryce I, 16. Cockburn, Journals II, 73 gives examples of the objections offered under the Scotch Benefices Act 1843, passed after the Disruption, but which may reflect the objections possible under the 1833 Declaratory Act. These included bodily infirmity, weakness of voice, stuttering, bad preaching style, intellectual feebleness, lameness, disagreeableness of manner, occasional exuberance of animal spirits, musical illiteracy and tone deafness. Cf. objections to the ordination of 'Jupiter' Carlyle in 1748, quoted by Clark, *supra*, n. 5, at 201, n. 3.
28 GA Act XII, 1834, Overtures and Interim Act on Calls, and Regulations; Acts of Assembly 1834, 31–6; GA Act IX, 1835. Bryce I, 21; Buchanan I, 255, note; Robertson Auchterarder I, App. 1; the First Auchterarder Case (1838) 16 S. 661 at 686; The Free Church Case [1904] AC 514 at 529. As to 'interim acts' see *infra* nn. 34 and 35.

a matter for Presbytery.[29] And so on: there were many arguments and much sophistry, all now dead. It may be that better drafting would have avoided some of the later difficulties, though that is a comment from hindsight. The Veto Act could have simply stated that the 'disapprovers' dissented from the settlement of a presentee and, were they a majority, presbyteries instructed not to take the presentee on trials.

The important point was that the Veto Act provided machinery to give the will of at least the heads of families in a congregation a crucial status in the selection and settlement of a minister. That their dissent should be conclusive that a man did not have the gifts appropriate to teach, edify and instruct that particular congregation seems elementary.[30] A presentee unable to discharge the pastoral duties involved was not qualified for that charge and the Presbytery ought not,[31] and should not induct him to that parish.[32]

Before the 1834 Assembly some doubted whether it was competent for the Assembly to enact the proposed Veto Act. Doubts even appear to have been expressed by Chalmers, the leader of the Evangelicals. It was, however, supported by the counsel, advice and active participation of men conversant with the law. Most notably the Lord Advocate (Jeffrey) and the Solicitor General (Cockburn) considered the Veto Act entirely competent, and the Report that gave immediate rise to the Act was moved by Lord Moncreiff, a Court of Session judge.[33]

The 1834 Assembly passed the Veto Act as an Interim Act by 184 to 139.[34] Three days later its mechanisms were set out.[35] One hundred and six members dissented from the step on grounds argued by Dr Mearns, Professor of Divinity in Kings College, Aberdeen.[36] His statement, adhered to by most of the moderate members of the Assembly, was subsequently repeatedly referred to in the civil courts. However, Mearns did not challenge the competency of the church to legislate as it had, just its wisdom. That challenge is only to be found in the 14 reasons for dissent given in separately by a single individual later pilloried by Buchanan as being the author of the Disruption since he later came to a position of eminence from which he could and did make his opinion felt. This was John Hope, Dean of the Faculty of Advocates. Hope dissented on the ground that in purporting to restrict the right of patronage the General Assembly had acted beyond its powers.[37] However, at this stage Hope did not suggest that the civil courts could do anything other than alienate the benefice,

---

29 Bryce I, 21–41.
30 It seems elementary, but even in the twenty-first century some ecclesiastics think differently. Cf. *supra* n. 10.
31 Buchanan I, 258. This view of 'qualification' was roundly dismissed by Lord Brougham in the House of Lords in the First Auchterarder Case (1839) McL. & Rob. 220 at 267–77, esp. 272; *infra* at n. 62.
32 At this time only men might be ministers. Women became eligible for the ministry in 1968 (GA Act 25 1968).
33 Bryce I, 25; Buchanan I, 262; Cockburn, Journals I, 160.
34 An Act of the General Assembly which affects doctrine, worship, government or discipline, requires the consent of a majority of Presbyteries to its enactment under Barrier Act procedure, the succeeding Assembly passing it into the law of the Church provided that it receives the appropriate level of Presbytery approval. During this procedure the Act is not in effect. In matters of urgency, however, an Act may be passed as an Interim Act and remains valid for one year. Cox 104.
35 These detailed procedures, who might dissent, and the compilation of rolls of possible dissentients. Buchanan I, 255 note; First Auchterarder Case (1838) 16 S. 661 at 668–91; Robertson's Auchterarder, I, App. I, 1–5. Although the 1834 Veto Act was converted into GA Act IX, 1835, the related regulations remained as Interim Acts, adopted year to year throughout the Ten Years' Conflict.
36 Buchanan I, 268.
37 Buchanan I, 268–9. Hope's father, Charles, then Lord President of the Court of Session, had been the first (in an Assembly debate in 1828) to suggest that, by reason of its establishing statutes, the powers of the Church were restricted: Buchanan I, 182–3.

that is award the rejected presentee the financial and civil rights stemming from the appointment, 'because I am clearly of opinion, in point of law, that a presentee, though rejected by a majority of heads of families, yet, there being no judgement of the church courts on his qualifications, will nevertheless be legally, validly and effectually presented to the benefice, and will have a clear right to the stipend and all other rights appertaining thereto'.[38] This restriction of the alleged incompetency of action of the church to civil matters should be borne in mind when considering the view Hope was to take in the later cases. It was not until he was advising in the First Auchterarder case that Hope sought to have the church compelled by the civil authority to act in accordance with the civil law.

The Chapel Act[39]

The Chapel Act, GA Act IX, 1834, was intended to give chapels of ease and their ministers a more effective place within the structures of the Kirk.[40] Chapels of ease were a response to history. Centres of population had grown remote, or at least detached, from the parish churches set up prior to or continued during the Reformation. The division of overgrown parishes and the erection of additional churches was the duty of Commissioners of Teinds authorised by the Scottish Parliament. The Act 1706 c. 10 transferred that jurisdiction to the Court of Session as a Court of Teinds and Plantation of Kirks but with limited powers. In particular a new parish and the consequent burdens connected with the church – the stipend of the minister, the duties and responsibilities in relation to the provision of schools, and so on – could be created only with the consent of heritors possessing at least three-quarters of the valued rent of the parish. Since this normally involved the heritors in increased expense, consent was not often forthcoming.[41] Accordingly, the Church had found it convenient to erect what were known as 'Chapels of Ease', located within parishes *quoad omnia*, but with only a preaching function. By the time of the Disruption in 1843 over 200 chapels of ease had been created.

Chapels of ease were not popular with the ruling authorities, particularly because they were normally served by evangelical ministries.[42] Equally important, they were usually created free of patronage, and government resisted attempts to impose that yoke. It followed that the ministers of chapels of ease and their congregations had a freedom of action not available to the normal *quoad omnia* church.[43] Although Buchanan puts the point extremely, Moderate dominated Assemblies of the period did impede development of chapels of ease and attempted to lessen the ecclesiastical status and influence of their ministers. The justification given was that there had to be a distinction between properly endowed ministries and those that were not. Ministers of chapels of ease could not sit in any of the courts of the church. They had no powers of discipline over their congregations, and monies collected for poor relief and so on were not under their control. The 'full parish', the parish *quoad omnia*,

---

38 Buchanan I, 269.
39 Reference point, *infra* n. 111.
40 Bryce I, 18–20; Buchanan I, 269–96.
41 Buchanan I, p. 229. The 1706 Act was modified by the Act 48 Geo. 3 c. 151, and the Judicature Act 1825. Heritors were owners of heritable property above a specific value in the parish. They were responsible for the erection and maintenance of church buildings and other parish matters.
42 On chapels of ease see *Presbytery of Edinburgh v De La Condamine* (1868) 7 M. 213.
43 Cf. W. Kennedy, *Annals of Aberdeen* (Aberdeen: Brown, 1818), I, 387, on the origin of Gilcomston Chapel of Ease.

continued to be responsible for civil matters, including funding education and poor relief as well as discipline in the 'territory' of the new charge. The effect was that chapels of ease had not developed as they might have done, nor had the Kirk as many full-status churches as it needed to properly serve growing and shifting centres of population. In the 100 years after 1730, the population of Scotland had doubled, but the religious needs of the additional inhabitants were met by an increase of only 40 full churches in the established Church, and the creation of 62 chapels of ease. In the same period about 100 churches had been erected by the non-established and poorer denominations.[44]

The 1833 Assembly had faced many overtures praying that chapels of ease should be given a more effective position within the Kirk and the status of their ministers be improved. By 153 to 103, the 1834 Assembly enacted that all ministers of chapels of ease were to be regarded and received as members of presbyteries and synods, were eligible to sit in the General Assembly and should enjoy the full powers of a parish minister – a return to the presbyterian doctrine of the parity of ministers, which had been ignored in previous years. Notwithstanding, the Moderate side opposed the enactment specifically on the competence of the Assembly so to legislate. Dr Cook of St Andrews, a leader of the Moderate party, said he adhered:

> to the opinion stated last year, that it is *ultra vires* of the Assembly to place chapels on the same footing as parish churches. The whole system of parish arrangements is the effect of the legislation of the country. There are certain civil privileges connected with them and ministers inducted by parishes have, in consequence of such induction, certain civil privileges which it is altogether out of the question to suppose that an ecclesiastical court could bestow on them. We sit in synods and in general assemblies solely and purely as ecclesiastical courts, but in presbyteries in the double capacity of spiritual and temporal courts: and as members of Presbytery we sit in judgement on manses and glebes and have certain temporal acts to perform which no man out of the church can perform and which we could not have been warranted to perform, had not the acts of the legislature made us the established church of the country.

This argument effectively meant that erastianism was of the essence of the principle of Church establishment – by establishing a church, the state necessarily becomes its lord and master. If the state confers any civil jurisdiction on the church courts then it has the power to determine the constitution of these courts.[45] Cook's argument was to prove valid. At that point in history much of the organisation of civil society at the local level was implemented through the parishes of the Kirk. Education and the Poor Law were matters for the parish under the supervision of Presbytery. Accordingly it should be for the civil authority in the form of Parliament, not the Kirk's General Assembly, to consider and if necessary alter the composition of the bodies (that is, presbyteries) that might take decisions in such matters.

Finally, before we turn to the cases themselves, one general point should be made. Although the Veto Act resulted in the greater volume of litigation, affected more individuals in more congregations, stirred the emotions, produced an easily grasped point of principle

---

44 Buchanan I, 230 – a rather scathing attack – and 233. Chalmers was a major figure in the response of the established church to the needs produced by the growth and relocation of the population, and was very active in that regard in the period 1834–49.

45 Buchanan, I, 282–3.

and in crude terms was a better political platform, as a matter of law the Chapel Act was the greater and more interesting innovation. Had the Chapel Act been acceptable to the civil authorities the Church of Scotland would have had a freedom of self-government that later had to be sought by legislative enactment. But the conflict became acute, and was largely conducted on the field of the Veto Act. When the Chapel Act came up for scrutiny in the civil courts many 'veto' cases had already been decided, and the monolithic concepts of John Hope and, let it be said, of a number of Episcopalian or sacramentalist judges, had been well aired. Reading the judgements *seriatim* it is difficult to escape the feeling that it had become more important to win the argument, or more accurately to enforce a particular view, than to do the best,[46] and all this at a time when judges were less concerned with precedent than they are today. At any event over the next years many cases were argued, and separate questions of the relationship between the established church and the state in Scotland submerged in the more vital one: whether the church had jurisdiction independent of the control of the civil authority.

II. The Conflict

On 7 June 1834, Lord Cockburn noted that the 'popular Veto on patronage' had been carried in the General Assembly:

> It has been sent to presbyteries for their approbation but has passed as an Interim Act. I have little doubt of its being agreed to by a majority of presbyteries; but it will be strongly resisted in the Civil Courts and otherwise by patrons and presentees. If the Courts of Law should overrule what the Assembly has done Parliament must interfere; otherwise there will be an indecent collision between the civil and ecclesiastical power in which the churchmen will probably stick to their point even though the spiritual cure should go to one presentee and the temporal benefice to another.[47]

His prediction of the 'indecent collision' proved accurate.

The intelligible presentation of the Disruption cases is not the least of the difficulties of this book. Over the next nine years the argument between the established Church seeking a greater degree of independence, and the state which had enacted the statutes which were its basis, was dissected. This occurred over what in legal practice is a very short period of time, with many cases proceeding simultaneously. The impact on both the general public and the more active disputants in the Conflict was therefore cumulative, but not linear. For ease of apprehension, however, it is best to consider a particular parish as a single unit, and only

---

46 After the Disruption Cockburn wrote: 'On looking back at the whole matter, what I am chiefly sorry for is the Court of Session. The mere purity of the Judges it would be ludicrous to doubt. They all delivered what each, after due inquiry, honestly believed to be the law; but passion sometimes invades the Bench, and when it does it obstructs the discovery of truth as effectually as partiality can. The majority of the court may have been right at first, and to a certain extent: but they soon got rabid, insomuch that there seemed to be no feeling except that at winging Wild-churchmen. The apology was that they were provoked by their law being defied; but a Court has no right to be provoked'. See Cockburn Journals II, 4–41. Later in Journals II, 56, in another connection 'Cocky' refers to 'these inexorable revolutionists – the steady Tories, who will change nothing voluntarily, and thus compel everything to change itself forcibly'.
47 Cockburn, Journals, I, 60–61.

later to arrange the cases in chronological order. At that stage the jurisdictional conflict can better be understood as the trend of decision became clear, majority judgements providing increasingly strong statements of a strict theory of state control.

The Veto Act cases[48]

Auchterarder

1 *Earl of Kinnoull and Rev. R. Young* v *Presbytery of Auchterarder* (1838) 16 S. 661; aff'd (1839) McL. & Rob. 220; 9 ER 78: C.G. Robertson, *Report of Court of Session Proceedings in the Auchterarder Case* (Edinburgh: Black, 1838).
2 *Earl of Kinnoull and Rev. R. Young* v *Rev. John Ferguson and others (a majority of the Presbytery of Auchterarder)* (1841) 3 D. 778: aff'd (1842) 1 Bell 662.
3 *Earl of Kinnoull and Rev. R. Young* v *Rev. John Ferguson and others (a majority of the Presbytery of Auchterarder)* (1843) 5 D. 1010.

August 1834 saw first test of the validity of the Veto Act. The minister of the parish of Auchterarder died. The patron, the Earl of Kinnoull, was required to present a successor to the charge within six months, otherwise by s. 3 of the Patronage Act 1711 the right to nominate would pass *iure devoluto* to the Presbytery of Auchterarder.[49] On 14 October, some six weeks after the vacancy had occurred, Presbytery received a presentation in favour of the Rev. Robert Young. This lay on the table of Presbytery until its next meeting on 27 October when Presbytery resolved to proceed in accordance with the Veto Act. They arranged for Young to preach in the parish so that the congregation should have opportunity to hear him and 'try his gifts'. The Earl's agent acquiesced in this procedure.

After Young had conducted a service a 'call' in the normal form was presented to the people for signature. This 'call' invited Young to take up the charge and oversight of the parish. Of the 3,000 parish residents, only two signed the 'call' and another added his signature invalidly. Then, in accordance with the Veto Act regulations the Presbytery gave opportunity to the male heads of families on the communion roll to dissent from the 'call'. Out of 330 entitled to exercise the privilege, 287 recorded themselves as dissentient. As required by the Act and regulations, Presbytery adjourned proceedings for a fortnight for the dissentients further to consider the matter. At a resumed meeting Presbytery found opinion had not altered. A motion was put that, since so few had signed it, the 'call' was not sufficient to allow Young's settlement and induction to proceed. Presbytery asked the 1835 General Assembly for guidance. By 131 to 91 it instructed the Presbytery to proceed in accordance with the Veto Act, but added that the proceedings were not to be liable to any further objection.[50] On 7 July 1835 the Presbytery rejected Young as presentee and decided to notify the Earl of its decision. Young's agent formally protested and appealed to the Synod of Perth

---

48 For the Veto Act see *supra* n. 6.
49 The charge was then within a separate Presbytery, Auchterarder. It is now part of the Presbytery of Perth.
50 GA Acts, 1835, 68–9. Buchanan I, 348–9; (1838) 16 S. 695; Robertson Auchterarder, I, App., 31–2, where the Assembly Minutes are narrated in the Minutes of the Auchterarder Presbytery; Buchanan I, 11 (Mr Whigham's speech).

and Stirling, but at this stage the matter passed from the courts of the Church. Before Synod could meet Young and the Earl took the matter into the civil courts.[51]

Auchterarder was ideal for testing the validity of the Veto Act. Clearly the overwhelming bulk of the congregation did not want Young as their minister. If a 'call' signed by only two out of 3,000 parishioners a sufficient basis for a minister to be settled then the 'call' was clearly simply a legal fiction. If the opposition of the bulk of the congregation and of 287 out of 330 heads of families did not bring into operation the principle that 'no pastor is to be intruded in a congregation contrary to their will', the Veto Act was ineffective, and perhaps invalid in civil law.[52]

Bringing the matter into the civil courts was not necessarily unusual. Civil courts were accustomed to dealing with questions of patronage in so far as they affected private right.[53] As originally drafted, the case would not have been remarkable. Trial of the action could have proceeded without difficulty as an inquiry into civil right. Indeed what was initially sought was a simple declaration that Young had been 'validly presented' (which was not in dispute), and that he had 'just and legal right' to the civil pertinents of the charge, the stipend, manse and glebe, 'during all the years of his life'. But the Dean of Faculty, John Hope, who had protested the legality of the Veto Act at the 1834 Assembly and separately dissented from its passing, was counsel for the Pursuers. He had the summons amended directly to raise the validity of the Veto Act and the powers and functions of the Church in what many considered spiritual matters. The amended summons sought to have it found *inter alia*:

> That the Presbytery of Auchterarder and the individual members thereof as the only legal and competent court to that effect, by law constituted, were bound and astricted to make trial of the qualifications of the pursuer and are still bound so to do; and if in their judgement after due trial and examination, the pursuer is found qualified, the said Presbytery are bound and astricted to receive and admit the pursuer as minister of the church and parish of Auchterarder according to law: that the rejection of the pursuer by the said Presbytery, as presentee foresaid, without making trial of his qualifications in competent or legal form and without any objections having been stated to his qualifications, or against his admission by the minister of the church and parish of Auchterarder, and expressly on the ground that the said Presbytery cannot, and ought not to do so, in respect of a veto of the parishioners, was illegal and injurious to the patrimonial rights of the pursuer and contrary to the provisions of the statutes and laws libeled.

The Court was asked, first, to hold that the Presbytery was bound to try Young's qualifications (which under the Veto Act in the face of the proportion of dissentient heads of families it could not do), and, second, to hold that the Presbytery's acting in accordance with the Veto Act was by statute law unlawful. That might have been enough for one day, but the court was also asked to declare that if the Presbytery found Young qualified, it was bound

---

51 There is some suggestion that this was done at the will of Mr Young and without the active support of Lord Kinnoull.
52 Buchanan I, 349.
53 For example *Dunse* (1749) Mor. 9911: *Culross* (1751), Mor. 9951: *Dick* (1752) Mor. 9954: *Unst* (1795), Bell's Cases 169: *Moncrieffe* (1735) Mor. 9909: *Strathbogie* v *Forbes* (1776) Mor. App. Patronage 3: Cf. other cases sub nom. Patronage in Morison's Dictionary; (1838) 16 S. 714 note; Stair, II.8.27–35; Dunlop, 299–308.

to admit him as minister of the charge.[54] The Presbytery was therefore not only to be told what it had done wrong, but also what it must do to do right. It was to be instructed in the performance of its duties. And, of course, underlying all the legal minutiae the base premise was that the civil courts had jurisdiction in the matter as thus presented, and the power to hold as was asked.

Since the case was clearly important, the Court of Session required it to be argued before the whole court, and eventually each of the 13 judges then on the Bench delivered a separate opinion. Pleading began on 21 November 1837 and concluded on 12 December. The Bench began delivering opinions on 27 February, concluding on 8 March. The size and complexity of the case and decision are therefore clear, and are underlined by several facts. In the sixteenth volume of Shaw's Session Cases the report begins at p. 661 with the summaries of the argument. The Opinions commence at p. 735 and run to p. 811, but at p. 735 the reporters regret that due to their unprecedented length they could only provide abridgements of the opinions. Full judgements are available only in the two-volume edition of the case report published by authority of the Court in 1838.[55]

By eight judges to five the decision of the Court of Session was substantially that in refusing to take Young on trials the Presbytery had indeed acted illegally and contrary to statute law, in particular the Patronage Act 1711.[56] The Church by law established had only such powers as were granted it under statute, and no other. Since statute did not sanction what the Church had done in passing the Veto Act, the Act and acts done in conformity with it were illegal.

The minority view was that the Veto Law was lawful, and, even were it not, the civil court lacked jurisdiction to interfere with the purely spiritual proceedings of the ecclesiastical courts.[57] The most that could be done would be to adjudge the temporalities (as the first form of the summons had intended), but the civil court could not compel the Presbytery to take Young on trials. Even in the majority, the Lord President, Charles Hope (father of John Hope) inclined to that view of the powers of the civil court. For him were the Presbytery to persist in refusing to take a presentee on trials, it was doubtful whether someone neither admitted as minister nor ordained could get the stipend; but he also thought it clear that no-one else could have right to it unless Young had been rejected as unqualified after due examination.[58]

The decision at first instance was unsatisfactory. The court was not unanimous, split by a non-compelling eight to five, and that head count was based only on the statement of each judge as to whether he found in favour of the pursuers or the defenders. The reasoning of each opinion varied, and it is difficult to harmonise even those that led to the same conclusion. Further, the decision did not leave it clear what could or would be done, although some of the majority warned that the Court might have to render its judgement effective.

In the resulting confusion many overtures asked the 1838 General Assembly to clarify the situation. Armed with the Court of Session decree, Young had demanded to be taken on trials. When the Presbytery demurred and asked synod for advice, he took a notarial protest,

---

54 Buchanan I, 353 (1838) 16 S. 661 at 696–7; Robertson Auchterarder I, App. II, 6 at 11.
55 C.G. Robertson, *Report of Court of Session Proceedings in the Auchterarder Case* (Edinburgh: Black, 1838).
56 Lord President Hope, Lord Justice Clerk Boyle, Lords Gillies, Meadowbank, Mackenzie, Medwyn, Cuninghame and Corehouse formed the majority.
57 The minority were Lords Fullerton, Moncrieff, Jeffrey, Cockburn and Glenlee.
58 Robertson Auchterarder, II, 20. Buchanan I, at 400 is inaccurate.

holding the members of the Presbytery jointly and severally liable in damages.[59] By 183 to 142 the 1838 Assembly affirmed the spiritual independence of the church and its competence in the exercise of its ecclesiastical authority to enforce obedience upon all office bearers and members of the church. The next day, the Synod of Perth and Stirling proposed that the Court of Session decision be appealed to the House of Lords and this was agreed.

In May 1839 the House of Lords had no difficulty in affirming the judgement of the Court of Session.[60] The judgement involved two positions expressed most cogently by Lord Brougham (247–315) and Lord Chancellor Cottenham (315–50). They considered that *by statute* and consequential case law the Church was the judge of the qualification of a presentee for the office of minister.[61] 'Qualification' was a technical term having reference to the doctrine, literature and life of presentee. In the absence of proven heresy, ignorance or immorality Presbytery could not reject a presentee. It followed that in requiring presbyteries to refuse to take on trials a presentee from whose 'call' a majority of the male heads of family dissented without reasons given, the Veto Act was illegal and *ultra vires* of the Church.

Beyond that point (and revealingly) the House of Lords considered that in inductions to a charge the Presbytery was in the same executive position as a bishop of the Church of England. In all matters where civil right was affected, the proceedings of church courts were subject to review in the civil courts. Lord Brougham in particular was explicit.[62] Only where a matter was proved to be of exclusive ecclesiastical competence would the civil courts be excluded.[63] He also dealt with the enforcement of the civil court's decree. For him the proposition that the Court of Session and the House of Lords might hold the Assembly and Presbytery to have acted in error and that either could or would persist in that error had only to be stated to be seen to be erroneous.[64]

Such reasoning was unacceptable to the Evangelicals. As Chalmers said to the General Assembly of 1839 meeting two weeks after the decision of the House of Lords, not only did the decision mean that the legislative power of the church in matters spiritual had been stated to be subject to the confines of civil statute, but the judicial power of the church had also been brought under the jurisdiction of the civil courts. Any decision of a Presbytery as to the qualifications of a presentee had a clear effect on his civil rights. If he were barred from induction to a charge, on the reasoning of the House of Lords the matter might therefore be taken from the church courts to the civil courts.[65]

Per contra the Moderates tried to revise church law to accord with the House of Lords decision. They argued that not to rescind the Veto Act would be rebellion against the law of the land and also dishonest. Since it was the church that had determined to go to the House of Lords in the hope that the validity of the Veto Act would be upheld, to defy the determination of the House of Lords indicated that the appeal had not been made with clean hands. The church had appealed to the House: integrity required obedience to the outcome.[66] However, by a majority of 49 the Assembly accepted Chalmers' view and affirmed the Church's intention to abide by the principle that a minister should not be intruded upon a congregation

---

59 Buchanan I, 401.
60 (1839) McL. & Rob. 220.
61 Reference point, *infra* n. 108.
62 Reference point, *supra* n. 31.
63 (1839) McL. & Rob. 220 at 307.
64 (1839) McL. & Rob. 220 at 314–5.
65 Buchanan I, 442–59.
66 Bryce I, 90; Buchanan I, 436–7.

against its will.[67] A committee was also appointed to negotiate a satisfactory solution to this conflict between the civil and ecclesiastical law. As far as Auchterarder was concerned, Presbytery was instructed to offer no further resistance to the claims to the temporalities but not to appoint a minister to the parish for the period. But the Assembly was not in control of events. Young had a court decree.

The Second Auchterarder case, *The Earl of Kinnoull and Rev. Robert Young v The Rev. John Ferguson and others (a majority of the Presbytery of Auchterarder)*, was decided on 5 March 1841.[68] It came about because the majority of the Presbytery of Auchterarder was unwilling to implement the result of the First Auchterarder case. On 8 June 1839 Lord Murray, the Lord Ordinary, issued a decree according with the decision of the House of Lords. The Presbytery was bound to try Young's qualifications as presentee, and, if found qualified, to admit him as minister to the Auchterarder parish.[69] This decree became final and the Earl and Young asked the Presbytery to comply with it. Presbytery therefore faced the instruction of the Assembly not to proceed to a settlement (although allowing Young the civil consequences of induction), and a court decree to a very different effect. Presbytery deferred the matter and asked the Commission of Assembly in August 1839, for advice. A claim for damages was intimated and a minority of the Presbytery expressed their readiness to comply with the court decree. The majority was then sued as individuals for £15,000, being £5,000 for the patron for interference with his rights and £10,000 for Young, made up of £8,000 for the wrongful refusal of the Presbytery to do its duty by taking him on trials and £2,000 in reparation for injury done to his character, usefulness and status in the Church of Scotland, and as recompense for injury done to his feelings (*solatium*) by the unlawful acts of the Presbytery.

The Presbytery defenders pleaded that the action was irrelevant, a technical Scottish defence to be understood as a plea that, even if all the facts alleged were proved, the law would not afford the remedy sought. First, the summons was improperly directed against them solely as individuals. Second, in referring the matter to Commission of Assembly the Presbytery had acted as legal court within its jurisdiction, not as an inferior court refusing to obey the order of a superior court. Lastly, the claim for damages was incompetent because damages were being asked for the non-performance of an obligation which the Court of Session could not enforce. Admission to the pastoral charge of a parish implied ordination, which was an exclusively ecclesiastical act. The Court of Session had no jurisdiction to compel ordination.

On grounds of its difficulty the Lord Ordinary referred the case to the Inner House, discussing in a lengthy Note whether the matter ought to be restricted simply to the temporalities or whether the judgement in the first case had gone beyond that.[70] This point was taken up particularly in the opinion of Lord Hope (senior), the Lord President, who elaborated his statements in the original Auchterarder case. While it was true that the Court of Session could not order the Presbytery to ordain, under the Patronage Act 1711 it could order to receive and admit a minister to a parish. Wherever persons are not only empowered but also may be ordered to act, 'it is necessarily implied that they are to take the means necessary

---

67 GA Act 39 1839; Buchanan I, 451–2, 466.
68 (1841) 3 D. 778 (1842), 1 Bell 662.
69 (1841) 3 D. 778 at 779.
70 (1841) 3 D. 778 at 782–92; (1843) 1 Bell 662 at 716–7. This contrasts with Lord Brougham's earlier statement that it was inconceivable that the Assembly and Presbytery would disregard the opinion of the House of Lords (1839) McL. & Rob. 220 at 314–5.

for accomplishing the end'.[71] If ordination were a necessary part of admittance to a parish, this amounted to the civil court having jurisdiction to order ordination. Further, what was at issue was simply one of failure to comply with a decree of the civil court. It was therefore unnecessary to aver malice and damages could be sought. Given the decision in the First Auchterarder case, the Presbytery could not refuse to give effect to the judgement. The decision of the majority of the Presbytery to disobey the judgement, therefore, exposed them to an action for damages.

This decision was also appealed to the House of Lords which, on 9 August 1842, had no difficulty in affirming the lower court's decision.[72] Decisions of the civil court have to be obeyed. This time, in marked contrast to his easy dismissal of the possibility of disobedience in the First case, the opinion of Lord Brougham concludes:

> it is fit that these men [sc. the majority] learn at length the lesson of obedience to the tribunals which have been appointed over them, a lesson which all others have long acquired, and which they, as learning it, should also practise. It is just that they should make reparation to those whom their breach or plain duty has injured. The duty is not doubtful. The Courts have laid it down. Their failure is not a mistaken opinion; their fault is not an error of judgement. They knew what they ought to have done, and they refused to do it. The penalty of their transgression is to make compensation to those whom they have injured by their pertinacious refusal to perform their duty and yield obedience to the law.[73]

Lord Campbell was similarly stringent in dealing with the argument that the majority had followed conscience, acting according to their deep-rooted beliefs as to the true relations between church and state:

> Finally, we were much pressed with the hardship to which the appellants (the majority) are exposed, by being held liable to actions for acting according to their consciences. I do not think, my Lords, that, where the law is clear, the hardship of being obliged to obey it is a topic that can be listened to in a court of justice. There can be nothing more dangerous than to allow the obligation to obey a law to depend upon the opinion entertained by individuals of its propriety; that opinion being so liable to be influenced by interest, prejudice, and passion, the love of power, still more deceitful than the love of profit, and that most seductive of all delusions, that a man may recommend himself to the Almighty by exercising a stern control over the religious opinions of his fellow men. Whilst the appellants remain members of the Establishment, they are, in addition to their sacred character, public functionaries appointed and paid by the State, and they must perform the duties which the law of the land imposes upon them. It is only a voluntary body, such as the Relief or Burgher Church in Scotland, self-founded and self-supported, that can say they will be entirely governed by their own rules.[74]

---

71 (1841) 3 D. 778 at 797.
72 (1843) 1 Bell 662.
73 (1843) 1 Bell 662 at 716–7.
74 (1843) 1 Bell 662 at 733–4.

If reform of the Church was impeded by Acts of Parliament, the Church should apply to Parliament for their modification or repeal:

> But a defiance of Courts of Justice and of the Legislature, inevitably leads to confusion and mischief; and perseverance in such ill-advised counsels must either end in the total subversion of the Establishment, or in a schism which would for ages impair its respectability and usefulness.[75]

The last stage in the Auchterarder proceedings, the Third case, *The Earl of Kinnoull* v *Ferguson* of 10 March 1843 arose from continued failure of the majority in the Presbytery to obey the injunctions of the civil courts.[76] The pursuers sought a court order that the minority willing to obey the courts might constitute the Presbytery to take Young on trials and to admit him as minister if found qualified. The majority of Presbytery was to be interdicted from interfering. The jurisdiction of the court and the competency of the action were sustained by a majority of six to three. At advising by eight to five, the court held there was nothing in law to hinder the action, and the remedies sought by Young and the Earl were appropriate to prevent and repair the wrongs been done to them. The matter was remitted to the Lord Ordinary to proceed.

This was the effective end of the Auchterarder dispute for the whole matter was swallowed up in the Disruption of the Church of Scotland, which occurred within two months of the decision being given.

Lethendy

> Clark v *Stirling* (1839) 1 D. 955; C.G. Robertson, *Report of the Proceedings in the Court of Session in the Lethendy Case* (Edinburgh, 1839)[77]

In Lethendy the facts were rather different. In 1835 the pursuer, Thomas Clark, had been presented by the Crown as patron as colleague and successor to the incumbent, Thomas Butter. The congregation 'vetoed' the settlement and when both the Presbytery of Dunkeld and the 1836 Assembly refused to induct him Clark raised a civil action. Shortly after trial of the action commenced in November 1837, Butter died and the Crown presented an Andrew Kessen to the vacancy, considering that because Clark had not been settled during the previous incumbency that presentation had lapsed. Kessen was acceptable to the congregation, but Clark sought to interdict his settlement. The Presbytery reported the interdict to the 1838 General Assembly which held that the induction of a minister was a purely spiritual act and of exclusively ecclesiastical competence. The Presbytery was therefore instructed to complete the settlement of Mr Kessen. The Court of Session then granted Clark another interdict prohibiting the Presbytery from proceeding. The Presbytery declined to appear before the civil court either to argue against the interdict or to attempt to have it removed. It did, however, refer the matter to the Commission of Assembly, which in August 1838 instructed it

---

75 (1843) 1 Bell 662 at 734.
76 (1843) 5 D.1010.
77 The facts are in the cited Reports, in Bryce 1, 73–80, and Buchanan II, 1–17. It appears from the Claim of Right, 1843, that there were four Lethendy cases, but only the one case is reported. The other cases were interdicts against Assembly and Presbytery proceedings. The 1 D. report is abbreviated, Robertson is full.

to take immediate steps to ordain and induct Kessen to the charge. The Commission also indicated that unless Clark withdrew his interdicts the Presbytery should cite him for the ecclesiastical offence of seeking to bring the government and discipline of the church under the control of the civil courts.

When the Presbytery met for the induction of Kessen, a letter was read to it containing the opinion of the Dean of Faculty, John Hope, as to the competence of their intended actions. Amongst other things this stated that 'the expectation that the supreme civil court will allow its interdict to be set at defiance, is the most vain and idle with which parties can delude themselves'. Hope further suggested that Presbytery members proceeding in defiance of the interdict would infallibly be committed to prison and that 'most justly, for an offence of the most grave nature, in the more aggravated in proportion of the status of the parties by whom it is committed'.[78]

The fulminations of the Dean strengthened the resolution of the Presbytery which proceeded to induct Kessen to Lethendy. Clark complained the breach of interdict to the Court of Session which ordered the Presbytery to appear before it. Whether Clark had title to apply for the interdicts, the jurisdiction of the civil court, and whether the respondents had been guilty of breach of interdict were fully rehearsed. It was decided that Clark had title to sue, that the Court had jurisdiction and that the breach of the interdicts was contempt of court. However, apparently by a majority, the Court decided simply to censure the Presbytery but made it plain that a future similar offence by the Presbytery would be treated more harshly.[79]

Clark subsequently obtained damages of several thousand pounds, but the Lethendy case was never fully settled. After the Disruption the Presbytery (or such of it as had not left the Church) might have inducted Clark to Lethendy, but found proved a libel (charge) that he was a drunkard, and deprived him of his licence to preach.[80]

Daviot[81]

MacIntosh v *Rose* (1839) 2 D. 253

Shortly after the Presbytery of Dunkeld was censured in the Lethendy case, the Second Division dealt with dispute arising from a vacancy in the parish of Daviot and Dunlichity in the Presbytery of Inverness. Patronage was vested in the Crown, which, in a minor genuflection to the Veto Act, had indicated that it would informally seek local opinion before exercising its rights of patronage. A list of two was circulated, the Crown intending to nominate whichever the heritors of the parish would select. Local feeling was in favour of an Archibald Cooke, whose name was not on the list. The heritors convened a meeting and invited to it the 10 heads of families entitled to act under the Veto Act. The meeting, attended by the heritors but only three heads of families, recommended a presentation in favour of MacIntosh, one of the listed men. The remaining seven heads of families intimated that Cooke should be the presentee.

---

78 Buchanan II, 8.
79 (1839) 1 D. 955 at 1020–1023; Buchanan II, 15.
80 Buchanan II, 16.
81 Reference point, n. 131 *infra*.

A presentation in favour of MacIntosh and his letter of acceptance was intimated to the Presbytery meeting on 27 November 1839 and the Presbytery appointed MacIntosh to preach in the churches of the united parish. The Presbytery was to meet on 19 December to moderate in the call. Believing that the seven heads of families who had proposed Cooke for the vacancy would dissent in terms of the Veto Act from his being inducted, MacIntosh asked the Court of Session to interdict them from objecting to his settlement without assigning any special objections to his life or doctrine. In support he relied upon the Auchterarder case as holding it contrary to law for a Presbytery to reject a presentee without cause shown.

The three judges of the Second Division were not as sweeping in their opinions as MacIntosh's application sought, but granted interim interdict two days before the Presbytery was due to meet. They took the position that the Auchterarder case had established the law of the land, and, as Lord Justice Clerk Boyle stated, it was their intention: 'to prohibit any attempt on the part of the respondents illegally to interfere with his [sc. MacIntosh] being taken on trials according to the laws of the church',[82] Boyle considered it his 'sacred duty' to grant an interdict to that extent. I have not been able to determine the actual outcome of the Daviot case, for the proceedings were overshadowed by the Strathbogie (Marnoch) case, an important stage of which was reached three days after Daviot.

Strathbogie (Marnoch)[83]

1 *Presbytery of Strathbogie and Rev. J. Cruickshank and Others, Suspenders* (1839) 2 D. 258
2 Same (1839) 2 D. 585
3 Same (1840) 2 D. 1047; id. 1380
4 *Rev. J. Edwards v Rev. J. Cruickshank and others (Majority of the Presbytery of Strathbogie and Rev. J. Robertson and others (Minority of the said Presbytery)* (1840) 3 D. 282
5 *Presbytery of Strathbogie* (1842) 4 D. 1298
6 *Rev. J. Cruickshank v Gordon* (1843) 5 D. 909
7 *Rev. J. Edwards v Rev. H. Leith* (1843) 15 Jur. 375.

Patronage of the parish of Marnoch in the Presbytery of Strathbogie was vested in the Earl of Fife and Huntly whose trustees presented John Edwards to the charge when the parish fell vacant in 1837. Only one parishioner, the local inn-keeper, was willing to sign the call and 261 heads of families dissented from the settlement in terms of the Veto Act. As Edwards had previously been an assistant in the parish, and had been withdrawn from the post at the request of the parishioners, their reaction to his proposed settlement should not have been unanticipated. However, the conflicting attitudes taken towards this presentation may be gathered from a juxta-position of the comments of Bryce and Buchanan. Bryce wrote:

---

82 (1839) 2 D. 253 at 256.
83 Bryce I, 101–58, 195–216; II, 53–80, 92–107, 120–70, 181–2, 203–4; Buchanan II, 17–52, 125–207, 245–85, 298–306, 345–56. The cases listed as 1–3 form the First Strathbogie case, nos 4 and 5 the Second Strathbogie case and no. 6 the Third Strathbogie case, corresponding with usual treatment. The cases are known in the literature as either 'Marnoch' (the name of the parish) or 'Strathbogie' (the name of the Presbytery).

The trustees of the Earl of Fife had presented a gentleman of the name of Edwards to the living of Marnoch within the bounds of the Presbytery of Strathbogie; the usual steps towards his induction had been taken and he had been dissented from or vetoed by a large majority of the parishioners. Although well known as a man of very great talents and erudition and having pulpit gifts of more than ordinary excellence. Such was the opposition got up against this gentleman that on the moderation of his call only one resident parishioner could be found to come forward and sign it, while there appeared a majority of the male heads of families being communicants dissenting from his settlement.[84]

Bryce goes on to write of Edwards in the highest terms. His encomium compares oddly with Buchanan's statement that,

[Edwards] having officiated as assistant to the former incumbent for a period of three years was well known to the parishioners. So little had they relished his services in that subordinate capacity that at their urgent request his employer had removed him from the situation altogether. It was not, therefore, to be wondered at, that when the representatives of the patron misinformed, it is believed, as to the facts of the case, made so injudicious a selection the people should have felt themselves seriously aggrieved.[85]

Both sides appealed for guidance, first to synod and then to the General Assembly. Both advised that Edwards be rejected. Presbytery complied. Edwards raised an action on the grounds that in refusing to take him on trials the Presbytery had acted illegally and in violation of the statute law of Scotland. The writ was served just after the court had decided the First Auchterarder case and the Presbytery, realising the import of that decision for their own problem, again applied to synod for advice. At this stage an intriguing development became apparent. Only a minority of the Presbytery wished to comply with the instructions of the higher courts of the church. They requested synod to instruct the Presbytery to reject Edwards. Synod did so and the majority of Presbytery complained to the Assembly. Without vote the 1838 General Assembly instructed the Presbytery to reject Edwards. In the meantime the patron, assuming that there was still a vacancy, presented a Mr Hendry to the living. Edwards was granted an interim interdict against Hendry being settled in the charge.

On 17 July 1838 the Presbytery decided, again by a majority, that its duty was to postpone the settlement at Marnoch until the Auchterarder question had been finally dealt with. The Presbytery minority dissented and complained to synod, which reaffirmed that admission to the pastoral charge was an entirely ecclesiastical act, but, rather than order the Presbytery to proceed with the Hendry settlement, it referred the whole case to the General Assembly of 1839, which itself passed the matter to the Commission of Assembly which met for the purpose as soon as the Assembly had adjourned. The Commission found the Presbytery censurable for having entertained the thought that the Court of Session might have any jurisdiction in the matter, and it specially forbad any steps towards the induction of Edwards. In the meantime, Edwards had obtained a further court order requiring the Presbytery to take him on trials. This interlocutor was served on the Presbytery together with a

---

84 Bryce I, 101.
85 Buchanan II, 18.

petition from Edwards that he be taken on trials.[86] It appears that the majority of Presbytery might well have obeyed the court order before the instructions of the Commission were formally received.[87] This was, however, forestalled by the then moderator of the Presbytery. The majority of Presbytery requisitioned a meeting asking for it to be held on 17 September 1839.[88] The moderator called it for 13 November. His action caused further dispute, aggravating the politics of the situation. At that meeting no decision on the settlement was made, but by a majority the Presbytery censured the moderator for not calling the meeting earlier. He appealed to the Commission, which ordered that parties should appear before it on 11 December. The Presbytery met for ordinary business on 4 December when, with knowledge of the court decree in Edwards' favour and the decisions of the General Assembly and its Commission prohibiting them from so proceeding, the Presbytery resolved by a majority of seven to three to take Edwards on trials and reported this to the Commission meeting on 11 December.

On 11 December, the Commission of Assembly thoroughly reviewed the Marnoch case and reversed the whole proceedings of the Presbytery of Strathbogie. It approved the conduct of the moderator, dismissed the petition of Edwards to be taken on trials under the court decree and prohibited him also for applying for this purpose to any Presbytery. It added that should he violate this injunction, he would be proceeded against for contumacy. The Commission further found that by resolving to take Edwards on trials the Presbytery had defied the General Assembly. It therefore suspended the seven ministers who had formed the majority of the Presbytery from their pastoral and judicial functions, a penalty less than deposition.[89] Lastly the Commission granted the four remaining ministers (three plus the moderator) full powers to act as a Presbytery, a step that may have been beyond the competence of the Commission.

The seven suspended ministers protested, and the Commission referred their protest to the next Assembly. Notwithstanding, they proceeded to meet as a Presbytery within four days of their suspension, disowned the authority of the Commission to act and sought the intervention of the Court of Session (*supra* case no. 1).[90] They asked the court, first, to order that no one should invade the exercise of their usual functions; second, that despite the decision of the Commission the minority should not have the full powers of a Presbytery; and third, that no-one should intrude into their parishes to intimate the suspension or to perform any of the normal duties of a ministry.

At first the Court of Session did not fully grant the orders asked for, restricting its decrees to interdicting service of the sentence of the Commission, and prohibiting others from using the churches, churchyards and school houses of the affected ministers.[91] This was wholly within the competence of the civil courts, being matters of civil rights alone. The ministers appointed by the Commission to intimate the suspension of the majority did so in the open country of the area and held church services in the open air within the bounds of the Presbytery. This last was too much for the suspendees and they asked for a further interdict to

---

86 The history to this point is not reported save in the narratives of the later proceedings.
87 Buchanan II, 18; Bryce I, 111.
88 Buchanan II, 20, gives 12 November as the requested date, but this appears to be an error.
89 This point was expressed at the Assembly by, for example, Principal Lee. However, it was countered by A.M. Dunlop who suggested that to suspend the ministers at this stage was less severe than to depose them at a future stage which would have been necessary had they proceeded to induct and ordain Edwards: Bryce I, 119.
90 *Presbytery of Strathbogie and Rev. J. Cruickshank and others, Suspenders* (1839) 2 D. 258.
91 (1839) 2 D. 258 at 267.

exclude other ministers of the established Church from all access to 'their' people. Refused by the Lord Ordinary (Murray), who continued the existing limited interdict, this was granted on appeal by the First Division, Lord Fullerton dissenting (*supra* case no. 2).[92] In fact the interdict of the Court of Session was broken freely without the civil courts seeking its enforcement.[93]

The matter came up again at the Commission of Assembly in March 1840 at which Chalmers gave notice that, if the interdicts in the Strathbogie case were continued, the church would accept whatever consequences flowed from disobedience.[94] A series of resolutions was proposed to the effect that the court interdict was 'contrary to the liberties of the Church' and that Parliament be petitioned for measures to protect the Church from the unconstitutional interference of the Court of Session.[95] In May 1840 the Assembly cited the seven ministers to appear before the Commission of Assembly in August, enjoining it to take disciplinary steps in the event of the ministers remaining contumacious. The seven ministers went back to the Court of Session and obtained a decree of suspension and interdict against the whole proceedings against them and therefore reponing them, that is cancelling their suspension as ministers and restoring them to full status (*supra* case no. 3).[96] The Assembly failed to lodge answers, so the decree was made perpetual on 11 July 1840.[97]

Consequent on the court decrees, when the Commission met in August 1840, the seven ministers informed it that they could not 'without acting inconsistently, recognise or sanction any part of the proceedings which had been suspended as illegal'. The Commission considered this in itself to be contumacious and accordingly libelled the seven Strathbogie ministers (that is charge them with a disciplinary offence) by a majority of 180 to 66.[98] Edwards was also similarly libelled.

At the meeting of the Commission of Assembly in November 1840, counsel for the seven ministers addressed the Commission and put forward written defences. In substance, these denied that the Commission had any lawful jurisdiction whatsoever in the matter, since it was not a court established by the laws of the land, and asserted that the Assembly sentence on which the libel proceeded had been suspended as illegal and was therefore itself void. It followed that the libel was a violation of the law of the land. Edwards' agent made similar defences. The Commission did not accept these arguments, upheld the relevancy of both libels and set proof for the March 1841 meeting of the Commission.[99]

Between the meetings of the Commission in November 1840 and in March 1841, there were further developments. Edwards had been examined and found qualified by the suspended ministers.[100] With the consent of the seven he raised an action against the Presbytery, both its suspended and unsuspended ministers, asking that the court order it forthwith to admit and receive him as the minister of the church and parish of Marnoch, or to pay damages. On 18 December 1840 the First Division of the Court of Session, with Lord Fullerton again dissenting, granted decree as asked for on the ground that it was the logical corollary

---

92 *Presbytery of Strathbogie, etc.* (1839) 2 D. 585.
93 Buchanan II, 48–9; Bryce I, 133–5.
94 Buchanan II, 49.
95 Buchanan II, 50–51.
96 *Presbytery of Strathbogie and Rev. J. Cruickshank and others*, 11th June 1840, 2 D. 1047.
97 Id. 11 July 1840, 2 D. 1380.
98 Buchanan II, 172.
99 Buchanan II, 182–3.
100 Buchanan II, 184–5; (1840) 3 D. 282 at 282 (see next note).

of their earlier proceedings (*supra* case no. 4).[101] Since the Court had jurisdiction to determine the duty of the Presbytery, it had also the power to order that duty be performed.[102]

Many presbyteries protested against the Court of Session decree. The seven 'suspended' ministers prepared to execute it. The 'Reel of Bogie', which inspired a famous cartoon, is still remembered in the annals of the area. The settlement was to take place in January 1841, the depths of winter. Despite the weather, many turned up at the church. The floor of the church was reserved for the parishioners, the gallery for spectators. Thompson of Keith, one of the suspendees, acted as moderator of the 'Court of Session' Presbytery and constituted the meeting by prayer. One of the elders of the congregation then challenged the authority of the 'Presbytery', an agent for the parishioners protested against the whole proceedings and the parishioners retired. Others then made it impossible for the settlement to proceed until a magistrate was called. He found no disturbance. Edwards was then admitted and received to the charge.[103]

The case against the seven ministers was presented to the General Assembly of 1841. The first act of that Assembly was indicative of its reception. Those commissioned by the suspended seven acting as the Strathbogie Presbytery were deleted from the Roll of Commissioners. When the case came up there was a wide-ranging discussion of the whole question of the power of the civil magistrate and the responsibility of ministers to obey (cf. Romans 13). But the majority accepted the arguments of Chalmers, Cunningham and A.M. Dunlop, a lawyer, that by obeying the civil power the ministers had violated their ordination vows through recognising a head of the Church other than Christ. Sentence of deposition was passed. The Moderates formally protested that the established Church was bound to 'be subject to the civil power in all matters declared by the supreme Civil Authorities of the country to affect temporal rights'.[104]

The next act was ludicrously inept. The Court of Session granted a further interdict to the seven, this time against the 1841 Assembly proceedings, and a court messenger at arms sought to serve it on the Assembly. He was refused admittance to the Assembly Hall and a deputation was sent to inform the Lord High Commissioner, the representative of the sovereign, of what had occurred. It was, of course, improper for the messenger at arms to seek to serve the papers in the presence of the Commissioner. After debate the interdict papers were allowed to lie on the table of the Assembly where they were ignored except for a protest at the attempted intrusion of the secular arm of the state into the ecclesiastical province.[105]

When the 1842 Assembly came round, the now deposed seven, constituting themselves the Presbytery of Strathbogie on the authority of the earlier decrees in their favour, sought again to send Commissioners. But the Assembly refused to countenance any representatives from Strathbogie other than those commissioned by the minority, also constituted as the Strathbogie Presbytery. Although the seven then obtained an interdict from the Court of Session against the minority's commissioners sitting, the Church refused to regard the civil authority, and once more complained of its interference (*supra* case no. 5).[106]

---

101 *Rev. J. Edwards* v *Rev. J. Cruickshank and others (the Majority of the Presbytery of Strathbogie) and Robertson and others (the Minority of said Presbytery)* (1840), 3 D. 282.
102 Per Lord President Hope (1840) 3 D. 282 at 308.
103 Buchanan II, 192–206; Bryce II, 100–101.
104 Buchanan II, 245–81; Bryce II, 120–160.
105 Buchanan II, 281–5; Bulloch I, 238.
106 *Presbytery of Strathbogie* (1842) 4 D. 1298.

The end of the Strathbogie cases came in 1843. In *Cruickshank* v *Gordon*, 10 March 1843 (1843) 5 D. 909, six judges of the Court of Session (Lords Medwyn and Cuninghame at great length and Lord Fullerton dissenting) held that the civil court had jurisdiction to declare that the prior interdicts were still operative, and that the court could also reduce (that is, quash) the depositions of the seven ministers by the 1841 Assembly. The majority had no time for any argument that the depositions were matters of ecclesiastical discipline and therefore the sole jurisdiction of the church courts. The supreme power of the state required the civil court to intervene where the church was contravening the statutes on which its power rested (*supra* case no. 6). The Lord Ordinary was ordered to proceed, and the very next day in *Edwards* v *Leith* (1843) 15 Jurist 375, held that the induction of Hendry to the parish of Marnoch by the 'minority' Presbytery amounted to a breach of interdict (*supra* case no. 7). However, all this was soon swallowed up in the Disruption itself, though it may be noted that Hendry had a very successful ministry as the Free Church minister in Marnoch.

Be that as it may, the Strathbogie cases underlined the conflict between church and state. The civil court had proved willing to intervene in all matters where a civil element was present, and, going beyond the First Auchterarder decision, it was prepared to instruct the Church how to act, and to review the internal proceedings of the Assembly. Cancelling the suspension of the seven ministers (case no. 3) and their deposition (case no. 6) took matters very far indeed. In addition the long saga crystallised attitudes on both sides, and arguably resulted in more extreme positions being taken up than were necessary, and from which neither side could extricate itself without at least the appearance of surrender.

Culsalmond

Middleton v *Anderson* (1842) 4 D. 957[107]

When in 1841 the incumbent of the parish of Culsalmond in the Presbytery of Garioch became too infirm to act, the patron presented William Middleton who had been acting as assistant in the charge. He was, therefore, known to the people. Out of a parish of around 1,000, 45 were willing to sign the call, and of the 139 heads of families, 89 dissented from the settlement in terms of the Veto Act. By this time such cases were supposed to be reported to the Assembly but the Presbytery considered that a sufficient proportion of the congregation and heads of families were in favour of the settlement for it to proceed. Aggrieved parishioners and Presbytery members appealed. Matters were then further complicated, for the dissentient parishioners not only sought simply to dissent, but put forward special reasons which would have fallen within the categories laid down as proper by the House of Lords in the First Auchterarder case.[108] They referred to Middleton's life and conduct.

The Presbytery dismissed these special objections and at a rather confused meeting on 11 November 1841 inducted Middleton to the charge.[109] Six days later on the complaint of

---

107 This case was also published separately in pamphlet form: *Report of the Opinions of the judges, and decision by the Court of Session (First Division) in the Cause the Rev. Wm. Middleton and Others, Suspenders, against Alex. Anderson and Others, Respondents* (Aberdeen: Cornwall, 1841: Edinburgh: Blackwood, 1842). However, the Dunlop report is full. See also Buchanan II, 313–23; Bryce II, 236–53. The facts resemble the settlement at Glass, which did not give rise to court action; Bryce II, 253.
108 See *supra* following n. 61.
109 Buchanan II, 315–8.

the 89 heads of families the Commission of Assembly took the matter up, and as an interim measure prohibited Middleton from acting as minister. Middleton, the majority of the Presbytery and the patron applied to the Court of Session to have the Commission proceedings suspended and the dissentients interdicted from molesting the Presbytery, or complaining to the church courts. The Lord Ordinary (Ivory) refused, considering that no civil question was involved as the acts of the Commission had not affected Middleton's civil rights. On appeal, however, the First Division (Lord President Boyle and Lords Gillies and Mackenzie and Lord Fullerton dissenting) reversed. Their reasoning was that the proceedings had to do with the Veto Act, an Act declared in previous court cases to be *ultra vires* of the Church. Any attempt therefore to operate the Act was *ipso facto* null, vitiating the whole proceedings. Further, Middleton's civil rights had been affected by the suspension, as suspension had unwarrantedly stigmatized him in his status as a minister of the gospel.

The latter ground of decision is very wide. No question of stipend, glebe or emoluments, or of the rights of the patron, were involved. Only the personal character of the minister was called in question. That would happen in any disciplinary proceeding held by the Church, and therefore the reasoning opened up new vast areas of the Church's jurisdiction to the reviewing powers of the civil court. An appeal to the House of Lords was marked, and in law the case ended by failure to prosecute that appeal, the judgement of the Court of Session therefore becoming final.[110] But the reason for the failure to continue the case was not acquiescence in the decision. As will be seen adopting the Claim of Right the Assembly of 1842 took a stand on the spiritual independence of the Church, requiring the state to make answer, and Culsalmond was overtaken by cases that more directly led to the Disruption.

The Chapel Act cases[111]

So far the cases dealt with have concerned the legality of the Veto Act and proceedings thereunder. The lawfulness of the Chapel Act did not come up for proper consideration until quite late in the Ten Years' Conflict, although hints of trouble to come were given *obiter* in a series of cases concerning rights to the Widow's Fund and in Poor Law matters.[112] The case of *Livingstone* (1841) 3 D. 1278 brought out more clearly the possibilities of trouble.[113]

Livingstone (1841) 3 D. 1278

In 1840 Archibald Livingstone, minister of Cambusnethan, North Lanarkshire, was libelled by the Presbytery of Hamilton for various acts of theft and found guilty of five of the charges. The Presbytery then petitioned the General Assembly to review the case on the grounds that, although Livingstone had appealed to the Assembly, he appeared to be deferring forwarding documents so that any final sentence would be delayed for a year. The Assembly cited Livingstone to appear but he asked the Court of Session to suspend the past proceedings and to interdict further action against him. Part of his argument was that the Presbytery meetings

---

110 Bryce II, 252–3.
111 For the Chapel Act see *supra* n. 39.
112 *Gordon* v *Trustees of the Widows' Fund* (1836) 14 S. 509; *Irvine* v *Trustees of the Widows' Fund* (1839) 16 S. 1024; *Panmure* v *Sharpe* (1839) 1 D. 840; *Bell* v *Bell* (1841) 3 D. 204.
113 Bryce II, 288–9. Cf. *Smith* v *Presbytery of Abertarff* (1842) 4 D. 1476, where interdict was granted by a majority on grounds of urgency and without fully argued opinions, against a Presbytery whose members included the minister of a parliamentary charge.

dealing with his case had been attended by ministers of chapels of ease. Their entitlement to attend was based on the Chapel Act. But, argued Livingstone, that Act was illegal, being *ultra vires* of the Church and contrary to statute law. The actions taken against him had therefore not been taken by a lawfully constituted court, but by some anomalous body consisting partly of members of the Presbytery and partly of others. The acts of such a body were incompetent, illegal, null and void.

Lord Ivory referred the question to the Inner House, observing that although the Chapel Act had been incidentally before the Court, its validity had not been pronounced upon and prior cases indicated some division of opinion in the courts. The Inner House decided to call the parties involved, Lord Gillies and Lord MacKenzie, indicating that they felt that the Church did not have power to change its constitution at its own hand by introducing new ministerial members, not being ministers of 'full' charges, into presbyteries. However, neither the Presbytery nor the Assembly responded and accordingly in their absence the interdict became final. The case only raised but did not settle the question of the Chapel Act.[114]

Wilson v Presbytery of Stranraer, (1842) 4 D. 1294

Livingstone's argument was next taken up by the pursuer in *Wilson* v *Presbytery of Stranraer*, (1842) 4 D. 1294, who sought to prevent a case against him being heard by the Presbytery on the ground that the decision to proceed had not been taken by a properly constituted Presbytery. A minister of a *quoad sacra* charge had been present. Again the legality of the Chapel Act was not settled as once more the church courts failed to respond and interim interdict was issued in absence. But it may be noted as indicative of the temper of the time that Wilson was summarily deposed from the ministry for contumacy in seeking the aid of the civil court in what the Assembly considered an ecclesiastical matter.[115] The legality of the Chapel Act was, however, by this time fully before the Court as the Stewarton case had begun.

Stewarton

Cuninghame v. *Presbytery of Irvine* (1843) 5 D. 427[116]

The Chapel Act admitted all ministers of *quoad sacra* charges, that is of churches created within the boundaries of the older parishes for preaching purposes only, to full membership

---

114 *Livingstone* is quoted for its place in the progress of the Conflict. In later proceedings ((1846) 8 D. 898, affirmed (1849) 6 Bell 469), the civil courts refused to reduce the sentence of deposition passed by the Church courts in Livingstone's absence, and in disregard of the interdict. The argument that the proceedings were vitiated *ipso facto* by the presence of 'ministers' whose rights to sit were based on the Chapel Act (which by then had been declared *ultra vires* in the Stewarton case, below) was held not valid. They had been acting *bona fide*, and had a colourable title to act. Cf. *Campbell* v *Presbytery of Kintyre* (1843) 5 D. 657, where the acts of a 'proper' Presbytery were held not vitiated by association with an Assembly and Commission partially composed of ministers of *quoad sacra* charges. The Presbytery had been instructed to proceed, but not how to proceed.
115 Bryce II, 286–8.
116 As in the First Auchterarder and Lethendy cases, the opinions were voluminous and were printed in full only in a separate volume: *W. Cuninghame, Mutual Cases, record and appendix in causa W. Cuninghame and others, Heritors of Stewarton v. Presbytery of Irvine*, 3 parts (Edinburgh: Presbytery of Irvine, 1842), J.M. Bell, ed. 1843 (the Stewarton Report). See also Buchanan II, 402–12.

of the courts of the Church. From 1834 the number of these churches had increased because the Evangelical party, following Chalmers' own earlier example, was diligent in their founding. In addition during the period a number of smaller non-established churches sought to unite with the established church, in part because through sympathy with the standpoint and efforts of the Evangelicals. Among these was the Associate Synod, which had seceded from the established Church in 1733 as part of the movement led by Ebenezer Erskine.[117] In 1839 the established church provided for the admission of ministers and congregations of the Associate Synod and, using the Chapel Act provisions, laid down procedures for the incorporation of Associate Synod churches as *quoad sacra* charges in the existing parochial system and their ministers as members of the appropriate Presbytery.

In August 1839 the Associate Synod church in Stewarton, a village within the bounds of the Presbytery of Irvine, sought to join the Church of Scotland under the new procedure. This was done. But when the Presbytery set up a committee to consider the creation of a parish *quoad sacra* within the boundaries of the existing parish *quoad omnia*, the patron of that charge, Cuninghame of Lainshaw, and others, heritors of the parish, decided to take action. They opposed both the subdivision of existing parish, doubtless as that would reduce the income in the older church, and the admission of the minister of the new church, James Clelland, to membership of the Presbytery of Irvine.

After procedures within the church courts Cuninghame and the others asked the Court of Session to interdict Clelland from sitting and acting as a member of the Presbytery of Irvine, and to interdict the Presbytery both from erecting the proposed new parish, and from giving Clelland any standing thereanent. They argued that by the Act 1706 c. 10 the power to create new parishes had been given to the Court of Teinds (by this time the Court of Session wearing another hat), and that the Church therefore did not have the power to create new parishes of its own motion. Decrees were granted on an interim basis until the matter could be fully argued. The church did not lodge answers, and these became permanent on 15 June. However, in the meantime procedures within the Kirk continued and in due course the Presbytery was instructed to proceed. When the Presbytery met on 1 September to do so, the interdicts of 15 June were served on it by agents for Cuninghame. The Presbytery offered to confer but this was refused. When the Presbytery met on 10 December the interdicts were again served on them but the Presbytery set up the new parish notwithstanding. It also adopted a resolution expressing puzzlement:

> The Presbytery cannot understand the interdict now served upon them to be intended to prevent them from doing any purely spiritual act, or to encroach at all on the spiritual discipline and government of the Church of Scotland as by law established, and secured by the Treaty of Union, but to refer entirely to the civil rights of the parties applying for the same; they declare and provide, as it is here expressly declared and provided, that no civil rights of these parties, or of any others whatever, shall be in any degree affect by the [the new parish boundaries *quoad sacra*]; and they further declare, that the effect of this allocation is limited exclusively to matters of spiritual discipline and government.[118]

---

117 These seceders had split on the question of the lawfulness of the Burgess Oath. The Associate Synod considered it lawful; Burleigh, 281–2. For the Associate Synod see Chapter % n. 50.
118 (1843) 3 D. 427 at 430.

Cuninghame complained to the courts but it was decided there was no urgency and matters could be deferred until his action was more fully tried. Accordingly the case proceeded with a variation. By the time the case came up, the Kirk had decided not normally to defend cases involving the disputed Acts lest it appear the church was acknowledging some right of the civil arm in such matters. However, it was decided to defend the Stewarton case to prevent the Presbytery being caught between the mills of the civil and ecclesiastical courts.[119] So, on 12 December 1840 the Procurator of the Church lodged answers for the Presbytery.[120]

Cuninghame and the other pursuers asked for the Presbytery proceedings to be suspended as illegal. Statute gave the power to create charges to the Court of Teinds. For the church to arrogate to itself the right to set up new parishes was therefore unconstitutional, and the Chapel Act *ultra vires*. The main defences of the Presbytery were the right of the Church to regulate the membership of its own courts and a want of jurisdiction of the Court of Session since the matters at issue were spiritual and therefore of exclusively ecclesiastical competence.

As in the Auchterarder case, the matter was referred to a Bench of the Whole Court, which decided by eight to five in favour of Cuninghame and the heritors. The ground of the majority's decision was far-reaching, and is best summarised by a short passage in the opinion of the former Dean of Faculty, John Hope, who had by now been raised to the bench as Lord Justice Clerk:

> I cannot admit that an establishment instituted by statute, can claim or legally possess any authority from a divine source, which the State, constituting the establishment, may not have thought fit to acknowledge as belonging to it; and of course, I cannot admit that an establishment can ever possess an independent jurisdiction, which can give rise to a conflict as between two separate and independent jurisdictions. The establishment being instituted by the State, the competency of all its acts must be subject to the determination of the supreme court of law. If it were admitted to possess any power as an establishment not sanctioned by the provisions of the State, and so, to possess from a separate source jurisdiction, producing a proper conflict of authority, then it would follow that the Church must be entitled to determine for itself the extent of that authority, and hence no one act which the Church chose to ascribe to that authority could be inquired into in a court of law.[121]

From such base the majority held that the proceedings of the Presbytery under the Chapel Act were void, because that act was *ultra vires* of the General Assembly of the Church having being passed without the authority of the state. The interdicts in the case were therefore made perpetual.

The decision in the Stewarton case was given in January 1843. It served as additional fuel to the opinions of those who felt that the authority claimed for the state over the church by the court decisions since 1838 was beyond tolerable bounds. The earlier cases holding the Veto Act unlawful were concerned with the judicial activities of the Church and with its

---

119 I suspect, but cannot prove, that another reason for the decision to defend was that the Church had no jurisdiction over the pursuers under which it could hold them as contumacious. As in *Strathbogie* the church courts generally took strong action against those of their flock who took them to the civil courts.
120 Buchanan II, 411.
121 Stewarton Report, *supra* n. 116, 53; Buchanan II, 407.

performance of its obligations. *Stewarton* now decided that in matters of legislating for its own internal constitution and composition, the church had only such powers as were laid down by the statutes constituting the establishment. This development, taken along with the Veto cases that were just approaching their conclusion, and with the new government's reply to the request for relief, indicated that radical steps would have to be taken.

A single flicker in the gloom came from the Court of Session on 21 February 1843 when the First Division unanimously, though only with the grudging assent of Lord President Boyle, decided not to intervene in the case of *Campbell* v *Presbytery of Kintyre* (1843) 5 D. 657. An appeal to the Assembly against the Presbytery's decision on an allegation of drunkenness had not been proceeded with and had been remitted back to the Presbytery. It was held that as the matter did lie within the competence of Presbytery and the Presbytery had no *quoad sacra* members, it was properly constituted in terms of the *Stewarton* decision of the previous month and the mixed membership of the Assembly was irrelevant. The Court therefore seems to have been striving to be dispassionate, but the main trend of its decisions was by then clear. On 10 March the Third Auchterarder and Third Strathbogie cases were decided, and the die finally cast.

III. The Disruption

We can now summarise the more important Disruption cases chronologically, both to illustrate the developing attitude of the civil courts, and to show that the cases, previously outlined as separate units, were more or less concurrent and formed an emerging pattern.[122] Indeed as time went on the pattern was made quite apparent within them by the frequent citation and explanation of previous opinions within the series.

The First Auchterarder case, the *Earl of Kinnoull* v *Presbytery of Auchterarder* (27 Feb. 1838 (1838) 16 S. 661, affirmed 3 May 1839 (1839) McL. & Rob. 220) held it unlawful for a Presbytery to reject a presentee under Veto Act procedure where the presentation by the patron was duly made. By doing so the Presbytery violated its duty and acted contrary to statute law. The Lethendy case, *Clark* v *Stirling* (14 June 1839, (1839) 1 D. 955) held that a preacher, rejected following the unlawful Veto Act procedure, could obtain an interdict against the Presbytery taking a second presentee on trials, and a declarator that he himself should be taken on trials and if found qualified, be admitted to the charge, all of which showed the civil courts willing to intervene in what was previously considered an exclusively ecclesiastical area. Further, the court could punish infringement of its decrees. In the undefended Daviot case, *MacIntosh* v *Rose* (17 Dec. 1839, (1839) 2 D. 253) interdicts were granted against heads of family dissenting from a settlement under the Veto Act without their proving special objections to the life or doctrine of the presentee. Being uncontested, *MacIntosh* is not particularly significant in the sequence of legal development, but was politically important in entrenching divergent viewpoints.

In the First Strathbogie case, *Presbytery of Strathbogie* (20 Dec. 1839, 14 Feb., 11 June and 11 July 1840 (1839–40) 2 D. 258, 585, 1047, 1380), the suspension by the General Assembly of ministers who had proposed to disobey the Veto Act because it had been declared unlawful in the First Auchterarder and Lethendy cases was itself suspended by the civil courts and the Church interdicted from acting on it ((1840) 2 D. 585). Interdict was also granted against the formal intimation of the church sentence, and other ministers were barred from preaching or otherwise intruding into church properties within the area.

---

122 In so doing I follow Innes I, 182; II, 89.

In the Second Strathbogie case, *Edwards* v *Cruickshank* (18 Dec. 1840, (1840) 3 D. 283), decree in absence had been given in favour of Edwards, the vetoed presentee, the courts holding that the Presbytery was bound take Edwards on trials and admit him to the charge if found qualified. The suspended ministers, whose suspension had been suspended in the First Strathbogie case, so found, and Edwards asked the court to order the Presbytery to admit him. The majority of the Presbytery (that is, the suspended ministers) consented to decree and it was granted in the face of argument by the minority of the Presbytery that the Court of Session had no jurisdiction so to order.

The Second Auchterarder case, *The Earl of Kinnoull* v *Ferguson* of 5 March 1841 ((1841) 3 D. 778; affirmed (HL) (1842) 1 Bell 662), decided that damages could be awarded, without proof of malice, for the refusal of the Presbytery to take Young, the presentee, on trials and admit him were he found qualified. The refusal of the majority of the Presbytery to comply with the decision in the First Auchterarder case rendered them liable as individuals. All that was involved was a simple disobedience of the authority of the civil court. The next year, on 10 March 1842, in *Middleton* v *Anderson*, the Culsamond case (1842) 4 D. 957), the Court of Session suspended an order of the Commission of the General Assembly suspending a presentee who had been settled by his Presbytery contrary to the Veto Act, and prohibiting him from officiating in the parish until the matter had been to the General Assembly. Interim interdict was also granted against other ministers intruding into the parish. The basis of these decisions was the invalidity of the Veto Act, which vitiated the proceedings against Middleton, and the civil effect of his suspension by the Church.

In January 1843 came the first proper decision on the Chapel Act. As had been foreshadowed in *Livingstone* (20 July 1841, (1841) 3 D. 1278) and *Wilson* v *Presbytery of Stranraer* (27 May 1842, (1842) 4 D. 1294), the decision was adverse. In the Stewarton case, *Cuninghame* v *Presbytery of Irvine* (20 Jan. 1843, (1843) 5 D. 427), the Chapel Act was held to be beyond the legislative competence of the General Assembly as that competence was set by statute law. Interdicts were therefore granted against the creation of a new parish *quoad sacra* within the boundary of a 'full' parish, against the constitution of the new kirk session to have jurisdiction over the proposed new parish and against the minister of the 'new' church sitting and voting as a member of the Presbytery. The previous procedures of the Presbytery were invalid by reason of the unlawfulness of the Chapel Act, and by the Presbytery being improperly constituted at the time through containing 'members' whose presence was justified only by that Act.

The final important decisions both came on 10 March 1843 when the Third Auchterarder and the Third Strathbogie cases were decided. In *The Earl of Kinnoull* v *Ferguson* ((1843) 5 D. 1010), the court declared that the minority of the Presbytery willing to obey the previous decisions in the Auchterarder series could constitute a valid Presbytery for the trials and induction of Mr Young, and the majority of the Presbytery were interdicted from interfering with such procedure. In *Cruickshank* v *Gordon* ((1843) 5 D. 909), the Court of Session asserted jurisdiction to reduce the deposition of the majority of the members of the Presbytery of Strathbogie by the General Assembly on account of their having disregarded the Veto Act and for contumacy in appealing to the civil courts.

Four things may be said about these cases; two distinctions and two comments. First, only the Stewarton case is concerned with the Chapel Act of 1834, the others being all occasioned by the question of patronage and the Veto Act. However, as said earlier when discussing the Acts, in a sense the Chapel Act was legally the more fundamental, and therefore the Stewarton decision is the most important. In the Chapel Act the Church was really seeking to legislate *de novo* by setting up new administrative areas and admitting a new category of membership to presbyteries. By contrast it is arguable that the Veto Act was simply an attempt to modify existing ecclesiastical procedures. However, in terms of popular opinion and impact the Veto Act cases were of more immediate effect.

Second, apart from the subject matter a different and equally useful distinction between the cases is to be found in the opinion of Lord Wood in the Stewarton case.[123] He suggested that the court had a twofold duty: first to declare what the Church was bound to do and to enforce its performance; and second, to declare what the Church was bound not to do and to enforce the restriction. Using such a classification the whole law arrived at in the Ten Years' Conflict may be summed up. Positive obedience, what the Church is bound to do comprises the three Auchterarder cases and the Second Strathbogie case. Negative obedience, what the Church is bound not to do, comprises the Lethendy and Culsamond cases, the First and Third Strathbogie cases and the separate case of Stewarton. In both categories, positive and negative, the statements of the majority of the civil court show an increasing willingness to intervene in church affairs to rebuke, to indicate correct conduct and then to require or facilitate that conduct.

The reference in the last sentence to 'the majority of the court' leads to the first comment. The decisions in the cases were generally by a majority. Of course at later stages judges, who earlier had dissented, had to work with the law as their brethren had decided it, and could no longer press their views. But the fact remains that views were expressed in the decisions that were sympathetic to the Church legislation being struck down, and which were against interference by the civil authority in matters within the ecclesiastical preserve. I have not gone into these in any detail as that would unnecessarily prolong matters, but in general they reflected the arguments put forward by the Church. What is important is that these dissentient notes appear and they indicate that the arguments put to the court were not absolutely unfounded and unsupportable: the cases were not open and shut, and the judiciary was not entirely hostile either to what the church had sought to do by the offending legislation, or to the view that the church did indeed have a jurisdiction into which the civil authority might not enter.

My second comment is that the parties seem to have confined their attention to the technicalities involved. Little consideration seems to have been given to a general constitutional point as to the Chapel Act. At the time local government in Scotland as to poor relief and elementary education was predicated on the parish system. The increase in *quoad sacra* parishes under the Chapel Act, the entry of their ministers into presbyteries, and the effect of altering the conditions on which a new minister would become moderator of a kirk session or Presbytery potentially altered the operation of civil local government. In retrospect some of the decisions may be explicable on those, unstated, unacknowledged and perhaps unperceived grounds.

But what was to be done? Various of the court opinions give indications that only two avenues of escape existed. Either the law would have to be changed by parliamentary enactment, or the dissentients would have to leave the Church of Scotland. Indeed, with the benefit of hindsight, the latter option begins to sound like a tocsin.

Three examples will suffice. The discussion of the appeal to the House of Lords, in the Second Auchterarder case above, quoted part of the Opinion of Lord Campbell dealing with the argument that the conscience of the majority of the Presbytery had compelled them to act as they had.[124] Immediately after the quoted extract Lord Campbell went on to state that the

---

123 Stewarton Report, *supra* n. 116, 73, quoted Buchanan II, 407.
124 *Supra* nn. 74 and 75.

freedom which the Church sought was available only to churches outside the establishment. They and they only could make up their own rules. 'Whilst the appellants remain members of the Establishment', they were bound by statute and statute could be amended only through by Parliament.[125]

In the Second Strathbogie case Lord Medwyn likened the establishment to a contract between church and state. An inherent condition of that concordat was that the state would be entitled to enforce its terms:

> This must have been an inherent condition, otherwise it would have been the most insane act on the part of the State to have given an irresponsible[126] power to a society that might become either a most useful and efficient ally, or a most tyrannical or oppressive opponent; and, further, to allow to this ally the right of saying, and that without review or control, that it is acting within its own province, when, in fact, it has failed in its duty to the State, by obstructing its lawful proceedings. This, however, was not done. On the contrary, the Church knew that it was intended to enforce the contract, with all its conditions, purchased by correspondent advantages. If the Church feels burdened with this condition, its remedy is not disobedience at its own hands, but a rescission of the contract, and a *restitutio in integrum* which is always within its power, however much to be deprecated.[127]

Finally, in the Lethendy case Lord President Hope stated:

> If the Church can prevail upon Parliament to repeal or modify the law of patronage, as shall be most agreeable to their views, good and well; but while patronage is the law of the land, it is also the law of the Church and it must be obeyed – *bona fide* and honestly obeyed. . . . As for those ministers of the Church whose conscience cannot submit to the law as long as it remains the law, I am afraid nothing remains for those ministers but to retire from the Established Church. It is impossible that they should remain ministers of the Established Church, and yet reject the law by which they have become an Established Church. . . . No man, I am sure, will regret more than I shall do, if that shall be the fate of some distinguished members of the Church; but, alas, I see no remedy. Either they must submit to the law, or they must retire from the Church. If any man chooses to remain a lay subject of the kingdom, he is bound by his allegiance to the Sovereign: if he cannot submit to that allegiance, he must retire to another country where that allegiance is not binding. In the same way, if a minister cannot conscientiously submit to the law of the Established Church, it is impossible that he should remain a minister of the Established Church.[128]

All this is not to say that Parliament and the government were inactive during the period. Following upon the 1832 Reform Act and the Representation (Scotland) Act representation of the people in a variety of contexts was of interest. The House of Commons *inter alia* set up a Select Committee on Church Patronage in Scotland. Before that Committee reported,

---

125 (1842) 1 Bell 662 at 733–4.
126 The term 'irresponsible' is here used technically, not pejoratively.
127 *Cruickshank* v *Gordon* (1843) 5 D. 909 at 964.
128 Lethendy Report, 217. This comment does not appear in the Dunlop version of the report.

the General Assembly passed the Veto Act. It is therefore, to say the least, interesting that the Committee recommended the defence and preservation of an establishment which, in its view, was intimately interwoven with the general prosperity and moral welfare of Scotland. No recommendations were made for change, and the Committee confined itself to rehearsing the evidence given to it. It does not appear that the Committee thought that the 1834 Acts required either legislative or judicial correction.[129]

During the currency of the dispute, the Melbourne Government indicated it would seek to remedy the situation. Thus in 1839 a Committee appointed by the Assembly after the First Auchterarder case did meet with government, but it appears that the government's political strength was not such as would allow satisfactory immediate action.[130] However, in August 1839 a letter from Lord Belhaven, who had been the Queen's Commissioner to the General Assembly, was read to the Commission of Assembly. This stated an intention that the Queen's patronage to be exercised 'in a manner congruent with the Veto Law'.[131] Further it was implied that the law of the land would be changed. This was strongly attacked by the Moderates. How was it possible that after a decision as to the law by the House of Lords was government going to act in a manner inconsistent with that law?[132] Similar views were expressed in the House of Lords, in particular by Lord Brougham. Finally, I cannot refrain from suggesting that the position was further exacerbated by a long pamphlet published by John Hope, the Dean of Faculty.[133]

According to Buchanan[134] one of the main reasons why the Church did not ask Parliament to amend the Patronage Law at the very beginning of the sequence was a distrust of the 1834 Parliament's ability to appreciate the Presbyterian viewpoint. Whether this was justified does not now matter. The important fact was that the Assembly proceeded with its own legislation with the results we have seen. Naturally this demonstration of a will to independence reinforced whatever anti-evangelical forces there were in Parliament, and, to borrow a metaphor from nuclear technology, the whole matter went critical.

Parliament did not come into the dispute again until things had gone far beyond patronage and the internal constitution and self-regulatory powers of the Kirk. The fundamental principles of church-state relations were by then the subject of dispute. At that stage government offered a solution to the patronage problem, which ultimately became the Scottish Benefices Act of 1843,[135] allowing members of a congregation simply to object to a presentee, or to give reasons why he was unsuitable for the charge. Presbytery was then to decide

---

129 *Report of the Select Committee on Church Patronage in Scotland*, 1834 HC 512, iii–iv.
130 Buchanan I, 472–3. On all governmental moves see G.I.T. Machin, 'The Disruption in British Politics' (1972), 51 Scot Hist. Rev. 20–51.
131 Buchanan I, 472–3. Cf. Crown procedure in the Daviot case, *MacIntosh* v *Rose* (1839) 2 D. 253, *supra* at n. 81.
132 Given the willingness of later governments to alter the law to elide court decisions which they find unacceptable, this argument is strikingly naïve. To go back some decades to avoid current debates, cf. *Burmah Oil (Burmah Trading) Ltd.,* v *Lord Advocate*, 1964 SC (HL) 117, and the War Damage Act 1965.
133 'A Letter to the Lord Chancellor, on the Claims of the Church of Scotland in regard to its Jurisdiction, and, on the proposed Changes in its Polity', by John Hope, Esq., Dean of Faculty (Edinburgh and London, 1839). The 'letter' is 290 pages long, plus 11 pages of appendices. However objective one may wish to be in discussing *lex lata* and *lex ferenda*, after reading the language of the letter, and reviewing the other acts of John Hope, one is left with the feeling that personal elements played a part in his conduct. In modern times, once on the Bench he would have had to recuse himself from the Disruption cases. That would have been interesting.
134 Buchanan I, 203. To follow all the negotiations and attempts at solutions would be to lose track of the point. They are all dealt with in Buchanan and Bryce. And see next note.
135 Church of Scotland Benefices Bill ('Lord Aberdeen's Act'), see particularly Second Reading, 1843 71 HC Deb. Cols 10–74; HL Committee Stage, 1843 70 HL Deb, Cols, 534–59. See also Buchanan II, 98–122,

what effect should be given to such objection. This was an improvement, but by ignoring other deeper questions, it did indicate that Parliament considered the *rationes* and *dicta* in the Disruption cases to be correct statements of the law. The state was the fount of all authority. Therefore although the Benefices Bill would have gone some way to approximate to Veto Act procedure, it implied a supremacy of state enactment which by this time was repugnant to an important section of the Church of Scotland leadership.

What the evangelicals wanted was state legislation giving effect to the church's claim to final powers of legislation and of judicial determination of spiritual matters as matters within the province of the Church alone. This is clear in the Claim of Right, that remarkable document adopted by the General Assembly of the Church by a majority of 131 in the early hours of Wednesday, 25 May 1842.

The Claim of Right[136] narrated the theological and statutory basis on which the Church claimed independence from the state, and the opinion of the Church that the civil courts had entrenched upon the rights of the Church. It went on to claim that independence of the civil arm for which it contended; declared that the ministers of the Church could not continue within the establishment unless it were suitably reconstituted to give effect to that view; and protested the Acts of Parliament which had led to this situation, while stating that these acts would continue to be obeyed within the civil realm. The Claim ended by calling on members of the Church if necessary 'to endure resignedly the loss of the temporal benefits of the establishment, and the personal sufferings to which they [might] be called' were Parliament to refuse to give relief by altering civil legislation so as to secure the spiritual independence of the Church.

The Claim of Right was intimated to Parliament, and other steps were taken to ensure that the government could not be ignorant of the consequences were the Claim not heeded and given effect to.[137] In this time, however, a series of court actions continued. In August 1842 the Second Auchterarder decision came from the House of Lords. In January 1843 the Court of Session struck down the Chapel Act in the Stewarton case. In the meantime, on 4 January the new government under Sir Robert Peel stated that the Claim was unreasonable and that the government 'could not advise Her Majesty to acquiesce in these demands'.[138] Despite this, on 31 January 1843 the Commission of Assembly resolved to make one further appeal to Parliament. This was done through the agency of Fox Maule in the House of Commons on 7 March 1843, who asked for a Committee of Enquiry, with perhaps an address to the Crown as its result, and for a declaratory Act in order better to define the jurisdiction of the Church, and confirming its jurisdiction within its own province. Though supported by a majority of the Scottish members the motion was lost.[139] Three days later on 10 March 1843 judgements in the Third Auchterarder and the Third Strathbogie cases were handed down.

218–23, 324–33: Bryce II, 2–37, 194–218; cf. Cockburn, Journals, I, 259–60; Bulloch I, 239–40. There was also a Bill prepared by the Duke of Argyle, but it was overtaken by events.

136 The Claim, Declaration, and Protest, by the General Assembly of the Church of Scotland, General Assembly 1842, Act XIX; SSFCS 235–55; Buchanan II, 471–85. See also the Free Church Case, *The General Assembly of the Free Church, Bannatyne and Others v Lord Overtoun and Others: MacAlister and Others v Young and Another* [1904] AC 515 at 737; Innes I, 162–7, II, 176–83. Cf. Sir H.W. Moncrieff, *A Vindication of the Free Church Claim of Right* (Edinburgh: Maclaren and Macniven, 1877).

137 Buchanan II, 398. Cf. the parliamentary debates cited *supra* n. 135, which post-date the Claim.

138 Buchanan II, 412.

139 Buchanan II, 419–27. 1843 67 HC Deb. Cols 354–422, 441–510. G.I.T. Machin, 'The Disruption in British Politics' (1972), 51 Scot Hist. Rev. 20 at 46–50.

Once it was clear that the Church was not to obtain redress from the state, preparation began for those ministers adhering to the Claim of Right formally to separate from the Church of Scotland. A Protest was drawn up narrating their view of the matter and laying the whole blame and responsibility upon the civil authorities.

The General Assembly met on Thursday 18 May1843. The Moderator, the Rev. Dr David Welsh, opened it with prayer. He then stated that instead of the Assembly passing as normal to make up the Roll of Commissioners, certain matters had to be dealt with. Since the liberties of the constitution of the Church had been infringed without redress, he protested against their proceeding further. He then read the Protest, laid on the table a copy signed by a body of others commissioned to the Assembly and withdrew from the chamber followed by those of like opinion.[140] They then walked to the Canonmills Hall, where they constituted themselves as the first Assembly of the Free Church of Scotland – a denomination having the legal status of a voluntary association.[141]

Was it all necessary? Could it have happened differently? Should the Disruption have been avoided? There are no answers to such questions. It happened. Certainly it was a part of a general change in Scottish life.[142] Yes, we can see certain crucial elements and turning points in the story. For example, it seems clear that successive governments of the day were either badly advised and unaware of the real seriousness of the situation (perhaps because their sources of information sympathised with the Moderates' position), or for political reasons they misconstrued the facts.[143] It may be that the success of the policy of inaction in coping with contemporaneous problems in the episcopal Church of England misled government into applying the similar policy in relation to the presbyterian Church of Scotland. Alternatively the Scottish policy may have been deliberate precisely to avoid stirring up the English situation again. At any rate the failure to see or permit that the will to participate in government that had manifested itself in the 1832 Reform Acts should also affect ecclesiastical government is certainly curious. Perhaps here, before his *Lectures* had received much publicity, we see in action John Austin's Sovereign, the ruler without superior, from whose unfettered will all authority within his state is derived.[144] Such could not allow the independence of the Church.

On the other hand some would argue that the governments of the day did the best possible thing in refusing to heed a strident and divisive minority, whose instability was proved by its readiness theatrically to quit the establishment. It is likely that the 1843 Assembly would once more have contained a majority of Moderates, who would have been willing to acquiesce in the Disruption judgements, and alter the ecclesiastical legislation accordingly, as indeed was done. The Disruption therefore can be presented as a pre-emptive strike by

---

140   GA Act I, 1843; SSFCS 257–62; Buchanan II, 485–8; the Free Church Case, *supra* n. 136 [1904] AC 514 at 741; Innes I, 167–71; II, 183–7.

141   Buchanan II, 431–49; Bryce II, 357–91; Cockburn, Journals II, 18–46; T. Brown, *supra* n. 1, 81–96. There is debate about exact numbers, but it is said that 474 ministers (about one-third of the then ministry) left the Church at this time. Bulloch I, 250, notes that had voting been by Presbyteries, 80 would have had a majority for remaining, and 18 would have voted to secede.

As a matter of law the Disruption was completed by the Act of Separation and Deed of Demission, GA 1843 Act IV, registered in the Books of Council and Session 8 June 1843 (Innes 1, 171–2); Free Church Case [1904] AC 515 at 532 n. 1) and a Supplementary Act of Separation and Deed of Demission, GA 1843 Act VI (SSFCS, 263–80).

142   Cf. Bulloch I, 25–74.

143   Bulloch I, 256–7.

144   J. Austin, *The Province of Jurisprudence Determined*, 1832 (many eds); J. Bentham, *On Laws in General*, H.L.A. Hart, ed. (London: Athlone Press, 1970).

the minority. But such an argument is not supportable. The Church could ill afford the loss of those who 'went out'. And the root of the matter goes deeper than that.

The Disruption was a tragedy for the Church of Scotland in that it absorbed so many energies both at the time and subsequently when both sides in succeeding years (especially the Free Church) sought to justify their stance. It is the cancer of schism that parties rarely put it behind them and get on with their immediate tasks. Rather they fight the old battles over and over again. Both the Free Church and the Auld Kirk were weakened by that tendency in the following decades, though in the long run the established church survived better.[145]

However, the Disruption was generally considered to be, and indeed was, one of the finest acts of principle that had been seen,[146] as ministers for conscience sake quitted the comforts and security of the establishment, and as members began the financial task of setting up a new church, providing it with buildings, a college system and so on. It was a fine example of a major element of the Scottish character. But it was also caused by other national characteristics. There were occasions early in the dispute when matters might have been solved by discussion and negotiation had first the Moderates, and later the Evangelicals, been willing so to do. Too soon, perhaps, stands were taken on principle, and the rights and wrongs of the situation, rather than its solution, contended for. The Moderates stood on statute law, the Evangelicals on theological doctrine. Arguing from different premises, they could not reach an accommodation without appearing to surrender principle. The result of that failure to discuss and negotiate before positions became entrenched is a warning to the heirs of both sides in the modern Kirk.

The post-Disruption period

The period following the Disruption need not take as much space as that relating to its occurrence. A greater recognition of the freedom and principles for which the seceding ministers and their followers had contended came to be granted by the state. The process was neither immediate nor without setback, but the trend was towards the recognition of an independent jurisdiction vested in the Church that was more extensive than that contemplated by the *dicta* of the Disruption cases. However, simultaneously, responsibilities for welfare and education were lost, being increasingly assumed by the Victorian state, and, seen in retrospect, a diminution of the influence of the Kirk.

*

After the Disruption procession had left, the remainder of the General Assembly swiftly brought the law of the Church into harmony with the statements of the courts. Much of this was regressive. The Veto Act and Chapel Act were repealed,[147] and the suspension of the majority of the ministers of the Presbytery of Strathbogie was treated as null and void. The Assembly also revived GA Act V, 1799, barring all but duly licensed Church of Scotland ministers from taking services in parish churches.[148] The only new development was a welcome for what was to become the Scottish Benefices Act, 1843. This required

---

145 Bulloch II and II, *passim*.
146 Cf. Cockburn, Journals II, 28–32, and his report of the reaction of his friend in his *Life of Lord Jeffrey* (Edinburgh: Black, 1872), 382.
147 Respectively, GA Acts IX and X, 1843.
148 There was much bitterness on both sides. Often the Free Church had problems in getting sites for its churches, landowners who favoured the established church being unwilling to sell land for the purpose: see *Reports of the Select Committee on Sites for Churches (Scotland)*, 1847, HC 247, 311 and 613; *Bain v Black* (1849) 11 D.

presbyteries to consider congregational opinion while deciding whether a minister ought to be taken on trials, which went closer to the Veto Act than many would have wished.[149]

The Kirk now effectively disavowed its competence to revise its own constitution, just as in the previous 10 years it had claimed that right. Further development of the law of the church would have to come through statute. At this point the state was theoretically supreme over the church, though how far this could have been pressed is doubtful. It does not appear, for example, that the state could have interfered substantively with the Confession of the Church, though the state was soon no longer to require that teachers should be subject to supervision by the Church, nor that they be required to sign the Confession.[150] On the contrary, such cases as made it to the civil courts make it plain that the church was supreme in its own sphere. These, however, do not contain the extravagant language to be found in the Disruption decisions, and fall to be distinguished from them as dealing with the judicial and not the legislative powers of the Church.

In 1849 two sets of cases discussed the Church courts acting in a judicial capacity. In *Dunbar* v *Stoddart* (1849) 11 D. 587, Dunbar, a parochial schoolmaster, claimed damages for alleged slander by the local minister, Stoddart. Malice was discussed, but it was decided that the facts did not raise questions of privilege. Later, however, the Presbytery deposed Dunbar from office following up on a complaint from Stoddart. Dunbar successfully sought to reduce that decision on grounds of procedural irregularity, but then sought damages from the Presbytery for their actings. In *Dunbar* v *Presbytery of Auchterarder* (1849) 12 D. 284,[151] issues were disallowed since it was clear that the complaint was one of error of judgement and not of malice.[152] However, in the latter case the question of the jurisdiction of the church courts was not properly looked into because the Presbytery was performing its duty under the then statutes as to the regulation of schools.[153]

More serious questions were raised by the normal disciplinary functions of church in respect of their members. *Sturrock* v *Greig* (1849) 11 D. 1220 involved another schoolmaster. Peter Sturrock, assistant schoolmaster at Blairgowrie, sought damages from the minister and members of the Blairgowrie kirk session who had acted against him in respect of a *fama* (a rumour of misconduct), and other faults. The case is complex. The session had ignored the reversal of its decisions by the superior courts of the church, and had failed in other duties. But the point for which it is here cited is the privilege of the Church courts and the finality of their actings. The first head note to the case summarises the decision succinctly:

> No action for damages will lie against a Church Court of the Established Church for any sentence or judgement pronounced by them in a proper case of discipline duly brought before them, regularly conducted, and within their competency and province as a Church Court, even although it be averred that the judgement was pronounced maliciously and without probable cause.

Lord Justice-Clerk Hope made it clear that, in law and when acting within the scope of their proper duty, Church courts were part of the constitutional structure of the judicial

---

1286; T. Brown, *supra* n. 1, 246–90. (There are also editions of 1883, 1884 and 1894.) For a fictional treatment see W.A. Alexander, *Johnny Gibb of Gushetneuk*, *supra* n. 1.
149 See *supra* n. 135 and Buchanan II, 450–462; Bryce II, 375–412.
150 See Chapter 6, 'Education'.
151 Reference point n. 157 *infra*.
152 A third case in this sequence is *Smith* v *Presbytery of Auchterarder* (1849) 12 D. 296, where a Mrs Smith failed to properly allege malice in an action for damages in respect of her being mentioned in the Presbytery proceedings against Dunbar.
153 Reference point n. 163 *infra*.

arrangements of the country and hence were not open to review, or to action in respect of their conduct. He said:

> ... in matters clearly within the cognisance of Church officers or Courts, as subject of Church censures ... when the Church judicatory is thus exercising the government so entrusted to it, [sc. by the State] its judicatories and its officers are not amenable to the civil courts for alleged wrong. They have been trusted as a separate government.[154]

Lords Medwyn and Moncreiff were of the same view, the latter stating:

> ... the action and proposed issue are incompetent, in so far as they are founded on the sentences or resolutions of the Kirk Session regularly convened, and ... no addition of malice or want of probable cause can render them competent.[155]

Lord Cockburn dissented on the apparently reasonable grounds that such statements meant that a kirk session had an absolute license of defamation.[156] But it is not clear whether this is so. The opinions of the majority speak in terms of 'proper' cases, 'regular' proceedings and the 'province' and 'competence' of the appropriate church court, language that would allow a later court if necessary suitably to interpret *Sturrock*.[157] Again other case law casts doubt on the wider language of *Sturrock*. *Dunbar* v *Presbytery of Auchterarder* (1849) 12 D. 284, is one.[158] The question does not seem to have been argued in respect of the established church since 1849, but I doubt whether *Sturrock* would readily now be followed.[159]

For present purposes the importance of *Sturrock* lies not so much in its discussion of the privileges of the established Church courts, but in the clear view that in the judicial area the Church courts were final. Indeed, as Lord Cockburn pointed out, *Sturrock* seemed to run counter to the wide statements of the previous Disruption cases. His Opinion concludes:

> It humbly appears to me that your Lordships' opinions amount to a reversal of the principle of these judgements. I am aware that this is not what your Lordships mean: but I suspect that it is the only construction that lawyers can put on what you are doing.[160]

In short, the majority held that within its province the Church court was supreme, but (and to a degree this accommodates Lord Cockburn) in the last analysis it was for the civil court to determine whether the Church court was acting within its exclusive jurisdiction.

---

154 (1849) 11 D. 1220 at 1231.
155 (1849) 11 D. 1220 at 1238.
156 (1849) 11 D. 1220 at 1238.
157 For example, in *Sturrock* itself an action was allowed in respect of the 'official' reiteration by the local minister on the authority of the session of the sentence of the kirk session although that sentence had been reversed by Presbytery and synod.
158 *Supra* at n. 151.
159 The preceding discussion is of the absolute privilege of the decision of a church court. Absolute privilege would not apply to communications within the court, or in the conduct of church business. Whether such communications are afforded qualified privilege (that is, actionable only if malice and want of probable cause are averred and proven) depends on the nature of the occasion: *Smith* v *Presbytery of Auchterarder* (1849) 12 D. 296; *Rankine* v *Roberts* (1873) 1 R. 225; *Croucher* v *Inglis* (1889) 16 R. 774; *Jack* v *Fleming* (1891) 19 R. 1; *A.* v *B.* (*Macleod* v *Munro*) (1895) 22 R. 984; *Doig* v *Thomson* (1898) 15 Sh. Ct. Rep. 59; *Barclay* v *Manuel* (1902) 10 S.L.T. 450; *Murray* v *Wylie* 1916 SC 356. See also *infra* at n. 172.
160 (1849) 11 D. 1220 at 1242.

Lord Justice-Clerk Hope stated that the principle of supremacy in disciplinary matters 'will not surround these courts with protection if they exceed their jurisdiction', and he cited the Disruption cases as illustration. These had shown that the church courts were not protected if they 'refuse to perform a duty imposed upon them by statute, as part of the ecclesiastical constitution of the Church'.[161] But Lord Hope dealt with the Disruption material only in that oblique way. In full agreement Lord Medwyn pointed to the separate jurisdiction of the Church courts so long as they acted within their sphere of competence. For him the only remedy for an unjust, as opposed to an illegal, sentence pronounced by a church court lay within the appellate procedures of the Church.[162] Lord Medwyn went on expressly to distinguish the Disruption cases on points of patrimonial interest but that does not seem valid. Previously the civil courts had been only too keen to right wrongs, and on that basis *Sturrock* seems to have had a relevant and competent case.

Despite the language of the majority, the Court of Session was no longer willing to make such extreme assertions of the subordination of the church to the state as they had for example in the Auchterarder and Strathbogie cases. An influential section of the Church had left the establishment because of those decisions. That seems to have cooled the ardour of the court. Their Lordships had now re-stated a principle which had effectively been mute in the Ten Years' Conflict; that there was an area within which the Church was final.

This principle was applied in *Lockhart* v *Presbytery of Deer* (1851) 13 D. 1296, where, without calling upon counsel for the respondents, the First Division refused a note of suspension brought by a minister against his deposition on the grounds of immoral conduct.[163] Lockhart alleged a variety of procedural deficiencies in the trial of his case which the General Assembly had refused to correct, but the court refused to consider the matter. Lord President Boyle stated:

> We are just driven to ask this question – does the Court of Session sit in review of the highest ecclesiastical court? We have just as little right to interfere with the procedure of the Church courts in matters of ecclesiastical discipline, as we have to interfere with the proceedings of the Court of Justiciary in a criminal question.[164]

Lord Fullerton said:

> The deliverances ... on the irregularity or informality of which the present application is founded, are deliverances by a Church court, in the undoubted exercise their own exclusive jurisdiction. ... I have always understood that a sentence of deposition pronounced by [the General Assembly] on an ecclesiastical offence, is beyond the reach of any interference by this Civil Court ...[165]

Lord Cuninghame was equally emphatic that the ecclesiastical courts had an exclusive jurisdiction in proper ecclesiastical cases, and it would be 'altogether unprecedented and unconstitutional' to review their judgements.[166] Given history, this language is interesting

---

161 (1849) 11 D. 1220 at 1231–2.
162 (1849) 11 D. 1220 at 1233–4.
163 This case differs from the reduction in *Dunbar* v *Stoddart* (1849) 11 D. 587 (*supra* n. 153) as it was a matter of discipline of a minister and not performance of statutory duty.
164 (1851) 13 D. 1296 at 1299.
165 (1851) 13 D. 1296 at 1299.
166 (1851) 13 D. 1296 at 1301.

and was commented on by Lord Ivory, who noted that the important question was the extent of the 'proper ecclesiastical' nature of any given case, which allowed the court to distinguish the Auchterarder and Strathbogie cases.[167]

Further examples exist in which the Court of Session refused notes of suspension and interdict against proceedings in the church courts on the ground that these bodies were acting within their powers. The effect of this pattern was slowly to establish an area of judicial activity within which the Church was supreme, thus removing many of the doubts that the wider pronouncements of the Disruption cases had caused.

In *Paterson* v *Presbytery of Dunbar* (1861) 23 D. 720, the court was asked to suspend the deposition of a minister on the grounds that a defence of insanity had not been properly dealt in the church courts. Lord Ivory put the point most succinctly. For the Court of Session to grant the note of suspension:

> . . . would be going contrary to the whole principles of independent jurisdiction which separate the Ecclesiastical from the Civil Courts. Each is independent of the other, and each has its own exclusive field of jurisdiction and within that field is paramount. No more can we interfere with the ecclesiastical jurisdiction, keeping it within its competency, than the ecclesiastical courts could interfere with us – keeping us within our competency.[168]

Again, in *Lang* v *Presbytery of Irvine* (1864) 2 M. 823, the court refused to consider the reduction of a Presbytery minute on the grounds of irregularity, because the pursuer had not exhausted the remedies open to him in the hierarchy of Church courts. Until that had been done the civil courts would not consider whether they were excluded by reason of the exclusive competence of the ecclesiastical court.[169] Finally, in one of the best-known formulations of the principle in *Wight* v *Presbytery of Dunkeld*,[170] after reviewing the averments Lord Justice Clerk Moncreiff stated:

> If, therefore, this were a case in which we were called upon to review the proceedings of an inferior Court, I should have thought that a strong case had been made out for our interference. But whatever inconsiderate dicta to that effect may have been thrown out, that is not the law of Scotland. The jurisdiction of the Church courts, as recognised judicatories of this realm, rests on a similar statutory foundation to that under which we administer justice within these walls. It is easy to suggest extravagant instances of excess of power, but quite as easy to do so in regard

---

167 (1851) 13 D. 1296 at 1302.
168 (1849) 11 D. 1220 at 1242.
169 Cf. the dicta of Lord Medwyn in *Sturrock* quoted *supra* at n. 162. This is comparable with the rule requiring 'exhaustion of local remedies' in questions of state responsibility in International Law.
170 Wight, minister of Auchtergaven, charged with fornication and indecent and scandalous familiarity with a female parishioner, pleaded guilty to the lesser charge of scandalous familiarity and not guilty to the others. He was suspended for six months. Nothing was officially done about the other charges, though Wight said he was told informally that they were to be dropped. No appeal was taken by any member of Presbytery. Four months later, on the petition of five elders of his congregation, the General Assembly ordered the remaining charges to be dealt with because of allegations of irregularity during the Presbytery proceedings. Wight argued that he had been tried and sentenced by a judgement which had become final, that the elders had no standing thus to petition and that matters were closed. He asked the Court of Session, therefore, to bar further proceedings against him.

to the one jurisdiction as to the other. Within their spiritual province the Church Courts are as supreme as we are within the civil; and as this is a matter relating to the discipline of the Church, and solely within the cognisance of the Church Courts, I think that we have no power whatever to interfere.[171]

The rest of the Bench agreed with Lord Moncrieff on general terms though expressing some doubts whether the civil court could not under any circumstances interfere with a church proceeding. Their restricted interpretation seems to be a more correct statement of the present law. So long as the courts of the Church do not act plainly *ultra vires*, or maliciously, or manifestly unjustly (not merely unjustly) or contrary to some civil enactment, no action will lie to reduce their proceedings, or to obtain redress for any injury they have caused. But this is not the same as a statement that the courts of the Church of Scotland have absolute independence from review by the civil courts. This would also accord with the possible restricted interpretation of *Sturrock*, using such concepts of 'proper jurisdiction', 'regularity of proceeding' and so on to allow the court freedom of manoeuvre round that rather exceptional case. Cases involving the judicatories of the non-established churches may also here be of persuasive authority in indicating that the privilege of any 'church court' is only of a qualified nature, that may be displaced.[172] A court acting maliciously would not be acting within its lawful province.[173] The question does not seem to have been argued in respect of the established Church since 1849, but, as said above, I am inclined to doubt whether *Sturrock* would now readily be followed.[174]

Clearly by the time of *Wight* in 1870 the nature of the courts of the Church of Scotland as recognised courts of the realm was being emphasised in a way not present in the Disruption *dicta*. This is underlined in the famous observations in 1874 of Lord President Inglis on the nature of the Presbytery as a court of the realm in *Presbytery of Lews* v *Fraser*:

We are dealing with a Presbytery, an established judicature of the country, as much recognised by law as the Court of Session itself. Its jurisdiction, indeed, differs widely from that of the civil courts, but it is just as much the creation of law as that of any other court in the kingdom.[175]

As such a court, church records are of like status to those of the ordinary civil courts, belonging to and held inalienably for the benefit of the public. The records are *extra commercium*, and cannot become private property by any means. Lapse of time does not bar their recovery by the court.[176] The same may apply to church bells.[177]

---

171 (1870) 8 M. 921 at 925.
172 Cf. the argument of the Pursuer in *Edwards* v *Begbie* (1850) 12 D. 1134, and the cases on the Church (Patronage) Scotland Act 1874, to which we are coming. Cf. *Dunbar* v *Skinner* (1849) 11 D. 945; *McDonald* v *Burns*, 1940 SC 376 but cf. also *Murray* v *Wyllie* 1916 SC 356. See Chapter 5.
173 This applies generally to all bodies that purport to act judicially, not just to church courts.
174 *Smith* v *Presbytery of Auchterarder* (1849) 12 D. 296; *Rankine* v *Roberts* (1873) 1 R. 225; *Croucher* v *Inglis* (1889) 16 R. 774; *Jack* v *Fleming* (1891) 19 R. 1; *A.* v *B.* (*Macleod* v *Munro*) (1895) 22 R. 984; *Doig* v *Thomson* (1898) 15 Sh. Ct. Rep. 59; *Barclay* v *Manuel* (1902) 10 SLT 450; *Murray* v *Wylie* 1916 SC 356.
175 (1874) 1 R. 888 at 892. Cf. *infra* n. 184.
176 *Presbytery of Edinburgh* v *University of Edinburgh* (1890) 28 SLR 567, where the public character of the records overcame a defence of possession for almost 200 years.
177 A.R.C. Simpson, 'Positive prescription of moveables in Scots law', 2009 Edin. L.R. 445.

The independent jurisdiction of the courts of the Kirk remains as outlined. Implicitly also the proceedings of the Kirk were sacrosanct, provided that they did not contravene statutory law. That view was to be taken forward into the twentieth century, but here I should note that the protection of the Kirk from the state was to be outflanked by modern concepts. We will come to the *Percy* case in a later chapter.[178]

So much for the courts of the Church. However, it should also be noted that ministers of the church should not stray from their proper sphere. In a case involving the Episcopal church, at 957 the Lord President noted that the courts had heard many cases involving clergyman, and cited two defamation cases where pleas of privilege and ecclesiastical jurisdiction had been disallowed.[179] Two years later *Lockhart* v *Cumming* showed that that position persisted.[180]

Matters were different as far as statute was concerned. During the post-Disruption period four major statutory innovations continued to show the subservience of the established church vis-à-vis the state. The first changed the law on the erection of new parishes *quoad sacra*, the second altered the powers of church courts, the third abolished patronage and the fourth liberalised the terms of subscription of the Westminster Confession by office-bearers.

First, the New Parishes (Scotland) Act 1844 modified the Act 1706 c. 10, easing the creation of new *quoad omnia* parishes. Subject to satisfactory endowments (s. 4), the Court of Session sitting as the Court of Teinds was empowered to erect new parishes, usually with the consent of the heritors.[181] The 1706 Act had required that a new parish have the consent of three-quarters of the relevant heritors. This was abolished (s. 1). Instead the Court could act with the consent of a majority, computed as including all those not actively objecting (s. 3) and, further, the consent of heritors might be dispensed with where there were 'good and sufficient reasons' for the new parish (s. 4). Finally, ministers and elders of such new churches were to have full status as office-bearers of the Church (s. 8).[182] The decision in the *Stewarton* case was thus avoided and many of the purposes for which the Chapel Act had been passed were achieved. However, the requirement of endowment and the intervention of the civil court in the proceedings meant progress in creating these new parishes was slow. Further, the whole development was by the courtesy and action of the civil authority, an intervention which would have been rejected by those who by then had formed the Free Church.[183]

Second, the Church of Scotland Courts Act, 1863,[184] made it clear that the church courts could suspend a minister from his parochial duties pending the determination of a libel

---

178 *Percy* v *Church of Scotland Board of National Mission* [2005] UKHL 73: 2006 SC (HL) 1; [2006] 2 AC 28, *infra* Chapter 4, at n. 56.
179 *Dunbar* v *Skinner* (1849) 11 D. 945 at 957. The cases Hope cites were, *Adam* v *Allan* (1841) 3 D. 1058 and *Dudgeon* v *Forbes* (1832–33) 11 S. 1014. *Dunbar* v *Skinner* is dealt with in Chapter 5 at n. 62.
180 (1852–53) 14 D. 452.
181 Delineating the actual new parochial boundaries was a matter for the Church.
182 See N. Elliot, *The Erection of Parishes Quoad Sacra and Feuing of Glebes under Authority of the Court of Teinds* (Edinburgh: Blackwood, 1879). Further developments and modifications, unimportant here, were contained in the United Parishes (Scotland) Acts of 1868 and 1876. The 1844 Act did not put an end to all difficulties and the hostility of many older churches to 'new' parishes persisted. *Hutton* v *Harper* (1875) 2 R. 893 (1876) 3 R. (H.L.) 9, a failed attempt to stop the calling of banns in *quoad sacra* charges, went as far as the House of Lords. Eleven out of 12 judges involved at various stages held banns to be *inter sacra*.
183 Statutory intervention was also needed for the reconstruction of certain parishes, for example Annuity Tax Acts 1860 and 1870. The Kirk could not act on its own initiative.
184 Fleming I, 125. To get the bill through Parliament a clause giving powers of compelling witnesses in ecclesiastical cases was dropped; but see *Presbytery of Lews* v *Fraser* (1874) 1 R. 888 (*supra* n. 175) where the Court

against him, and clarified procedures in cases of insanity. A minister charged with immoral conduct or error in doctrine could be suspended from the exercise of his ecclesiastical functions and, until the matter had been fully resolved, the parish dealt with as if the minister had died (s. 1). Suspension, however, did not affect the right to stipend. Presbytery was to appoint a temporary assistant to a suspended minister, the assistant receiving up to half the stipend during the period of the assistantship (s. 3). Section 2 made similar provision for the appointment of an assistant were a minister found to be unable to function because of insanity. That appointment subsisted until the Presbytery was satisfied that the minister's mental condition had improved or the charge had been declared vacant.

The 1863 Act showed the civil authorities willing to afford the Kirk a greater liberty of action in its disciplinary and internal governmental functions. Disappointingly however, and perhaps tellingly, the Free Church of Scotland petitioned against the legislation at the Bill stage on the ground that these moves clearly showed the erastian nature of the establishment of the Church of Scotland. For the Free Church such legislative clarification and innovation was an unacceptable intrusion into what should have been the inherent power of a Church. But the Free Church really ought to have welcomed the development. That it did not rather diminished its pretensions.

Third, patronage was abolished, again by the act of the civil arm, but as the result of a petition by the Kirk itself following much discussion in the 1860s.[185] Section 3 of the Church Patronage (Scotland) Act, 1874, enacted that: 'the right of electing and appointing ministers to vacant churches and parishes in Scotland is hereby declared to be vested in the congregations of such vacant churches and parishes . . . subject to such regulations . . . as may from time to time be framed by the General Assembly of the Church of Scotland . . .' Further, '. . . the courts of the said Church are hereby declared to have the right to decide finally and exclusively upon the appointment, admission, and settlement in any church and parish of any person as minister thereof. The ministers . . . [so settled] . . . have in all respects the same rights, privileges and duties which now belong to or are incumbent on the ministers of the said Church'. Compensation for the loss of rights was to be paid only to private patrons, and only if the patron so requested within six months of the passing of the Act. Compensation was determined by the local sheriff (s. 4) and was normally one year's stipend taken as the average of the preceding three years (s. 5).[186] Finally, arrangements had to be made for the filling of a vacancy. The right to appoint was transferred to the congregation, but were the congregation to fail to act within six months of a vacancy, the right devolved to the Presbytery of the bounds (s. 7).

Devolution of the right of appointment soon gave rise to court action that clearly showed the extent of the concession to church autonomy made by s. 3. *Stewart* v *Presbytery of Paisley* (1878) 6 R. 178 considered whether the congregational right to appoint to Paisley Abbey had devolved on Presbytery. The six-month time limit had lapsed because the minister initially selected by the congregation declined the call. Two parishioners sought to stop the Presbytery acting *iure devoluto* in the vacancy. This was refused as being out of time, and because in the meantime both the Assembly and Presbytery had

---

of Session held, without the need for statute, that the civil authorities could compel witnesses to attend courts of the established Church and give evidence.

185 Innes II, 115. The Assembly Committee on Patronage published an examination of the topic in 1870 and this served as the basis on which the Bill was drawn.

186 See *Paterson* v *Paterson* (1888) 15 R. 1060; *Earl of Strathmore* v *Heritors of Rescobie* (1888) 15 R. 364.

determined that no valid appointment had been made. In terms of s. 3 of the Act that determination was final.

Apart from the merits of the decision in *Stewart*, the opinion of the Court, delivered by Lord President Inglis, contains observations as to the nature of the legislation and the relations of the civil and ecclesiastical courts. The Presbytery had argued that under s. 3 the courts of the Church were final, excluding any recourse to the civil judicatories. The Lord President held the right to appoint under the Act to be a statutory right and not one of patronage. Jurisdiction to determine disputes as to statutory right rested with the civil courts of the country unless expressly excluded, and this had not been done. As he put it:

> Being legal rights dependent upon statute their enforcement or a challenge of their validity in any particular case can only be tried in the tribunal which is appointed to interpret and enforce the statutes of the realm, that is, the supreme civil court, unless the jurisdiction and duty have been conferred and imposed on some other tribunal. If the Legislature had thought fit they might have committed this jurisdiction to an inferior civil court, or the Legislature, being omnipotent, might in like manner have conferred this jurisdiction upon the courts of the Church, though an enactment conferring upon these courts power to adjudicate in a competition of statutory rights would have been so entire a novelty that it would have required very clear words in such a case to oust the ordinary tribunals.[187]

It followed that while the church courts could determine whether a valid appointment had been made, but whether the consequence of that decision was that devolution to Presbytery had occurred was for the civil court to decide. In the ordinary event the church courts might decide, but if two statutory rights collided – the one that of the congregation under s. 3 and the other that of the Presbytery under s. 7 – the ordinary courts could intervene, because they had not been excluded.

Within a fortnight the decision in *Stewart* was reinforced by *Cassie v The General Assembly of the Church of Scotland* (1878) 6 R. 221. There Lord Justice Clerk Moncreiff explicitly adopted the reasoning of the Lord President in *Stewart* although without directly referring to that case.[188] The other judges similarly approved the decision in *Stewart*, holding the civil court not to be excluded from taking jurisdiction in matters of a competition between interests emergent under the 1874 Act. However, in *Cassie* the Division refused a note of suspension where would-be members of a congregation had sought to be placed on the electoral roll during a vacancy. The making-up of the roll was for the church courts to decide, and the civil courts would not interfere, no relevant case having been stated. But the court was careful to preserve its role were church courts to abuse their powers. Thus: 'It is unnecessary, however, to hold, and I do not hold that there might not be such an abuse or excess of the powers of the Church courts as to warrant the interference of this court'.[189]

Following these decisions, a series of cases showed the civil courts not unwilling both to take jurisdiction and determine issues properly brought before them. In *McFarlane v Presbytery of Coupar* (1879) 16 SLR 480 Lord Young held that a right of appointment had

---

187 (1878) 6 R. 178 at 183.
188 (1878) 6 R. 221 at 237.
189 Per Lord Ormidale (1878) 6 R. 221 at 238.

not fallen to Presbytery *iure devoluto* because the running of the six-month period under the Act had been interrupted by an erroneous ruling by the person appointed by the Presbytery to moderate in the call. In *Dunbar* v *Presbytery of Abernethy* (1889) 26 SLR 517 Lord Wellwood held that the right of appointment had not devolved because the Presbytery had materially misled the congregation, resulting in the calendar period expiring without an appointment being made. These actions interrupted the period in which the congregation had opportunity to appoint a minister.

Not all cases went against Presbytery,[190] but where the Presbytery effectively precluded the timeous exercise of the congregational right of appointment, the civil courts intervened. Where Presbytery was not at fault, in a competition between the right of the congregation to appoint under s. 3 and the power of the Presbytery *iure devoluto* under s. 7, the Court upheld the devolution if the six-month period had elapsed. In *Craig* v *Anderson and the Presbytery of Deer* (1893) 20 R. 941 the First Division reduced a minute of the congregation purporting to appoint Anderson as minister of the parish of Old Deer. Anderson had been 'appointed' during the six months but had then declined appointment, so the Presbytery ruled this first appointment invalid. A second 'appointment' of Anderson by the congregation was made more than six months after the date of the vacancy. The court held that the initial 'appointment' had not interrupted the running of the six months within which the congregation could act, and therefore their acting after that period was incompetent. The Presbytery decision that the initial 'appointment' had been invalidated by Anderson's refusal was determinative. Under s. 3, that decision was final, and it was for the civil courts to decide what the effect of that decision was. The rules of the church debarred the civil court from holding that there had been a valid appointment followed by a resignation.

Fourth, the legislature intervened to liberalise the terms of the subscription of the Westminster Confession required of ministers and office-bearers. This showed that the established church remained bound to the terms of the statutes which were the ground of its privileges.

Subscription of the Confession was required of ministers under the Ministers Act 1693 c. 38. The actual terms of subscription were set by the church itself, which the next year required subscription by elders as well as ministers. In 1711 the church had made the terms of subscription for ministers much stricter than required by the 1693 Act.[191] With the changing theological opinions in the nineteenth century, particularly through German theologians such as the Tübingen School,[192] many aspects of the Confession came under fire, and the strict Calvinism of certain of its portions came to be disavowed by many. Accordingly the church was faced with a demand to revise the terms of the required subscription.

One solution proposed was a return to the formula of the 1693 Act, and this was effected in part by GA Act 17, 1889.[193] But this raised questions as to the propriety of the church's acting, and whether, if the church could so act, it could not go farther and enact a formula of subscription in even freer terms, and therefore more congenial to 'modern' theology. Opinion was given to the 1900 Assembly by A. Asher, QC, Dean of Faculty, John Rankine, QC and A.H.B. Constable that the church was still bound by the 1693 Act, and that the 1711

---

190 See Note by Lord Kyllachy. in *Craig* v *Anderson* (1893) 20 R. 941 at 944.
191 GA 1711, Act X. See the *Free Church* case (1904) AC 515 at 536n.
192 The Tübingen School saw a distinction between Jewish (Petrine) Christianity and Gentile (Pauline) Christianity, the two having come together in the second century.
193 The Church acquiesced in the change: Innes II, 136–7.

formula could not be revived because it was not sanctioned by that Act. Assuming that the 1693 statute was still authoritative, the Church could not proceed to a more liberal formula; though were the Opinion were wrong on the vitality of the 1693 Act, the contrary decision would be possible.[194] The 1900 Assembly resolved to explore the matter further, and in 1901 by a narrow majority restricted itself to receiving the Report of an enlarged 'Committee on the Powers of the Church with regard to the Confession', which stated that, statute *obstante*, the Church did not have power further to alter the terms of subscription of the Confession. Against this view a large body of opinion led by Dr Story and Sheriff R. Vary Campbell argued that by reason of its spiritual independence the Church did have power to define the relation of its office-bearers to the Confession without the intervention of the state. That power was stated in the Confession which itself had been made part of the law of the land.[195]

Opportunity to deal with the matter came with the parliamentary proceedings in consequence of the Free Church cases of 1904. Section 5 of the Churches (Scotland) Act 1905 enacted that the formula of subscription to the Confession of Faith for ministers should be such as was prescribed by the General Assembly following Barrier Act procedure.[196] The Assembly responded, GA Act III, 1910, enacting a formula of declaration of belief of the fundamental doctrines contained in the Westminster Confession, but without defining which doctrines were fundamental. In so doing the church approached the 'liberty of opinion in matters not of the substance of the faith', already adopted as an escape from the strict totality of the Confession by other Scottish churches.

*

The developments covered later in this chapter moved towards a greater freedom for the church, but always on the basis that any grant of greater freedom was through the intervention of the state. Patronage was abolished, but by the state, and the civil courts continued to have an important role in disputes under that legislation. New parishes were more easily established and their ministers were given full status, but only under statute. Even the doctrinal profession of ministers was a matter in which the state had the last say. Although power was granted to the Assembly, yet 'what Caesar gives, Caesar may take away'. The established Church was therefore gaining freedom, but freedom on a lead. Such powers as it had were given to it by the state, and were not inherent in it *ex natura*.

Amid such consistency of attitude in case law and in the statutory interventions just outlined, it is unsurprising that, especially in the last quarter of the nineteenth century, there was considerable agitation for the disestablishment of the Church of Scotland.[197] This reflected

---

194 The Opinion is printed in the Proceedings of Assembly 1900; Innes II, 138–9; and as an appendix to Sheriff R. Vary Campbell, 'Spiritual Independence Constitutionally Considered' (1900), 12 Jur. Rev. 194, who reviews the whole question, as does Innes. See also C.N. Johnston, 'Doctrinal Subscription in the Church of Scotland' (1905), 17 Jur. Rev. 201.
195 Innes II, 187–202 prints the minute of the debate. See also *supra* n. 194.
196 See Johnston *supra* n. 194. The 1905 Act s. 6 and Sched. 2 repealed two important provisions: 1. that part of the 1693 Act requiring that a minister had to subscribe the Confession declaring 'the same to be the Confession of his faith, and that he owns the doctrine therein contained to be the true Doctrine, which he will constantly adhere to', and 2. that part of the Protestant Religion and Presbyterian Church Act 1706 c.6 requiring ministers to acknowledge and profess the Confession as the confession of their faith. See also the Second Reading Debates, 1905 148 HC Deb. Cols 1003–70; 1905 105 HL Deb. Cols 840–82.
197 See Sjölinder, 84–92; Fleming II, 26–34; Burleigh, 335–6, 364–6, 398–9; and next note. Disestablishment Bills were introduced annually from 1883 but did not progress.

similar moves in respect of the Irish and Welsh churches,[198] but was a well-grounded native Scottish movement as well. Many Free Church figures, as well as the United Presbyterians, held that the only way for a true reconstruction of the Church of Christ in Scotland was for there to be a strict separation of church and state. Again moves to unite denominations including the Kirk were for the time frustrated. Church union was in the wind, but if the Kirk continued on the terms on which it was established, a general union within the Presbyterian tradition was not possible.[199] The established Church, still by far the largest church, could not accommodate itself to the ideas of the lesser bodies, and they were unwilling to unite in its form. That was understandable: after all the very ground of existence of many of the smaller denominations was disagreement with the then ruling principles of the establishment. The crusade against establishment was fierce, and of grave importance, affecting the political life of the nation in addition to its church life, but in the end of the day the question faded from general attention. As will be seen in Chapters 4 and 5, a major step was the union of (most of) the Free and the United Presbyterian churches in 1901 to form the United Free Church, and discussion between that Church and the Church of Scotland was eventually to bring about Union in 1929. In order to achieve that result, however, the whole question of the relationship between the church and the state had to be resolved and restated.

---

198 P.M.H. Bell, *Disestablishment in Ireland and Wales* (London: SPCK, 1969). These churches were respectively disestablished by the Irish Church Act 1869, and the Welsh Church Act 1914. That they are both Episcopal in their polity may be irrelevant.

199 On moves towards church union in this period see next chapter; D.M. Murray, *Rebuilding the Kirk* (Edinburgh: Scot. Acad. Press, 2000), 18–26; Sjölinder, 58–104; Fleming II, 35–55, 81–94, 103–25; Bulloch III, 298–322.

4 The Church of Scotland today

The relationship between the established Church and the state is now regulated by the Church of Scotland Act 1921 and nine 'Articles Declaratory of the Constitution of the Church of Scotland in Matters Spiritual' declared to be lawful by and scheduled to it.[1] The Articles Declaratory were formulated through consultations and negotiations between the Kirk and the United Free Church to allow the union of the two largest of the presbyterian denominations in Scotland. Following mutual acceptance of a Basis and Plan of Union and with the Articles as fundamental to it, the present Church of Scotland came into being in May 1929.[2] Given history, getting there was understandably lengthy, not to say tortuous. To narrate and discuss the negotiations would take a separate treatise.[3] It will suffice to summarise what is of interest for the present study.

The later nineteenth century saw proposals for the re-uniting of the several divisions of Presbyterianism in Scotland.[4] By the early 1900s there was much to recommend the development. There was little basic doctrinal divergence between the main denominations. Most subscribed the Westminster Confession of Faith, though each with variable reservations reflecting the then current theologies. In government the churches were alike. A conviction of the duty to seek corporate unity with each other had grown. Finally, there was also an element of sheer practicality. It was inefficient that they should compete when there was the whole of Scotland to be served.

A rapprochement between the United Presbyterian Church and the Free Church of Scotland was the first major attempt to heal the divisions of Presbyterianism. The former was a union of a number of small groupings,[5] and the latter the result of the Disruption of 1843.

---

1 Church of Scotland Act 1921; Cox 470.
2 Basis and Plan of Union, 1929, Cox, 392.
3 Sjölinder; D.M. Murray, *Rebuilding the Kirk: Presbyterian Reunion in Scotland 1909–1929* (Edinburgh: Scot. Acad. Press, 2000); and his *Freedom to Reform: the 'Articles Declaratory' of the Church of Scotland 1921* (Edinburgh: T&T Clark, 1993); G.M. Reith, *Reminiscences of the United Free Church General Assembly (1900–1929)* (Edinburgh: Moray Press, 1933); M.A. Maclean, *The Crown Rights of the Redeemer* (Edinburgh: St Andrew Press, 2009) 106–35.
4 Fleming I, 72–6, 123–39, 174–90; II, 35–56, 81–94, 103–25; Murray, *Rebuilding*, supra n. 3, 18–26.
5 See Chapter 6 at n. 8, 'Presbyterian churches'.

However these moves were halted in 1869 by opposition led by James Begg of the Free Church.[6] Proceeding further would have led to a schism of the Free Church without offsetting benefit. Union was, however, merely deferred, coming to fruition in 1900 in the United Free Church.[7]

The impetus to union persisted. Many felt that more might be accomplished through the re-invigoration of the ancient Kirk, but it was floundering. Its arrangements mimicked the 'unwritten constitution' of the civil state, and the patchwork of its own legislation coupled with various cases and civil statutes of the later 1800s was proving unhelpful. A single simple constitutional document might provide a solution. During the 'disestablishment controversy' in the later nineteenth century a House of Commons Bill to 'Declare the Constitution of the Church of Scotland' was introduced by R.B. Finlay in 1886.[8] This would have affirmed the spiritual independence of the Church, but it satisfied neither the Kirk nor those attacking it. A wider-ranging document, backed by and including other denominations might have had more success. In 1912, on the initiative of the Procurator of the Church of Scotland, C.N. Johnston (later Lord Sands), the Kirk approached the United Free Church to seek a way forward through a re-constituted national Church. Negotiations produced a Memorandum suggesting that the Church of Scotland should seek a reformulation of its constitution to meet all the difficulties standing in the way of union with that reformulation to be approved by the state.[9] The spiritual independence of the Church, continuity of its traditions and identity, and so on, were all to be safeguarded. On this basis and subsequent discussions it was found possible to proceed to plan for union. Three sets of draft Articles for the new Church's constitution were considered over the next five years.[10] Eventually a Bill was presented to Parliament scheduling the Articles that had been agreed by the two churches, and in due course these were declared lawful by the 1921 Act.[11] The thorny question of the endowments of the Church was dealt with separately, the Church of Scotland (Property and Endowments) Act, 1925, reconstructing the bulk of the Kirk's financial and property arrangements.[12]

The processes had been difficult. The new settlement had to secure three points; legislative freedom as to doctrine, worship, government and discipline, independence from state control and the avoidance of a damaging legal dispute.

Legislative freedom was the contribution of the United Free Church. A degree of freedom to amend its constitution had to be part of the new arrangements to allow such change as might be thought good in future years. The union of the Free and United Presbyterian churches had given rise to a major property case, the Free Church case.[13] Fear of a similar case overhung the negotiation of the projected union. The 1900 union had engendered much

---

6 T. Smith, *Memoirs of James Begg*, 2 vols (Edinburgh: Gemmell, 1885–88); J.W. Campbell, *Trembling for the Ark of God: James Begg and the Free Church of Scotland* (Edinburgh: Scottish Reformation Society, 2011).
7 See Chapter 5 at n. 123 ff.
8 Reference point, *infra* n. 93.
9 Memorandum, annexed to the 'Report of the Committee of the Church in Conference with the Representatives of the United Free Church of Scotland', *Reports to the General Assembly of the Church of Scotland*, 1912, 1205 at 1216. See Murray, *supra* n. 3, 290–294; Sjölinder, 214–33.
10 Sjölinder, 252–306; Murray *supra* n. 3, 63–142.
11 Sjölinder, 309–58. Second Reading, Commons, 1921 143 HC Deb. Cols 1397–469: Lords, 1921 45 HL Deb. Cols 1339–64.
12 Murray, *supra* n. 3, 115–42.
13 *Bannatyne and Others* v *Lord Overtoun and Others*: *MacAlister and Others* v *Young and Another* (1904) 7 F. (HL) 1, [1904] AC 515. For detail see Chapter 5 at n. 122.

bitterness. The new United Free Church had sought to take over all the property of the Free Church and to expel from their manses and charges Free Church ministers who declined to enter the new united church. This was resisted both as a matter of principle and of law. *Inter alia* the dissentients from union argued that the new United Free Church allowed members to affirm both or either Calvinist and Arminian theologies, while the Free Church held solely to Calvinism and that as an original fundamental principle. They won. In 1904 the House of Lords held that by their departure from the 'original principles' of the Free Church, those of the Free Church who had entered the United Free Church had forfeited right to the property and endowments of the Free Church.[14] The difficulties caused by this decision had been mitigated by the Churches (Scotland) Act 1905, and the appointment of a Commission to divide the property between the two factions.[15] However, in consequence of the reasoning of the House of Lords the United Free Church Act I 1906 'Anent the Spiritual Independence of the Church' had affirmed as basic principles the right to independent and exclusive jurisdiction in spiritual matters, and the right 'through her courts to alter, change, add to or modify her constitution and her laws, her subordinate standards, and formulas . . .'[16] This had grafted into the constitution of the United Free Church a degree of freedom that the House of Lords had determined not to be present in the Free Church constitution. Freedom to legislate and the ability to adjudicate in worship, doctrine, government and discipline had therefore to be part of the constitution of the new church, both to satisfy the United Free Church, and to ensure that the property of both churches would be carried into the union.

Another element to be safeguarded was independence from state control. Potentially this was contentious. The United Free Church was in part the successor of the Free Church, which although created in 1843 to avoid the alleged erastian establishment of the Church of Scotland, held a doctrine of establishment – the duty of the state to support the church – as had been made clear in the Free Church case. However, the United Free Church was also in part the successor of those 'Voluntaryist' churches which had come together in 1847 to form the United Presbyterian Church, the other partner in the 1900 union. The United Free Church therefore also contained elements of opposition to any form of establishment.[17] Clearly the independence of the new church from the state was to be sought. The establishment of the Church of Scotland of the early 1900s was unsatisfactory from a United Free Church viewpoint. On the other hand, as indicated at the end of the previous chapter, the Church of Scotland had survived a long campaign for its dis-establishment and dis-endowment and c/would not have entered a union that required the complete dissolution of its ties with the state.

The result was a compromise and the retention of an establishment of sorts. This involved a national recognition of religion, but without the odious appurtenances of the former system. In fact most of the prior faults of establishment (basically its privileges) were already being elided through the development of the law relating to non-established churches, and the assumption by the civil authorities of many social responsibilities that had previously

---

14 *General Assembly of the Free Church of Scotland* v *Lord Overtoun (Bannantyne* v *Overtoun)*: *MacAlister* v *Young* (1904) 1 F. (HL) l; [1904] AC 515. The negotiators of the 1910s wanted to avoid a similar re-run.
15 See Chapter 5 at n. 144.
16 See Murray *supra* n. 3, 288–9; the Appendix to the Basis and Plan of Union, 1929, Cox, 392. On the Basis and Plan see Murray, *supra* n. 3, 165–204.
17 For detail of the churches which had entered the United Presbyterian Church, see Chapter 5 at n. 8, 'Presbyterian churches'.

been those of the established Church.[18] Additionally, in the eventual compromise it proved possible formally to state that the position accorded to the national Church in no way derogated from the standing of other denominations – rather different from the view of the Reformers that there was 'na uther face' of the Kirk than their own.[19] That said, unfortunately the 1921 Act was not satisfactorily framed. By its s. 1 all previous statutes and laws as to the 'matters spiritual' of the Kirk are to be construed in conformity with the Articles Declaratory, and insofar as inconsistent with the Articles are 'repealed and declared to be of no effect'. Further, without further specification or definition of content, Declaratory Articles I and V affirmed 'fundamental doctrines' of the faith. Such language has all the appearance of the negotiated fudge of an awkward area of divergent views.[20] Proceeding by consensus can be dangerous.[21]

*

To repeat: the relationship between the Church of Scotland and the state is now regulated by the Church of Scotland Act 1921 and Articles Declaratory of the Constitution of the Church of Scotland in Matters Spiritual declared to be lawful by and scheduled to the Act. That way of putting things is important. From the point of view of the Kirk the Articles were recognised by the state as lawful: they were not legislated for it by the state. When in 1926, and prior to the bringing into force of the 1921 Act, the Kirk adopted the Articles Declaratory as its constitution in matters spiritual, it considered that it exercised inherent powers: it was not being given that constitution by an external authority.[22] It continues to assert that standpoint.[23] With the Articles as a foundation and an agreed Basis and Plan of Union,[24] the present Church of Scotland was formed through the union of the bulk of the United Free

---

18 In later Victorian times many social responsibilities, including poor relief and education, were assumed by the state.
19 Section 2 of the 1921 Act, headed 'Other Churches not to be prejudiced', provides that: 'Nothing contained in this Act or in any other Act affecting the Church of Scotland shall prejudice the recognition of any other Church in Scotland as a Christian Church protected by law in the exercise of its spiritual functions'.
20 It was the view of Prof. T.B. Smith, Q.C., that some passages of the Act and the Declaratory Articles were 'drafted with more ambiguity than candour to create in churchmen the sense that the legislature and judiciary could not pronounce, and should not have pronounced, on matters affecting the Church', 'Legal Opinion of Counsel for the Presbytery of Lothian', Edinburgh, 25 January 1983. Cf. the observation of Megarry J. in *Barker* v *O'Gorman* [1971] Ch. 215 at 220, that 'in discussing doctrinal matters of some complexity I necessarily do so with a relative brevity; and if in so doing I falter, or express myself with less than accuracy, or with a want of felicity, it must be remembered that in considering ecclesiastical doctrines a lawyer untrained in theology may find himself in seas as heavy as those likely to be encountered, if I may say so, by theologians who embark upon a discussion of the arcana of the law'. Cf. D.M. Murray, *Freedom to Reform* (Edinburgh: T&T Clark, 1993).
21 Cf. from a different area, F. Lyall, 'The Role of Consensus in the ITU', in M. Hoffman ed., *Dispute Settlement in the Area of Space Communication* (Baden-Baden: Nomos, 2015) 33–42.
22 The 1921 Act was brought into force on 28 June 1926 (SR & O 1926, No. 841) following the approval of the Declaratory Articles by the General Assembly of the Church of Scotland following Barrier Act procedure.
23 *In gremio* of GA Act V, 2010, a 'Declaratory Act anent the Third Article Declaratory of the Constitution of the Church of Scotland in Matters Spiritual', s. 2 asserts that, while the Kirk's commitment to a national mission had been recognised by the state in the 1921 Act, the 'true origin and entire basis' of that commitment lay 'not in civil law but in the Church's own calling by Jesus Christ, its King and Head'. It may be indicative that the Assembly felt the need to make this assertion.
24 Basis and Plan of Union, Cox 386–433. The Uniting Act of 1929 is at 386–90.

Church and the Church of Scotland in May 1929.[25] To avoid strife the few United Free congregations unwilling to enter the union were omitted from the union, and continued to hold their property.[26] A small United Free Church still exists.

The Declaratory Articles sought to balance and harmonise the different attitudes and traditions of the churches that were to unite on their basis. There had to be freedom for the Church to govern itself in its institutional framework, and at a deeper level in its doctrinal formulations. The nine Articles present the church as an entity, deriving its authority and standing from God and recognised as such by the state. It is not the creature of the state as depicted in many judgements in the Disruption cases. At the same time the historic identity of the Church of Scotland is preserved.

The main burden of Article I is the general and fundamental doctrines of the Faith professed by the Church. Lineally these are those carried down through the centuries from the primitive Church. Narrated almost in creedal form, orthodox Trinitarian doctrine is provided for. Article I also identifies the reformed Protestant nature of the Church of Scotland for it refers to adherence to the Scottish reformation. The terms of the Article are incompatible with an interpretation based upon un-reformed doctrine, or with non-trinitarian dogma. Doubt was cast upon whether this represented a restriction upon the freedom of the church to formulate doctrine, a power not present in the 1906 United Free Church Act I anent Spiritual Independence, but Opinion of Counsel was to the contrary.[27] The ordinary principles of the law of trusts required that the property of the church be held on an ascertainable trust purpose, and the Trinitarian and Protestant purposes were already present in the United Free Church constitution. Of the Articles Declaratory only Article I is declared to be unalterable by the Church and adherence to that Article, as interpreted by the Church, 'is essential to its continuity and corporate life'.[28] The ground of being of the Church of Scotland is therefore to be found in the First of the Declaratory Articles.

It is possible here to deal summarily with some of the other Articles before turning to those that concern the relation of the two powers. Article II places the Westminster Confession of Faith in position as a subordinate standard. It goes on to affirm the presbyterian nature of the government of the church, though reserving the right of the church to alter its system of government, principles of worship, orders and discipline by Acts of Assembly or by consuetude (custom).[29] In that Article II is not fundamental in the way that the First Article is, it is clear that Presbyterianism is not essential to the identity of the church, thus reflecting the church prior to the settlement of its polity in 1592. Nonetheless Article III

---

25 The United Free Church had gone through an equivalent procedure. The union of the two churches was accomplished in 1929. A minority of the United Free Church remained outwith the union.
26 Murray, *supra* n. 3, 205–45.
27 The Memorial and Opinion of Counsel: Appendix to the 'Report of the Committee for Conference with the Church of Scotland on Union', *United Free Church Reports*, No. XXVII, 1928, at 13–31. See also Sjölinder, 365–6.
28 Article VIII. On the arguments and debate as to the relations between Article I and Article VIII see Sjölinder, 252–308.
29 Consuetude is the opposite of desuetude. It is not a word common in the law reports, Westlaw identifying 11 instances of its use in Scots cases, and Lexis only 4. None define it. The Latin tag, *consuetudo pro lege servatur*, means that established custom may serve when there is no legislation. Instances of its use allow emergent custom to trump common law. Here it indicates the constitution of a practice different from a former practice through being engaged in without opposition for a considerable period. In effect it is established by a consensus of active practice. This is to be deduced from the discussion of its opposite in *Brown* v *Magistrates of Edinburgh*, 1931 SLT 456 – disuse is not the same as desuetude.

affirms the historical continuity of the Kirk with that reformed in 1560, whose liberty was ratified in 1592 and for whose security provision was made in the 1707 Treaty of Union and related legislation. Despite this affirmation of identity, however, Article VII recognises the duty of the Kirk to 'seek and promote union with other churches' . . . 'in which it finds the Word [of God] purely preached, [and] the sacraments administered according to Christ's ordinance and discipline rightly exercised'. The Article therefore claims the right so to unite 'without loss of its identity on terms which [it] finds to be consistent with' the Articles. Article IX once more ratifies and confirms the constitution of the Church.

Articles IV, V, VI and VIII contain the provisions of greatest importance in settling the alterations to the constitution of the church and its relation to the civil power. Articles IV, V and VIII give doctrinal freedom, and Articles IV and VI independence.

As noted above, one objective of the United Free Church negotiators was to see that the constitution for the new church would reflect their own stand on spiritual independence as enunciated in 1906. The Kirk on the other hand was bound by legislation to the Westminster Confession of Faith, though as seen in the previous chapter, some steps had been taken under the power granted by s. 5 of the Churches (Scotland) Act 1905 to modify the terms of subscription of the Confession required of ministers. The cumulative effect of the Articles cited is to give that doctrinal freedom which was sought by the United Free Church negotiators. Article IV gives '. . . the right and power subject to no civil authority to legislate. and to adjudicate finally, in all matters of doctrine, worship . . .' Article V states that,

> The Church has the inherent right, free from interference by civil authority, but under the safeguards for deliberate action provided by the Church itself, to frame or adopt its subordinate standards, to declare the sense in which it understands its Confession of Faith, to modify the forms of expression therein, or to formulate other doctrinal statements, and to define the relation thereto of its office-bearers and members, but always in agreement with the Word of God and the fundamental doctrines of the Christian Faith contained in the said Confession, of which agreement the Church shall be sole judge . . .[30]

Article VIII allows the interpretation or modification of the Articles, with the exception of Article I, subject to modified Barrier Act procedures. In this way the freedom of the Church from interference by the state in doctrinal matters was laid down.

In the same way the right of the Church to deal with its own organisation and structure independent of the state was set out. Just after the portion quoted from Article IV is the right to legislate and adjudicate:

> . . . in all matters of . . . government, and discipline in the Church, including the right to determine all questions concerning membership and office in the Church, the constitution and membership of its courts, and the mode of election of its office-bearers, and to define the boundaries of the spheres of labour of its ministers and other office-bearers.

---

30 By GA Act V 1986 (a Declaratory Act) the Kirk now no longer affirms certain passages and phrases of the Westminster Confession that condemn the Pope, Roman Catholics, Roman Catholic practice or marriage to infidels or other idolators. It dissociates itself from them and does not require its office-bearers to accept them.

The inclusion of this statement in that Article, and its being followed by a statement that the recognition of the separate and independent government and jurisdiction of the church by the civil authority does not affect the character of that government and jurisdiction as derived from Christ alone, shows clearly that, according to the church's constitution, all such matters are spiritual matters. There is no place for the *rationes* of the Disruption cases.

Apart from the affirmation of the spiritual independence of the Church, Article VI also contains a statement of the relation between the Church and the civil authority:

> This Church acknowledges the divine appointment and authority of the civil magistrate within his own sphere, and maintains its historic testimony to the duty of the nation acting in its corporate capacity to render homage to God, to acknowledge the Lord Jesus Christ to be King over the nations, to obey His laws, to reverence His ordinances, to honour His Church, and to promote in all appropriate ways the Kingdom of God. The Church and the State owe mutual duties to each other, and acting within their respective spheres may signally promote each other's welfare. The Church and the State have the right to determine each for itself all questions concerning the extent and the continuance of their mutual relations in the discharge of these duties and the obligations arising therefrom.

The constitution of the Church of Scotland therefore asserts the coordinate jurisdiction of church and of state, each supreme within its own sphere, but leaving the actual determination of each sphere to each of them. That left room for conflict. The Disruption cases contained frequent affirmations by the civil court that the church was independent within its sphere, but that where civil right was affected the civil court had jurisdiction. That difficult boundary can still arise on a construction of the 1921 constitution, and questions may again emerge as to the correct forum.[31]

The body of the 1921 Act is simple but far-reaching. Section 1 states that the scheduled Articles Declaratory are lawful for the Church to hold, and that the constitution of the Church of Scotland in matters spiritual is as there set forth. In all questions of construction the Declaratory Articles are to prevail, and all statutes and laws in force at the passing of the Act are to be construed in subjection thereto, and in conformity therewith. In-so-far as statute and other laws were inconsistent with the Articles, they were repealed and declared to be of no effect. However, s. 3 preserves the place of the civil court:

> Subject to the recognition of the matters dealt with in the Declaratory Articles as matters spiritual, nothing in this Act contained shall affect or prejudice the jurisdiction of the civil courts in relation to any matter of a civil nature.

In so declaring the lawfulness of the Articles as providing for the constitution of the church in matters spiritual, the state seems to have accepted what had been negotiated between the churches concerned in the projected union and did not act of its own initiative. From the point of view of the new church, what has been granted is *recognition* of the church's constitution:

---

31 Cf. observations in recent cases involving other churches such as *Free Church of Scotland (Continuing)* v *General Assembly of the Free Church of Scotland* [2005] CSOH 46, 2005 SC 396; *Smith et al* v *Morrison et al.* 2009 CSOH 113; 2009 SLT 973; *Smith, Moderator of the General Assembly of the Free Church of Scotland, et al.* v *Morrison, et al.* [2011] CSIH 52, 2012 SC 79, 2011 SLT 1213. See Chapter 5 following n. 148.

76 The Church of Scotland today

the church has not been *given* a constitution. Any remnant ideas of the church being constituted by the state and deriving its powers and jurisdiction from the state may therefore have been laid to rest by the declaratory formulae of the Act, at least in the mind of the ecclesiastics.

The settlement of the property question may be dealt with shortly. The principal legislation is the Church of Scotland (Property and Endowment) Act 1925 dealing with the tenure of most of the property of the church and matters of teinds and stipend.[32] Former burdens on heritable property exigible for the upkeep of the church were to be redeemed at a standard monetary valuation.[33] All endowments were to pass into the ownership of the united church. The provision and upkeep of churches were to be taken over by the new church itself, and were no longer to be the responsibility of heritors.[34] In addition the administration of the Kirk's financial affairs was to become a matter for the church alone, property being dealt with through the Church of Scotland General Trustees, and with the civil courts excluded from these matters.[35] The rendering of matters of property and endowments as domestic for the church makes them part of general internal church law, and hence largely outside the scope of the present enquiry. Suffice it to say that this move made the independence of the church more complete.[36]

*

32 A.H.M. Gibson, *Stipend in the Church of Scotland* (Edinburgh: Blackwood, 1961); Murray, *supra* n. 3, 115–42. The Act has been amended by Church of Scotland (Property and Endowment) Acts of 1933 and 1957.
33 Standardisation resulted in a loss to the Church of around one-sixth of its income from these sources. Sections 2, 4 and 5 of the Land Tenure Reform (Scotland) Act 1974 prohibited the creation of new teinds and similar feudal burdens, and provided machinery for the redemption of any remaining at the option of the person liable, or on the first transfer for value of the burdened land. All feudal burdens were abolished by the Abolition of Feudal Tenure etc. (Scotland) Act 2000, asp 5.
34 The procedures for phasing out the responsibility of heritors laid down in ss. 26–33 of the Church of Scotland (Property and Endowment.) Act 1925, ended a system of support for the church which had given rise to many court cases. A search of Westlaw brings up over 1,000 reported cases, many involving the maintenance and repairs of church buildings. The general view was that it was anomalous that heritors should be liable for the upkeep of a church and parish particularly if they were not members there.

An unreported case contributed to the general demand for abolition of heritors' liability. In the 1890s John White, then minister of Shettleston Church, Glasgow, later a leading figure in the union negotiations, secured a court order for a new church to be built largely at the expense of heritors, they denying liability and having refused an offer to limit their contribution to only one-third. Many strands, including disestablishment, were drawn into the general argument and agitation surrounding the case, but the law was simple. See C.A. Muir, *John White* (London: Hodder and Stoughton, 1958); A. Gammie, *Dr John White; a Biography* (London: Clarke, 1929).

As noted above, the duty of heritors disappeared in the arrangements for the 1929 Union. Contrast for England the persistence of the duties of lay rectors until the end of 2013: *Aston Cantlow with Wilmcote with Billesley Parochial Church Council* v *Wallbank and another* [2003] UKHL 37, [2004] 1 AC 546. The English liability was removed by the expiry of para 16 of both Scheds 1 and 3 of the Land Registration Act 2002 in October 2013: Art. 2.2 of the Land Registration Act 2002 (Transitional Provisions) (No. 2) Order, 2003 SI 2431.
35 *Church of Scotland General Trustees, Petitioners*, 1931 SC 704; 1931 SLT 526. The General Trustees are presently constituted under the Church of Scotland (General Trustees) Order Confirmation Act 1921, c. cxxv, as amended, the Church of Scotland Trust Order Confirmation Act 1932, c. xxi, as amended, and other Acts relating to particular Trust funds.
36 As part of the Basis and Plan of Union, the terms on which property was held was preserved in the union. Thereafter the new Church adopted a Model Constitution which congregations were invited to adopt. Where individual trusts held former United Free Church property subject to control by a central body, these could be transferred to the General Trustees. In 1995 by private legislation procedure the Church of Scotland (Property and Endowments) Amendment Order Confirmation Act 1995 c. xi enacted that property held on such terms be used as the General Assembly and other central bodies of the church might determine. Former United Free Church property held by local trustees and not subject to central control was exempted from this provision (1995 c. xi, s. 3(1)). The option remains for the relevant congregations to adopt the new system. Not all have.

The 1921 settlement in the courts

Down to 2014 the ambit and application of the 1921 Act and the Declaratory Articles have been considered in only three reported cases, *Ballantyne* v *Presbytery of Wigtown*, 1936 SC 625, *Logan* v *Presbytery of Dumbarton*, 1995 SLT 1228, and *Percy* v *Church of Scotland Board of National Mission* [2005] UKHL 73, [2006] 2 AC 28, 2006 SC (HL) 1. A fourth case, *Buchan* v *Brodie*, came to the Court of Session in 1984, but that case was without an issued opinion and is known only through it being mentioned in the *Logan* case. The paucity of cases might be taken to indicate the success of the 1921 legislation. While I would concede the point in respect of the last 90 years (I write in 2014) the future may destabilise the situation. 'Human rights' may yet have its effects, although the Kirk has adapted many of its procedures in ways that may protect it from the civil courts.

Ballantyne v Presbytery of Wigtown, 1936 SC 625[37]

Ballantyne was the first case to construe the effect of the 1921 Act. The judges had to cope with the vagueness of the repeal of all statutes and laws inconsistent with the Declaratory Articles by s. 1 of the Act. Under the 1874 Church Patronage (Scotland) Act, congregations of the Church of Scotland played a role in the election of their minister. In *Ballantyne* the charge of Kirkmabeck in Wigtownshire had vaiked (a wonderful word – sc. 'fallen vacant') on the death of the incumbent minister on 8 November 1932. Procedures under the 1874 Act had been begun but were suspended by the local presbytery. Ballantyne and a majority of the Kirk Session objected and took their complaint to the courts, urging that the right of a congregation to elect a minister was a civil right under the 1874 Act unaffected by the 1921 Act and the Declaratory Articles. Both parties conceded that by s. 3 of the 1921 Act it was for the civil court to determine whether the matter lay within its competence.

A majority of the Inner House held that the matter was indeed outwith the competence of the civil authority. However, Lord Justice Clerk Aitchison drew attention to the comprehensive sweep of the first section of the 1921 Act. The purpose of the Act was 'to declare the right of the Church to self-government in all that concerned its own life and activity'. It followed that the:

> question must therefore be – Is the particular matter complained of, . . . a matter which on reasonable construction, falls within the Declaratory Articles. If so, the matter is at an end, and neither the statute nor the common law nor previous judicial decision, whether upon statute or upon the common law can avail to bring the matter within the jurisdiction of the civil authority.[38]

This meant that any argument that the 1921 Act was merely declaratory and not innovative, fell. It could not be assumed that all matters that had been civil before the Act continued civil in character despite the Act, for s. 1 'is the only and the final test'. Of the conferral of the power of government in Declaratory Article IV, Lord Aitchison observed: 'No more comprehensive words could have been devised'.[39]

---

37 Reference point, *infra* nn. 54, 83 and 119.
38 *Ballantyne* v *Presbytery of Wigtown*, 1936 SC 625 at 654.
39 1936 SC 625 at 655.

In a 20-page dissent, Lord Mackay challenged these arguments. In his view the 1921 Act did not exclude the jurisdiction of the civil court from the particular area under dispute. In times past the court had often taken precisely such jurisdiction. To hold it now excluded by an extended interpretation of an Act which was expressed to be declaratory was erroneous. Declaratory legislation was enacted simply to avoid doubts by declaring what the law was, not to change the law:

> Beyond that reasonable interpretation must not go. If it had been intended by Parliament to make the Church independent (as some zealots had always claimed. but unsuccessfully) of all State control, other terms and other means must have been found. If it was intended to carve out a well-defined piece of what (with so much benefit) had been found to be civil jurisdiction and to give it over. it would have been easy to do so. Nothing of that kind is done.[40]

The Act repealed prior statutes on the basis of their inconsistency with the Article (s.1), but for Lord Mackay a very restricted interpretation of 'inconsistency', amounting to a presumption against, ought to be applied.[41]

Lord Pitman, the judge at first instance, had dismissed the action on grounds of relevancy of averment.[42] He had not therefore dealt expressly with the issues raised in the appeal. He had, however, observed that the 1921 Act was unfortunately formulated since it left for determination by the civil courts precisely which prior law had been replaced by the Declaratory Articles:

> It is now said by the defenders that the right to elect a minister is a spiritual matter with which the Law Courts have nothing to do, and not a civil right at all. It is difficult to understand why, in view of the clear words of the [Abolition of Patronage] Act of 1874, the pundits responsible for the drafting of the 1921 Act did not have inserted into it a clause specifically repealing the 1874 Act, if, as counsel informed me, that was one of the moat important things they had in mind when drawing up the Act . . .[43]

Towards the end of his dissent Lord Mackay indicated his belief that the Lord Ordinary would have held for the pursuers had he not felt compelled to dismiss the action on grounds of relevancy.[44] It would therefore have been useful if this case had gone further than the Second Division on such an important matter. It is a pity that the decision should stand simply on the basis of the opinion of two judges, with one lengthy dissent and an open question as to the potential view of the Lord Ordinary on a crucial point.

But Lord Mackay was in the minority and the Second Division held that all the matters enumerated in the Declaratory Articles had been declared by statute to be spiritual matters under the jurisdiction of the Church, to the exclusion of the jurisdiction of the civil court.

---

40 1936 SC 625 at 678.
41 1936 SC 625 at 679. Lord Mackay's opinion in the *Church of Scotland General Trustees, Petitioners* 1931 SC 704 at 711–12 makes the same point about repeal, though there, based on the facts of the case, he came to a different conclusion.
42 Sc. even if you prove what you allege, as a matter of law you would not get the result you seek.
43 1936 SC 625 at 642. Lord Mackay at 678–9 makes the same point. However, cf. his view in 1931, *supra* n. 41.
44 1936 SC 625 at 689.

Accordingly the *Ballantyne* action failed. The election of a minister was a spiritual matter and therefore a matter for the Kirk alone.

Buchan v Brodie, 1984 (unreported)[45]

The sweeping phrases of Lord Aitchison in *Ballantyne* seemed to have settled matters. It was almost 50 years before the 1921 Act again turned up in the civil courts. However, in the meantime legal attention had turned to what is now known as 'judicial review', a court procedure in which actions are re-examined to check that a body has acted within its competence and complied with appropriate procedures when there is no further formal right of appeal. It has to be said that 'judicial review' was not new in Scotland. Without using the term, that was what the courts had been doing in the Disruption and other church cases as well as disputes involving the administration of Poor Law and decisions of school boards, highway authorities and others.[46]

In *Buchan* a minister appealed to the Judicial Commission of the General Assembly following a disciplinary procedure. However, when the Commission met it was inquorate. On the advice of its legal adviser, the Procurator, the General Assembly held the Commission proceedings null and void and sent the case back to the Commission to be re-heard. Pleading natural justice Buchan asked the Court of Session for interim interdict against the Commission resuming proceedings.[47] Members of the Commission participant in the earlier hearing would have already made up their minds.[48] In answers Brodie, for the Kirk,[49] citing Declaratory Article IV and the 1921 Act, argued that the civil court had no jurisdiction. Interdict was refused, but without a reported opinion. However, one may deduce that the plea of 'no jurisdiction' was effective.

Logan v Presbytery of Dumbarton, 1995 SLT 1228[50]

A decade later in 1995 a reported decision fully turned on the 1921 settlement. By Kirk rules, a minister holding a charge may engage in business only with the permission of the local Presbytery. Logan, minister of Abbotsford, Clydebank, who had been conducting a business, applied to his presbytery for retrospective permission. This was refused but Logan continued to run his business. He was suspended and an interim minister was appointed to the charge. Logan asked the civil courts judicially to review these decisions. As it happened

---

45 *Buchan* v *Brodie*, is referred to in the *Logan* report, *infra* n. 50.
46 Cf. A.O. Deas, *Digest of Decisions relating to Poor Law and the Local Government in Scotland* (Glasgow: Adshead, 1897). See also the discussion of history in *West* (*infra*, n. 51). Judicial review was reintroduced to public attention, and its major principles highlighted, by S.A. de Smith, *Judicial Review of Administrative Action* (1st ed., London: Stevens, 1959). For Scotland an important case in its revival was Brown v Hamilton District Council, 1983 SC (HL) 1. See also J. St Clair and N.F. Davidson, *Judicial Review in Scotland* (Edinburgh: Greens, 1986); T.J. Mullen, K. Pick and A. Prosser, *Judicial Review in Scotland* (Chichester: Wiley, 1996); J.J. Clyde and D.J. Edwards, *Judicial Review* (Edinburgh: Greens, 2000).
47 An interim interdict prevents matters proceeding until the case is fully heard, and permanent interdict is issued or refused.
48 It may be inferred that the Commission had not been reconstituted with a different membership, but whether this was the case is unknown.
49 Brodie was immediate past Moderator of the General Assembly. In the year after presiding over the Assembly a moderator (after a fashion) represents the Church.
50 Reference point, *supra* n. 45, and *infra*, n. 72. *Logan* was an Outer House (single judge) decision.

the court procedures in judicial review had recently been reformulated,[51] and the powers of the court authoritatively set out in *West* v *Secretary of State for Scotland*, 1992 SC 385. There Lord President Hope had set as the first principle determining application of the supervisory jurisdiction of the court as being that:

> [t]he Court of Session has power, in the exercise of its supervisory jurisdiction, to regulate the process by which decisions are taken by any person or body to whom a jurisdiction, power or authority has been delegated or entrusted by statute, agreement or any other instrument.[52]

However, that power was held insufficient to allow Logan's case to be heard in the civil courts. As in *Ballantyne*, parties had conceded the right of the civil court under s. 3 of the 1921 Act to determine whether it had jurisdiction. Lord Osborne affirmed that right, but then ruled that the court had no power in the matter. The terms of the 1921 Act were such that the courts of the Church could not be said to have 'a jurisdiction, power or authority . . . delegated or entrusted by status, agreement or any other instrument' to them.[53] Rather than the 1921 Act conferring power, Parliament had by it recognised a pre-existent power inherent in the Kirk. Lord Osborne did allow that there might be other instances when the civil court might intervene in ecclesiastical disputes, but parties had agreed that the matter under consideration was one of discipline – a spiritual matter in terms of the Declaratory Articles. The civil courts were excluded. Lord Osborne therefore recalled interim measures which he had granted, and, no doubt to counsel's chagrin, regretted that counsel had failed to draw to his attention either the 1921 Act or its discussion in *Ballantyne*[54] when the matter had first come before him.[55]

Percy v Church of Scotland Board of National Mission [2005] UKHL 73; 2006 SC (HL) 1; 2006 SLT 11; [2006] 2 AC 28; [2006] 2 WLR 353; [2006] IRLR 195; [2006] 2 WLR 353; [2006] 4 All ER 1354; [2006] ICR 134[56]

In 1994 the Presbytery of Angus decided to link six parishes. Given the responsibilities and the extent of the territory involved, it decided that an Associate Minister should be appointed to help the minister. The 'Aims and Duties' of the post as advertised involved the conduct of worship together with a nine-hour-per-week commitment to the chaplaincy at HM Prison Noranside which lay within the linked parishes. Related 'Terms and Conditions' indicated that the appointment was for a five-year period at minimum stipend, together with a manse and travelling expenses. The appointee, Helen Percy, was sent an extended set of 'Terms and Conditions of Appointment'.[57]

---

51 Then by Rule of Court 260B. See now (2015) the Rules of the Court of Session, Chapter 58 'Applications for Judicial Review'.
52 1992 SC 385 at 412–3. The authoritative status of this decision is marked by the uniting of the three judges in a single judgement.
53 *Logan* v *Presbytery of Dumbarton*, 1995 SLT 1228 at 1235.
54 *Supra* n. 37.
55 F. Lyall, 'Logan v Presbytery of Dumbarton', 1996 Jur. Rev. 71–3.
56 See also H. Percy, *Scandalous, Immoral and Improper: The Trial of Helen Percy* (Glendaruel, Argyll: Argyll Publishing, 2011).
57 Women have been eligible for the Church of Scotland ministry since 1968 (GA Act 25, 1968), having been eligible for the eldership since 1966 (GA Act 28, 1966).

In 1997 it was alleged that Ms Percy had had an affair with a married elder of the parish. She offered to resign, but then withdrew that offer. Presbytery began disciplinary procedures and suspended Ms Percy. Following consultations Ms Percy demitted her office and ministerial status and presbytery proceedings ended. However, in February 1998 she reconsidered and applied to an employment tribunal alleging unfair dismissal and discrimination under the Sex Discrimination Act 1975 on the grounds that she had not been treated in the same way as male ministers who were 'known to have had/are still having extra-marital sexual relationships'.[58] The counter-arguments were, first, that the Employment Tribunal did not have jurisdiction because discipline was reserved to the Church under the 1921 Act, and, second, that as a minister Ms Percy was not an employee and hence the anti-discrimination legislation was inapplicable.

Both the Employment Tribunal and the Employment Appeals Tribunal held that the civil authority had no jurisdiction, the matters complained of being disciplinary and therefore reserved to the Church by the 1921 Act.[59] On appeal the First Division of the Inner House of the Court of Session took a different line, holding that the arrangements for Ms Percy's appointment had not been intended to create obligations enforceable in civil law.[60] The absence of a contractual relationship meant the appeal must be refused, and it was unnecessary to consider either the ambit of the 1921 Act or European Law.[61] In the leading Opinion, Lord President Rodger considered that, before any effect of the 1921 Act had to be determined, the nature of the relationship between the appellant and her alleged employer had to be identified. Only were she 'employed' under a 'contract personally to execute any work or labour' would the 1975 Sex Discrimination Act arise and only at that point would any effect of the 1921 Act come into play. Lord Rodger carefully reviewed the arguments of counsel. Certainly it was clear that the appellant held an office within the Church. That did not of itself mean that there was no relevant contractual relationship with the Board of National Mission. However, he adopted the approach of Mummery L.J. in *Diocese of Southwark* v *Coker*, an English unfair dismissal case which had reviewed a number of cases involving clergy.[62] As summarised by Lord Rodger, Mummery had considered there to be a rebuttable presumption that: 'where [an] appointment was being made to a recognised form of ministry within the Church and where the duties of that ministry would be essentially spiritual, there would be no intention that the arrangements made with the minister would give rise to obligations enforceable in civil law'.[63] Lord Rodger noted that the documentation relating to Ms Percy's appointment was formal to a degree, but considered that not of major importance. Rather it was to be expected from a church whose procedures 'are replete with terminology which is familiar to practitioners of Scots law'.[64] Since there was no contract of employment the question of sex discrimination did not arise.[65] It was therefore unnecessary

---

58 Statement of Claim, *Percy* v *Church of Scotland Board of National Mission*, Employment Appeal Tribunal, Edinburgh, EAT/1415/98.
59 See n. 58.
60 *Percy* v *Board of National Mission of the Church of Scotland*, 2002 SLT 497.
61 Alan Rodger, then Lord President, later confessed that he was 'glad to decide the case on that basis and to be relieved of the need to deal with the Church's first argument, that the matter did not lie within the jurisdiction of the civil courts': A. Rodger, Lord Rodger of Earlsferry, *The Courts, the Church and the Constitution: Aspects of the Disruption of 1843* (Edinburgh: Edinburgh UP, 2008) 92.
62 [1998] ICR 140.
63 2002 SLT 497 at para 13.
64 2002 SLT 497 at para 14.
65 2002 SLT 497 at para 24.

to consider a further argument as to any applicability of the European Union's Equal Treatment Directive (Directive 76/207/EC) on the interpretation of the 1921 Act.[66] Lords Cameron and Caplan concurred and the appeal was refused. At this stage, therefore, it looked as though the Kirk remained protected by the 1921 Act. The General Assembly appointed a legally qualified special commission to hear Ms Percy's complaint as to sex discrimination, with power to award compensation if necessary.[67] However, she decided to take the case to the House of Lords.

The majority of the House of Lords disagreed with the unanimous decision of the Inner House. Only Lord Hoffman would have refused the appeal. In his view Ms Percy did hold an office, her relationship with the Kirk was therefore not one of employment and hence the laws as to discrimination in employment could not apply. However, all five judges considered that the Mummery presumption was overstated.

For the majority the Percy facts easily overbore the Mummery presumption.[68] The history of the appointment disclosed an employment relationship, a civil matter, which meant that the civil courts had jurisdiction by s. 3 of the 1921 Act. Lord Hope's Opinion was the most extensive, using Scots authorities to establish that a contractual relationship had been created. That relationship carried with it a duty not to discriminate on grounds of sex: a contract of employment could not disapply or negate the law on sex discrimination.[69] The contractual relationship involved rights and obligations of a civil character. *Ex natura* these were not spiritual matters.[70] Ms Percy's duties had been defined by the terms of her employment, not by her office as a minister.[71]

The majority was careful explicitly to note that the rights of the Church as to discipline were preserved.[72] However, although the complaint of unlawful discrimination arose out of disciplinary proceedings, Ms Percy's complaint was not as to the conduct of the discipline process.[73] That process was itself subject to the ordinary law. That an ecclesiastical disciplinary procedure was involved, therefore, did not carry with it the immunity from the civil courts that many had thought it did.[74] The Lords therefore remitted the case back to the Employment Tribunal, Lady Hale expressing the hope that the matter might be resolved by a settlement acceptable to both parties, as did in fact happen.[75]

The reasoning of the House of Lords in *Percy* is therefore simple, and undermines previous sweeping assertions of the extent of Kirk's jurisdiction as separate from that of the civil courts. The implications could run wide. Ms Percy did not press her argument on unfair dismissal but that would now appear to be open in a similar case.

---

66 2002 SLT 497 at paras 25–6.
67 GA Reports 2004: Report of the Special Commission.
68 [2005] UKHL 73; 2006 SC (HL) 1; [2006] 2 AC 28. Lord Nicholls at paras 23–6; Lord Hoffman at para 63; Lord Hope at para 121; Lady Hale at para 151.
69 Per Lord Hope at para 106.
70 Per Lord Nicholls at para 41.
71 Lord Scott at para 137. Lord Nicholls at para 34 stated that the associate minster post had no content other than that defined in the contract, not by an 'office'.
72 Per Lord Nicholls at para 41. *Logan* v *Presbytery of Dumbarton*, 1995 SLT 1228 (*supra* n. 50) was cited.
73 Per Lord Nicholls at para 40; Lord Scott at para 138.
74 Cf. Lady Hale at para 152.
75 Per Lady Hale at para 153. Ms Percy accepted £10,000 as compensation, and £10,000 as legal expenses repayable to the Scottish Legal Aid Board; sec. 2.2 of the Report of the Legal Questions Committee, GA Reports, 2007, 6.4/4. Cf. *Percy, supra* n. 56.

As yet Scots law has seen no direct successors to the *Percy* case in its interpretation of the settlement of the 1921 Act and its avoidance of the Kirk's Declaratory Articles. However, it has been referred to or construed in a number of cases to do with other Scottish churches as well as in English cases. Suffice it here to note that in one of those, *The President of the Methodist Conference* v *Preston (alt. Moore)* [2013] UKSC 29, [2013] 2 AC 163, the Supreme Court held that where the duties of a 'minister' were prescribed in the constitution of a church rather than in a prescribed or itemised list particular to the appointment, a contractual arrangement did not exist. Such questions were again traversed in *Sharpe* v *Worcester Diocesan Board of Finance Ltd* (2013–5). Sharpe, having resigned from his charge, claimed unfair dismissal arising from detrimental treatment following his having made protected disclosures. An Employment Tribunal held there was no contract of employment. On appeal a rehearing was ordered on the basis that, although an ordained Church of England minister and subject to its Canon Law, Sharpe might indeed be an employee within the terms of the relevant legislation. However, in a further appeal the Court of Appeal held that no contract of employment had been constituted by Sharpe's appointment. Employment law was therefore not involved.[76]

Ministry may well be an 'office', but many forms of the exercise of ministry (and that not only in the Church of Scotland) are surrounded by terms and conditions. In *Percy* the ultimate judges did not find the concept of 'office' as opposed to 'servant' particularly helpful and it may be that that distinction is becoming outmoded in modern conditions.[77] Lady Hale for example found it 'difficult to discern any difference in principle between the duties of the clergy appointed to minister to our spiritual needs, of doctors appointed to minister to our bodily needs, and of the judges appointed to administer the law . . . in respect to whether these appointments were intended to create legal relationships or not'.[78] The future may lie that way. Certainly 'who is a minister' or 'what is a minister', and what that label 'minister' may imply requires further exploration. At present it is muddled. There is also the problem of how the claim to be a 'minister' is to be substantiated. No longer can minister be considered a status, though it may label an occupation.[79] For the purposes of the law it should be so considered, whatever the belief groups that use the term might choose to infer by its use.

*

So much for the cases. Other questions remain as to the interpretation of the Articles Declaratory and how far the freedom of the Church of Scotland extends. It is noticeable that the Kirk has integrated itself with the normal processes of the governance of society and its expectations. One such was retirement from the ministry of the Kirk. Age and infirmity were long grounds on which a minister might retire. However, in 1972 a compulsory retirement age of 70 was introduced for ministers inducted to a charge after the Act that introduced it.[80]

---

76 *Sharpe* v *Worcester Diocesan Board of Finance Ltd and another* [2015] EWCA Civ 399. F. Cranmer, 'Case Note: Sharpe v Worcester Diocesan Board of Finance', 2014 16 Ecc LJ 256. The initial decision (UKEAT/0243/12/DM, [2014] ICR 9) is noted at 2012 14 Ecc LJ 459. See also the progress of *Davies* v *Presbyterian Church of Wales* [1986] 1 All ER 705.
77 Cf. the *Percy* case [2005] UKHL 73; 2006 SC (HL) 1; [2006] 2 AC 28, Lord Nicholls at paras 14–22; Lady Hale at paras 141–8.
78 Lady Hale at para 151.
79 The trade-union (labour union) Unite has a section for faith workers, including ministers of religion. There are many self-proclaimed ministers, bishops and up.
80 GA Act III, 1972.

This was an innovation.[81] Previously a minister was inducted to a charge *aut vitam aut culpam* (during life and good behaviour).[82] The requirement to retire would appear to interfere with civil right because it truncates the period in which a minister would have had right to a full stipend. However, Declaratory Article IV affirms the right of the Kirk to define the spheres of labour of its ministers. To take an analogy, the majority in *Ballantyne* would consider the dating of ministerial retirement as ecclesiastical, although it has civil overtones.[83] On Lord Mackay's argument it is civil, having been civil before the passing of the Act, and not being inconsistent with the provisions of the Articles, but only inconsistent with what the Church purported to enact under those Articles. However, 40 years on it is too late to make such an argument. *Mora*, taciturnity and delay have worked their work, extinguishing any such claims by a failure timeously to prosecute them.[84]

The Kirk has brought other aspects of its working into conformity with the general patterns of civil law, albeit sometimes under protest. Thus, while ministers may consider themselves to be employed by God, not by the Kirk as a denomination or by a particular congregation, in the 1970s it was agreed with the Inland Revenue (now Her Majesty's Revenue and Customs) that for tax purposes ministers should be treated as employed by the church rather than as self-employed (or employed by God).[85] Stipends (salaries) were thereafter centralised and paid from the central church offices. Again, all churches, not just the Kirk, are subject to the requirements of the Disability Discrimination Act 1995 as to access to premises and facilities for the disabled. In 1998 the government overrode Church of Scotland objections to its courts falling into the category of 'public authority' and therefore subject to the new Human Rights Act.[86] Thereafter the Kirk modified its disciplinary procedures to comply with the requirements of the Act as to trial by an independent tribunal.[87] The emergence of statutory protection against discrimination has been mirrored by Kirk legislation that conforms to the general law on such questions. In 2007 the Kirk codified its rules as to discrimination, banning discrimination on grounds of age, gender,

---

81 Under the Consolidating Act anent Ministry (GA Act II, 2000, as amended), a minister is now normally inducted to a charge to serve until age 65, with the possibility of an extension to age 70 governed by Regulations for Continuing Beyond the Age of 65 (Regulations II, 2004, as amended). See GA Act II, 2000, s. 33.1.
82 The triggers for the 1972 Act were several notorious instances where a minister served on long after his effectiveness had, by reason of senility, ceased. Although Presbytery had (and has) the power to remove a minister on grounds of incapacity, this was never done. It remains possible for a minister to retire earlier, usually on grounds of health. Since 1986 (GA Act II, 1986, currently provided for under the Consolidating Act anent Ministry, GA Act II, 2000, as amended) it has been possible for a minister to retire with a church pension at age 65. As to the status of ministers appointed *aut vitam aut culpam*, see the Opinion of Lord President Inglis in *Hastie* v *McMurtrie* (1889) 17 R. 715 at 730–732; Lord Mackay in *Ballantyne* v *Presbytery of Wigtown* 1936 SC 625 at 686–7. But cf. the Opinion of Lord President Clyde in *Church of Scotland General Trustees* v *Inland Revenue* 1932 SC 97 at 101.
83 *Ballantyne* is reviewed *supra* n. 37.
84 On '*mora*, taciturnity and delay' in a recent ecclesiastical case see the Opinion of Lord Grieve in *MacDonald* v *Free Presbyterian Church* [2010] CSOH 55; 2010 SCLR 475.
85 Previously assistant and student ministers were not 'employed' persons within the tax system, though lay missionaries were: *Scottish Insurance Commissioners* v *Paul and another*, 1914 SC 16.
86 House of Commons Committee Stage debate, 20 May 1998, 312 HC Deb. 977–1076, esp. at 1056–8 and 1063–9. Ss. 6–12 of the Act deal with public authorities.
87 GA Act III 2001 'Anent Discipline of Ministers, Licentiates, Graduate Candidates and Deacons'. Under the previous procedures the local Presbytery was the investigating authority, the prosecutor and the trial court, with an appeal lying first to the Judicial Commission and then to the Assembly. The Church of England has similarly amended its procedures.

marital status, colour, racial group, ethnic origin, national origin, nationality, sexual orientation or disability and combating harassment or victimisation.[88] The *Percy* case itself shows that on occasion employment and discrimination legislation may be applicable to the Kirk. It is to be hoped that the 2007 GA legislation may avoid future problems. Other steps have been taken to avoid potential problems. Thus in 2011 a circular was issued by the Church offices, giving guidance as to how the Kirk and its components should conduct business so as to comply with the Bribery Act 2010, should it be found applicable in a church activity or extended to bodies such as the Kirk.[89]

*

Questions remain. Fundamental is the identity of the Church. As an association in law the church has and must have an identity. Within that identity, how free is the Kirk to change doctrine, discipline or governance? At what point might an attempted change in these areas ground an argument that it has departed from its 'original principles', leading to property consequences?[90] Or, as we will come to, might the time have come to recognise that stresses and strains that in the shadow of I Cor. 6: 1–6 should lead to the resolution the emergent situation by negotiation?

First, a general point.[91]

The interpretation of the Articles has limits. The Declaratory Articles do not recognise the Kirk as having a total freedom to do as it will. That emerged during the debates on the 1921 Act. In the House of Commons, Solicitor General Murray was asked whether the phrase 'as interpreted by the Church', modifying the reference to Article I in Article VII, could be used to get round the provisions of the Articles. He replied:

> My legal opinion has been asked whether that [phrase] means that the Church as a Free Church has a power of interpretation. In law, if my opinion was asked, I think there must be a limit. It must at least be 'interpretation', and in the long run, of course, you have to have recourse to judicial interpretation. Provided that the Church loyally and *bona fide* interprets its standard as there set forth, it has the right to determine that standard. That right is only limited by the right of the judiciary, where there has been misinterpretation or absence of interpretation, to control.[92]

---

88 GA Act V, 2007, 'Protection against Discrimination Act', subsequently amended by Acts VIII and IV 2014. Note: this legislation post-dates the *Percy* case.
89 The Bribery Act 2010, s. 17(1)(b) abolishes the Scots common law as to bribery. Bribery is now a statutory offence only.
90 See in the next Chapter, 'III Property', and in particular discussion of the 1904 Free Church cases, *Bannatyne and Others* v *Lord Overtoun and Others*: *MacAlister and Others* v *Young and Another* (1904) 7 F. (HL) 1 [1904] AC 515, together with *The Free Church of Scotland (Continuing)* v *General Assembly of the Free Church of Scotland* [2005] CSOH 46, 2005 SC 396, and *Smith, Moderator of the General Assembly of the Free Church of Scotland, et al.* v *Morrison, et al.* [2009] CSOH 113; [2011] CSIH 52.

Questions might also be raised as to the Baird Trust, constituted by Deed of Trust dated 24 July 1873 and registered in the Books of Council and Session, which referred to the Westminster Confession and conservative principles as being those 'sound religious principles', on which purposes and institutions to be supported are to be judged. Perhaps prophylactically, the Kirk has secured private legislation on the Baird Trust and it has been re-constituted as a company limited by guarantee: Baird Trust Reorganisation Act 2005, asp 11.
91 Reference point, *infra* nn. 112 and 145.
92 1921 143 HC Deb. Col. 1461.

In the House of Lords, Viscount Finlay who, prior to elevation, had been active in attempts satisfactorily to solve the situation stated:

> The power of interpretation may be dangerous, and it has been asked: If the interpretation is in the eyes of lawyers erroneous, will not the Civil Courts interfere? I say without hesitation that on the terms of this Bill the Civil Courts could not interfere. The whole scope of the Bill is to oust any interference by the Civil Courts by way of suspension or anything of that kind.[93]

Lord Parmoor noted that the formula in the Bill did everything necessary to ensure the spiritual independence of the church.[94] However, Viscount Haldane, who in 1904 had been counsel for the United Free Church in the Free Church case, noted that while spiritual independence was assured, under some circumstances there might be property difficulties. He observed:

> When you get to property you cannot altogether oust the Civil Courts, and therefore to that extent I think the Civil Courts always must come in. Whether it be the United Free Church or the Established Church of Scotland, they must have the right to see whether identity has been preserved.
>
> If a number of burglars got into the Carlton Club . . . ousted the committee and declared it an institution for the promulgation of Bolshevism, I think it would not be in vain that appeals would be made to the Courts, notwithstanding that there would be a new committee or majority of members to mould the constitution, and I think that the Courts would say that identity had ceased and continuity was nonexistent, and at an end between the two bodies. So it may be if the Church of Scotland or even the United Free Church were to go over to the creed of Mahomet or even to adopt the jurisdiction of the Bishop of Rome, that the Civil Courts might intervene and say: 'Are the people who have this property people who are continuous with those who have hitherto enjoyed the title?' That might be the case. But it is abundantly clear that so far as doctrine is concerned, so far as the spiritual side of the constitution is concerned, so far as doing everything which can appertain to its continuity of existence and is consistent with it is concerned, the Church of Scotland will have under this constitution the most unlimited power of determining in its own Courts, and free from intrusion from the Civil Court, the doctrine which will be taught. No Civil Court can intrude. That principle has been conceded in its fullest form, and, speaking for myself, I have no doubt that the misgivings which have been expressed are misgivings which amount to nothing.[95]

Viscount Haldane may have overstated. Changing theological views has led to a wide spectrum of belief within the Church. While divergent theologies are nothing new, the question has become one of tolerance: when does divergence justify separation? The General Assembly of 2014 referred to the 'interests of the peace and unity' of the Kirk.[96] However, some

---

93 1921 45 HL Deb. Col. 1161. In 1886 Finlay had attempted to introduce a Bill declaratory of the constitution of the Church of Scotland: *supra* n. 8.
94 1921 45 HL Deb. Col. 1164.
95 1921 45 HL Deb. Cols 1151–2.
96 *Infra* at n. 158.

ministers (together with all, or some members of their congregations) have already taken steps to leave the Kirk, being of the view that tolerance has gone too far and that fundamentals of the faith are being departed from.

The term 'fundamentals of the faith' and a similar expression 'the substance of the faith' have become significant in theological discussions of the last century and a half. Briefly to summarise: the eighteenth-century Scottish Enlightenment encouraged questioning attitudes in many fields, including theology.[97] Deism, scepticism and even atheism became respectable. For a time most Christian churches stood by their traditional doctrinal beliefs. But change was to come. Charles Lyell's *Principles of Geology* (1830–33) came to new conclusions as to the age of the earth. Darwin's *Origin of Species* (1859) was popularised by T.H. Huxley, and the semi-hysterical reactions of some ecclesiastics to the 'new' ideas, contributed to debate. In 1844 Karl Marx observed that 'religion is the opiate of the people', and he and his friend Engels were to question the foundations of society. In 1882 Nietzsche proclaimed 'God is dead'. Biblical criticism, in particular the Germanic 'Higher Criticism' began to erode traditional theologies and ideas of 'revelation'. All this had tectonic effects on theological opinion.[98]

Ecclesiastical institutions had to accommodate the new views.[99] Churches came to appreciate that not all the new discoveries and theories had major or direct impact on basic doctrine. Thus in 1892 the Free Church Declaratory Act (No. 8 of Class II) allowed liberty of opinion on parts of the Westminster Confession which did not enter into the substance of the faith, the Free Church reserving to itself the right to determine what points fell within that category.[100] Later, liberty of opinion, with its corollary that some doctrines are indeed fundamental, formed part of the common ground between the Church of Scotland and the United Free Church during the negotiations of the 1929 Union.[101] Article I of the

---

97 J. Rendall, *The Origin of the Scottish Enlightenment* (London: Macmillan, 1978); R.B. Sher, *Church and University in the Scottish Enlightenment* (Edinburgh: Edinburgh UP, 1985); G.E. Davie, *A Passion for Ideas: Essays on the Scottish Enlightenment* (Edinburgh: Polygon, 1994); P.B. Wood, ed., *The Scottish Enlightenment* (Rochester: University of Rochester Press, 2000); A. Broadie, *The Scottish Enlightenment* (Edinburgh: Canongate, 2001); A. Herman, *The Scottish Enlightenment* (London: Fourth Estate, 2002).

98 J.L. MacLeod, *The Second Disruption* (East Linton: Tuckwell Press, 2000), Ch. 2, 'The Free Church Response to Biblical Criticism and Darwinian Science', 38–124.

An 1878 spectacle did much to diminish general respect for theologians and ecclesiastical politicians. William Robertson Smith, Professor of Hebrew at the Free Church College in Aberdeen, was arraigned for heresy for his articles in the Ninth Edition of the *Encyclopedia Britannica* (1875), which had adopted some of the techniques of the emerging 'Higher Criticism' and *inter alia* discussed the authorship of Isaiah. The indictment was dropped but Smith was warned not to express incautious opinions. A further article in the *Encyclopedia* queried the authorship of Deuteronomy so in 1881 the Assembly deposed him. He went to Cambridge as Reader in Arabic. Smith's views, now subject to criticism on substance but not as to concept, remained influential, particularly through a series of three lectures on 'The Religion of the Semites' and books on *The Old Testament in the Jewish Church* (Edinburgh: Black, 1881 and 1892), *The Prophets of Israel* (Edinburgh: Black, 1882, 1895) and *Kinship and Marriage in Arabia* (Edinburgh: Black, 1885, 1903). See J.S. Black and G.W. Chrystal, *The Life of William Robertson Smith* (London: Black, 1912); W. Johnstone, ed., *William Robertson Smith: Essays in Reassessment* (Sheffield: Sheffield Academic Press, 1995).

99 Not all do. Cf. the rise of 'creationism': R.L. Numbers, *The Creationists: The Evolution of Scientific Creationism* (London: Harvard UP, 2006).

100 'Act anent the Confession of Faith', GA Free Church, 1889–93, 478–9; Macleod *supra* n. 98, 211–2, cited in the Free Church case at [1904] AC 543. The Act was modified in 1894, [1904] AC 544. Cox 436–7. Tensions as to 'liberty' between the traditional (and occasionally rigid) theologies, and modern knowledge, remain. There can be a cognitive dissonance.

101 Curiously the concept of 'liberty of opinion' had been taken over from the Free Church into the United Free Church. The 2015 Free Church does not appear as tolerant as the phrase might imply.

Declaratory Articles refers to 'the fundamental doctrines of the Catholic faith', and Article V to 'the fundamental doctrines of the Christian Faith', with that Article going on to assert the right of the Church to interpret such matters 'with due regard to liberty of opinion in points which do not enter into the substance of the Faith'.[102] The problem for the Kirk (and for other denominations that have adopted 'liberty of opinion') remains that the category 'fundamental/substance' has not been defined.[103]

Increasing use came to be made of the 'liberty of opinion on such matters as do not enter into the substance of the Faith' until it began to seem that virtually any opinion might be classed as not being of the substance of the Faith, and so not proscribed by reference to the Confession.[104] The 2013 Report of the Theological Commission on Same-sex Relationships and the Ministry proves how traditional and liberal views within the Kirk now differ significantly.[105] The result may be a further task for the civil courts, where from the legal point of view the lucubrations of theologians and ecclesiastics as to the content of the 'substance of the faith' are irrelevant. On the basis of the Free Church cases of 1904 and others discussed in the next chapter,[106] should questions arise, the function of the civil court will be simply to determine as a matter of fact what are the original principles for which the property of Kirk is held, and whether these have been departed from.[107] If there has been a departure, the Law of Trusts means those continuing to hold to the 'original principles' would be entitled to the property of the Kirk, though perhaps, short of court action, a division of property might be agreed.[108]

What is the identity of the Church? What are its parameters? This has several aspects. The Reformed tradition is one and the position of the Westminster Confession of Faith another. Could the Church reconstitute itself on a creedal rather than a confessional basis to avoid those difficulties? The matter of practising homosexuals in the ministry has also

---

102 See para 12 'Preamble', in *Services of Ordination and Induction to the Ministry of Word and Sacrament*, published by the Ministry and Discipleship Council, Church of Scotland, Edinburgh (available from the Church's website); cf. *Preamble, Questions, and Formula to be used for Admission to Office in the Church*, Cox, 568.

103 A limited understanding of 'fundamental' may emerge, albeit framed in the negative, as some matters may come to be classified as 'non-fundamental', but this does not solve the problem. Cf. the removal by GA Act V, 1986, of the requirement to believe the Pope is Anti-Christ: *supra* n. 30, and the assertion in GA 2015 Act I that sexual matters are not 'of the substance of the faith', *infra* n. 159.

104 As then a member of the Presbytery of Aberdeen I took part in discussions with one minister whose views on the Resurrection were decidedly unusual.

105 GA Reports, 2013, 'Report of the Theological Commission on Same-sex Relationships and the Ministry', 20/1. Both the 'traditionalist' and 'revisionist' points of view are well-argued. But see the Smith Opinion (*supra* n. 20) that the theologs do not appreciate that a legal understanding of the terms involved may blow apart their vacuities.

106 *Bannatyne and Others v Lord Overtoun and Others*: *MacAlister and Others v Young and Another* (1904) 7 F. (HL) 1, [1904] AC 515; *The Free Church of Scotland (Continuing) v General Assembly of the Free Church of Scotland* [2005] CSOH 46, 2005 SC 396; *Smith, Moderator of the General Assembly of the Free Church of Scotland, et al. v Morrison, et al.* [2009] CSOH 113; [2011] CSIH 52.

107 Note 'as a matter of fact'. Cf. the cases *supra* n. 106. In 2014 in *Shergill and others v Khaira and others* [2014] UKSC 33, the Supreme Court held unanimously that where questions of property or other civil issues were involved, UK courts would objectively consider religious issues in order to decide the matter. Note also the unwillingness of court to enter into theology and belief in questions of human rights: *R (Williamson et al.) v Secretary of State for Education and Employment* [2005] UKHL [2005] 2 AC 246, a case on corporal punishment of children.

108 United Free Church congregations unwilling to enter the Union of 1929 were allowed to retain their property. See *supra* following n. 25. The UFC denomination still exists.

emerged as a stress point. Last, how might the settlement of 1921 be unpicked to permit the major strands of the underlying tensions to go their separate ways?

*

The Reformed tradition

The Reformed tradition is basic to the identity of the Church of Scotland as presently constituted. Under Declaratory Article VIII adherence to Declaratory Article I, as interpreted by the Church, is 'essential to its continuity and corporate life'. By Article I the Church 'adheres to the Scottish Reformation'. What does that mean?

In the 1970s debate might have resulted in the displacement of the Westminster Confession as 'the principal subordinate standard' of the Church (Art. II). A collection of papers was published to which I was asked to contribute.[109] I expressed the view that the combination of the Art. I reference to the Church's adherence to the Scottish Reformation and the Art. II reference to the Confession as 'containing the sum and substance of the reformed church' meant that the Confession could not be wholly displaced. Other subordinate standards might be added and declaratory Acts could interpret the Confession within limits.[110] However, the language of Art. II declaring the Confession to express the 'sum and substance' of that Reformation binds the Church to the Scottish Reformation. This view was not wholly well received, but legal opinion, though given with some regret, was that my view was correct.[111] In short, my view remains that the Church of Scotland is constitutionally required to remain within the tradition of the Scottish Reformation, and its expression in the Westminster Confession. It is free within its identity, but is not free of itself to change that identity.[112]

The Westminster Confession of faith

The Confession has been criticised as being too clear and rigid, and reflecting views conditioned by its time and not by modern thought. Such criticism, though overstated, has some force. However, the Confession has not recently been so applied in the Kirk, and some of its more pointed denunciations have been muted or detoxified.[113] On the contrary, my impression is that there is a greater rigour in the way in which the ephemeral fashions of some modern theologies are insisted upon and traditional formulations facilely dismissed.[114]

'Liberty of opinion' in matters not of the substance of the faith has eroded the authority of the Confession of Faith, albeit that by Declaratory Art. II it is the Church's principal

---

109 A. Heron, ed., *The Westminster Confession in the Church Today* (Edinburgh: St Andrew Press, 1982).
110 The sparser Scots Confession of 1560 would be one, and there is a raft of other confessions within the reformed tradition. However their inclusion could be unhelpful as they often differ in minor aspects.
111 F. Lyall, 'The Westminster Confession: the legal position', in Heron, ed., *supra* n. 109, 55–71. T.B. Smith, QC, 'Legal Opinion of Counsel for the Presbytery of Lothian', Edinburgh, 25 January 1983. Cf. F. Cranmer, 'Christian doctrine and judicial review: the Free Church case revisited', 2002 Ecc LJ 318 at 331.
112 See text *supra* following n. 91.
113 See GA Act V, 1986, *supra* n. 30.
114 Another accusation is that not all the 'proof texts' attached to the Confession support the propositions for which they are cited. Such criticism reveals ignorance. The Confession was agreed by the members of the Westminster Assembly as their understanding of the teaching of the Bible. Originally there were no proof texts. It was only when Parliament asked for them that texts were later adduced. But the Confession was not thus drafted, and the validity of its propositions was not based on scraps of verses.

subordinate standard. In the later 1960s one solution canvassed was that certain doctrines be specified as being of that substance. The Panel on Doctrine suggested that the Declaratory Articles be amended to remove the concept of a subordinate standard and that the Confession cease to hold its position. Instead a stricter formulation of doctrinal belief would be substituted in the Preamble for Ordination of ministers and elders, affirming particular doctrines as being 'of the substance of the Faith'.[115] Discussions were lengthy and for various reasons confused. Two legal opinions were made available as to the powers of the Church so to act.[116] In 1974 the Assembly did not proceed with the Panel's suggestion and by a narrow vote in 1978 resolved to depart from the matter until a new statement of belief had been adopted. That statement has not emerged.[117]

The then Procurator of the Church was asked about the Panel's initial proposals to displace the Confession.[118] Relying on Lord Justice-Clerk Aitchison's statements in *Ballantyne*,[119] his view was that Declaratory Art. IV permitted alteration to the status of the Confession. A different view is possible. First the precise power of the Church under the Articles is uncertain. Second, a standard of belief is necessary within the present identity of the Kirk. Third, the relation of the 1921 Act to previous statutes and the Treaty of Union legislation does not permit such a step.[120] Last, such a change would involve a transition from a confessional to a creedal church, a step that I consider separately.

First, the Procurator's Opinion did not distinguish between the Confession as a statement of belief and its use as the standard of belief to be subscribed by office-bearers of the Church – a test of orthodoxy.[121] The power under Declaratory Article VIII is to modify or add to subordinate standards. That is not the same as their elimination. To remove the Confession as a standard of belief while retaining it as a historic statement does not lie within such language. In departing from the concept of a subordinate standard the Church of Scotland would alter its identity and breach the terms under which it holds its property. Even were the Confession (and maybe others[122]) retained as historic affirmation of the Church's belief, there would have been a departure from the Reformed tradition discussed above. Relegation of the Confession to a 'historic' status would carry profound implications.

---

115 This might have gone some way to eliminating heresy, but raised the spectre of disciplinary hearings in which the content of words would be explored.

116 See *infra* at n. 118.

117 In retrospect, that the Panel was unable to formulate an acceptable statement was symptomatic of the theological divergences then already present within the Kirk. On the process and discussions see in Heron, *supra* n. 109, R. Pettigrew, 'The recent debate in the church of Scotland', 72–81.

118 Opinion of the Procurator, GA Reports 1970, 171 at 180–182. It, and one secured by the National Church Association taking a different view, are Appendices III and IV to F. Lyall, *Of Presbyters and Kings: Church and State in the Law of Scotland* (Aberdeen: Aberdeen UP, 1980). Both are on early versions of the Panel's proposals, but later amendments were not such as to render them irrelevant. Cf. *Barker v O'Gorman* [1970] 3 All ER 314, [1971] Ch. 215 (also known as *Re Methodist Church Union Act, 1929*) for observations on the then English Methodist position on doctrinal standards and doctrines.

119 *Supra* n. 37.

120 Cf. Opinion of Counsel obtained by the National Church Association, dated 3 October 1971. See *supra* n. 118.

121 At one point the Procurator used the phrase 'subordinate standards' as a term of art, and at another as a simple label capable of different meanings, for example a 'standard' that can flourish in battle or at a demonstration. The two are not the same.

122 Other Confessional documents including the Scots Confession of 1560 might have been listed for the purpose, but see supra n. 110. Any addition or substitute would have to reflect the 'sum and substance' of the Scottish Reformation, which the current text of Art. II states that the Confession already does.

Second, the constitution of the Kirk consists of the Articles Declaratory, the legislation of the General Assembly and the constitutional practice of the Kirk – in effect its common law.[123] The Articles, and in particular Article I, are fundamental, but not to the exclusion of all else. Article I is not 'the constitution'. Article I is not self-executing. Its terms are insufficiently clear to be interpreted without recourse to other instruments. It is silent as to structures and their relationships. It is also silent as to the content of the beliefs of the Kirk, but the identity of the Church includes those beliefs. The Westminster Confession, even with 'liberty of opinion', provides detail as to the content of what Article I describes as 'the fundamental doctrines of the Catholic faith', thus setting the parameters of orthodoxy within the denomination. In the absence of such an articulation the General Assembly would have to consider on a case-by-case basis whether a particular belief is consonant with the holding of office in the Kirk. Even were elements of the 'substance of the faith' included in ordination vows, there would be disputes as to shades of meaning. Heresy and quasi-heresy trials would be necessary – an unattractive prospect.[124]

Third, the National Church Association raised the position of previous legislation and the safeguards for the Kirk built into the Union of 1707.[125] How far does the language of s. 1 of the 1921 Act run? Previous legislation is to be construed subordinate to the provisions of the Articles, and all 'statutes and laws in so far as they are inconsistent with the Declaratory Articles are hereby repealed and declared to be of no effect'. But what does that mean? In *Ballantyne* Lord Mackay's point was that a wide implied repeal of prior legislation by s. 1 of the 1921 Act is not to be presumed, but must be proved.[126] Wherever possible the Act should be interpreted not to conflict with prior statute: that changes of such magnitude are not to be implied is a well-known principle of statutory interpretation.[127]

If a true interpretation of the 1921 Act is that it over-sets the pre-1707 legislation then it could be argued that the 1921 Act was *ultra vires* of Parliament. The Protestant Religion and Presbyterian Church Act 1706 c. 6 held that the polity of the Church of Scotland, including the Confession of Faith, was to be 'held and observed in all time coming as a fundamental and essential condition of any Treaty or Union' between the two Kingdoms and that Act was inserted in both the (Scottish) Union with England Act 1706 c. 7 and the (English) Union with Scotland Act 1706 of the English Parliament. That protection is still sensitive. During the debates on the reconstruction of the judiciary in the nineteenth century, the Treaty of Union was expressly cited as requiring that the Scottish Courts be omitted from the proposals.[128] This was accepted by the government of the day. In 1963 the Confession of Faith Ratification Act c. 1 and the Papal Jurisdiction Act c. 2, both of 1560, were among the 'spent, obsolete and unnecessary' enactments proposed to be swept away by a Statute Law Revision (Scotland) Bill. Both were dropped from the final form of the legislation. They were not 'spent, obsolete and unnecessary'. Another more equivocal point lies in the 1937 Regency Act, where, under s. 4(2) the Regent is barred from assenting to the repeal of the

---

123 See the reference to consuetude at the end of Declaratory Article II.
124 In 1976 Second Baptism was discussed in the Assembly, and found unacceptable. For the Kirk baptism, whether adult or of infants, is once and for all: Appeal, *Presbytery of Hamilton v Synod of Clydesdale*, 23 May 1976, GA 1976, Sess. 7, and relative Minute.
125 *Supra* n. 118.
126 *Supra* n. 41.
127 *Nairn v University of St. Andrews* 1909 SC (HL) 10; *Viscountess Rhondda's Claim* (1922) 2 AC 339.
128 Thus MacCormick, *infra* n. 130 (1972) P.L. 174 at 177 quotes 1872 210 HL Deb., Col. 1990; 1873 214 HL Deb., Col. 1738.

1706 Act of Security. That might be argued to indicate that the true Monarch may so assent but *per contra* it could be construed simply as clarificatory of the Monarch's powers. Finally account must be taken of the express concession by the Lord Advocate, and the assertion by the Court in *MacCormick*, to which we are just coming, that Parliament cannot lawfully alter or repeal the fundamental conditions of the Union.[129] If there is any force in the argument that parts of the Union arrangements are enforceable limitations upon the power of the Westminster Parliament, the question of the Westminster Confession could raise it.[130] And if the Westminster Parliament is so limited, its devolution of legislative competence to Holyrood by the Scotland Acts 1998 and 2012 could not free Holyrood from that limitation. You cannot devolve a power that you do not have.

That a Westminster Act of Parliament might be held *ultra vires* inheres in the opinions of the First Division in *MacCormick* v *Lord Advocate* 1953 SC 396.[131] The Pursuers were held to have no *locus standi* in a matter of public right, but that defect could be avoided in a case involving the 1921 Act and the Confession. The matter could be made justiciable by the secession from the Church of a congregation holding its own property through local trustees and not through the Church of Scotland General Trustees, and the congregation raising an action against the General Trustees for transfer of their buildings and property. Alternatively the General Trustees themselves could present a special case for clarifications of their powers and duties. In all these instances the argument would be analogous to that in *Bannantyne* v *Lord Overtoun* (1904) 7 F. (HL) 1; [1904] AC 515, and others, that in altering the status of the Westminster Confession the Church had broken the terms on which the property of the Kirk is held. Involving private right, this would avoid the flaw in *MacCormick*. Once the matter was so brought before the civil courts, a full discussion of the powers of the Westminster and Holyrood Parliaments could take place. Argument would start from the observation of Lord Cooper in *MacCormick*, 1953 SC 396 at 411, that: 'The principle of the unlimited sovereignty of Parliament is a distinctively English principle which has no counterpart in Scottish constitutional law'. Other *dicta* in Scottish cases could also be adduced to show that the terms of the Treaty of Union were intended to be fundamental, particularly in relation to the Kirk.[132]

On this point Scots and English law might usefully be held to diverge, and the doctrine of parliamentary sovereignty which we are told 'is almost entirely the work of Oxford men' could be returned whence it came.[133] Were such argument accepted, the judicial oath of

---

129 1953 SC 396 at 409 (Argument of Respondent); Opinion of Lord President Cooper at 411–2.
130 T.B. Smith, *The British Commonwealth: the development of its laws and constitutions, Vol. 1, The United Kingdom, Part 2, Scotland, Channel Islands* (London: Stevens, 1955) 641–50, 'Two Scots Cases' [1953] 69 LQR 512; 'The Union of 1707 as Fundamental Law' [1957] 2 PL 99: K.W.B. Middleton. 'Sovereignty in Theory and Practice' (1952) 64 Jur. Rev. 135; 'New Thoughts on the Union between England and Scotland' (1954) 66 Jur. Rev. 37; G. Marshall, 'Parliamentary Supremacy and the Language of Constitutional Limitation' (1955) 67 Jur. Rev. 62. Cf. his 'What is Parliament? The Changing Concept of Parliamentary Sovereignty' (1954) 2 Pol. Stud. 193; D.N. MacCormick, Review of S.A. De Smith, 'Constitutional Law', 1972 PL 174–9.
131 The pursuers sought to prevent the new monarch being designated Queen Elizabeth II since Scotland had not had a Queen Elizabeth I.
132 *Minister of Prestonkirk* v *Earl of Wemyss* (1808) Mor. App. 'Stipend' No. 6. The Opinions are reprinted in full from Session Papers in J. Connell, *The Law of Scotland regarding Tithes and the Stipends of Parochial Clergy*, 1815, vol. III, 310 ff. J.D.B. Mitchell, *Constitutional Law*, 2nd ed. (Edinburgh: Green, 1968) 71–2, n. 34, notes several cases from the Disruption. See also T.B. Smith, *supra* n. 130, [1957] 2 P.L. 99 at 115.
133 R.F.V. Heuston, 'Sovereignty', in A.G. Guest, ed., *Oxford Essays in Jurisprudence* (London: Oxford UP, 1961, at 198. There is no reason why Scotland should not adopt a position 'completely contrary to the whole tenor of English authorities on the point' (*ibid.*, 206). The doctrine is merely a theoretical extrapolation designed

office would require effect to be given to the terms of the fundamental law limiting the power of Parliament rather than any mere Act of Parliament.[134] But difficulty would arise as to the remedy to be sought. Lord Cooper did express doubt as to the authority of the Court of Session to entertain such an action.[135] The English courts refused to intervene when the Irish Church was disestablished.[136] On the other hand, the Scottish courts have always sought to give a remedy where there is a wrong. Again it is not unknown for a court to take to itself the right of judicial review of legislation. That is the basis of the United States Supreme Court's actings since *Marbury* v *Madison* (1803) 1 Cranch 137, though the US Constitution is silent as to the matter.[137] The development of such a power by the Court of Session would be useful and might commence with the position of the adherents of the Confession.

But against this line of approach there lie strong arguments. The fact that there have been few cases involving construction of the 1921 Act argues that there has been acquiescence in its propositions. However desirable it might be to introduce judicial review, the conduct of the Church and its members – *Percy* notwithstanding – has stemmed from the conviction that the 1921 Act was constitutive, sweeping aside the earlier restrictions upon action of the Kirk. It can therefore be argued that the Scottish Acts in the Union settlement have fallen into desuetude in their prohibitory aspect.[138] Other parts of the Union settlement have vanished without their unalterable nature being invoked.[139] Most cogently, 40 years ago in *British Railways Board* v *Pickin* [1974] AC 765 the House of Lords held the supremacy of Parliament to be unassailable, according with the general English doctrine. Their Lordships refused a remedy even though it was alleged that Parliament had been misled during the passing of a Private Act, and declined reliance on an old Scottish appeal where a remedy had been given.[140] *Pickin* therefore re-asserted the 'traditional' English doctrine of Parliamentary supremacy, and the English courts failed to take advantage of a useful opportunity to introduce judicial review of parliamentary legislation. The possibility that the Supreme Court would arrive at a different decision in a Scottish appeal must be remote.[141]

---

to justify and dignify the exigencies of government. It would be proper to decide this matter on utility and justice, not doctrinal theory.

134 T.B. Smith, *supra* n. 130, [1957] 2 P.L. 99 at 114.

135 1952 SC 396 at 411. Cf. Mitchell, *supra* n. 132, 82–91.

136 *Ex parte Canon Selwyn* (1872) 36 J.P. 54. P.M.H. Bell, *Disestablishment in Ireland and Wales* (London: SPCK, 1969); O. Chadwick, *The Victorian Church*, vol. I (London: Black, 1966), 47–60. The passing of the Roman Catholic Emancipation Act 1829 and the Irish Church Act 1869 show that the Sovereign's Accession Oath to protect those ecclesiastical interests was without legal weight (cf. Chadwick, 14-15).

137 The Israel Supreme Court took a similar step: *Bergman* v *Minister of Finance* (1969) 23 P.D. 693 (I), known to me only through M.B. Nimmer, 'The Uses of Judicial Review in Israel's Quest for a Constitution' (1970) 70 Col. L.R. 1217.

138 Cf. Lord Russell in *MacCormick* v *Lord Advocate* 1953 SC 396 at 417.

139 For example by the 1711 Patronage Act, and the abolition of University Tests by the Universities (Scotland) Act 1853. T.B. Smith, *supra* n. 130 (1957) 2 P.L. 99 at 112, goes rather far in suggesting that patronage was not covered by the Union Agreements. By the time of the Universities (Scotland) Act, 1889, the Church seems not to have pressed the question of University Tests, and in its evidence to the Committee on University Tests in Scotland (1892, C. 6970), acquiesced in their removal. See Chapter 6 at n. 20 and ff.

140 *M'Kenzie* v *Stewart* (1754) 1 Pat. 578, Mor. 7443 and 15459. The House considered that there was no reported judgment sufficient to make clear its ground of decision.

141 More recently see *R. (Countryside Alliance and others)* v *HM Attorney General and another* [2007] UKHL 52; [2008] 1 AC 719, for a similar unwillingness to overset an Act of Parliament, and *AXA General Insurance Ltd and others* v *H.M. Advocate and others* [2011] UKSC 46; 2012 SC (UKSC) 122; [2012] 1 AC 868 on the powers of the devolved Scottish Parliament. But cf. *Recovery of Medical Costs for Asbestos Diseases (Wales) Bill: Reference* [2015] UKSC 3, for a different result. *Cf. RM* v *The Scottish Ministers* [2012] UKSC 58;

In any event, to return to the idea that the law may be fixed for all future generations by express formulation is not to be welcomed. It is better to recognise that the language of the Treaty of Union indicated that legislators should proceed with caution in this area, and reflect rather than lead Scottish opinion.[142] If the Kirk is to be seen as an organism, developing and reformulating doctrine, its right to act within the Declaratory Articles should be construed widely. For an alteration of the Declaratory Articles Art. VIII requires Barrier Act procedure in two successive years which perhaps brings the 'evident utility of the subjects within Scotland' of Article XVIII of the Treaty of Union into play, and diminishes the plain words of the entrenchment of the religious settlement. Thus C.H. Johnston, the then Procurator of the Church, wrote that the Treaty of Union deprived Parliament of all moral right to disestablish the Church without either 'substantial unanimity, or else a distinct reference back to the people of Scotland, who only assented to that Treaty on the condition that Parliament should not interfere with the Church'.[143] Such reasoning might also apply to the position of the Westminster Confession, the Barrier Act procedure constituting a 'reference back' to the people. Where the Kirk itself desires the change that change ought not to be frustrated, but only so long as it remains within its known identity.

Some consider that the Article VIII right to interpret allows the Church to do as it pleases.[144] But that point has already been canvassed. It goes too far. During the passage of the 1921 Act it was asked whether the Church could, by a judicious use of its power to interpret, avoid the provisions of the Articles. Although there were statements in the House of Lords to the contrary, the observation of the Solicitor General in the House of Commons that ultimately questions of such interpretation would require resolution by the civil courts is cogent.[145]

Of course, such sentiments settle nothing. The question will still remain at what stage alteration to the Church's constitution is such that the Church has become something other than the Church with which the state dealt, and whose constitution in matters spiritual the state declared to be lawful in 1921. In Viscount Haldane's terms, at what stage would it be considered that 'the robbers have entered'?[146] At that stage those unwilling to move from the existing identity of the Church would be entitled to its property and funds.[147]

Madzimbamuto v Lardner-Burke [1969] 1 AC 645. C. Himsworth, 'The Supreme Court reviews the Review of Acts of the Scottish Parliament', 2012 P.L. 204; A. Page, '"Not law that the courts will recognise": Axa in the Supreme Court', 2012 Jur. Rev. 224; A. McHarg, *'Axa General Insurance Ltd v Lord Advocate'*, 2012 Edin. L.R. 224.

142 A.V. Dicey and R.S. Rait, *Thoughts on the Scottish Union* (London: Macmillan, 1920) 252–4. This seems to modify Dicey's previous statement in his *Introduction to the Study of the Law of the Constitution*, 10th ed. by E.C.S. Wade (London: Macmillan, 1959), 64–70, see Wade at lxiv–lxvi. Cf. Innes I, 126; II, 66 to the effect that one generation cannot bind another.

143 C.N. Johnston, *A Handbook of Scottish Church Defence*, 203, a comment quoted by T. Johnston during the Second Reading of the Church of Scotland (Property and Endowments) Bill 1925, 1924–25 180 HC Deb., Col. 58.

144 Sjölinder, 351 and 356. Cf. Murray *supra* n. 20.

145 For the 1921 parliamentary debates see *supra* following n. 91. See also Viscount Haldane, *supra* n. 95.

146 *Supra* n. 95.

147 See *supra* n. 90.

Homosexuality

In common with other churches the Kirk has had to consider homosexuality, including in its ministry.[148] As noted above, it has adopted rules forbidding discrimination on grounds of sexual orientation.[149] In the past active homosexuality has been prosecuted in the Kirk as a disciplinary offence. However, as the attitudes of society have changed there have been moves to recognise a difference between promiscuous homosexuality and a stable exclusive relationship. The introduction of civil partnership in 2004 first raised such matters.[150] Some ministers wished to conduct a 'blessing service' for couples that had entered into such arrangements. However, it was questioned whether such a service might expose the minister to disciplinary procedures for breach of church doctrine, the inference being that such a service implied approval of homosexual activity. In an attempt to clarify the situation the General Assembly of 2006 adopted a measure to allow, but not require, ministers to conduct such services without incurring disciplinary action. As affecting discipline, it was sent down to presbyteries under the Barrier Act. A majority of presbyteries disapproved, and the matter was departed from.[151]

In 2009 an Aberdeen church called as its minister someone who in correspondence with that church had stated that he was in an active homosexual relationship. That should have raised a question of discipline.[152] However, instead of asking Presbytery to refer this evidence to the minister's then Presbytery to be dealt with as a matter of discipline, a minority of the Presbytery of Aberdeen chose to oppose his settlement in the calling church.[153] Unsuccessful, they appealed to the General Assembly.[154] The matter thus concentrated on the right of a congregation to call a minister, not on the ecclesiastical offence. A Special Commission was set up to consider same-sex relationships, which, after wide consultations,[155] reported in 2011.[156] The 2011 Assembly agreed a future 'trajectory' that might permit change. A Theological Commission, representative of different theological views on human sexuality, was established. Its extensive report of 2013 included history and views of human sexuality together with separate statements of the traditional and the revisionist attitudes.[157] The Assembly instructed the Legal Questions Committee to bring forward proposals to the 2014 Assembly. The resultant proposal was accepted by the 2014 Assembly and sent down to

---

148 GA Reports 2007, Working Group on Human Sexuality, 'A challenge to unity: same-sex relationships as an issue in theology and human sexuality'. Cf. the Report to the House of Bishops, by the Working Group on Human Sexuality (London: Church House, 2013).
149 See *supra* at n. 88.
150 Civil Partnership Act 2004. See also the Marriage and Civil Partnership (Scotland) Act 2014, asp 5. See Chapter 7.
151 Nine presbyteries were in favour, 36 against.
152 Homosexual activity remained an offence in church law, though homosexual acts were decriminalised. In the 1970s the Presbytery of Aberdeen had prosecuted a minister for active homosexuality.
153 As one commentator noted, the effect was to 'entangle' the question of homosexuality with the congregational right to call. But for that the conservative view might have won at the Assembly: R.D. Kernohan, 'Will the Kirk split?', *The Scottish Review.net*, Feb. 2011.
154 F. Cranmer, 'Human Sexuality and the Church of Scotland: *Aitken et al* v *Presbytery of Aberdeen*' (2009), 11 Ecc LJ 335.
155 Consultation Paper, Special Commission on Same-sex Relationships and the Ministry, GA 2009. Responses to the questions posed by the Commission were given by secret ballot among the members of presbytery and kirk session.
156 GA Reports, 2011, 'Special Commission on Same-sex Relationships and the Ministry', 23/3.
157 GA Reports, 2013, 'Theological Commission on Same-sex Relationships and the Ministry', 20/1.

presbyteries under the Barrier Act.[158] It begins by affirming the traditional view of the Kirk on such matters, but in the interests of 'the peace and unity' of the Kirk, states in para 2.2 that:

> For the avoidance of doubt, the historic and current doctrine and practice of the Church in relation to human sexuality, their application to ministers and deacons of the Church and the provisions of this Act are points on which there is liberty of opinion in accordance with Article Declaratory V. Departure from the doctrine of the Church is permitted to this extent.[159]

The Act then sets out procedures under which a congregation may choose to depart from the traditional doctrine, and call a minister or deacon who is in a civil partnership. This accords with what is called a 'mixed economy' in various of the reports.[160]

A majority of presbyteries voted in favour of the legislation, and it was enacted as Act I of the 2015 Assembly.[161] Five days later the Assembly of some 700 Commissioners voted by 213 to 205 to modify the new Act to include ministers and deacons in a same-sex marriage, and by 215 to 195 to send that amendment down to presbyteries under the Barrier Act. The result will come back to the 2016 Assembly. In debate it was said that this extension was explicitly on the basis that the term 'same-sex marriage' was informed by the civil law, and did not reflect or contain any conclusion as to the theological doctrine of marriage held by the Kirk. That matter was referred to the Theological Commission for report to a later Assembly. Whether a 'mixed economy' solves the Kirk's problem remains to be seen.

A question is whether the new Act lies within the power of the Kirk. Can the Kirk both assert traditional doctrine and allow a clearly contradictory exception from it while still adhering to the Scottish Reformation as provided by Declaratory Articles Arts I and II? Is this departure from biblical teaching indeed within the 'liberty of opinion' sanctioned by Declaratory Article V? Or is this an example of interpretation disavowed by Murray and Haldane?[162] However, I doubt whether there will be a legal challenge. Disapproving of the recent developments, some ministers and members have already left the Church. These have not sought to take property with them. Others have covenanted together to remain within the Kirk and work within it despite their reservations.[163]

A creedal Kirk?

In the 1960s and 1970s the adoption of a simple creedal formulation as the statement of the faith of the Church was suggested. As the National Church Association pointed out,[164] the effect of the 1974 proposals to displace the Confession would have been to alter the Kirk

---

158 GA Reports, 2014, Legal Questions Committee, 7.4 and Appendix B.
159 Reference point, *infra* n. 166.
160 For example GA Reports, 2013, 'Theological Commission on Same-sex Relationships and the Ministry' 20/36.6; GA Reports, 2014, 'Legal Questions Committee', 7.4.3.4.1, 2; GA Reports, 2015, 'Theological Forum', 22.1.2.
161 The Barrier Act result was that 33 presbyteries were in favour with 13 against: 1,391 presbyters were in favour with 1,153 against.
162 See text *supra* accompanying nn. 91–6.
163 I have to say that, although I went with my congregation when it left the Kirk, at the time I would have preferred this solution.
164 *Supra* n. 120.

from one where orthodox doctrine was acknowledged in the form of the Confession to one in which office-bearers would, without further explication, simply assent to identified but simple propositions. Others would go further and, in pursuit of the peace and unity of the Kirk, suggest that the Kirk should simply acknowledge doctrine in creedal form. This is what ordinary members do. Why should office-bearers have an additional level of orthodoxy imposed on them? The Kirk could operate on the basis of the ancient creeds.

Such a step would allow doctrinal heterodoxy and may in due course prove to be a solution for the Church of Scotland as an extension of its 'mixed economy'. However, it would take the Kirk outwith the tradition of the Scottish Reformation, and would be better served by legislative intervention amending the 1921 Act following upon decisions within the Kirk on the Articles. To legislative action I now turn.

A future scene?

Before concluding this chapter with a general summation, I want to consider a possible future. The debate on homosexuality has revealed the fractures within the Kirk, the Report of the Theological Commission making these very apparent.[165] Sections hold very different views of the authority of Scripture. Declaratory Article I says simply that the Kirk 'receives the Word of God which is contained in the Scriptures of the Old and New Testaments as its supreme rule of faith and life'. For some, the biblical proscription of homosexuality cannot be avoided. For others, humanity has moved on from time-bounded attitudes. These differences are not new – the debates in the 1960s and 70s as to the Confession contain variants of the argument. The stresses may become intolerable. What does Declaratory Article I mean by the Word of God? And, from the language of GA Act I 2015, what is the substance of the faith that defines the identity of the Kirk and where does liberty of opinion come in?[166]

Any future split in the Church of Scotland should be coped with by an orderly disentanglement of property based on an acceptance of divergent doctrinal conviction rather than resort to legal dispute. Church property cases feel wrong. 'Dare any of you go to law with one another?' (I Cor. 6: 1). Following the 1904 Free Church case the state stepped in. A Commission was established to allocate to the Free Church properties and assets where at least one-third of a Free Church congregation wished to remain in that church.[167] That procedure could be inverted to help unpick the divergent theologies within the Kirk. In a future split a two-thirds majority within a congregation could be held to have the ability to leave the Kirk. Alternatively any question of schism could be settled as was done for the 1929 Union where United Free churches unwilling to enter the new Church of Scotland were not required to do so. Those congregations unwilling to modify existing doctrine could be allowed to leave, with the property they occupy. In either case the powers of the Church of Scotland General Trustees would have to be amended to allow a transfer of property under these circumstances.

*

---

165 *Supra* n. 157.
166 I do not enter into such matters as 'inspiration', 'inerrancy' or 'infallibility'. 'Authority' is far enough here. See *supra* n. 159.
167 Churches (Scotland) Act 1905, s. 1(2). By s. 1(2) account could also exceptionally be taken of the density of church properties in a neighbourhood.

Assuming that the doubts expressed in previous pages are not pressed too far, the Articles Declaratory of the Constitution of the Church of Scotland in Matters Spiritual, and the 1921 Church of Scotland Act leave the Church of Scotland with a much greater degree of freedom of action, and freedom from state control than it had under previous law. There is a clear contrast between the language of Lord Aitchison in *Ballantyne* above and those of the majority in any of the Disruption cases.[168] The definition of the Kirk in Declaratory Article I is sufficiently wide to allow full development within the Protestant reformed tradition. At the same time the position of other churches is not diminished, they being also protected by law in the exercise of their functions.

The Church of Scotland is not 'established' in the way that the Church of England is.[169] However, its position is recognised. That the Church of Scotland remains the National Church is made plain in a variety of ways. On accession to the Throne the Sovereign takes an oath to preserve the settlement of the true Protestant Religion and the Government, Worship, Discipline, Rights and Privileges of the Church of Scotland (though its legal worth may be dubious).[170] In Scotland the monarch is without special ecclesiastical powers or standing. The Moderator of the General Assembly of the Church of Scotland participates in the Coronation ceremony and in Scotland takes precedence after the Lord Chancellor.[171] Clear signs of the accommodation between church and state are to be seen at the General Assembly. A Lord High Commissioner appointed by the sovereign attends each Assembly,[172] but he or she is not member of the Assembly, and sits in a gallery which is not entered from the Assembly Hall, and technically is not part of the Hall. Basically the Lord High Commissioner listens in to Assembly proceedings through a window. Though the Lord High Commissioner is given opportunity to address the Commissioners,

---

168 '. . . the right claimed by the Church of Scotland to legislate and adjudicate finally, in all matters of government is now the law of the Church, declared by the Church itself, and recognised by Parliament. The General Assembly is not something alien to the Church; it is the Supreme Court of the Church, and the guardian of the Church's rights and liberties.

. . . I have endeavoured to resist the temptation, in construing the Act, of being influenced by any preconception of what the law should be. But I may be allowed to make this observation. If the pursuers' construction of the Act were to prevail, the result, in my opinion, would be simply to open a new chapter of confusion in the history of the Church. It would involve once more interference by the civil magistrate in matters that properly belong to the Church itself. If past history affords any guidance for the future, such an interference could not be other than calamitous'. per Lord Aitchison, *Ballantyne* v *Presbytery of Wigtown*, 1936 SC 625 at 657.

169 M.A. Maclean, 'The Church of Scotland as a National Church', 2002 149 Law and Justice 125, and her *The Crown Rights of the Redeemer* (Edinburgh: St Andrew Press, 2009), 121–5; C.R. Munro, 'Does Scotland have an established church?', 1997 Ecc L.J. 639; R. King Murray, 'Church and State', Stair Memorial Encyclopedia (1994), Vol. 5, paras 679–705, and his 'The Constitutional Position of the Church of Scotland', 1958 PL 155; T.M. Taylor, 'Church and State in Scotland', 1957 Jur. Rev. 121.

170 See n. 136 *supra*.

171 In England the Moderator takes precedence after Bishops of the Church of England but before Barons; Cox, 782. Technically the Coronation is an Anglican ceremonial, some would say arrogantly so. See C. Garbett, *Church and State in England* (London: Hodder and Stoughton, 1950); T. Beeson, *The Church of England in Crisis* (London: Davis-Poynter, 1973). The form and substance of the next Coronation remains to be seen.

172 The Lord High Commissioner may not be a Roman Catholic; Roman Catholic Relief Act, 1829, s.12. The Commissioner's allowance is regulated under the Lord High Commissioner (Church of Scotland) Act 1974 and, following the Scotland Act 1998 (Consequential Modifications) (No. 2) Order 1999, 1999 No. 1820, paid by the Scottish Ministers.

neither she nor he or the Crown has the right to initiate business or to control the proceedings of the Assembly in any way. Even the former conflict as to the right of the Crown or the Assembly to fix the date and place of the next meeting of the Assembly has been elided since 1927, the Lord High Commissioner undertaking to inform the monarch of the Assembly's own decision.[173] In such small, formal and ceremonial ways the *modus vivendi* of the national church and the civil authority is indicated.

---

173 S. Mechie, *The Office of Lord High Commissioner* (Edinburgh: St Andrew Press, 1957).

5   Outside establishment

At the end of the nineteenth century Taylor Innes recognised that the law relating to the non-established denominations was important and difficult.[1] Its importance lies in the role of religion in the life of many. In the past, difficulty lay in developing how the civil court might deal with such bodies given there was an established Kirk. In the present, difficulty can lie with the unincorporated voluntary association. Religious bodies that are incorporated are not relevant for this chapter.[2] Only the Church of Scotland has particular recognition in UK public general statutes, while s. 2 of the Church of Scotland Act 1921 acknowledged the existence of other Christian denominations that merely recognised what already emerged rather than gave them statutory being.[3] Otherwise the Methodist Church and the United Reformed Church have secured private Acts to facilitate the various unions now comprised within them.[4]

*

History has produced a plethora of Scottish denominations and churches. That has been augmented by the introduction of non-Christian religions and faith groups.[5] Three sets of Christian denomination can be classified according to the form of their government, Presbyterian Churches, those with an Episcopal base and a miscellaneous grouping of other movements. With a membership of c. one million out of a population of 5.35 million, Protestant denominations are a minority of the population. Roman Catholics number some 250,000.[6]

1 A.T. Innes, *The Law of Creeds in Scotland*, I, 242; II, 209.
2 See Chapter 8, 9. Charities.
3 See *infra* n. 168.
4 Methodist Church Acts, 1976 c. xxx, and 1939 c. xxvi. The United Reformed Church Act 2000, c. ii, regulates the union of the Congregational Union of Scotland with the United Reformed Church.
5 C. MacLean and K. Veitch, eds, *Religion*, Vol. 12 of *Scottish Life and Society: A Compendium of Scottish Ethnology* (Edinburgh: Donald, 2006).
6 Protestant churches count adult members; the Roman Catholic Church counts baptisms.
   A general 'Directory' of Scottish Churches is D.P. Thomson, ed., *The Scottish Churches Handbook* (Edinburgh: Lassodie Press, 1933). See also John Highet, *The Churches in Scotland Today* (Glasgow: Jackson, 1950), and *The Scottish Churches* (London: Skeffington, 1960). For more modern data see R. Currie, A. Gilbert and L. Horsley, *Churches and Church-goers: Patterns of Church Growth in the British Isles since 1700* (Oxford:

Presbyterian churches[7]

The Kirk considered itself the 'only trew and haly Kirk' in the land.[8] That claim was ineffective.[9] The dominance of the Kirk did not prevent the development of other groups, and their existence became plain in the eighteenth century. Some came into being through secession from the Kirk. Others were separately instituted.[10] Some stemmed from dissatisfaction with the organisation of the Kirk, or sometimes through objection to doctrine.[11] A frequent impulse was dissent from change, the objectors sticking with the former arrangements or doctrine.[12] Thus the Cameronians, descendants of the Covenanters, 'came out' from the Kirk in opposition to its alleged departure from covenanting principle in the 1690 settlement.[13] In 1733 a group left the Kirk over the right to nominate a minister when the patron had not acted timeously. They formed the Associate Presbytery. Others similarly began the General Associated Synod. The Relief Church began in 1761. Implicit in its original name, the Presbytery of Relief provided 'relief' from patronage.[14] Such groups were to merge and split, in particular over the Burgess Oath,[15] and as to elements of the Westminster Confession. However in 1820 most coalesced into the United Secession Church,[16] which, along with other traditions, fused into the United Presbyterian Church in 1847. In 1901 that Church joined with the Free Church of Scotland, becoming the United Free Church of Scotland.[17] In 1929 the bulk of that Church joined the re-constituted Church of Scotland.

Not all unions of Presbyterians were complete.[18] Not all the United Free Church entered the 1929 union with the Church of Scotland. There is still a Free Church of Scotland, birthed by the Disruption of the Kirk in 1843, and now descended from those who did not join the

---

Clarendon Press, 1977); P. Brierley and F. MacDonald, *Prospects for Scotland: From a Census of the Churches in 1984* (Edinburgh: National Bible Society, 1985); J.N. Wolfe and M. Pickford, *The Church of Scotland: An Economic Survey* (London: Geoffrey Chapman, 1980); S. Bruce, *A House Divided: Protestantism, Schism, and Secularization* (London: Routledge, 1990).

7 For diagrams of the principal schisms and unions in Scotland see Burleigh, insert; Sjölinder, 379, and (to its date) Innes, *supra* n. 1, I, 418. See also Wikipedia sub nom. 'Scottish religion in the nineteenth contoury'.
8 The Church Act 1567 c. 6.
9 H.R. Sefton, 'Presbyterianism', in MacLean *supra* n. 5, 127–42.
10 Cf. N.M., *Annals of the General Assembly of the Church of Scotland from the Origin of the Relief in 1752 to the Rejection of the Overture on Schism in 1766* (Edinburgh: Johnstone, 1840).
11 Cf. D. Lachman, *The Marrow Controversy* (Edinburgh: Rutherford House, 1988); E. Fisher, *The Marrow of Modern Divinity* (Fearn: Christian Focus, 2009).
12 Innes, *supra* n. 1, II, 212.
13 For the history of the Cameronians see Lord President Inglis in *Wallace* v *The Ferguson Bequest Fund* (1879) 6 R. 486 at 501, and more extensively the Note of Lord Curriehill, the Lord Ordinary, at 495 ff. In 1843 they adopted the name the 'Reformed Presbyterian Church'. The bulk joined the new Free Church of Scotland in 1843. See also http://website.lineone.net/~davghalgh/churchhistorytext.html#cameronians
14 *Annals*, *supra* n. 10; G. Struthers, *The History of the Rise, Progress and Principles of the Relief Church* (Glasgow: Fullarton, 1843).
15 See more fully *infra* n. 50. See also M'Kerrow, *infra* n. 16. Cf. Adam Gib's case, *infra* nn. 48 and 50.
16 J. M'Kerrow, *The History of the Secession Church* (Edinburgh: Oliphant, 1839; Glasgow: Fullarton, 1841, 1848); A. Thomson, *Historical Sketch of the Origin of the Secession Church* (Edinburgh: Fullarton, 1848); D. Scott, *Annals and Statistics of the Original Secession Church* (Edinburgh: Elliot, 1886); W.H. Macfarlane, *'Twixt the Land and the Moss: The Story of a Northern Church in Its Historic Relations (1773–1922)*, 2d ed. (Edinburgh: Elliot, 1922).
17 United Free Church of Scotland: http://www.ufcos.org.uk
18 The Reformed Presbyterian Church of Scotland is descended from congregations that did not re-enter the reconstituted Church of Scotland in 1690: http://www.rpcscotland.org/constitution-of-the-rpcs/. See also *supra* n. 13.

United Free Church in 1900.[19] The Free Church of Scotland itself has had two schisms, the Free Presbyterian Church of Scotland (1893)[20] and the Free Church of Scotland (Continuing) (2000).[21] The Free Presbyterian Church of Scotland itself further split in 1989, a minority forming the Associated Presbyterian Churches.

Episcopal Churches

Varieties of the Orthodox Church have a small presence in Scotland, as has the Old Catholic Church in the United Kingdom.

The Episcopal Church in Scotland

The Scottish Episcopal Church is small, but has a long history. The struggles between Episcopalianism and Presbyterianism were severe. Although the *Greenshields* case of 1710 and the Scottish Episcopalians Act (the Toleration Act) of the following year gave it some standing,[22] Acts of 1746 and 1748 prohibited Episcopalian worship in Scotland except in premises licensed for the purpose and only if conducted by clergymen of Irish or English orders. Restrictions were relaxed in 1792, but the Episcopal Church in Scotland has remained a small denomination.[23] Last century it engaged in a number of conversations with the Church of Scotland, which some hoped would bring about a united Church of Scotland with an episcopal form of governance. These foundered.[24]

The Roman Catholic Church

Like other denominations the Roman Catholic Church regulates its affairs in accordance with its own Canon Law and through its own structures.[25]

---

19 J.L. MacLeod, *The Second Disruption: The Free Church in Victorian Scotland and the Origins of the Free Presbyterian Church* (East Linton: Tuckwell, 2000).
20 *A Catechism of the History and Principles of the Free Presbyterian Church of Scotland* (FP Church, 1943, rev. ed. 2013); A. McPherson, *History of the Free Presbyterian Church of Scotland (1893–1970)* (Inverness: F.P. Church, 1975); MacLeod, *supra* n. 19.
21 In 2011 a very small group left the Free Church of Scotland when that body decided to allow the singing of hymns as well as the psalms. Based in Stornoway it calls itself the Reformed Presbyterian Church of Scotland (RPCS).
22 See *infra* n. 45.
23 F. Goldie, *A Short History of the Episcopal Church in Scotland* (Edinburgh: St Andrew Press, 1976); G. Grubb, *A History of the Church in Scotland*, 4 vols (Edinburgh: Edmonston and Douglas, 1861); W. Mutch, *A Manual of Scottish Ecclesiastical History* (Aberdeen: W. Mutch, 1907)); I. Guild, 'Synodical Government in the Scottish Episcopal Church', 1996 Ecc LJ 493; A. Maclean 'Episcopalians' in MacLean, *Religion, supra* n. 5, 191–234. Not all 'Episcopalians' were members of the Episcopal Church in Scotland: see the narrations of fact in *Dunbar* v *Skinner*, (1849) 11 D. 945 (*infra* n. 63), *Peake* v *The Association of English Episcopalians in Scotland* (1884) 22 SLR 3, and *Burnett* v *St. Andrew's Episcopal Church* (1888) 15 R. 723 (*infra* n. 161).

   In Aberdeen in 1784 the Scottish Episcopal Church consecrated Samuel Seabury, the first bishop of the Episcopal Church in the US. Seabury had been elected as bishop in Connecticut, but there being no Anglican bishop in the US he came to the UK to be consecrated. However, as a US citizen he could not take the oath of allegiance to the English monarch which was required of bishops consecrated in England. The Scottish Episcopal Church, a non-established denomination, had no such impediment. It is intriguing to find that one of the consecrators was Bishop Skinner, as to whom see *infra* n. 63.
24 A. Herron, *Record Apart* (Edinburgh: Scottish Academic Press, 1974) 49–61; I. Henderson, *Power without Glory: A Study in Ecumenical Politics* (London: Hutchinson, 1967).
25 G.A. Read, 'The Catholic tribunal system in the British Isles', 1991 Ecc LJ 213.

While the Reformation in Scotland was in one way abrupt, the replacement of the Catholic structures was slow. Following the legislation of 1560, steps were taken not so much to disendow the Roman Catholic Church as progressively to take over its funds and benefices.[26] Patronage of benefices remained in the hands of existing patrons, but with the Reformed Church as the judge of the qualifications of a presentee. In fact many of the ministers of the new reformed Church had formerly been Roman Catholic priests.[27] At first there was no overt persecution. With the exception of schoolmasters, none of the Bishops, clergy or laity were immediately required to subscribe the 1560 protestant Confession of Faith, and subscription was not made obligatory for holding a benefice until 1573. Old Catholic practices simply faded out and the general population went over into the new system without much difficulty. Priests unwilling to go along with the new system left the country. One by one the Bishops of the Scottish Church died off – the last, Archbishop Beaton, died in Paris on 15 April 1603. Thereafter the Roman Catholic Church in Scotland virtually ceased to exist although pockets of Catholicism persisted.[28]

The bull *Ex Apostolatus Apice* of 1878 of Leo XIII restored the hierarchy of the Roman Catholic Church in Scotland.[29] At that time the old statutes against Roman Catholicism remained on the statute book. However, it was the opinion of senior Counsel that although restoring the hierarchy was contrary to statute law the newly appointed prelates would not incur penalty.[30] The matter was never put to the test. Today most of the old Scots anti-papal statutes remain on the statute book but their penal clauses have all been repealed.

Other groups

Non-Episcopal and non-Presbyterian Churches are well rooted in Scotland. Numbers in each are not particularly large but they are not without effect.[31] There are a few Meetings of the Society of Friends.[32] A small number of Congregational Churches are banded together in the Congregational Union.[33] Scotland is served by Baptist[34] and Methodist Churches,[35] as well as by the Salvation Army.[36] Pentecostal churches are present, as are a number of

---

26 Sc. charges providing income for their incumbents.
27 G. Donaldson, 'The Parish Clergy and the Reformation', in D. McRoberts, *Essays on the Scottish Reformation 1530–1625* (Glasgow: Burns, 1962), 129–44.
28 Peter F. Anson, *Underground Catholicism in Scotland 1622–1878* (Montrose: Standard Press, 1970); D. McRoberts, 'Modern Scottish Catholicism, 1878–1978', 39 *Innes Rev* (sep. pub. Glasgow: Burns, 1979); in MacLean, *Religion, supra* n. 5; J.R. Watts, 'Roman Catholics in Scotland: Late Sixteenth to Eighteenth Centuries, 143–69'; J.F. McCaffrey, 'Roman Catholics in Scotland: Nineteenth and Twentieth Centuries', 170–190.
29 D. McRoberts, 'The Restoration of the Scottish Catholic Hierarchy in 1878', 1978 29 *Innes Rev* 1–29. The Bull is Appendix 1 to the *Acta et Decreta Concilii Scotiae Plenarii Primi Post Redintigratum Hierarchiam* (Edinburgh, 1888) and an extract is Appendix 19 to A. Bellesheim (trans. D.O. Hunter Blair) *History of the Catholic Church of Scotland*, 4 vols (Edinburgh: Blackwood, 1887–90). See also G. Read, 'The Catholic Tribunal System in the British Isles', 1990 2 Ecc LJ 213.
30 Innes II, 288.
31 J.A. Whyte, 'Other Christian Groups', in MacLean, *Religion, supra* n. 5, 235–55.
32 See www.quakerscotland.org
33 H.S. Escott, *A History of Scottish Congregationalism* (Glasgow: The Congregational Union of Scotland, 1960). See also *supra* n. 4.
34 D.W. Bebbington, ed., *The Baptists in Scotland* (Glasgow: Baptist Union, 1988).
35 There have been moves for the Methodist Church in Scotland to unite with the Church of Scotland, but these moves have stalled. Doctrinally there might be little difficulty, but the major Church proved unwilling to incorporate a Methodist system of 'circuits' within its own Presbyterian system.
36 www.salvationarmy.org.uk

independent churches that trace their roots to Nigeria. The 'Plymouth Brethren' is significant particularly round the North and East coasts.[37]

Scotland has its fair share of other faith groups. Some are organised on denominational lines and some are independent gatherings. Practising Jews have been present in Scotland for a long time, and the Jewish community received a boost with the Nazi persecutions. However, synagogues are few.[38]

The Church of Jesus Christ of the Latter Day Saints, the 'Mormons', has been in Scotland for many years, as have the Jehovah Witnesses.[39] There are many varieties of spiritualist churches. Scientology has its followers. The Findhorn Community outside Nairn is but one of a number of 'New Age' groups.[40] All such may on occasion produce problems classifiable as matters of Church and State, for example, on the question of medical procedures, refusal to take oaths, registering as required by civil law for various purposes and so on.

Partly because of the British Empire and immigration after the Second World War, Scotland has a large number of non-Christian religions.[41] There are several Buddhist establishments. Varieties of Hinduism are active. The largest non-Christian faith in Scotland is, however, Islam.[42]

*

Three major sets of problems arose for the unincorporated ecclesiastical voluntary association. First, the existence in law of non-established churches had to come about. Second, what 'jurisdiction' they might have over their members had to be settled, including when and how the civil courts might intervene. Third, questions of property and trust law arose from ecclesiastical schisms and unions, traceable to the nature of these churches as developing organisms. Throughout, the renowned ability of Scots to stand on a point of principle is manifest.[43] It may be that modern legal developments will afford other more satisfactory arrangements, but that remains to be seen.[44]

I. Legal existence

The root of the problem was that the notion of an association as an entity with legal personality separate from that of its members had not been developed when the question of 'churches' emerged. Partnerships were known, but companies did not exist in their modern form. Guilds had competence over various kinds of business, but operated as quality-control and often as a cartel, their members being independent traders. A religious grouping was something else.

---

37 F.R. Coad, *A History of the Brethren Movement*, 2d ed. (Exeter: Paternoster Press, 1976); N. Adams, *Goodbye, Beloved Brethren* (Aberdeen: Impulse Books, 1972). Following the difficulties outlined in the latter book some Brethren Halls have changed their names, designating themselves as independent Evangelical churches.
38 K. Collins, 'The Jews in Scotland', in MacLean, *Religion, supra* n. 5, 256–80. There is one Jewish school within the state educational system.
39 In *Walsh v Lord Advocate* 1956 SC (HL) 126, 1956 SLT 283, Walsh, a Jehovah's Witness, unsuccessfully sought exemption from National Service on the ground he was a minister. See Chapter 8, n. 290.
40 S.J. Sutcliffe, 'Alternative Beliefs and Practices', in MacLean, *Religion, supra* n. 5, 313–31.
41 Sutcliffe, *supra* n. 40.
42 M. Siddiqui 'Islam in Scotland after 1945', in MacLean, *Religion, supra* n. 5, 281–94.
43 For contenders see http://website.lineone.net/~davghalgh/churchhistorytext.html
44 See *infra* at n. 167.

Churches operated, but without official status. For reasons of history and its own belief in its calling, the established Church was not willing that other churches should be recognised in law. Well-known statute law affirmed and secured its position as the true church. As a result, development of the law took time.

The first move was the successful appeal to the House of Lords in *Greenshields* v *Magistrates of Edinburgh* (1710) Rob. App. 12.[45] Greenshields, an Episcopalian, had been ordained in England after the 1690 abolition of Scottish episcopacy. In 1710 Greenshields opened a place of worship within the boundaries of the Edinburgh presbytery. Because he was an Episcopalian, the presbytery held him not qualified to act as a minister within their jurisdiction. The magistrates therefore ordered it closed and the Court of Session refused to disturb that order. The House of Lords reversed. Soon after, Westminster enacted the Scottish Episcopalians Act 1711, the 'Toleration Act'. This required the Scottish courts to recognise the Episcopalian denomination as a church, thus affording it a degree of civil protection. However, the Act did not confer on the Episcopalian Church any standing in law comparable with that of the established Church with a jurisdiction independent of the civil authority. As Lord President Boyle put it in *Dunbar* v *Skinner* (1849) 11 D. 945 at 958: '. . . there exists in Scotland no Episcopal Church whatever except as a distinct sect, fully recognised and protected under the Toleration Act'.[46] One modern principle in relation to non-established denominations was therefore adumbrated – that such denominations are voluntary associations, which the law may regard, but which do not by law necessarily have independence of the civil courts.

The next step was the extension of tolerance in practice (if not in law) to non-established churches other than the Episcopalians. There was, however, no change by legislation or in the common law for decades. Indeed, for a decade ecclesiastical titles were banned.[47] But tolerance is not the same as a legal existence. It took many years to establish that non-established religious denominations were legal entities. Progress was obtained mostly in property cases. These disclosed that congregations were indeed operating as associations, often within a denominational structure, but the civil courts paid no heed to that latter fact.

The first reported case is *Bryson* v *Wilson*, of 1752.[48] Title to a Secession Church meeting-house was held by trustees who had undertaken to denude in favour of any new trustees that the congregation might elect.[49] The congregation split over the Burgess Oath, the majority going with the minister against the Oath.[50] The congregation elected new trustees, who

---

45 Reference point, *supra* n. 22.
46 Reference point, *infra* n. 64.
47 The Ecclesiastical Titles Act, 1851, repealed by the Ecclesiastical Titles Act, 1871.
48 Also known as *Adam Gib's Case*, Elchies' Decisions, *voce* Title to Sue, 487, 30 June 1752. *Pollock* v *Maitland*, *ibid.*, 488, 8 July 1752 is to like effect. Cf. D.M. Forrester, 'Adam Gib, the Anti-Burgher' (1941) VII RSCHS 141-69; M'Kerrow, *supra* n. 16.
49 As its name indicates, the Secession Church was first composed of a group who seceded from the Kirk in 1733 over the question of the election of a minister to a charge when the patron had not timeously exercised his right. See also next note.
50 The burgesses of a city or town were entitled to engage in commerce, belong to a trade guild and vote in local matters. Becoming a burgess involved taking the Burgess Oath. In 1744 the form of the oath in Edinburgh, Glasgow and Perth was amended in ways which some thought designed to approve the then form of government of the Church of Scotland, the Church which some had recently left to form their own associations, notably the Associate Presbyteries (Associate Synod). Others felt that Christians could take the oath considering it to be directed only to exclude Roman Catholics. Those opposed to the new oath were known as 'Anti-Burghers'. Their presbyteries had formed the Secession Church (*supra* n. 49). Those who considered the oath

called on their predecessors to comply with their undertaking. However, on appeal it was held that the new trustees had no title to sue, 'their constituents being no legal congregation'.

Almost 20 years later in *Wilson* v *Jobson* (1771) Mor. 14555, and followed in *Allan* v *Macrae*, (1791) Mor. 14583, *Bryson* was overruled. In *Wilson* Jobson had taken title to the meeting house of the Associate Congregation in Dundee but without acknowledging that he held the property in trust.[51] At that time the congregation professed Anti-Burgher principles. The minister, and amongst others Jobson, 'departed from' these principles, and the minister was suspended by the Associate Presbytery. The remnant of the congregation brought action to compel Jobson to transfer title to those who remained 'Anti-Burgher'. Jobson argued that the pursuers had no title to sue, being qualified neither as individuals nor as representing a corporation. However, the pursuers argued that 'the Law of Toleration' made them a legal society, capable of enforcing the trust. Their title to sue was upheld, and Jobson was ordered to denude in their favour since he had admitted that he held the property in trust. The Court therefore recognised the existence of the congregation as a society. However, the Court required the designation of the pursuers as being 'subject to the Associate Synod' to be struck out since the phrase was without legal meaning.

Ten years later *Drummond* v *Farquhar*, F.C. 6th July 1809, maintained a similar attitude where the designation of the pursuer as 'one of the bishops, or senior clergymen of the superior order of the Episcopal communion in Scotland' was struck out 'as not recognised by the Court'. However, in *The General Assembly of the General Baptist Churches and Evans* v *Taylor* (1841) 3 D. 1031 it was held competent for an action to be raised in the name of that Assembly and of persons delegated by it to carry on the action. It had been argued that the action was improperly brought because it was at the instance of an unincorporated association, and therefore by individuals who did not themselves have title to sue. This argument was repelled.

The Titles of Religious Congregations Act 1850 was a major development, allowing the title to property held for religious purposes to be taken in the names of relevant office-bearers and their successors in office, as trustees, without the need for a regular assumption of new trustees.[52] Despite this, in the first of the Free Church cases, *Bannantyne* v *Overtoun* (1902) 4 F. 1083; (1904) 7 F. (HL) 1, as well as the relevant trustees, the Third Defenders included all the members of the United Free Church General Assembly of 1900, designated individually. This was because the whole funds and properties of the former Free Church were at stake. The new United Free Church formed by the union of the Free and United Presbyterian churches in 1900 had claimed to have taken over all these assets.[53]

While the identity of non-established churches had become clear in the area of property, it took longer to establish their amenability to suit in other cases, and it may not yet be fully established in all instances.[54] Thus the Third *Cardross* case, *MacMillan* v *The General Assembly of the Free Church of Scotland* (1864) 24 D. 1282, held that the Assembly of the Free Church could not be sued as such for damages conjoined with the action for reduction of the deposition of MacMillan from the ministry. The Assembly was a body of changing

---

lawful for Christians were called 'Burghers'. Further splits gave rise to the 'Auld Licht' [Light] and 'New Licht' versions of their origins. These centred on interpretations of the duty of the civil magistrate as stated in Ch. XXIII of the Westminster Confession of Faith. See M'Kerrow and Scott, both *supra* n. 16.

51 An Associate congregation was part of the Secession Church, *supra* n. 49.
52 Now s. 26 of the Titles to Land Consolidation Act, 1868.
53 See *infra* at n. 123 ff.
54 It may be difficult to sue a church as such for debt, *Aitken* v *Harper* (1865) 4 M. 36.

composition that met infrequently, and the Assembly of 1858, whose acts were complained of, had ceased to exist. In the Fourth *Cardross* case, *Macmillan v The Free Church of Scotland* (1864) 2 M. 1444, the Lord Ordinary decided that the Free Church itself could not be sued due to want of specification of persons, the changing membership of the Church and so on, rendering it impossible to hold either that that body or its members had committed a delict, or (more dubiously) to mulct it or them in damages. The case did not go further because MacMillan consented the refusal of his appeal, but it seems likely that the Lord Ordinary would have been sustained. At that point, therefore, to sue the governing body of a non-established church with a Presbyterian conciliar structure, or the denomination itself, for reparation appeared impossible, though it was possible to sue named individuals. However, such bodies can raise actions, normally delegating the prosecution of the action to named persons. In some peculiar way, therefore, these bodies were, and may perhaps still be, transparent to the law, unless they choose to be actors.

Other forms of church structure may be amenable to court action. In episcopacy, where the individual members of the General Synod are known, and the Synod is continuous in membership, they may be sued, as in *Forbes v Eden* (1865) 4 M. 143.[55] In *Skerret v Oliver* (1896) 23 R. 468, it was held possible to raise an action against the Synod of the United Presbyterian Church through its officers, because it was a permanent body though not in permanent session.[56] At (1896) 23 R. 468, 474 Lord Kincairney ruled:

> But if it be impossible to call [such a body] it cannot be necessary to call it . . . It acts and is, I think, represented by its duly appointed tribunals and administrative and executive bodies.

However, whether the development of the law in *Skerret* would allow an action against the more traditionally structured Presbyterian churches remained moot for many years. In *Bridge v South Portland Street Synagogue*, 1907 SC 1351, Lord Salvesen repelled a plea that it was incompetent to sue an unincorporated body for damages through its officials. He considered that cases such as *Skerret* and *Murchison v Scottish Football Union* (1896) 23 R. 449 revealed a departure from the former law on grounds of expediency. Provided that the office-holders were also called as individuals, he was willing to allow the action. Fifty years later in *McGonagle v Glasgow Unitarian Church*, 1955 SLT (Sh. Ct.) 25, the congregation was sued through its office-bearers and competency was not raised.

In more recent years this matter has been solved by mutual concession. In *Brentall v Free Presbyterian Church of Scotland*, 1986 SLT 471, an action lay against the Synod of that Church (its highest body), the moderator and treasurer of the Synod both as its members and as individuals, together with the southern presbytery of the Church, its moderator and clerk again both as members of that presbytery, and again as individuals. However, to avoid the old debate a joint minute of the parties was lodged conceding that the Synod and Presbytery had been properly convened as defenders. By the twenty-first century matters had gone further. In the 2005 Free Church case, *Free Church (Continuing) v Free Church*, 2005 SC 396,[57] it was acceptable to designate the pursuers and defenders as respectively the General Assembly of the respective parties and others, and a similar solution was adopted at the

---

55 For Cardross see *infra* n. 68ff. For *Forbes* see infra n. 74.
56 For *Skerret* see *infra* following n. 74.
57 See *infra* n. 150.

appeal stage in *Smith, Moderator of the General Assembly of the Free Church of Scotland, et al.* v *Morrison, et al.* [2011] CSIH 52.[58] Both are property cases to be returned to later.

II. Legal nature, and the jurisdiction of non-established churches

What authority has a non-established church, and what jurisdiction has it over its members? As unincorporated voluntary associations founded upon contract, do they form communities having, *ex natura*, a jurisdiction over their members exclusive of that of the civil courts? Can an action lie against the judicatories or legislatures of such bodies in respect of their acts, and what restrictions may there be on such an action? The general position was fairly easily established, although relevancy of averment remained a more complex theoretical problem.

In practice most of the cases that have made it to court have had to do with discipline and the self-regulation of the association. How the entity acts to ensure compliance with doctrine, competency or expectations as to the behaviour of ministers and members will affect whether the civil courts intervene or decline so to do.[59]

Matters begin with the refusal of Lord Braxfield in 1793 to review the findings of the Associate Synod 'so far as they regarded an ecclesiastical offence'. In *Auchinloss* v *Black*, he did:

> not consider it competent for this court to review the proceedings of the Associated congregation, commonly called Burghers, when sentences are pronounced by them in their ecclesiastical character.[60]

Braxfield's stance was sustained on appeal, the Inner House refusing to permit the case to continue unless malice was alleged. However, the House also considered it competent for a related property action to proceed, thus underlining its refusal to look into the ecclesiastical realm.[61]

The doctrinal basis of this attitude is identified as that of contract in the interlocutor and Note of Lord Moncreiff in 1831 in *Osborne* v *Southern Reformed Presbytery*.[62] Principle requires that where a person has submitted to the 'jurisdiction' of an association, he may not tear up the contract and then have recourse to the ordinary courts, except in exceptional circumstances. In practice civil action is competent, but unusual. A case will fail if facts relevant to bring it within the exceptional category are not averred.

---

58 For the case see *infra* n. 151.
59 Thus a minister of the United Presbyterian Church was proceeded against because he had met and walked with a Miss A.B., a member of his congregation, after evening services and on other occasions, the complaint against him specifying the routes: *Skerret* v *Oliver* 1896 23 R. 468, fn. at 470–471. Cf. F. Cranmer, 'Church Courts in the Law of Scotland', 1998 13 *Denning L.J.* 49 at 53, n. 17. The Minutes of the Kirk Session of Gilcomston Free Church, Aberdeen (an antecedent of my own church) contain many proceedings against members for ante-nuptial fornication.
60 *Auchinloss* v *Black*, Hume, *Decisions*, 6th March 1793, 595. At 596 Hume notes the case of *Brownlee and Scott* v *Kirk-Session of Carluke* as being to the same effect, and cf. *Grieve* v *Smith*, Hume, *Decisions*, 631. Braxfield was famous for his severity in other matters. See Michael Fry, 'Macqueen, Robert, Lord Braxfield (1722–1799)', *Oxford Dictionary of National Biography* (Oxford: Oxford UP, 2004).
61 See the note of *Auchinloss* in *Dunn* v *Brunton* (1801) Mor. App. Soc. 10 at 16.
62 Unreported, footnoted Innes I, 263. Innes II, 217 n. 3 refers to a later page, but there is no later reference.

Dunbar v *Skinner* (1849) 11 D. 945,[63] the first case after the Disruption to consider the basis and limitations of the authority of a non-established church, contains statements of general application. Dunbar, an Episcopalian, licensed in England, had subscribed the Canons of the Scottish Episcopal Church and undertaken to submit to its bishops when he came north to minister at St Paul's Chapel in Aberdeen. There he used the English liturgy. Skinner was the Episcopal Bishop of Aberdeen. He insisted on the Scottish forms of worship, which did not accord with the English Book of Common Worship. Eventually Dunbar withdrew his subscription of the Scottish Canons, and he and most of his congregation seceded. Sentence of deposition followed in strong terms. In court Dunbar argued that the sentence had 'been pronounced illegally, irregularly and without authority, and that the same was null and void'. He also asked for damages for defamation contained in correspondence – there had been other contentions between the two – and in the sentence of deposition.

The Bishop argued, first, that the court lacked jurisdiction as his acts were of a regular ecclesiastical character and therefore not subject to review in the civil court, second, privilege, and, third, that had voluntarily placed himself under the authority of the Scottish Episcopalian hierarchy. The court unanimously rejected the argument that the Court of Session had no jurisdiction. The Episcopal Church in Scotland did not have a 'jurisdiction' to the exclusion of the civil court because its powers were not conferred by the state. Toleration under the Scottish Episcopalians Act of 1711 did not confer jurisdiction, the '*potestas iudicandi et exsequendi causas iure magistratus competens*'.[64] Dunbar's submission to the 'jurisdiction' of the church required proof, which had not yet been met.[65]

In view of the then very recent series of decisions in the Ten Years' Conflict, a different decision was not possible.[66] That would have meant allowing to the non-established churches an authority and power, not based on statute or common law, which statute had reserved to the established Church. Indeed, the non-established churches would have had a power and authority wider than was then available to the established Church.

Dunbar v *Skinner* showed that the 'jurisdiction' of non-established churches did not necessarily exclude the civil courts. However, the Court was cautious as to whether a limited 'jurisdiction' might arise from the voluntary consent to the rules of an association (prorogation), and indicated that were such proved in an appropriate case the result might be different. Lord Fullerton stated:

> There is no doubt that all parties entering into an association for purposes not prohibited by law, may effectually bind themselves to submit without appeal to the determination of certain matters and even to the infliction of certain censures, by the official authorities to whom such power is committed by the terms of the association; and if it could be instantly shown that, by the admitted or proved circumstances of this case, the defender had absolutely bound himself to submit to such a sentence as that for which he now seeks redress, the defence in the second

---

63 Reference point, nn. 23, 70, 73. The Lord President (1849) 11 D. 945 at 957, cites *Adam* v *Allan* (1841) 3 D. 1058 and *Dudgeon* v *Forbes* 1833 3 S. 1014 where pleas of privilege and ecclesiastical jurisdiction had not stopped the court from considering whether the plea was valid. Cf. Lord Jeffrey at 964–5.
64 Per Lord Fullerton (1849) 11 D. 945 at 961; cf. Lord President Boyle, at 958, quoted *supra* n. 46.
65 Bishop Skinner abandoned an appeal to the House of Lords. Issues were approved, with damages laid at £1,500: (1851) 13 D. 1217. The case seems to have been settled.
66 See Chapter 3, The Disruption.

plea in law might have been sustained [sc. submission by contract] and the case sent out of Court.[67]

A series of decisions soon refined these views, although at the end of *Cardross* the law had not been advanced.[68] The facts are contorted.

MacMillan, minister of the Free Church at Cardross, was accused of misconduct. Presbytery found part of the case against him proven. MacMillan appealed to Synod against the part of the deliverance of presbytery unfavourable to him. Synod sustained his appeal, and the presbytery appealed to the General Assembly. It, having a full print of the prior proceedings, re-opened the whole question, which they were not asked to do, and found proven a major portion of the original libel. MacMillan was suspended from office *sine die*, and loosed from his charge. As his civil interests were affected he went to the civil court which issued a Note suspending the Assembly proceedings. This was served on the Assembly. The Assembly summoned MacMillan and required him simply to state, without explanation, whether he had authorised the civil court action. On receiving an affirmative answer the Assembly immediately deposed him from the Free Church ministry. MacMillan raised actions to reduce the two sentences of the Assembly, and for damages in respect of the effects of both.

The First Cardross Case, *MacMillan v The General Assembly of the Free Church of Scotland*, (1859) 22 D. 290, established that the Free Church of Scotland, like every church other than the Church of Scotland, was in law simply a voluntary association. If a member of an association claimed unlawful interference with his civil rights, a remedy in the civil courts was not necessarily excluded just because the acts complained of were done by a 'court' of that church. Lord Deas was succinct:

> Now, if anything be clear in the case, it is that the defenders are invested with no jurisdiction whatever, ecclesiastical or civil. All jurisdiction flows from the supreme power of the State. The sanction of the same authority which enacted the laws is necessary to the erection of courts, and the appointment of judges and magistrates to administer the laws. The Established Church of Scotland had, and has, this sanction. The statute law of the land conferred upon it ecclesiastical jurisdiction . . . But there is no such statute law applicable to the association called the Free Church. When the defenders separated from the Establishment, they left all jurisdiction behind them.[69]

The court was therefore not barred from intervening and would examine both the sentence complained of and the contract that was the basis of the defence, although the actual content of the contract was reserved for future debate.

In the Second Cardross Case, *MacMillan v The General Assembly of the Free Church of Scotland and Beith and Others* (1861) 23 D. 1314, the Assembly claimed its actions were 'spiritual acts' and since they did not affect civil matters, they were not subject to review. The Court repelled this plea without difficulty, though in terms less sweeping than in the first

---

67 (1849) 11 D. 945 at 962.
68 *Macmillan v The General Assembly of the Free Church of Scotland* (1859) 22 D. 290; (1861) 23 D. 1314; (1862) 24 D. 1282; (1864) 2 M. 1444.
69 (1859) 22 D. 290 at 323.

case.[70] Other defences, however, were of more substance, notably that the 'jurisdiction' of the Free Church was founded on contract. MacMillan had subjected himself to its judicatories. However, since the parties could not agree on what the constitution of the Free Church was, and the court was not willing to hear debate on the theological concept of a church, the matter was remitted for proof.

In the Third Cardross Case, *MacMillan v The General Assembly of the Free Church of Scotland and Beith and Others* (1862) 24 D. 1282, the court, *ex proprie motu*, raised the difficulty that the major defenders, the General Assembly of the Free Church, were not capable of being sued. As a body of changing composition, the General Assembly was not a proper defender, and any action for damages could not be insisted in. It followed that the action for reduction of the sentence of the Assembly could not proceed. Other questions as to malice were raised but were not essential to the case at that stage, and the action was dismissed.

At this stage the case came to a rather unsatisfactory end. In the Fourth Cardross case, *MacMillan v The Free Church of Scotland*, (1864) 2 M. 1444, in a final attempt to press his case MacMillan sued the Free Church of Scotland itself for its interest, and various individuals including its then Moderator and principal clerks as representing the association, together with particular members of the 1858 General Assembly who had been most active in his deposition. The Lord Ordinary sustained the defence of the Free Church and those called as representing it, observing that it would be impossible to determine of what that body consisted. No decree could be given against it. Its individual members could not be properly ascertained, nor could they be attacked through representatives. For other purposes he was disposed to let the case proceed, and both sides reclaimed (appealed). However, by this time MacMillan, apparently weary of the conflict, consented to his appeal being refused, and the defenders assoilized (liberated from the action).[71]

Cardross was unsatisfactory because it collapsed when far advanced; yet it clearly shows developments in the attitude of the civil courts towards voluntary associations. The Free Church, which had left establishment in order to find freedom, discovered itself to be still amenable to the jurisdiction of the civil court. Indeed, it appeared that there was less independence outside establishment than inside, for at the time the independence of the established Church courts within their own jurisdiction had recently been reaffirmed.[72] Had the *Cardross* series proceeded further, the contract between MacMillan and the Free Church could have been clarified and whether it had been breached or whether its terms excluded the civil courts determined, thus allowing the court to continue or dismiss the case as *Dunbar v Skinner* had indicated.[73]

However, the *Cardross* saga did make it clear that non-established churches could be open to the scrutiny of the civil courts, and this has been the subsequent pattern. The Court of Session can take jurisdiction in ecclesiastical cases, and will consider the 'internal' workings of

---

70 A harbinger of the decision was *Mathers v Laurie* (1849) 12 D. 433, where it was held that an extract of a Free Church Kirk Session minute was not evidence since that kirk session was not recognised by law as a court. Eventually the point had to be proved by parole evidence; the clerk not having been present at the meeting, the minute book itself was not evidence. Cf. *Dunbar v Skinner* (1849) 11 D. 945, *supra* n. 63.

71 On the whole saga see Fleming I, 127–30; N.L. Walker, *Chapters from the History of the Free Church of Scotland* (Edinburgh: Oliphant, Anderson and Ferrier, 1895), 'The Cardross Case and Spiritual Independence', 212–25; A.M. Hunter 'The Cardross Case' (1941) VII RSCRS, 247–58.

72 *Sturrock v Greig* (1849) 11 D. 1220, and *Lockhart v Presbytery of Deer* (1861) 23 D. 120. See Chapter 3 following n. 148 and at n. 158.

73 *Supra* n. 67.

denominations. But when exactly will the Court intervene, and when not? What is required for a relevant case?

First, to succeed in an action against a church judicatory a pursuer must have a patrimonial interest. In *Forbes* v *Eden* (1865) 4 M. 143; (1867) 5 M. (HL) 36, one reason for Forbes' failure to get the civil court to reduce certain canons of the General Synod of the Scottish Episcopalian Church was that he could show no patrimonial interest.[74] *Skerret* v *Oliver* (1896) 23 R. 468 is to like effect. Skerret sought reduction of a decree of a Commission of the United Presbyterian Synod suspending him from the ministry.[75] He did not plead, but expressly reserved, the question of damages. The judges unanimously threw the case out because no patrimonial interest had been made out and no specific remedy other than reduction was asked for. Lord President Robertson said:

> Courts of law, as I understand, take no concern with the resolutions of voluntary associations, except in so far as they affect civil rights. If a man says merely, 'such and such a resolution of an ecclesiastical body is a violation of its constitution, on the faith of which I became a member or a minister', and stops there, the court will have nothing to do with his case, and will not declare the illegality or reduce the resolution. But, if the same man says, 'I have been ejected from a house, or have been deprived of a lucrative office, under cover of this illegal resolution, and I ask possession of the house, or I ask £500 of damages', then the court will consider and determine the legality of the resolution, on its way to the disposal of the demand for practical remedy. There is there a specific claim of a specific remedy for invasion of patrimonial rights.[76]

Second, there must be an irregularity in the church's procedure, but not just any irregularity will ground an action. The irregularity must be gross, undermining the integrity of the proceedings, perhaps involving malice or breaching natural justice. Only then will the Court consider whether the contract under which the person became a member of the association has been breached. The terms of the contract must be established. If they are not properly condescended on (alleged in the pleadings) and proved, the action will still fail.[77]

The major authoritative opinion remains that of Lord Justice Clerk Aitchison in *McDonald* v *Burns*, 1940 SC 376.[78] Trustees of a convent had asked for the removal of five Roman Catholic nuns who had been expelled from their Order but refused to vacate the premises. The nuns argued that their expulsion was invalid, the investigation of their conduct having been a mere pretence. Allegations of prejudice and irregularity were also put forward. The

---

74 There was also no procedural irregularity. Cf. *McGonagle* v *Glasgow Unitarian Church* 1955 SLT (Sh. Ct.) 25, an attempt to assert membership of the Church; *Mackintosh* v *The Trustees of the Scottish Episcopal Fund* (1801) (unreported: noted A. McWhirter, 'Lesser Known Church Law Cases' (1955) 11 RSCRS 149–59, at 149); *Aitken* v *Associated Carpenters and Joiners of Scotland* (1885) 12 R. 1206. Following the property cases discussed *infra* Forbes would have been better to claim the property of the Scottish Episcopal Church arguing that the new canons meant Eden et al. had forfeited right to the property because they had departed from the original principles of the Church.
75 See *supra* n. 59 as to his offence.
76 *Skerret* v *Oliver* (1896) 23 R. 468 at 490.
77 *Skerret* v *Oliver* (1896) 23 R. 468, Lord Kincairney at 481–2; *Mulcahy* v *Herbert* (1898) 25 R. 1136; *Brook* v *Kelly* (1893) 20 R. 470, 20 R. (H.L.) 104; *MacMillan* v *General Assembly of the Free Church* (1859) 22 D. 290 (1861) 23 D. 1314.
78 Reference point *infra* n. 89.

Second Division continued the case for proof of averments, with limitations, but the importance of the case lies in the statements of the right of the court to review the functioning of the internal proceedings of the Roman Catholic Church. According to Lord Justice Clerk Aitchison:

> ... the intervention of the court in disputes arising out of the decisions of religious associations, and affecting the relations between them and their members has always been regarded as subject to certain very clearly defined limitations. The judicatories of religious bodies in Scotland are not in the position of ordinary civil judicatories whose decisions are reviewable by appeal or suspension. They have their own exclusive jurisdictions, and their decisions, within their own sphere and in matters pertaining to their own life and discipline, are final and binding on their own members, and are not open to review unless in exceptional circumstances.
>
> It is true that the judicatories of dissenting bodies are not Courts in the technical sense in which the judicatories of the National Church, which had their foundation in, statute, have always been regarded as Courts of the realm, but, whatever contrary views may at one time have been entertained and expressed, it can scarcely now be doubted that they have privative jurisdiction within the limits of their own constitution, in questions affecting their own members who, by becoming members, have voluntarily undertaken to submit themselves to and abide by the constitution of the church to which they belong, although not entering into any express contract or covenant to do so.[79]
>
> In the case of *Oliver* v *Skerret*, (1896) 23 R. 468, the right of the Courts to concern themselves with the resolutions of dissenting religious associations, where patrimonial interests are injuriously affected, was generally accepted, but subject, as I read the opinions, to recognition that there must be clear illegality, and not mere irregularity, in what is complained of.

Further,

> The internal discipline of any such body [sc. a non-established church] is a matter of domestic concern, notwithstanding that status, or civil rights, may be involved, and it is only in extraordinary circumstances that the Courts will regard it as within their competence to intervene.[80]

> Speaking generally, [these circumstances are] in either of two situations – (first) where the religious association through its agencies has acted clearly and demonstrably beyond its own constitution, and in a manner calculated to affect the civil rights and patrimonial interests of any of its members and (secondly) where, although acting within its constitution, the procedure of its judicial or quasi-judicial tribunals has been marked by gross irregularity, such fundamental irregularity as would, in the case of an ordinary civil tribunal, be sufficient to vitiate the

---

79 1940 SC 376 at 382.
80 1940 SC 376 at 383.

proceedings. But a mere irregularity in proceedings is not enough. It must be so fundamental an irregularity that it goes beyond a mere matter of procedure, and becomes something so prejudicial to a fair and impartial investigation as to amount to a denial of natural justice, as, for example, of a conviction of an ecclesiastical offence were to take place without an accusation being made, or without allowing the person accused to be heard in his defence. In short, the irregularity must not be simply a point of form, or a departure from prescribed regulation, but must go to the honesty and integrity of the proceedings complained of. Thus, if there has been 'such a gross and wilful violation of the rules of the body, in order to effect a purpose which could not be attained without it, as shall amount to an entire breaking up of the contract, on the faith of which any jurisdiction was committed to these Courts' there may be a point 'not undeserving of the consideration of the Court', per Lord Moncreiff (at p. 671) in *Smith* v *Galbraith* (1843) 5 D. 665. It is perhaps unnecessary that the violation should be wilful, but, at least, it must be fundamental. There must be some vital disconformity to the law and constitution of the religious association whose decision is being impugned, or some flagrant departure from elementary justice in the conduct of its proceedings, or some usurpation of jurisdiction, or, to put it generally, something against the essential faith of the contract by which the members of the body by entering into association have expressly, or impliedly agreed that they shall be bound.[81]

These remarks encapsulate the principles worked out in a long series of cases, beginning with Lord Braxfield in *Auchinloss*.[82] In the ordinary instance the civil court will not intervene, but will do so to do justice where clearly necessary. However, the court will not give an abstract decision. An effective remedy must be possible, such as requiring the rehearing of a case of discipline. And if in the ultimate it is not possible to sue for damages, then the whole claim will fail.[83]

When the civil court intervenes it will not itself review the sentence of the ecclesiastical judicatory. The church court is expected to rectify the matter. Only if it does not will other consequences potentially arise. However, a correlative rule is that the Court will not force a voluntary association to receive back someone whom it has expelled. In such an instance only damages may be appropriate. In the second *Cardross* case, Lord Deas observed:

Nobody contemplates that the defenders are to be ordained to receive the pursuer back into their association; to allow him to sit and vote in their Presbyteries, Synods and General Assemblies; or that the Free Church Congregation at Cardross are to be compelled either to listen to his sermons or to absent themselves from the church, and leave him to preach to empty benches. The principle on which we should decline to take that course is a very ordinary principle. If a master unwarrantably dismisses his servant, we give pecuniary redress; but we do not compel the master to take the servant back into his service. If I engage a teacher in any department of science, literature, or art, the law will compel me to pay him, but the law will not compel me

---

81 1940 SC 376 at 383–4.
82 *Supra* n. 60.
83 See the Cardross cases generally; *Gall* v *Loyal Glenbogie Lodge of the Oddfellows Friendly Society* (1900) 2 F. 1187 (1900) 8 SLT 140; *Skerret* v *Oliver* (1896) 23 R. 468.

to be taught by him. It is not because the office of a clergyman is a holy office – it is not because those who ordained or deposed him did so by divine authority – that we decline to interfere further than I have indicated. It is simply because this Court deals only with civil or patrimonial interests and consequences and, while vindicating or giving redress for these, refuses to go beyond them.[84]

That noted, however, there are no cases where there has been a final decision by the court in a non-established church case. In the *Brentnall* and *Macdonald* cases the parties agreed a settlement.[85] But where major irregularity is pleaded the civil court may have to consider carefully how to proceed. One remembers the confident assertions of Lord Brougham in the First Auchterarder case that it was inconceivable that a church court would defy the civil law – and the resulting Disruption. It might be that damages would be the only effective remedy, but that could be a difficult remedy to obtain. Some church structures make it difficult, if not impossible, to call parties who may be liable in damages. If a church judicatory refuses to re-hear a case, or were directed so to refuse, by a superior court of inconstant membership and existence, against whom would an action lie? The appropriate procedure would seem to be to sue the several individuals constituting the body that has wrongfully acted, as well as the body itself, leaving them to seek such remedy as they may have from the funds of the association. It is noticeable that in the recent cases involving ecclesiastical voluntary associations the parties have accepted that they have been properly designed and called.[86]

It remains possible that a member's submission to the courts of a church is final, barring any appeal to the civil authorities. In *Sturrock* v *Gregg*, Lord Justice Clerk Hope narrated the statutory and doctrinal basis of the Church of Scotland, then stated:

> From this, I think it necessarily follows that in matters clearly within the cognisance of the Church officers or courts . . . its judicatories and officers are not amenable to the civil courts of the country in damages for alleged wrong . . .
>
> The inquiry into their motives . . . is absolutely repugnant to the freedom which must belong to the Church in matters of discipline . . .
>
> The view that may be taken of this matter by independent religious bodies, unless their constitution is very express, may go much further; and it may be that their Church courts may have, as against their own ministers, the sole right to decide what is a competent matter for Church government and ecclesiastical discipline.[87]

The Lord Justice Clerk went on to indicate that in the case of the then established Church, that to the protection afforded to its courts were they to act *ultra vires* might have limits, and that a similar limit would apply in the case of other churches, but the general point might be

---

84 *Macmillan* v *The General Assembly of the Free Church of Scotland* (1861) 23 D. 1314 at 1345–6.
85 See respectively *infra* nn. 94 and 98.
86 See the Free Church and Free Presbyterian Church cases below: *Brentnall* v *Free Presbyterian Church of Scotland* 1986 SLT 471; *MacDonald* v *Free Presbyterian Church of Scotland*, 2010 CSOH 55; *Free Church of Scotland (Continuing)* v *General Assembly of the Free Church of Scotland* [2005] CSOH 46, 2005 SC 396; *Smith* v *Morison* 2009 CSOH 113; 2009 SLT 973; *Smith, Moderator of the General Assembly of the Free Church of Scotland, et al.* v *Morrison, et al.* [2011] CSIH 52, 2012 SC 79, 2011 SLT 1213.
87 (1849) 11 D. 1220 at 1231.

drawn that, in submitting to the jurisdiction of the courts of the dissenting church, a person gave up his right to recourse to the civil courts.[88] In *Dunbar* v *Skinner* Lord Fullerton indicated that prorogued jurisdiction might be determinative of a case, but in *McDonald* v *Burns* Lord Aitchison left open the situation where the church court had acted in an irregular and oppressive manner or out of malice.[89]

Even if a church court is not final in an absolute sense, it may be that when it acts quasi-judicially the occasion is qualifiedly privileged. To displace qualified privilege, malice must be both averred and proved for a successful case. It was so averred in *Edwards* v *Begbie* (1850) 12 D. 1134, and the Court approved of the issues. But in the various stages of the *Cardross* case, malice was averred only against the particular members of the Free Church Assembly who had been active in Macmillan's deposition. However *Cardross* terminated before it was fully discussed whether malice ought to have been averred against all the Assembly members. In the case of action against a judicatory of the established Church, it is clear that malice must be averred for proceedings to be competent, but in one of the cases on that point, *Lang* v *Presbytery of Irvine* (1864) 2 M. 823, Lord Deas went out of his way to comment on *MacMillan* and position of the non-established church. After noting that malice had to be alleged in an action against a court of the established Church, he went on at 836–7:

> The only other observation I have to make is this, that as we are dealing with the procedure of a constituted court of this country, the principle is different from the principle applicable to a voluntary association, different as respects their right to regulate their own procedure and power of process, and as respects the principles of their constitution. In the case of a voluntary association, the question resolves itself into a breach of a civil contract, and I know no law for holding that malice is necessary to render parties liable for a breach of a civil contract. That was the sort of question that occurred in the case of MacMillan against the Free Church.

At the end of his judgement Lord Ardmillan challenged this view:

> In consequence of what has fallen from Lord Deas, I feel it to be my duty to state my deliberate opinion that, in this matter of privilege in judicial proceedings, there is no difference between . . . the church court of the Established Church, and the church courts of non-conforming bodies, provided there is jurisdiction which by law or by contract the parties are bound to recognise, and a judgement pronounced by Judges whom by law or by contract the parties are bound to obey. In both cases I think that the judgement is privileged and that malice must be alleged. . . . Whether the grossness of the irregularity of a judicial proceeding might or might not be held as sufficient to infer the malice which the law required is a question which is not now before us; . . . But I think it right to add, that, as at present advised, I am not satisfied that any mere irregularity would be sufficient; and I am disposed to think that it would be necessary to instruct special malice, apart from the irregularity of the procedure . . .[90]

---

88 Cf. the arguments to this effect in the Cardross cases.
89 1940 SC 376 at 383–4, quoted *supra* n. 81.
90 *Lang* v *Presbytery of Irvine* (1864) 2 M. 823 at 838.

Lord Deas responded:

> I must explain that I did not give any opinion as to what would be the law in the case of a civil contract with a voluntary association acting within the contract. The case to which I referred was one in which it was distinctly alleged, and offered to be proved, that the parties had acted not according to, but in violation of the contract. It was of that case alone that I spoke.[91]

Lord Ardmillan noted that he himself referred to no particular case, but considered that the broadly stated dictum of Lord Deas was not one in which he concurred.

A divergence of opinion as to the nature of the ecclesiastical court is inherent in these comments. At various times Lord Deas had stated that the courts of the non-established churches did not have 'jurisdiction', and his view follows from that.[92] For him only state-established courts had jurisdiction and therefore immunity from action against their proceedings. Other informal bodies could not claim immunity or privilege. But the developed law has not followed his view, preferring that of Lord Ardmillan. Lord Curriehill stated the point succinctly in *MacMillan* v *The Free Church of Scotland*, (1862) 24 D. 1282 at 1295:

> Parties upon whom judicial functions are lawfully conferred and who in the exercise of these functions over parties subject to their authority, fall into errors in judgment, are not liable in damages to those parties in consequence of such errors. *Humanum est errare*. . . . But such functionaries have immunity from liability for errors in judgment, unless their errors arise from corruption or malice. The law unquestionably confers such immunity upon judges officiating in the public judicial institutions of the country, whether civil, criminal or ecclesiastical, upon whom jurisdiction is conferred by the State. It also extends such immunity to private persons, upon whom the parties, by voluntary agreement, confer authority to adjudicate in certain matters among themselves; it being the policy of our law to encourage and support the settlement of disputes by such private arrangements . . . In like manner, when voluntary associations, constituted for religious purposes, confer upon some of their own members authority to adjudicate among them in certain matters, the law extends to the persons so appointed immunity from claims of damages, on the part of members of their respective associations, for errors into which these functionaries may fall in the *bona fide* exercise of the authority so entrusted to them. They enjoy such immunity . . . because these members by voluntarily conferring such judicial authority upon them are held to confer likewise the privilege which the law itself attaches to the *bona fide* exercise of judicial functions. This is a principle which is of great importance in this country, as, in my opinion, it enters into the constitution of most, if not all, of the voluntary religious associations which have been formed in Scotland under the protection of the Toleration Acts.

---

91 *Lang* v *Presbytery of Irvine* (1864) 2 M. 823 at 838.
92 Cf. his observations in *MacMillan* v *The General Assembly of the Free Church of Scotland* (1865) 22 D. 290 at 323, quoted *supra* n. 69. Lord Ardmillan is generally broader. In *Presbytery of Lews* v *Fraser* (1874) 1 R. 888 at 894, he would have the civil power compel witnesses for non-established as well as established Church courts.

These statements, as those of Lord Aitchison in *McDonald*,[93] make it clear that a plea of malice would allow an attack on the regular proceedings of a duly constituted court of a non-established church. The subsequent development of the concept of natural justice in other contexts has added the possibility that a plea of privilege would not be sustained in the face of gross or fundamental irregularity. Exactly when irregularity becomes fundamental, breaking up the contract of association of a non-established church allowing recourse to the civil court, is something which until relatively recently (in legal terms) had not required decision. But, after a period of quiescence such questions have re-emerged.

In *Brentnall* v *Free Presbyterian Church of Scotland*, 1986 SLT 471,[94] John Brentnall and H.R.M. Radcliff, ministers of the Free Presbyterian Church, had sought to protest (as opposed to dissent from) a 1978 decision of the Synod, the highest body of that church. 'Protest for conscience sake' had exercised that Church over many years. In 1944 Synod had decided that while protest was a competent in some circumstances, continuing in protest after the decision of the supreme court of the Church 'may and usually does' involve the self-exclusion of the protester from the Church.[95] In 1980 without discussion the Synod dismissed a move by Brentnall and Radcliff to re-open the 1978 decision. The move was held to be contrary to the Synod decision of 1944, and they were asked to undertake to desist from spreading their view of continuing protest. They declined to do so. Synod suspended them from ministry, but with their consent. In 1981 Synod recalled Brentnall. He stated that he remained of his earlier view. This was viewed as disrespect and a continued defiance of the Synod. His suspension was continued, but in addition the pastoral tie between him and his congregation in Dumbarton was dissolved.

In the Outer House Lord Dunpark dismissed Brentnall's action to reduce the decisions of the Synod, holding that the Synod had acted within its powers, and that no question of natural justice arose.[96] Brentnall had been properly disciplined. The Inner House thought differently. Lord Justice Clerk Ross considered that no relevant averments of contumacy sufficient to justify the Synod action had been made. Further, while in 1980 Brentnall and Radcliff had been asked whether they were prepared to desist in spreading their views, they had not been ordered so to do. The suspensions and other decisions therefore lay outwith the power of Synod. Lord Ross also observed that, even if he had held the Synod to have acted *intra vires*, it had breached natural justice by not affording the ministers opportunity to know the charge against them and to make representations thereanent in the 1980 proceedings. That in 1981 some opportunity had been given to argue did not mend the irregularity of 1980.[97] Ross's two colleagues were more forthright, holding that natural justice had indeed been breached. The case was remitted for proof of damage. The Free Presbyterian Church entered an appeal to the House of Lords, but settled the case before the appeal went ahead.

---

93 1940 SC 376 at 383–4 (*supra* n. 77).
94 Reference point, *supra* n. 85.
95 I summarise the 'five points' regarding protest as given in the Opinion of Lord Justice-Clerk Ross, 1986 SLT 471 at 472. For later consideration of 'The Right of Continued Protest' by the Free Presbyterian Church see the Finding of its Assembly of May 2013, http://www.freechurchcontinuing.org/about/other-documents/item/the-right-of-continued-protest
96 Brentnall's case was the one argued, parties accepting that Radcliffe's case would have the same result.
97 Other non-ecclesiastical cases involving questions of natural justice were cited in both argument and the judgments, including *Malloch* v *Aberdeen Corporation*, 1971 SC (HL) 85, *St Johnstone Football Club* v *Scottish Football Association Ltd*, 1965 SLT 171, and *Barrs* v *British Wool Marketing Board*, 1957 SC 72; 1957 SLT 153.

A later Free Presbyterian case might have raised similar matters.[98] Over a period the Rev. A.J. MacDonald had been critical of another minister. Synod suspended him temporarily from the ministry in 2007. A year later the suspension was confirmed *sine die* and the pastoral tie with his congregation severed. He sought recourse through two avenues. An Employment Tribunal rejected an application to it on the ground that he was a minister and not an employee in terms of the Employment Rights Act 1996. This decision was upheld on appeal.[99] MacDonald also petitioned the Court of Session judicially to review the Synod's decisions on a variety of grounds including natural justice. The criticised minister and his father-in-law had taken part in some of the proceedings, and MacDonald alleged he had not been given adequate opportunity to respond to charges. In *MacDonald* v *Free Presbyterian Church* [2010] CSOH 55; 2010 SCLR 475, Lord Grieve easily repelled a defence of *mora*, delay and taciturnity (that is, that matters had not been raised soon enough) and allowed the case to proceed. The Church considered an appeal, but settled with MacDonald without conceding either liability or that in so doing it was somehow complying with the orders of the civil authority.[100]

Finally, some might argue that submission to the courts of a church implied by membership would be conclusive in such affairs were the church's constitution contractually and explicitly to bar any appeal to the civil authorities.[101] This is mistaken. The civil courts will strike down on grounds of public policy any attempt to exclude them from dealing with breaches of natural justice.[102]

III. Property

Property has been a major area in which the civil courts have had to consider the constitution, tenets and beliefs of non-established churches. In the main, churches have taken the view that, however much they might object to the intervention of the courts in matters of spiritual jurisdiction, they were not opposed to the civil courts regulating matters of property. A long line of cases comes to a climax in the House of Lords decision in 1904. Thereafter saw a lull as the law as then stated was coped with. In the 2000s further Free Church cases re-examined the law, but have not departed from the 1904 principles.

Rights to property have concerned, perhaps over-concerned, non-established churches over the years.[103] Until recently churches have not sought incorporation or other legal

---

98 Reference point *supra* n. 85.
99 *Rev Allan J. MacDonald* v *Free Presbyterian Church of Scotland*, Appeal No. UKEATS/0034/09/BI: BAILII case number: [2010] UKEAT 0034_09_1002. But cf. *Sharpe* v *Worcester Diocesan Board of Finance Ltd*, UKEAT/243/12, [2014] ICR 9, where, on the basis of the (Church of Scotland) *Percy* case (see Chapter 4 at n. 56), whether a Church of England clergyman was an employee within the employment protection legislation, was referred back for further consideration. However, the Court of Appeal reversed, considering that there was no contract of employment to be founded upon: *Sharpe* v *Worcester Diocesan Board of Finance Ltd and another* [2015] EWCA Civ 399.
100 *The Free Presbyterian Magazine*, Vol. 115, no. 11, Nov. 2010, 350–351.
101 I note that the Free Church of Scotland (Continuing) did consider whether recourse to the civil courts should bar or exclude a minister from its association: http://www.freechurchcontinuing.org/about/other-documents/item/the-right-of-continued-protest. Cf. the action of the Assembly in the first *Cardross* case, *supra* following n. 68.
102 For example from the cases discussed earlier, *McDonald* v *Burns*, 1940 SC 376, 1940 SLT 325; *Brentnall* v *Free Presbyterian Church of Scotland*, 1986 SLT 471. Cf. secular cases such as *Smith* v *Nairn Golf Club* 2007 SLT 909; *St Johnstone Football Club Ltd.* v *Scottish Football Association Ltd.*, 1965 SLT 171 and *Lee* v *Showmen's Guild of Great Britain* [1952] 2 QB 239, [1952] 1 All ER 1175.
103 Cf. Matt. 5: 40; Luke 6: 29; I Cor. 6: 1–8.

devices. As voluntary associations, their property had therefore to be held by individuals in trust for the purposes of the congregation or denomination. In essence, when the matter arises the court, therefore, simply applies the terms of the relevant trust. The court does not create the trust, but it will enforce that trust which, on the evidence before it, it finds to exist. This has caused problems over the years, but these may be elided by suitable trust deeds and appropriate statements of principle by the ecclesiastical governing bodies. The problems may be simply stated. Where the constitution of a church or congregation does not contain an expressed inherent right of doctrinal deviation – the right to alter fundamental doctrines and their statements over the years – the civil court will hold that that church forfeits its property if it deviates from its original principles.[104] Any minority continuing to adhere to the original principles, doctrine or constitution will be entitled to the property held in trust for that church.

At root, many early cases on the recognition of the non-established churches as legal associations involved property.[105] In most there had been schism in the original body and trustees unwilling to convey the property to one or other of the factions.[106] The bigger cases involved denominations, the others title to single properties. Recent cases stand in their line.[107]

The first major reported case that deals precisely with property, and argues the facts, is *Dunn* v *Brunton* (1801) Mor. App. Soc. 10. It involved the Burgher Seceders and the 'New Light' controversy.[108] However, the court sidestepped the issue. It was invited to consider the terms on which the minister of a church in Aberdeen held tenure, and his conduct in replacing the locks on the church when a majority of the congregation failed to follow him into the 'New Light'. But, being 'much divided in the opinion', the court simply stated that: 'The Court can enter into no investigation as to the religious grounds of the schism here, and if they did, they must presume the majority in the right'.[109] Apparently in other unreported cases of the time the Court of Session had considered that questions arising from change of objects by the majority of a church were not matters to concern the court. But the court was not fully satisfied with that a position and selected the *Craigdallie* case 'to try the general point again more deliberately'.[110]

Craigdallie v *Aikman*,[111] 'was taken up and determined with the very view of fixing and settling a general question'.[112] The process took 20 years. It is unnecessary here to discuss its several parts,[113] but the general principle enunciated by Lord Chancellor Eldon in the House of Lords was simple in concept, if difficult of application. Church property is held in trust for the principles of that Church. The concept of the prior cases, that the will of the majority should prevail, was swept aside in the House of Lords without apparent difficulty,

---

104 Of course, this steps round the question of what is 'fundamental'.
105 See Section II, above.
106 *Bryson* v *Wilson* (1752), Elchies Decisions, 487; *Pollock* v *Maitland*, ibid. 488; *Wilson* v *Jobson* (1771) Mor. 14555; *Allan* v *Macrae* (1791) Mor. 14583, See *supra* n. 48 and following.
107 See the Free Church cases of 2005 and 2011, *infra* nn. 150 and 151.
108 See *supra* n. 50.
109 M. App. Soc. 10 at 17. It may be noted that this is the principle to an extent adopted in the US. See *infra* n. 114.
110 Per Lord Justice Clerk Hope in *Craigie* v *Marshall* (1850) 12 D. 523 at 536.
111 *Craigdallie* v *Aikman* (also known as *Davidson* v *Aikman*) (1805) Mor. 14584; (1813) 1 Dow 1, 3 ER 601, 5 Paton 719; (1820) 2 Bligh 529, 4 ER 435, 6 Paton 618.
112 Per Lord Meadowbank in the Campbelltown case, *Galbraith* v *Smith* (1837) 15 S. 808 at 827.
113 These are reviewed Innes I, 327–43, II, 222–31, in Lord Meadowbank's opinion *supra* n. 112, and in the opinions in *Smith, Moderator of the General Assembly of the Free Church of Scotland, et al.* v *Morrison, et al.* [2011] CSIH 52, *infra* n. 151.

although it had not so been in the Court of Session.[114] *Craigdallie* established that questions of ecclesiastical property were to be decided according to the ordinary rules of the law of trusts. That meant that where a union involved a change in the church's basic principles, a minority could block it and retain the property.

The principles of *Craigdallie* were applied in later cases. *Galbraith v Smith*, the Campbelltown case (1837) 15 S. 808; (1839) 5 D. 665, added little to the law in that the court applied the 'original principles' test, but decided that it had not been proved that the Relief Church had departed from its original principles. The case is of main interest in the observations of Lord Meadowbank in the earlier stage of the case since he had been counsel for the Synod in the *Craigdallie* case.[115] What was important was not numerical superiority, or a greater sum contributed by parties, but: 'their adherence to the original principles which it was their professed object to maintain in the constitution of the trust'. There might be limits in that it was possible that a church might have the power to reform its doctrines through its governing body.[116] Lord Meadowbank was, however, of the view that it could be assumed that the governing body of a church will adhere to the principles of the sect, and hence adherence to it, and therefore in Presbyterian systems the will of the majority involves adherence to the original principles. That view was roughly treated by Lord Justice Clerk Hope in *Craigie v Marshall* (1850) 12 D. 523, the Kirkintilloch case, as confusing adherence to a governing body of a church with adherence to original principles.[117] Lord Meadowbank must, therefore, be treated with extreme caution. Later cases have followed the Justice-Clerk.

Craigie v Marshall is subsequent to the Disruption cases, and differs from the earlier cases. In it the title in issue placed main emphasis upon the congregation. It was held by: 'trustees and fiduciaries for behoof of the members of the Associated congregation in Kirkintilloch, commonly called Seceders, and presently in connection with the United Secession Church'.[118] Had the congregation to go into a proposed union? The weight of judicial opinion took matters well beyond congregational affiliation indicating that the question at issue was the adherence of the congregation to the original principles, and not adherence to a formal church structure, or to the judicatures of a given church.[119]

Craigie has other important elements, for part of the question at issue was the very propriety of church union. In short, the Court saw no duty to seek union. The Lord Justice Clerk stated:

> . . . any congregation in the circumstances of this one is entitled to refuse to submit themselves to any such changed government, or to concur in any such union. This is in my opinion the leading and most fundamental principle of all such congregations . . .

---

114 Contrast the US position where the courts are (I believe) more reluctant to enter into such matters: *Watson v Jones*, (1872) 13 Wall. 679; *Presbyterian Church v Hull Church* (1969) 393 U.S. 440; *Jones v Wolf* (1979) 443 U.S. 595. See generally 'Notes: Judicial Intervention in Disputes over the Use of Church Property' (1962) 75 *Harv L. Rev* 1142–86; L.J. Sirico, Jr, 'Church Property Disputes: Churches as Secular and Alien Institutions', 1986 55 *Fordham L. Rev* 335–62; J.T. Noonan, *The Believer and the Powers That Are* (New York, London: Macmillan, 1987).
115 It may be noted that at the end of his opinion, Meadowbank confesses that he had only opened the papers in the case on the previous day: (1837) 15 S. 808 at 831.
116 For some this has provided a way out of the difficulties inherent in an unduly strict application of the 'original principles' concept.
117 Per Lord Justice Clerk Hope, *Craigie v Marshall* (1850) 12 D. 523 at 539–43.
118 *Supra* nn. 16 and 50.
119 See particularly Lord Justice Clerk Hope, *Craigie v Marshall* (1850) 12 D. 523 at 539–43.

The desire to keep separate – to keep one sect apart from all others – as in itself a good way strictly to maintain certain peculiar opinions, especially if of a severe and stern character – may be unreasonable – it may be to many unintelligible – it may appear idle caprice: But it is the first privilege of every congregation of such a body.[120]

Lord Moncreiff thought similarly. Property remained with those who adhered to the original principles. They might refuse to concur in any union of churches and might stay out without penalty of losing their buildings and assets. The union proposed in *Craigie* would clearly have involved a departure from original principles, but even without that the congregation was not bound even to inquire into the differences between the sects. The fact that the two were separate was proof enough of difference, and justified their refusal to go with the ruling judicatories of their own sect into union.[121]

A further step was taken in the Thurso case, *Couper* v *Burns* (1850) 22 D. 120. Church union was again involved. Principle was again expanded. The unanimous decision of the Inner House was that a dissentient minority was not bound to unite even with a body whose principles were the same as their own. It was, however, necessary that the dissentients should act timeously, otherwise they would be presumed to have acquiesced in the union. In the Carnoustie case that was not done.[122]

It is of course possible to consider these cases from a different viewpoint. On one plane the question is of trust and change of trust purposes, but, viewing the church as a developing organism, the identity of the church was at issue. That is seen where churches have been regarded as keeping or losing their individual identities in relation to 'third party' property. The point arose in relation to the Ferguson Bequest Fund, but unfortunately was not fully clarified. In 1856 the Ferguson Bequest was left to Trustees for particular purposes. In *Wallace* v *The Ferguson Bequest Fund* (1879) 6 R. 486 a question arose over the share of the Fund appropriate to the Reformed Presbyterian Church. In 1863 that church split on members' involvement in civil functions, and the Trustees recognised the majority as the church to benefit from the Trust. In 1865 and 1876 the minority sought participation in the Fund's benefits, but were refused. However, in 1876 the majority united *quoad sacra*, though not *quoad civilia*, with the Free Church. The minority then argued they were entitled to participate in the Fund to the exclusion of the majority. The Trustees applied for directions. The Court eventually decided that the principles of the Reformed Presbyterian Church should not be narrowly construed, and that both forms of that church ought to participate in the Fund in proportion to their respective numbers. Despite the schism, there had not been such a departure from identity as took either part of the former church outwith the purposes of the trust.

Later in *The Ferguson Bequest Fund* v *The Congregational Union* (1899) 1 F. 1224, 6 SLT 236, the tenets of would-be participants in the Fund were investigated. It was decided that irrespective of name, and of entry into the federal union of the Congregational Union of Scotland, only congregations that held principles according with those of the Congregational Church as designated in the trust deed ought to participate in the Fund. The question was once again one of identity. The 'Congregational Union' included congregations holding beliefs different from those held by the congregations designated by the testator. The

---

120 *Craigie* v *Marshall* (1850) 12 D. 523 at 547–8.
121 *Craigie* v *Marshall* (1850) 12 D. 523 at 558–61, 567.
122 *Cairncross* v *Lorimer*, or *Cairncross* v *Meek* (1858) 20 D. 995; aff'd (1860) 22 D. (HL) 15, 3 McQ. 827.

'newcomers' did not come within the scope of his provision and therefore could not share in the benefits of the Fund.

The Free Church cases, 1904

The union in 1900 of the Free Church and the United Presbyterian Church produced a major statement as to 'original principles'. *Bannatyne and Others* v *Lord Overtoun and Others*: *MacAlister and Others* v *Young and Another* (1904) 7 F. (HL) 1 [1904] AC 515[123] did not itself develop, amend or alter the law, and may be taken more as an application of the principles set out by Lord Eldon in the *Craigdallie* case. However, apart from its effect on the parties, its other historico-ecclesiastical importance lies in the effect it had on the new United Free Church, and on the eventual negotiations between it and the Church of Scotland leading to the union of 1929.

The facts derive from history.[124] In 1900 the United Presbyterian Church united with the major part of the Free Church to form the United Free Church of Scotland. The Free Church had been created by the Disruption of the Church of Scotland in 1843. The United Presbyterian Church had come into existence in 1847 as a union of the Relief Church and the United Secession Church.[125] As such it contained almost all the former congregations whose basis had been opposition to the principle of connection with the state. This, known as 'Voluntaryism', not only implied that a Christian church was to be self-supporting without state connection, but also active hostility to the principle of an establishment of religion for any church.

The controversy between establishment and a voluntary system was of long standing. To some extent it appears in positions taken up by not a few of those active in the Ten Years' Conflict, but at the Disruption the Free Church had set its face against Voluntaryism as a principle, albeit it had separated itself from the establishment of the time. Over the years, however, the Free Church had come to consider that schism was to be avoided, and wherever possible annulled. The presbyterian duty to unite with all who preach the Gospel purely was reasserted, and discussion began with the United Presbyterian Church as to the possibilities of union. These discussions had come to a halt in 1871 after it became clear that a large element in the Free Church were opposed to union, but they re-started in 1896, leading to the union of 1900. A minority of the Free Church Assembly dissented from that union, and ministers adhering to this group were deposed, actions being raised by the majority to evict them from their churches and manses. The minority constituted themselves as the General Assembly of the Free Church to continue the work of that church and raised actions against the Trustees of the Free Church, claiming the property of the Church, or a proportion of it.

---

123 The Appeal Cases report is more satisfactory than that of Session Cases as it prints and indexes all the documentary material in the case. The case is also printed, with full argument of counsel, in R.L. Orr, ed., *The Free Church of Scotland Appeals* (Edinburgh: Macniven and Wallace, 1904). Orr is not easy to use as it prints material *in gremio* of the speeches.
124 A. Stewart and J.K. Cameron, *The Free Church of Scotland, the Crisis of 1900* (Edinburgh: Hodge, 1910, Knox Press, 1989); K.R. Ross, *Church and Creed in Scotland: The Free Church Case, 1900–04, and its Origins* (Edinburgh: Rutherford House, 1988); F. Cranmer, 'Christian doctrine and judicial review: the Free Church case revisited', 2002 Ecc LJ 318.
125 The United Secession Church was formed in 1820 of the Associated Synod and the General Associated Synod, basically the New Light elements of the Burgher and Anti-Burgher Seceders.

Two actions were involved. *Bannantyne* v *Overtoun* (1902) 4 F. 1083 was raised by the continuing Free Church Assembly and officials delegated to prosecute the action against the General Trustees of the Free Church as individuals and as holding office within the United Free Church. It sought payment or transfer of the whole assets of the property held in trust for the Free Church. *Young* v *MacAlister* was initially raised by the Trustees for the United Free Church and its officials against the trustees of the Free Church in whose name title to the Free Buccleuch and Greyfriars Church stood in terms of the Free Church Model Trust Deed.[126] The two cases, therefore, dealt with virtually the whole assets of the Free Church, the property held centrally by its General Trustees, and the property held by local trustees in terms of the Free Church Model Trust Deed. Beyond that there were some churches whose title was taken in special terms, but these were not the subject of action at this time.

Because they proceeded substantially upon the same grounds, the two actions were conjoined. The Free Church argued that the United Free Church had no title to the property because the property of the Free Church had been held in trust, requiring in terms of the Summons, 'In the First Place', that:

> no part of the said lands, properties or funds so vested might lawfully be diverted to the use of any other association or body of Christians, or at least of any other association or body of Christians not professing, adhering to, and maintaining the whole fundamental principles embodied in the constitution of the said Free Church of Scotland without the consent of the said Free Church of Scotland, or at least without the unanimous assent of the members of a lawfully convened General Assembly of the said Free Church . . .

Since:

> . . . the association or body of Christians calling itself the United Free Church of Scotland is an association or body of Christians associated under a constitution which does not embody, adopt, and provide for maintaining intact the whole principles which are fundamental in the constitution of the said Free Church of Scotland . . .

it followed that

> . . . the said United Free Church of Scotland has no right, title or interest in any part of the said lands, property or funds . . .

and former members of the Free Church adhering to the new church had lost their beneficial interest in both the funds and property.

Other claims were made in both cases, but the whole issue boiled down to whether the United Free Church held to the whole original principles of the Free Church of Scotland as constituted in 1843. If it did not, then it had no right to the property that it had purported to take over from that Church along with the bulk of its members and ministers.

---

126 Young was selected from four cases raised as test cases by the United Free Church. One of these is reported: *The United Free Church of Scotland* v *McIver* (1902) 4 F. 117, which was simply decided in accordance with *Bannantyne*. The Free Church Model Trust Deed is discussed Innes II, 249–53.

The question had two grounds. In the first place, the Free Church contended that, based on the Twenty-third Chapter of the Westminster Confession, the principle of a National Establishment of Religion was a fundamental tenet of the Free Church. Because that was a fundamental, essential and distinctive principle, the General Assembly had had no power to unite with a church which did not hold to that principle, or to admit persons who did not hold such principle to share in the Free Church trust funds and properties. Nor could it deprive the dissentient minority of the right to share in the funds. On the contrary, union with the United Presbyterians necessarily involved the forfeiture of all right, title and interest in and to the funds, by reason of breach of trust.

In the second place, the Free Church drew attention to the terms in which the United Presbyterian Church required subscription of the Westminster Confession of Faith. At its inception in 1847, that Church had, by Head 2 of its Basis of Union, declared that the Westminster Confession of Faith and the two catechisms (the Longer and Shorter Catechisms) were the authorised faith of that church, and 'contain the authorised exhibition of the sense in which we understand the Holy Scriptures'. No approval was given to anything in these documents that taught intolerant principles in religion.[127] In 1879 there had been a further modification, which was made compulsory in the formula of subscription.[128] In particular this Act departed from the doctrine of pre-destination as set out in the Westminster Confession in favour of an Arminian view.[129] In 1892 the Free Church Declaratory Act (No. 8 of Class II) had recognised liberty of opinion on matters in the Confession which did not enter into the substance of the faith, the Church having the power to determine what points fell within such category.[130] These contradictory elements from the uniting churches were both included in the constitution of the United Free Church, its members being able to choose their own standpoints. This allowed doubt to be cast upon the whole relation of the new church to the Westminster Confession itself, adherence to which was stated to be a fundamental principle of the Free Church.

The United Free Church argued that the establishment principle had not been a fundamental, essential and distinctive principle of the Free Church, and that even if it had been, the Free Church General Assembly had had power to depart from that principle, and had exercised it. The 1892 change in the Declaratory Acts had not altered the Confession, being not inconsistent with it, and merely declaratory of its meaning as understood by the United Presbyterian Church. The proper procedures for union had gone through in the two churches, and the minority of the Free Church were bound either to accede to the union, or to forfeit their right to the property involved.

The Lord Ordinary, Lord Low, and the Second Division of the Court of Session (Lord Moncreiff being absent) decided in favour of the United Free Church.[131] Lords Trayner and Low, and the Lord Justice Clerk, Lord Kingsburgh, considered that the establishment principle was not one fundamental to the Free Church, and might therefore be departed from. Lord Young went further. There was nothing in law 'to prevent a dissenting church from abandoning a religious doctrine or principle, however essential and fundamental, or from

---

127 United Presbyterian Church Basis of Union, [1904] AC 515 at 752, App. J; and more fully United Free Church 1900, Act I; Cox, 441.
128 U.P. Church Declaratory Act 1879, [1904] AC 539: Cox, 435–6.
129 Orr's Report, *supra* n. 123, 254–5, speech of Mr Johnston.
130 'Act anent the Confession of Faith', GA Free Church, 1889–93, 478–9; Macleod *supra* n. 20, 211–2 [1904] AC 543. The Act was modified in 1894 [1904] AC 544. Cox 436–7. See *supra* n. 19.
131 (1902) 4 F. 1083.

returning to it again without qualification or modification'.[132] There might indeed on occasion be property effects, but where the property was given *ex facie* absolutely to a church, the court ought not imply a condition that the property was to be held in trust for original principles. Lord Trayner considered that the establishment principle had existed at the inception of the Free Church, but that it was not fundamental and had been departed from.[133]

The appeal to the House of Lords in both cases was heard twice due to the death of Lord Shand.[134] There was some evidence that at the end of the first hearing before six Lords of Appeal their Lordships were equally divided, in which case the decision of the Court of Session would have stood. Lord Shand, who was said to be in favour of the United Free Church, died before he had signed his judgement. There had to be a re-hearing. This and the 'altered result' are common grounds of criticism of the decision among church writers. But, whatever the facts as to the change, I am of the opinion that the 'second decision' was both right and legally correct. As Lord Robertson stated, the re-hearing had left the House in a much better position to deal with the question because at it the judges had been given copies of all the historical documents relied on in argument.[135] Incredibly it appears that this had not happened during the first hearing, though it seems elementary that a decision on a complex matter – which the case was – is better taken if one sees the text of the documents involved.[136]

The ratio of the decision was clearly a holding that the establishment principle was an original principle of the Free Church, from which, constitutionally, it did not have power to depart against the wishes of a minority. This fundamental and essential principle had been breached by the purported union, and, in the opinion of the five judges in the majority in the House of Lords, it followed that the United Free Church, and those former members of the Free Church who had joined it, had lost their right title and interest in and to the whole funds and properties held in trust for the Free Church.[137] Lords James and Alverstone did not feel it necessary or desirable to go beyond the question of establishment for the decision. Lords Davey and Robertson stated that the case might have been disposed of not only on the matter of establishment, but also on the question of the modified relationship of the office-bearers of the United Free Church to the Westminster Confession. The change from owning the Confession as the confession of the faith of the office-bearer, to acknowledging it as expressing the sense of Scripture, as acknowledged by the Church, was a fundamental change, removing the Westminster Confession from its place of authority as a standard.

The Lord Chancellor, Lord Halsbury, gave the widest ranging judgement, favouring the Free Church on the question of establishment like his colleagues. He also took up the departure from the Calvinist doctrine of predestination under the Declaratory Acts of the United

---

132 (1902) 4 F. 1083 at 1110.
133 (1902) 4 F. 1083 at 1114.
134 A. Rodger, Lord Rodger of Earlsferry, *The Courts, the Church and the Constitution: Aspects of the Disruption of 1843* (Edinburgh: Edinburgh UP, 2008) at 100–101 and related footnotes highlights the curiosity that the first appeal was set to be heard by only six judges, allowing the possibility of an equal split. The re-hearing was set for eight judges – raising the same possibility. However, Lord Kinross, then Lord President of the Court of Session, who had been invited to sit, withdrew the night before the second hearing. A letter to *The Times* of 2 June 1904 (reprinted (1904) 12 SLT (News) 31–2) had disclosed that, consulted at an earlier stage, he, then Balfour, QC, had indicated that 'there was no risk whatever' of the UF Church not being able to retain the property of the Free Church. Kinross' withdrawal resulted in the second appeal being heard by seven judges, only one, Lord Robertson, with a Scottish background.
135 Lord Robertson, 1904 7 F. (HL) 1 at 53; [1904] AC 515 at 686.
136 T.M. Taylor, 'Church and State in Scotland', 1957 Jur. Rev. 121 at 131; Fleming II, esp. 64–5.
137 I have not sought to refer to particular parts of these judgements as they require to be read as units.

Presbyterian Church of 1877 and of the Free Church in 1892, holding this to be incompatible with the Free Church principles. He went out of his way to state that the opinion of Lord Young that the court ought not to read in an implied term of principle into a transfer of property in trust could not stand in the instant case. There was no proof an argument put to the House, following Lord Young, that the Free Church had had an inherent right to change its doctrines or principles and yet retain its property. Lastly, he considered the Basis of Union of 1900, allowing the former members of the Free and United Presbyterian Churches freedom within the new United Free Church to retain their original views, made the union a 'colourable union'. The Trustees of the Free Church were not at liberty to admit to the use and benefit of the trust funds and property persons who did not hold to the principles of the Free Church.

The decision was of considerable political importance, and as has been shown in the previous chapter, affected the union of the Church of Scotland and the United Free Church of 1929. As far as the law was concerned, one may agree with the observation of Lord Ferguson, that '[t]he recent judgement applies but does not alter or amplify the existing law'.[138] Lord Eldon's statement in the *Craigdallie* case, that a trust will be enforced for the benefit of those adhering to the original principles of the trust, irrespective of their number, was applied. The Free Church case applied it to a denomination rather than a congregation for the first time, but there was no hint in the earlier cases that a different result would attach to church property as opposed to congregational property, and Lord Eldon's words could not easily be forced to bear such a meaning. The principle, therefore, was and is clear. The terms of a trust will be enforced, though it is obvious that in any given case it may be arguable as to what the original purposes and principles may consist.

In the light of the decision in the Free Church cases, many churches have been careful to write into their constitution, either in a plan and basis of union, where there has been union, or by way of Declaratory Act, the right of the church to modify its doctrinal standards, and fundamental principles. In so doing, the church does not necessarily affect property held at the time of the change – and the change itself might be challenged as a breach of the principles of the original trust – but lapse of time settles the question for prior property, and newly acquired property is held on the new form of constitution.[139] It follows that in such cases it would be much more difficult to set up an argument of fundamental breach of trust than in the Free Church case. A good example of such an avoidance of future difficulty is the United Free Church Declaratory Act, the Act anent the Spiritual Independence of the Church (1906 Act I), stating *inter alia* that the United Free Church:

> has the sole and exclusive right and power from time to time as duty may require, through her courts to alter, change, add to, or modify her constitution and laws,

---

138 J. Ferguson, 'The Scottish Church Case' (1904) 16 JR 347; cf. A.T. Innes, 'Church Law and Trust Law' (1904) 16 J.R. 314. E. Peck 'American versus British Ecclesiastical Law' (1905–06), 15 Yale LJ 255 at 262, superciliously concludes that the different US rules on such matters left US churches as living not dead branches. Cf. *supra* n. 114.
139 *Kennedy* v *Morrison and Lee* (1879) 6 R. 879, which also illustrates the point that even where a Model Trust Deed is not adhered to by a congregational title, that title may nonetheless separately provide for union or schism. A deed of trust may similarly provide: *Bannerman* v *Bannerman's Trustee* (1896) 23 R. 959. Where the constitution is a private Act of Parliament it may so provide. In other cases a private Act of Parliament may be required. Thus the difficulties of the Methodist Church in *Barker* v *O'Gorman* [1971] Ch. 215, and in the discussions between that Church and the Church of Scotland as to union (*supra* n. 35) were met in the Methodist Church Act 1976, c. xxx.

subordinate standards and formulas, and to determine and declare what these are, and to unite with other Christian Churches.[140]

It may be noted in passing that this form of language influenced that of the Articles Declaratory of the Constitution of the Church of Scotland in Matters Spiritual, the effect of which is discussed elsewhere. But where no such steps have been taken and been acquiesced in by the whole church concerned, the courts continue to apply the clear statements of the *Craigdallie* case, as reiterated by the House of Lords in 1904.[141]

The decision in the Free Church cases naturally gave rise to much controversy. It appeared that a small minority were to have property which had been contributed by many but whose descendants had chosen to join the United Free Church. Nothing daunted, the Free Church asked for the judgement of the House of Lords to be applied, and this was allowed.[142] Other actions were raised for the transfer back to its remaining adherents of the assets of the former Free Church.[143] But it was quite apparent that the 30 remanent congregations of the Free Church could not either support or administer all the property which they had just successfully claimed. Parliamentary action was the only way out. A Royal Commission found that only the United Free Church was in any position to fulfil the purposes of the trusts involved.[144] In 1905, therefore, the Churches (Scotland) Act set up a special Commission to allocate property between the Free and United Free Churches on an equitable basis.[145] In general, where one-third of a former Free Church congregation wished to remain in that denomination, the property was allocated to the Free Church, but s. 1(2) gave power to vary from this norm where the presence of numerous buildings in a locality or other circumstances made this sensible. Under s. 2, Orders made by the Commission were registrable in the appropriate Sasine Register and operated either as transfers of property to the United Free Church or as confirmation of the title of trustees for the Free Church as required. The Commission took 10 years to cover all the properties in dispute, but eventually the Free Church was left adequately financed with a manageable number of church properties, and with college property sufficient to train the number of ministers required for its size.[146]

Given the stramash of the 1904 Free Church cases, it was prudent that at the union in 1929 between the United Free Church and the Church of Scotland there was no question

---

140 See Appendix to the Basis and Plan of Union, 1929, Cox, 392.
141 *Ness* v *Miller* (1912) 2 SLT 263.
142 *General Assembly of the Free Church* v *Lord Overtoun* (1904) 7 F. 202. Overtoun asked for delay as there were moves to overrule the decision by parliamentary action, which eventually produced the 1905 Churches (Scotland) Act as described below.
143 *General Assembly of the Free Church* v *Johnston* (1904) 7 F. 517, *General Assembly of the Free Church* v *Rainy* (1904) 12 SLT 387. A list of the actions was compiled for the House of Commons (*United Free Church and the Free Church of Scotland (Litigation)* 1905 HC 148), for the use of Sir John Cheyne's Commission to settle interim possession of the properties at issue pending final determination; see the *Interim Report of the Departmental Commission on the Free and United Churches*, 1905 Cd. 2510. A number of Free Church ministers unwilling to join the new United Free Church were served with notice of eviction from their manses; see Second Reading Debates, *infra* n. 145.
144 Report of the Royal Commission on Churches (Scotland) 1905, Cd. 2494 (Evidence printed Cd. 2495).
145 Second Reading: Commons, 1905 148 HC Deb. Cols 1003–70; Lords, 1905, 150 HL Deb. Cols 840–882; Lords Ctee stage 1905 151 HL Deb. Cols 231–8. These summarise the whole matter. There were ancillary problems as to Income Tax and its recovery: *Free Church of Scotland* v *Macknight's Trustees*, 1914 2 SLT 236, 1915 3 SLT 237.
146 Report of the Royal Commission appointed under the Churches (Scotland) Act 1905, 1910 Cd. 5060; its Proceedings, Cd. 5061.

of court action, provision being made for the minority of the United Free Church which decided to stay out of that union.[147]

There followed a lull.

In 1952 property questions recurred in an unreported case, *MacKay* v. *MacLeod*. There had been a schism in the local congregation and a claim was made to property of the Free Presbyterian Church in Inverness. It was not successful.[148]

Half a century later such questions still trouble the courts. In 2000 a division within the Free Church gave rise to two sets of court cases. Their shared basis was that in the 1990s a disciplinary process had been initiated against one of the staff of the Free Church College (later to be elected principal of the College). Following its own investigations, and after a parallel case in the Edinburgh Sheriff Court, the General Assembly of the Free Church decided the evidence in the matter was insufficient. It declared the matter closed and directed that no further action be taken. Later it decided that any further pressing of the question would constitute contempt of the Assembly. Notwithstanding, some continued to argue that the matter had not been fully dealt with, thus damaging the work and witness of the Free Church. A disciplinary process was initiated on the ground that this was divisive and a potential breach of ordination vows to be subject to the decisions of the Church. Those cited in that process then withdrew from the Free Church and formed the Free Church (Continuing).[149]

In *The Free Church of Scotland (Continuing)* v *General Assembly of the Free Church of Scotland* [2005] CSOH 46, 2005 SC 396, the Free Church (Continuing) lodged a claim to the entire centrally held assets of the Free Church of Scotland.[150] Mirroring the argument of the Free Church in 1904 it argued that it represented the true Free Church. The 'other' Free Church and its Assembly had failed properly to exercise its functions and in particular had not recognised the right of continued protest. These flaws meant that the 'Free Church' was no longer true to its basic principles and was in contravention of the constitution of the Free Church. Alternatively it asked for an appropriate share of the assets. They were unsuccessful. Lady Paton held that no relevant case had been pleaded. Although questions of religion were involved as to which she expressed no view, they had to be viewed as facts in a property case. Neither side had departed from the fundamental tenets of the Free Church. A right of continued protest did not form part of these principles. The Free Church continued to hold its property. Further, while in terms of fundamental tenets the pursuers had not generally forfeited their rights in the Free Church assets, their failure to comply with the discipline and government of the Church meant there was no relevant case for the apportionment of those assets between the parties. The action was dismissed. The decision was not appealed.

The 2005 case had had to do with the central assets of the Free Church of Scotland. In *Smith, Moderator of the General Assembly of the Free Church of Scotland, et al.* v *Morrison,*

---

147 Fleming II, 121.
148 See para 51 of the Opinion of Lady Paton in the 2005 Free Church case, [2005] CSOH 46, *infra* n. 150; para 54 of the Opinion of Lord Uist in the later Free Church case [2009] CSOH 113, and paras 19–25, 31, 69, and 117–20 of the judgments in the Inner House, [2011] CSIH 52, *infra* n. 151. Cf. para 52 of *Shergill* v *Khaira* [2014] UKSC 33.
149 Twenty-six ministers and about 650 members formed the 'Continuing' Free Church. The remaining 'old' Free Church had 147 ministers and c. 4,500 members. F. Cranmer, 'Christian doctrine and judicial review: the Free Church case revisited' 2002 Eccles. LJ 318 at 329–30 gives more background data.
150 Reference point, *supra* nn. 57 and 107. F. Cranmer, 'The Free Church of Scotland (Continuing): a note', 2007 Eccles LJ 94; G. Junor, 'Church heritage – law and religion' 2008 SLT (News) 167.

et al. [2009] CSOH 113; [2011] CSIH 52, the property in issue was specific – the church and manse of the Strath Free Church at Broadford on the Isle of Skye.[151] This had been donated in 1869 by a feu disposition to trustees for the Free Church congregation at Broadford. In 2001 that congregation had united with the neighbouring congregation at Sleat. In 2002 the Rev. Allan McIver, the minister, and some of the congregation joined the Free Church (Continuing) and the Free Church suspended him from its ministry. Notwithstanding, McIver and his group continued to occupy the properties until he retired in 2007. As the local members of the Free Church (Continuing) proposed to continue to use the property, the Free Church sought a declarator as to its ownership and interdict against its unlawful use by the Free Church (Continuing).

In the light of Lady Paton's decision in 2005 as to the central assets of the Free Church, the Free Church (Continuing) did not argue that the Free Church had departed from its original principles. They did, however, argue that the Free Church intended the property to be held for a congregation that was meeting at Sleat, not one meeting at Strath. By contrast they themselves continued to use the property at the Sleat location and for the purposes defined by the Feu Charter. In a lengthy Opinion Lord Uist held these arguments unfounded.[152] The united Strath/Sleat congregation did still fulfil the purposes of the trust constituted by the Feu Charter. Further, he considered that a group leaving an association while still holding to the original fundamental principles of the larger body did not retain rights in property that they might in fact occupy, if the original association continued to adhere to those original principles. By setting up a structure separate and distinct from the Free Church, the Free Church (Continuing) had lost right in the property. The Free Church (Continuing) was not the Free Church identified in the feu charter. To hold otherwise would allow successive groups, while adhering to the fundamental principles of the Free Church, to leave that denomination on whatever grounds they considered sufficient, and carry with them any properties of which they had possession. Accordingly Lord Uist concluded that there was nothing to go to proof and that the defences of the Free Church of Scotland (Continuing) were irrelevant. He granted decree for the Free Church.

The Free Church of Scotland (Continuing) appealed. Lords Osborne and Drummond Young delivered long and exhaustive opinions with which Lord Bonomy concurred.[153] The appeal was refused. Both Lords Osborne and Drummond Young carefully analysed that long line of previous church property cases, drawing out their reasoning and background circumstances. Their conclusion was that in such cases, all depends upon the particular terms of the trust under which the property is held.[154] In *Strath/Sleat* the parties were not divided in theology and, within their separate existences, followed the practices and procedures of the pre-2002 Free Church. However, the title provided for the property to be held in trust for

---

151 Reference point *supra* nn. 58 and 107. More extensively see F. Lyall, 'Non-established church property in Scotland: a further case' (2010), 14 Edin. L. Rev. 113–6.
152 *Smith et al.* v *Morison et al.* [2009] CSOH 113: 2009 SLT 973.
153 *Moderator of the General Assembly of the Free Church of Scotland* v *Interim Moderator of the Congregation of Strath Free Church of Scotland (Continuing)* [2011] CSIHH 52; 2012 SC 79. F. Lyall, 'Non-established church property in Scotland: the Sleat appeal', 2012 Edin. L.R. 259; G. Junor, 'Church heritage, law and religion: an update', 2012 SLT 54.
154 Cf. *Shergill* v *Khaira* [2014] UKSC 33, where in a case as to a Sikh Trust the Supreme Court unanimously decided that where questions of property were involved, UK courts could on an objective basis consider religious issues in order to determine such questions. To that extent and as previous cases had demonstrated, questions of religious belief were not non-justiciable.

Outside establishment 131

those acting in accordance and complying with the institutional structures and procedures of the Free Church. As Lord Uist had held, by setting up its own structure the Free Church of Scotland (Continuing) had separated itself as an institution from the Free Church. Title to the property remained with the Free Church, which was entitled to occupy its property.[155] So much for the law. However, in his last paragraph Lord Drummond Young pointed out that different Christian denominations have cooperated even in the face of doctrinal divergence. Perhaps, he suggested, given their lack of doctrinal difference the disputants should consider cooperation. The suggestion would appear to underestimate the thrawness (sc. obstinateness) of Scots who, without fundamental theological doctrinal divergence, are prone to stand on a matter of 'principle'.

Modification of trust purposes

On occasion the trust purposes may be unduly restrictive, perhaps because of change in the situation they were intended to deal with. Under these circumstances legislation can be promoted appropriately to modify the terms of the trust. In the area of religion the obvious example is the successive modification of the Baird Trust, the most recent being the Baird Trust Reorganisation Act 2005, asp. 11.[156] Secular examples exist.[157]

Failure of trust purposes

What happens when the trust purposes for which the property of a church or religious charity is held fail? In law there would be no difference between property held for a congregation, for a denomination or, indeed, for any secular trust. The property would be considered to be held for a general charitable purpose, and in the ordinary case a *cy prés* scheme would be possible.[158] Under such circumstances and in exercise of its *nobile officium* or its statutory powers[159] the Court of Session may authorise the appropriate replacement of the beneficiaries of the trust.[160] Thus in *Burnett* v *St. Andrew's Episcopal Church* (1888) 15 R. 723, a trust fund existed for the benefit of a particular Episcopal church in Brechin. A majority of the members of that congregation decided to join the Relief Church, which later joined

---

155 Though clear on the simple law, this decision is also politically intriguing. The depth and length of the main judgments raises a suspicion that the Court might have been preparing for (or attempting to discourage) the emergence of cases were the Church of Scotland to split on the question of active homosexuality in the ministry, and recourse made to the reasoning of the 1904 Free Church case.
156 The Baird Trust Order Confirmation Acts of 1939, 1957 and 1971, repealed by the 2011 Act. The Baird Trust was constituted in 1873 to support religious purposes and institutions. In its original form it refers to the Westminster Confession of Faith and 'conservative religious principles' as the basis on which potential recipients were to be judged. I have not seen its current text. Whether developments in the Church of Scotland fall within its terms is an interesting question.
157 The Burrell Collection (Lending and Borrowing) (Scotland) Act 2014, asp 4, permits items from the Collection to be loaned to other institutions although when constituting the Trust upon which the Collection was left to the City of Glasgow Sir William Burrell's Will prohibited the making of loans from the Collection.
158 Cy prés = 'near to it'.
159 Law Reform (Miscellaneous Provisions) (Scotland) Act 1990, s. 9, and the Charities and Trustee Investment (Scotland) Act 2005, asp 10, ss. 39–42.
160 In the past interested parties, occasionally the trustees involved, might approach the Court. Now, in addition, OSCR may bring the matter to the court: Charities and Trustee Investment (Scotland) Act 2005, asp 10, s. 40. See Chapter 8, 9. Charities.

132 Outside establishment

the United Presbyterian Church, and the original Episcopal church ceased to function.[161] In a *cy prés* hearing, the United Presbyterian Church claimed the fund, as representing the majority of the former members who had benefitted under the trust. However, another Episcopal church had been established in Brechin, and some members of the former church had joined it. Further, the new church was the sole Episcopalian church in the town. The court sanctioned a scheme in its favour without allowing the United Presbyterian Church a proof of its averments, on the ground that it was the only body that represented Episcopalians in Brechin and the trust had been in favour of that persuasion. This seems an eminently fair decision.

In such cases all would depend on the precise terms of the trust that is claimed to have failed.[162] The Court has not been anxious to step in and authorise schemes in cases involving churches. For example in *Thomson* v *Anderson* (1887) 14 R. 1026, the Court refused to act on the application of the Original Secession Church, holding that trust purposes had not failed in respect of a particular church, although no services had been held in its buildings for some years, and it did not appear likely that services would be resumed. Again in *The Pringle Trust Petitioners*, 1946 SC 353, the Court refused to rewrite the terms of a trust deed which could continue to operate, although it was argued that a change in church law had reduced the benefit which the testator had intended to confer. In *Macleod* v *Clacher* 1993 SLT 168 the court did not intervene to appoint when the trust had no extant trustees but remitted the case for proof before answer.

A *cy prés* scheme is not always possible. The terms trust might be found to be so restrictive of charitable intention that the *cy prés* doctrine could not be applied. In that event the fund would fall either to the original donors or to their representatives by way of resulting trust.[163] Were either not ascertainable the property would ultimately fall to the Crown.[164] It is, however, unlikely that property would so fall where there is any credible connection to an existing body. Eventually in one reported case a multiple-poinding was

---

161 The Relief Church was one of the constituent elements of the United Presbyterian Church created in 1847 by the union of a number of small denominations.
162 Cf. *Gibson, Petitioner*, 1900 2 F. 1195, 8 SLT 157; *Burgess's Trustee* v *Crawford*, 1912 SC 387; *Anderson's Trustees* v *Lyon*, 1914 2 SLT 157; *Clutterbuck, Petitioner*, 1961 SLT 427, *Ballingall's Judicial Factor* v *Hamilton*, 1973 SC 298. If the petition is unnecessary the Court will not intervene: *Edinburgh Young Women's Christian Institute* (1893) 20 R. 894, 1893 1 SLT 104.
163 *Connell* v *Ferguson* (1857) 19 D. 482, a multiple-poinding involving claims to the whole fund, or a part (see note 165). But cf. *Bain* v *Black* (1849) 11 D. 1286, where the established Church was held entitled to a Fund originally collected to build a church, although one of its purposes had been to erect a church under the Chapel Act, the Act which had been overturned by the *Stewarton* case. This decision was not well-received, the Free Church claimants feeling harshly treated since they considered that they more truly represented the intentions of the contributors. Cf. also *Peake* v *The Association of English Episcopalians in Scotland* (1884) 22 SLR 3, where a minority was held entitled to interdict against the dissolution of the Association because its purposes had not failed. Lord Mclaren, *obiter* at 5, suggested surplus revenue might be redistributed to contributing congregations without recourse to the civil courts. Later, in *Stuart's Executors* v *Colclough* 1900 8 SLT 236, the executors of the Treasurer of the Association raised a multiple-poinding in which some former contributors claimed. The funds were held to remain the property of the Association. Cf. also *Edinburgh Young Women's Christian Institute* (1893) 20 R. 894, 1893 1 SLT 104.
164 See *dicta* of Lord Cullen, in *Anderson's Trustees* v *Scott*, 1914 SC 942; Lord Dunedin in *The Incorporated Maltmen of Stirling*, 1912 SC 887 at 891; Lord Sands in *The Caledonian Employers Benevolent Society*, 1928 SC 633 at 637. I know of no reported cases in which such trust property has actually fallen to the Crown. See A.R.G. McMillan, *The Law of Bona Vacantia in Scotland* (Edinburgh: Green, 1936); N.D. Ing, *Bona Vacantia* (London: Butterworths, 1971).

raised.[165] There the court repelled the claim of the Crown as *ultimus haeres* and allowed the United Original Seceders to try to establish their claim, which failing a *cy prés* scheme might be sanctioned.[166] One would hope that competent lawyers ensure that no similar problems trouble the courts in future.

IV. Modern forms of association[167]

Lastly, it might be considered that a way out of the difficulties traversed in the previous sections would have been for the non-established churches to seek incorporation, as have many churches in the USA. When I first wrote on these matters the short answer was that the different Christian churches and denominations saw their existence as being founded upon Christ. To seek powers and a constitution under or from the state would have been considered inconsistent with this view. Further, when most of the then non-established churches were coming into being there was little advantage to be obtained by incorporation. Their position in law was worked out in such a way that, for many, incorporation was unnecessary. Section 2 of the Church of Scotland Act, 1921, provides that 'nothing in the [1921] Act or the other Acts affecting the Church of Scotland is to prejudice the recognition of any other Church in Scotland as a Christian Church protected by law in the exercise of its functions'.[168]

Matters have now changed. New congregational groupings have appeared. Their property, heritable and moveable, can be held for each by a company limited by guarantee, which, if appropriately constituted, can also qualify as a charity within the legal requirements for such institutions.[169] The spiritual element of the new congregation continues to be the responsibility of its elders. However, the office bearers of such seceders, familiar with former structures, may find operating under secular concepts difficult. Were proposals for a statutory form of a 'Scottish Association with Limited Personality' (SALP) ever to be implemented, these matters may be reconsidered.[170] In the meantime the Scottish Charitable Incorporated Organisation, the SCIO, may also provide a suitable legal form.[171]

---

165 In a multiple-poinding any person (including trustees) holding property or funds asks the civil court to determine its beneficial ownership. Anyone with an interest is free to claim.
166 *Anderson's Trustees* v *Scott*, 1914 SC 942. I do not know the eventual outcome.
167 Reference point, *supra* n. 44.
168 This solution for non-established churches was first suggested by C.N. Johnston (later, Lord Sands), then Procurator of the Church of Scotland, in his Memorandum on how the union negotiations between the Church of Scotland and the United Free Church might proceed and the union carried through. See *Reports to the General Assembly of the Church of Scotland*, 1912, 1216–21. Cf. *supra* n. 3.
169 See Chapter 8, 9 Charities.
170 See Scottish Law Commission: *Report on Unincorporated Associations*, 2009 (SLC No. 217); *Discussion Paper on Unincorporated Associations*, 2008 (SLC Discussion Paper No 140); *Discussion Paper on Supplementary and Miscellaneous Issues relating to Trust Law*, 2011 (SLC Discussion Paper No.148). The 2009 Report contained a draft Bill which would have introduced a 'Scottish Association with Limited Personality' (SALP), which associations might choose to adopt. In March 2010 the then Scottish Minister for Community Safety indicated that since the proposals would relate to types of business association and that such matters were reserved to the Westminster Parliament under the then constitutional arrangements progress would have to await its action. Cf. the Scottish Charitable Incorporated Organisation (SCIO), the new legal form for Scottish charities registered with the Office of the Scottish Charity Regulator, the Scottish Charitable Incorporated Organisations Regulations 2011, SSI 2011 No. 44, and http://www.oscr.org.uk/about-scottish-charities/scio/, and 'Charities' *infra* Chapter 8, 9 Charities.
171 See Chapter 8 at n. 278.

6 Education

General

Education is an area within which church and state interact. The extent to which religious belief is reflected in schools and universities is important and can cause argument. In recent years the question has manifested in international treaties to which the UK is party,[1] and accordingly Scots education law complies with the UK international obligations.

Scottish education, whether primary, secondary or tertiary, has always been separately treated within the UK, and education in general is not reserved to Westminster under the Scotland Act 1998.[2] The bulk of education is broadly secular, although allowance is made for religious sensibilities. Education outwith the state system is supervised and standards are checked by the state. That is rather different from the original historical position.

---

1 1. (UN) Covenant on Economic, Social and Cultural Rights, 1966, 993 UNTS 4; 1977 UKTS 6, Cmnd. 6702; 1967 6 ILM 360: Art. 13.2 primary education to be compulsory and free, and accessible and available to levels thereafter. 2. (UN) Convention on the Rights of the Child, 1989 1577 UNTS 3, 1989 UNGA 44/25; 1992 UKTS 44, Cm. 1976; 1989 28 ILM 1456: particularly Art. 28.1 on the right to education (compulsory and free at primary level, desirable thereafter). See also *infra* at n. 117. 3. (UNESCO) Convention against Discrimination in Education, 1960, 93 UNTS 44; 1962 UKTS 44, Cmnd. 1760. Art. 1 prohibits discrimination on a variety of grounds including religion that deprives a child of the same standard of education as is generally available. Art. 2(b) permits separate educational systems or institutions for religious or linguistic reasons, offering an education in keeping with the wishes of parents, provided participation is optional, that the education conforms to standards approved by the competent authorities, in particular of the same level. 4. (European) Convention for the Protection of Human Rights and Fundamental Freedoms, Rome, 1950, ETS 5; 1953 UKTS 71, Cmd. 8130, Arts 8–11. 5. First Protocol to the European Convention on Human Rights, 1952, 213 UNTS 262: 1954 UKTS No. 46, Cmd. 9221; 1952 ETS 9; 1999 38 ILM 482. Art. 2, 'No person shall be denied the right to education. In the exercise of any functions which it assumes in relation to education and to teaching the State shall respect the right of parents to ensure such education and teaching in conformity with their own religious and philosophical convictions'. The UK has intimated a Reservation that the second sentence of Art. 2 is accepted 'only so far as it is compatible with the provision of efficient instruction and training, and the avoidance of unreasonable public expenditure': Cmd, 9221, 7.
2 Research Councils remain under Westminster: the Scotland Act, 1998, Sched. 5, C12.

History

In the beginning, education and the Church were closely connected. The arrival of the Dominican Order in the thirteenth century stimulated the Church to provide educational facilities connected with the monasteries. Soon there developed 'sang schools' and lecture schools, as well as grammar schools (often established under the auspices of a burgh administration rather than any particular ecclesiastical foundation).[3] At a higher level the universities of Scotland came into being, the pre-Reformation institutions all being founded pursuant to papal bulla.[4]

Until the late fifteenth century education was a privilege: it was neither a right nor a duty. The Roman Catholic Church was not unmindful of the importance of education even during the grosser periods of corruption, but it was civil authorities that introduced the first education statute. The Act 1496, c. 3, ordained under penalty of 20 pounds Scots, that all barons and freeholders of substance should send their eldest sons and heirs to school: 'fra thay be [from the age of] six or nine years of age, and till [to] remaine at the grammar schules quhill [schools until] thay be competentlie founded, and have perfite [perfect] Latine, and thereafter to remaine three zeirs [years] at the schules [schools] of art and jure [law], swa [so] that they have understanding of the lawes'.[5]

The Reformation was stimulating, spreading the advantages of education through the community. The doctrine of the priesthood of all believers meant that all should have access to the Word of God in their vernacular: any notion that 'the Word' was only for the few – particularly priests – was intolerable. Translation of the Bible into local languages was therefore fostered.[6] Further, the Gutenberg invention of printing by moveable type allowed both sides of the Reformation – and sectaries within each – to set out their arguments, defences and attacks in many a book and pamphlet.[7] The Scottish Reformers were keen that the youth should 'have knowledge and erudition' particularly to profit through 'the comfort . . . [of] the kirk and spouse of our Lord Jesus'. Because God no longer directly revealed things to men, the youth had to be educated so that they could read the Bible for themselves.[8] But what was taught in the schools and universities had to be 'sound', and the teachers trustworthy. Education in Scotland was therefore to be controlled by the Kirk.

---

3 My old school, Aberdeen Grammar School, dates back to 1418, and perhaps to 1157: R.W. Lockhart and J.L. McCombie, *Bon Record: A History of Aberdeen Grammar School* (Edinburgh: Birlinn, 2012), 8.
4 See below, Universities.
5 One function of the Act was to produce at least partially educated personnel to staff the lower courts of the time: W.C. Dickinson, 'Introduction' to *The Sheriff Court Book of Fife. 1515–1522*, Scot. Hist. Soc., 3rd Ser., Vol. XII (1928), ciii.
6 Luther produced a Bible in German (1522–34). English translations had begun with Wycliffe c. 1380–95, prior to the invention of printing. Thereafter publication of English translations was forbidden without ecclesiastical permission, which was refused. Printed English translations begin with William Tyndale's translation of the New Testament from the Greek and of various Old Testament books, including the Pentateuch. Tyndale was burnt at the stake in Brussels in 1536 for heresy, 14 months after Thomas More, his vengeful main antagonist, had been executed at the Tower of London for refusing to take the Oath of Supremacy to Henry VIII as Head of the Church of England: B. Moynahan, *If God Spare My Life* (London: Little, Brown, 2002). The 47 translators of the King James Bible of 1611 drew on previous efforts including, to a significant extent, Tyndale's translation. G. Campbell, *Bible: The Story of the King James Version, 1611–2011* (Oxford: Oxford UP, 2010); A. Nicolson, *When God Spoke English: The Making of the King James Bible* (London: HarperPress, 2010) – as *Power and Glory: Jacobean England and the Making of the King James Bible* (London: HarperCollins, 2003).
7 The Act 1525, c. 4 prohibited the importing of Lutheran books.
8 J.K. Cameron, ed., *The First Book of Discipline* (Edinburgh: St Andrew Press, 1972), 130 (Head V(3), para 20).

The Fifth Head of the *First Book of Discipline*, 1560/1561, sets out the financial affairs of ministers and how church assets should be used in the reformed Church. Heads V(4) to V(10), assume that education is a duty of the reformed Church. The necessity of schools is affirmed and their provision and curriculum at different levels discussed before passing on to the courses, stipends, expenses and privileges of the universities. However, although the *Book* was approved by the General Assembly, the legislature failed to enact it as law. Acts of the Privy Council as to Thirds of Benefices were substituted for the proposed financing of ordained ministers,[9] and nothing was done about education.[10] Rejection of the *First Book* was not, however, objection to its educational provisions as such, but rather turned on an unwillingness to meet the expense, including for education, it would have involved. The *Book* envisaged the surrender of former ecclesiastical properties, which many nobles had seized.[11] Also an aversion to the wide powers that the *Book*'s proposals would have given to the clergy should not be underestimated.

The *First Book of Discipline* was nevertheless significant. It took the long view, and contained many notions of which later Scottish educationists have been proud: a country-wide school system, a bursary system for 'clever poor' and a university system with entry based on merit. Grounded on a proper moral and spiritual core, education was to be compulsory for all and available to whatever level one could attain.

A basic motive of the scheme was the education of the populace in the beliefs of the Reformed Kirk. All should be able to study the Bible, and themselves come to proper convictions based on informed understanding. Anything else would have been a reversion to a system under which knowledge of the Bible was the prerogative of the few, with attendant dangers. The youth was to learn good habits through the Geneva Catechism and from being taught by approved and godly men. Their elders would also be affected: 'the exercise of the children in every church shall be great instruction to the aged' (Head V (5)). To that end Head IX 1–3 provided that every Sunday before noon the Word should be preached and in the afternoon the children should be catechised.

Elements of Head V are repugnant to modern ideas. For example, entry to a university was to be conditional not only on educational promise and proven aptitude, but also upon the production of a certificate from one's minister and teacher regarding one's 'learning, docility, age and parentage' – a system open to abuse.[12] On the other hand, though reflecting a different viewpoint today, there is familiarity in the assertion that: 'this must be carefully provided, that no father, of what estate and condition that he ever be, use his children at his own fantasy, especially in their youth-head; but all must be compelled to bring up their children in learning and virtue'.[13] Clearly the framers of the *First Book* anticipated that their

---

9 'Thirds of Benefices' was a tax levied on the income of former church estates that had been taken over by laymen at the Reformation. The revenue was supposed to help defray ministers' expenses, but was usually insufficient. See J. Kirk, ed., *The Books of Assumption of the Thirds of Benefices* (Oxford: Oxford UP, 1995); G. Donaldson, ed., *Accounts of the Collectors of Thirds of Benefices*, 1949 Scot. Hist. Soc., 3rd Ser., Vol. 42.
10 Knox, *History*, Appendix IX.
11 Marischal College, Aberdeen, was founded in 1593 by George Keith, Earl Marischal, using part of the proceeds from the Abbey of Deer, north of Aberdeen, which his family had seized following the Reformation. Marischal College was fused with Kings College, the university in Old Aberdeen in 1494, to form the current University of Aberdeen: see below, n. 15.
12 Head V (8). 'Docility' means aptitude or teachability.
13 Head V (5) *ad fin* (Head V (6) *ad med.* in some eds); P.F. Fraser, *The Law of Scotland Applicable to Personal and Domestic Relations*, 1st ed. (Edinburgh: T&T Clark, 1846), Vol. 2 (Parent and Child), 30–31; *Parent and Child*, 3rd ed. by S. Clark (Edinburgh: Greens, 1906), 89–91, cite instances of such 'compelling'.

ideas on learning and virtue were to have precedence – the core of the conflict between a parent and any educator.

Eighteen years later the *Second Book of Discipline* of 1578 ranged less widely, apparently accepting that the *First Book* would not be implemented. As to education, its comments are limited to the duty of the 'doctor' (a term embracing the function of teaching the catechism and the rudiments of religion in schools, colleges and universities) to see that the purity of the gospel was not corrupted through ignorance or evil opinions (Head V (1)-(4), (6)). In that the doctor had to be an elder of the Kirk his orthodoxy would (at least at first) be assured.[14] However, the doctor was not to preach or minister unless properly and separately qualified (Head V (6)). In addition, and crucially, schoolmasters were added to those to be alimented from the funds of the Kirk (Head IX (4)).

Such were the intentions of the Reformers. How did they work out? What follows outlines the changing responsibilities for the provision and maintenance of education, before turning to control of content.

*

Education of Scotland now has major two parts, the universities and the schools.

Universities

At the Reformation in 1560 Scotland had three universities, St Andrews, Glasgow and Aberdeen.[15] Edinburgh was to come into being in 1583.[16] The *First Book of Discipline*[17] made extensive recommendations for each of the three then existent (Head 5 (9)-(10)).[18] University officers and teaching staff were to be exempted from normal taxation, civil actions against them were to be dealt with by the university itself not the civil courts, and in criminal cases staff were to be assisted by an assessor from their university (Head V (11)).

Education should go beyond the level of schools. Head V (5) of the *First Book* stated that: 'in every notable town, and especially in the town of the Superintendent, [there] be erected a College, in which the arts, at least Logic and Rhetoric, together with the tongues be read by sufficient Masters, for whom honest stipends must be appointed'. Finance should be provided for those that needed it. The scholastic ideal was carried through for the clever into the universities. Twenty-four bursaries were recommended for every college in every

---

14 Reference point n. 39 below.
15 St Andrews was founded in 1412 by Bishop Wardlaw under a Bull of the Antipope Benedict XIII (1328–1423): R.G. Cant, *The University of St Andrews* (Edinburgh: Oliver & Boyd, 1946; rev. ed., Scot. Acad. Press, 1970). Glasgow was founded in 1451 by Bishop Turnbull under a Bull of Pope Nicholas V: J.D. Mackie, *The University of Glasgow: 1451–1951* (Glasgow: Jackson, 1954). Aberdeen was founded in 1494 by Bishop Elphinstone under a Bull of Pope Alexander VI (the Borgia Pope): R.S. Rait, *The Universities of Aberdeen* (Aberdeen: Bisset, 1895); L. Macfarlane, *William Elphinstone and the Kingdom of Scotland, 1431–1514: The Struggle for Order* (Aberdeen: Aberdeen UP, 1995).
16 R.D. Anderson, et al., *The University of Edinburgh: An Illustrated History 1582–Present* (Edinburgh: Edinburgh UP, 2003): D.A. Horn, *A Short History of the University of Edinburgh, 1556–1889* (Edinburgh: Edinburgh UP, 1987).
17 Supra n. 8.
18 The recommendations for St Andrews are the most detailed, perhaps reflecting a greater familiarity with that institution.

university: 'that is, in Saint Andrews, seventy-two bursars; in Glasgow, forty-eight; in Aberdeen, forty-eight; to be sustained only in meat upon the charges of the college' (Head V (8) ad fin).

At first professors and other university officers were assumed to be 'sound' through their being elders of the Kirk, but in due time this was tightened by requiring appointees to be approved by a commission established in the seventeenth century, to supervise the universities. Later the commission required appointees and office-holders to subscribe the Westminster Confession of Faith – a theological test – and to conform themselves to church government and the local presbytery – an ecclesiastical test.[19] At the Union this procedure was reinforced, being directly referred to in the Act of Security of 1707,[20] and it persisted for many decades thereafter. However, at his induction as Professor of Humanity (Latin) at Marischal College, Aberdeen, in 1839 J.S. Blackie signed the Confession but with express reservation that, while he signed in his public professional capacity, he did not have the theological expertise to decide on many of its articles.[21] A court case followed and Blackie was allowed to retain his post.[22] This was not acceptable to Moderates who wanted to use the theological test to debar members of non-established churches and non-believers from university posts. However, their complaints backfired, resulting in the Universities (Scotland) Act, 1853.[23] By ss. 1 and 2 the holders of lay (that is, non-theological) chairs were asked only to declare they would not seek to subvert church doctrine, and subscription of the Confession was made compulsory only for holders of the theological chairs, defined as chairs of Divinity, Church History, Biblical Criticism and Hebrew – a not unjustifiable requirement since a degree in divinity satisfied the educational requirements of the Kirk. Subscription was also retained for the holders of the office of Principal, except those of Marischal College, Aberdeen, and the United College of St Leonard's and St Salvator's at St Andrew's.[24] The position was not, however, stable. In 1859 the Lord Advocate watered down the requirements on non-theological professors, asking them only to undertake, not to oppose the Confession, or subvert the Kirk.[25]

Thereafter, theological and ecclesiastical tests in universities, colleges and schools became confused, not being finally dealt with for universities until 1932. Colleges and bodies of equivalent status, including those of the Free Church after the Disruption in 1843, operated without regard to the 1707 Act. Universities expanded the range of the courses they offered without reference to theological or ecclesiastical tests. The Universities (Scotland) Act, 1889, revised the general structure and financing of the Scottish universities.[26] The requirement of benevolence towards the Confession and the established Kirk was abolished except for theological chairs (s. 17). A commission took evidence as to the propriety and necessity of tests for university officers, principals and professors (s. 18). In 1892 it

---

19 Despite their attachment to the Confession some lost a university position because they adhered to a different denomination and would not subject themselves to presbytery. See Innes, below n. 21, at 305.
20 Quoted below at n. 46. See also Chapter 2 at n. 84.
21 A.T. Innes, 'University Tests in Scotland' (1892), 4 Jur. Rev. 301 at 304–6.
22 The case is unreported, but is noted in Innes I, 122–3 and 158–61 and Innes, *supra* n. 21, at 305–6. The jurisdiction of the civil court was not disputed.
23 Cf. Innes, *supra* n. 21; Cockburn, Journals II, 49–53; Bryce II, 172–3.
24 The universities differed as to who could present or appoint to chairs in their divinity faculties.
25 Innes, *supra* n. 21, at 306.
26 J. Kirkpatrick, 'The Universities (Scotland) Act, 1889' (1889), 1 Jur. Rev. 344.

recommended that the Declaration continue in abeyance for lay chairs.[27] Time passed. Then as part of the settlement after the Free Church case of 1904,[28] s. 5 of the Churches (Scotland) Act 1905 empowered the Church of Scotland to frame the declaration required of the holders of chairs of theology in the Scottish universities but this was removed by the Universities (Scotland) Act 1932 and the patronage of theological chairs was transferred to the relevant university courts (s. 1).[29] Further, it provided that the Declaration required by the 1707 Act 'shall no longer be necessary' (s. 5).[30] Now, the Church of Scotland is represented on committees of appointment to theological chairs, but not on appointments to lectureships.[31] However, many of the old theological chairs have fallen into abeyance, being replaced by chairs in schools of theology to which the Act does not apply.[32] The Kirk plays no role in appointment to these. The Kirk and some other denominations accept university passes in appropriate subjects as satisfying their educational requirements.[33] However, it is noticeable that most students in religious studies now intend social work, teaching and similar careers, not full-time posts in churches. All universities have chaplaincies devoted to different Christian and other faiths. Finally, several other independent institutions offer qualifications acceptable to various denominations. Some universities validate their courses.

Schools

Any national school system requires, first, the provision of educational facilities; second, an approved national curriculum; third, control of the qualifications and performance of the teaching profession, and last, decision as to the place of religious subjects within the curriculum. In Scotland cooperation between church and state has been worked out. A state school system with both denominational and ordinary schools is the distinctive element of the 'Scottish solution'. However, given the history from which it stems, it may not be a model attractive to other jurisdictions.[34]

In Scotland the influence of religion on education has declined. The state system is largely secular. Only a few privately run 'religious' schools exist and they are subject to state supervision. Within the state system ecclesiastical control has declined in curricula and in the qualifications of teachers with the limited exception of teachers in 'denominational'

---

27 *Report of the Committee on University Tests in Scotland*, 1892, C. 6970. See Innes, *supra* n. 21.
28 See Chapter 5 at n. 122.
29 D.M. Murray, *Rebuilding the Kirk: Presbyterian Reunion in Scotland 1909–1929* (Edinburgh: Scot. Acad. Press, 2000), 199–204. The 1932 Act left for local negotiation how the colleges of the former United Free Church in Aberdeen, St Andrews, Edinburgh and Glasgow were incorporated in the appropriate university. Arrangements vary. The Master of Christ's College in Aberdeen is often a local minister of the Kirk.
30 Presumably the Declaration remains optional, though I have not heard of the Declaration being made during my time. On my own appointment in 1973 I was not asked whether I wished to make it.
31 An Agreement between the Kirk and those universities with divinity faculties was registered in the Books of Council and Session on 28 March 1951. See Ordinance No. 284 (General No. 10) of the University of Aberdeen, *Acts and Ordinances Affecting the University of Aberdeen, 1858–1965* (Aberdeen: Aberdeen UP, 1966). Appointees to theological chairs need not be members of the Kirk, or Presbyterian. James P. Mackey, a laicised Roman Catholic priest, was appointed to the Thomas Chalmers Chair in the University of Edinburgh in 1980. Chalmers, a staunch Presbyterian, had led the Disruption of 1843. See Chapter 3.
32 'Theological chairs' dealt with subjects such as Dogmatics.
33 The proportion of students in divinity or theological studies that intend entry to a denominational ministry is small, and declining.
34 J. Murphy, *Church, State and Schools in Britain, 1800–1970* (London: Routledge & Kegan Paul, 1971), 112–3; J.J. Robertson, 'The Scottish Solution', in *Yearbook of Education*, 1951, 329–48 at 335.

schools. However, even that altered.[35] In state schools religious instruction as a subject is excluded from the supervision of Her Majesty's Inspectorate, though the modern curriculum now includes 'religions' as a permissible element.[36]

The Scottish solution is the product of a long process, but not a smooth development. The broad outline is, however, reasonably simple. Over the years the roles of church and state in education reversed. As state provision and financing of education increased, so the contribution of the Kirk declined. As state control of the curriculum increased, so church control dissipated. Denominational schools privately run by churches (usually non-established) and those of other civil authorities (the 'burgh schools') long resisted State encroachment unless on terms they approved. The result is an educational structure that contains elements of previous compromises and concordats.[37]

Facilities

As noted, the Reformers were keen on education. The *First Book of Discipline* (1560/1561) stressed the necessity of schools, the basic scheme of Head V (5) being that: 'every several [i.e. each] Kirk [ought to] have a Schoolmaster appointed, such a one as is able, at least, to teach Grammar and the Latin tongue, if the town be of any reputation'. In rural parishes the Reader or Minister was to teach children the basic rudiments, especially the Catechism. Needy scholars should be alimented throughout their studies through 'provision for those that be poor, and be not able by themselves, nor by their friends, to be sustained at letters, especially such as come from landward (sc. outside the towns)' (Head V (6)(4)).

Notwithstanding good intentions, the proposed parish school system did not come to full fruition. Financial backing was often lacking, but the idea was not without traction. Influential men had proposed it and schools were established in many parishes and elsewhere. The Kirk itself planted some and often petitioned the civil authorities to use the assets of the old (Roman) Church for the purpose.[38] In these efforts the Kirk was also anxious to retain authority over teachers and instructors.[39]

A Privy Council decree of 1616 directed the establishment of schools in each parish where possible, the salary of the schoolmaster being a charge on parishioners.[40] This was, however, not entirely altruistic. In part it was intended to suppress continuing Highland unrest through the teaching of English and the abolition and removal of Gaelic from schools.[41] The Act 1633 c. 5 ratified the 1616 decree and permitted the territorial bishop,[42] with the assent of the heritors, to impose a stent (a local assessment) to meet the costs of providing

---

35 *McNab v. Glasgow City Council* [2007] IRLR 476, *infra* at n. 125.
36 *Moral and Religious Education in Scottish Schools: Report of a Committee Appointed by the Secretary of State for Scotland*, Chairman W.M. Millar (HMSO, 1972) noted that the 'Scottish solution' had led to a decline in religious education in the State school system. That has continued.
37 For the early period cf. J. Durkan and J. Reid-Baxter, 'Scottish schools and schoolmasters, 1560–1633', Scot. Hist. Soc. Ser. 5, v. 19 (Woodbridge: Scot. Hist. Soc, 2013).
38 J. Scotland, *The History of Scottish Education*, 2 vols (London: Univ. London Press, 1969), I, 46–8. Many abbeys, monasteries and other estates were seized.
39 See *supra* at n. 14 as to the qualification and duties of the 'doctors'.
40 Dunlop, 461–2.
41 Another 1616 Privy Council decree ordered the principal clansmen to have their children educated in the Lowlands, a common method of ethnic absorption. Scotland, *supra* n. 38, I, 51–2.
42 This was during the period of the imposition of Episcopalian church government.

the school.[43] The Act was not particularly successful since the country was going through a period of political and religious turmoil. It should, however, be given due weight in the development of the present school system, being the first time the state, as such, authorised payment from civil revenues for the establishment of parochial schools. The two powers were approaching harmony on the dissemination of education. The next step was the Act 1646, c. 46, which required the establishment of parish schools, the duty to provide falling on the heritors (whom failing a local presbytery committee), with powers to impose an assessment to meet costs of buildings, and the schoolmaster's salary. Unsurprisingly, again given the times of its enactment,[44] the Act was also not particularly effective.[45]

Once the instabilities of the seventeenth century were past, the Act 1696 c. 26, 'an act for the settling of schools', appeared in the government's legislative programme. Largely repeating its predecessor, it began by stating as its justification, 'how prejudicial the want of schools in many places has been, and how beneficial the establishing and settling thereof in every parish will be to this church and kingdom' – an interesting co-mingling of interests. The only major change from the 1646 Act was that were the heritors to default, the local presbytery could apply to the Commissioners of Supply to settle the school and salary, such settlement being effective as if performed by the heritors themselves. The 1696 Act was much more successful than its predecessors and contributed to a large increase in the distribution of schools throughout Scotland.

At the Union in 1707 concern for educational arrangements can be seen in the extent to which they occupy the Act of Security, the Act 1707, c. 6, the 'Act for Securing the Protestant Religion and Presbyterian Church Government', passed by the Scots Parliament immediately prior to ratifying the Union with England 1707, c. 7.[46] After confirming the worship and doctrine of the Kirk, the Act continued that:

> further for the greater security of the foresaid Protestant Religion and of the Worship, Discipline of this Church as above established Her Majesty [Anne] . . . Statutes and Ordains That the Universities and Colledges of Saint Andrews Glasgow Aberdeen and Edinburgh as now established by Law shall continue within this Kingdom for ever. And that in all time coming no Professors, Principals, Regents, Masters or others bearing office in any University college or School within this Kingdom be capable or be admitted or allowed to continue in the exercise of their said functions but such as shall own and acknowledge the Civil Government in manner prescribed or to be prescribed by the Acts of Parliament. As also that before or at their admission they do and shall acknowledge and profess and subscribe to the foresaid [Westminster] Confession of Faith as the confession of their faith, and that they will practise and conform themselves to the worship presently in use in this church and submit themselves to the Government and Discipline thereof and never endeavour directly or indirectly the prejudice or subversion of the same and that before the respective Presbyteries of their bounds by whatsoever gift presentation or provision they nay thereto be provided'.

---

43 A 'heritor' was the owner of immoveable property above a certain value in a parish. The owner of separate properties might be liable several times. The stent might vary with the size of the property.
44 This was the time of the struggle between Crown and Parliament in England, followed by the occupation of Scotland by the Parliamentary forces, since for a time the Scots had supported Charles I.
45 It was rescinded at the Restoration of the Monarchy in 1660.
46 Reference point, *supra* n. 20.

Though not universally successful, the pre-Union arrangements were the legal basis of the broad spread of education in Scotland in the eighteenth century. The Act of Security remained law for over 100 years until its education provisions were repealed so far as inconsistent by the next major education Act, that of 1803.

The Parochial Schools (Scotland) Act, 1803, sought to improve the education system. However, the state confined its interest to the provision of educational facilities and establishments through local not central financing. The era in which the state would itself establish, maintain and pay for the school system, with consequent difficulties with the church, had yet to come. The Act raised the salary of schoolmasters to between 300 and 400 merks,[47] the salary was to remain fixed for 25 years and thereafter be tied to the local price for meal. Parish heritors were to provide the schoolmaster with a schoolhouse, a dwelling-house and a garden of at least a quarter of an acre.[48] To avoid the heritors prolonging a situation to save money, they were required speedily to fill a vacancy in the post of parish dominie.[49] In addition a fund was set up for the widows of schoolmasters.[50] In larger parishes 'side schools' were to be established, but the heritors were responsible only for paying their schoolmasters, and did not have to provide a house or garden for any second schoolmaster.

Education was not wholly provided by the parochial schools. Almost all burghs ran their own educational establishments, and the burgh schools were important. Owing their origin to local effort, these were not subjected to the same degree of rudimentary state control and interference. As a result they do not leave many traces in public statutes until the nineteenth century. They may be seen to exist in local legislation, and in the Kirk supervision of education.[51] This obscurity was to disappear in the new state approach to education in the reign of Queen Victoria.

In the nineteenth century the state began to take a more active role in the organisation of society. The franchise was extended. New laws were brought in to regulate the operation of factories, water pollution and so on.[52] Indeed, to ignore the general movements of the time when viewing educational development is to make that development seem extraordinary, while in fact it was a natural concomitant of other changes. Indeed, occasionally some educational developments were introduced as part of that other legislation.[53]

Interest in education was stimulated by the Commission on the Education of the Lower in the Metropolis, chaired by Lord Brougham in 1816.[54] This, which became a general Commission on the Education of the Poor at least partially thanks to the very wide interpretation given to its terms of reference by its chairman, did much to alert responsible

---

47 Between £16 and £20 Scots. The teacher was also entitled to fees from his pupils.
48 An acre is 4,840 square yards, or .404 of a hectare.
49 Possession of land at least £100 Scots in the parish attracted a share in the duty, s.22. 'Dominie' was the affectionate name for a parish schoolmaster.
50 The Act 41 Geo. Ill, c. 85 (2nd sess.) (1800) had already set up such a Widow's Fund.
51 Scotland, *supra* n. 38, I, 1–21, II 1–87, 209–27. J. Grant, *History of the Burgh and Parish Schools of Scotland* (Glasgow: Collins, 1816) gives a full picture. See also Argyll I and II, *infra* n. 67. Private schools were also active, Scotland I, 90–113, 261–301.
52 F. Lyall, 'Law and the Environment', in M. Mulhern, ed., *The Law* (2012), Vol. 13 of *Scottish Life and Society: A Compendium of Scottish Ethnology* series, 459–78.
53 Early statutes on the employment of children required that they were given basic schooling, for example the Labour in Factories Act, 1844, ss. 38 and 39.
54 Reports of the Select Committee on the Education of the Lower Orders in the Metropolis, 1816 H.C., 427, 469, 495, 491 and 498.

opinion. The evidence it gathered ranged over the whole UK, including Scotland.[55] In 1818 Brougham followed up with a Commission on Educational Endowments, which, it appears due to his conduct, tended to alienate the legislators and leaders of opinion. The French Revolution was still in the back of their minds, and in part at least their guiding idea was to keep the masses quiet.[56] An English Educational Bill introduced by Brougham in 1820 failed, both thanks to a fear lest the populace become unruly, but also because it left education in England under the general control of the Church of England, a situation abhorrent to Dissenters and Nonconformists.[57] Nonetheless, the two Brougham Commissions helped change attitudes.

The next manifestation of state interest in education was almost surreptitious. The 1832 Exchequer Estimates included £20,000 to aid local efforts in school building.[58] Scottish 'grants in aid' began two years later, and were channelled through the minister and kirk session of each *quoad omnia* parish.[59] State aid to education from public funds thus became established. This was a great help particularly to the efforts of the Kirk, the one institution then capable of taking a general view of Scotland's needs.[60]

In 1838, on the initiative of the Church, an 'Act to facilitate the foundation and endowment of additional schools in Scotland' authorised payments for the running of schools in certain Highland areas out of the monies allocated for education in Scotland. This allowed schools to be set up in new parishes whose creation had been provided for in 1823 and 1824.[61] Provision of the schoolhouse and accommodation remained the duty of the heritors, but the government was to pay the schoolmaster.

1839 saw an increase in the annual sums disbursed for education by government, and the creation of a special supervisory department. An Order in Council gave educational responsibility to a Special Committee of the Privy Council. Most importantly, grants were to be given only to schools that were open to government inspectors. The Committee had power to issue Minutes regarding the conduct of schools and for ancillary purposes. These guidances were eventually consolidated in 1860 as a Revised Code, and thereafter were issued with revisions annually, all grant-aided schools being required to conform to the Code.[62]

The number of schools increased following the 1843 Disruption of the Church of Scotland.[63] Many leaders of the new Free Church had, while in the Church of Scotland, been interested in education, and many teachers were closely linked to the new Church.[64] Given

---

55 Reports of the Select Committee on the Education of the Lower Orders, 1817 HC 419; 1818 HC 136, 356, 426, 421,428. 1819 HC 224, 3 vols, prints a digest of the Parochial Returns to the Committee's questions.
56 H. Craik, *The State in Its Relation to Education* (London: Macmillan, 1896), 12 (the author had been the Secretary to the Scotch Education Department; see Scotland, *supra* n. 38, II, 25–7).
57 Craik, *supra* n. 56, 13.
58 Craik, *supra* n. 56, 15–17.
59 A *quoad omnia* parish had responsibilities for preaching, for poor relief and for education.
60 The Kirk had been put on its mettle by the evidence accumulated by the Brougham Commission and in 1824 had set up its own Educational Committee, which had settled schools in various parts of the country. State grants are always useful.
61 The Churches in Highlands Act, 1823, as amended by the Church of Scotland Act, 1824. The new schools were known as 'Parliamentary Schools' by reason of their genesis.
62 Evidence of Ralph R.W. Lingen, Secretary of the Privy Council Committee on Education, *infra* n. 67, Argyll I, 32 ff.; Argyll II, lii–cxii; Scotland, *supra* n. 38, I, 231–9. The Privy Council Committee later became the Scotch Education Department under s. 1 of the Education (Scotland) Act, 1872.
63 On the Disruption see Chapter 3.
64 In his massive *Annals of the Disruption* Thomas Brown devotes a full chapter and many other comments to education: T. Brown, *Annals of the Disruption* (Edinburgh: MacNiven & Wallace, 1892), 309–26. See also

the manpower among the teachers who 'came out' in 1843 and also given, at first at any rate, a leadership intent on building up its movement, it is not surprising to find that at the end of 25 years,

> there are connected with and supported by the Free Church 598 schools (including two normal [secondary] schools), with 633 teachers and 64,115 scholars. The results of the examination of schools receiving grants from the Privy Council by Her Majesty's inspectors, according to the revised code, show that the Free Church schools stand at the top of the elementary schools both in Scotland and in England.[65]

Nonetheless, even with the Free Church, the Kirk, special societies, such as the Gaelic Schools Society and the Scottish Society for the Propagation of Christian Knowledge, the burgh and parliamentary schools and those run by individuals, the mid-Victorian picture of Scottish education, while comparatively speaking good, was not yet sufficient. Educational facilities were not yet available throughout the country, and educational standards varied greatly. Further, while elementary education was fairly widely accessible, secondary education was of more limited availability.

Some defects of the educational system were attacked in an Act of 1861, which is better considered in connection with the control exercised over educational content.[66] Here it is enough to note that teachers' salaries were raised. The next major step was the establishment of a Royal Commission on Education in Scotland under the Duke of Argyll, which sat from 1864 to 1867, publishing three reports and volumes of evidence. The two main reports of the Commission dealt with elementary schools and burgh and middle-class schools, and in each category comprehensive surveys were carried cut by Assistant Commissioners who actually visited many of the schools concerned.[67]

The Argyll Commission made a series of wide-ranging and radical recommendations.[68] These included: a Board of Education to supervise the building of schools and to advise the Privy Council Special Committee on the distribution of the grant in aid; public schools to be established and partially supported by the rates (local property taxes); annual school inspections by a government inspectorate; and a new system of educational streaming from elementary school to employment.

In 1869 Argyll introduced a Bill to give effect to most of the Commission's recommendations, but it lapsed, as had other less important education bills in previous years. It was not until 1872 that a Scottish Education Act was passed. To a degree this was in the train of a similar Act for England based on the continuing work of the English Education Commission

---

N.L. Walker, *Chapters from the History of the Free Church of Scotland* (Edinburgh: Oliphant, 1895), 113–30. Cf. Statistics of Schools in Scotland collected by the Registrars of Births, Deaths and Marriages (1867 H.L. 3845 – V) and Digest of Parochial Returns to the Brougham Committee, 1818 (1819, HC 224, Vol. 3, 1275–1450).

65 Brown (*supra* n. 64), 324, quoting an official report. Thus Moray House College of Education, Edinburgh, was founded as a Free Church teachers training college in 1847, Walker (*supra* n. 64), 128. See also D.J. Withrington, 'The Free Church Educational Scheme, 1843–50' (1966) XV RSCHS, 103–16.

66 Parochial and Burgh Schoolmasters Act 1861, *infra* at n. 94.

67 Argyll I, II and III. Reports of the Education Commission (Scotland), Chairman, The Duke of Argyle. First Report: Evidence. 1865 [PP 3483 and 3858]; Second Report: Elementary Schools. 1867 [PP 3845] with Reports of Assistant Commissioners [3845 – I to IV]; Third Report: Burgh and Middle Class Schools, 1867–8 [PP 4011].

68 Argyll II, *supra* n. 67, clxxiii–clxxxv.

reports initiated by Lord Brougham.[69] However, strenuous efforts secured that the Scottish Act did not simply translate the ideas of the English Commission into Scottish terms. Indeed the delay between the English and Scottish Acts allowed defects of the English Act to be avoided.[70]

The Education (Scotland) Act, 1872, marks an important stage in the development of education in Scotland, being the point at which the state took over major responsibilities for the provision and maintenance of the school system.[71] From it state interest becomes paramount, with a consequent diminution of the role of the Church. Private schools and independent denominational establishments continued, particularly those run by the Roman Catholic Church and the Episcopal Church in Scotland, but over the years differences in scholastic standards and training between these and the State schools began to have effects.

The 1872 Act was a wider enactment than the English Act of 1870. It envisaged a complete system of education and not merely a filling in of gaps in the existing system. Education was to be universal (ss. 26–36), and, at the elementary level, compulsory (ss. 9, 70 and 72). Teachers had to be of proven competence if they were to occupy positions of authority (s. 56), and a system of certification of teachers was introduced (ss. 57–9). Last, provision was made for further education (s. 40) and for industrial schools (s. 41) within the State system.

The 1872 scheme was put into operation by a radically reconstructed educational system. The Privy Council Committee on Education for Scotland became the Scotch Education Department with general supervisory functions (s. 1). A Board of Education was set up to see to financial and administrative matters (ss. 3–7). At the local level, school boards were created for school districts, largely based on the former parish and burgh school areas (ss. 8–11), board members being elected by local government electors by cumulative vote (s. 12).

School boards were to provide and maintain public schools adequate for the needs of their area (ss. 26–37). They took over all existing burgh and parish schools and all powers of presbytery over these schools were abolished (ss. 23–4). In addition s. 38 permitted private schools, including those run by non-established denominations, to be transferred to the new authority. However, while the managers of those schools might transfer them to the local school board and thereafter escape liability for their maintenance and upkeep, such transfer could only be by way of gift. School boards were prohibited from purchasing such institutions. This led to less use of the s. 38 provisions than had been hoped. Many private schools simply went out of existence, their premises sold rather than being given away.[72] Where a school was transferred under s. 38 its endowments and funds passed with the property, and former contributors to such schools were not relieved of their liability (ss. 39, 46). If endowments were insufficient to meet the needs of a board, to make up the deficiency a school

---

69 Elementary Education Act, 1870. Craik, *supra* n. 56, 88–105.
70 Craik, *supra* n. 56, 154–60 gives comparisons, as does Scotland, *supra* n. 38, I, 366. On the formation of the Scottish Act see J.D. Myers, 'Scottish Nationalism and the Antecedents of the 1872 Education Act' (1972, 4 Scot. Educ. Stud. 73–92; B. Lenman and J. Stocks, 'The Beginnings of State Education in Scotland' (1972), 4 Scot. Educ. Stud. 93–106; D. Withrington, 'Towards a National System, 1867–1972: The Last Years in the Struggle for a Scottish Education Act' (1972), 4 Scot. Educ. Stud. 107–24; and his 'The Making of the 1872 Act', Times Educational Supplement, Scotland, 18 August 1972.
71 Reference point, *infra* n. 100.
72 Scotland, *supra* n. 38, II, 41–3. Some of the premises were not worth taking over. It was easier for the school boards to expand the premises of the larger local institutions.

rate might be levied as part of the usual local rating assessment (s. 44). The school board was to appoint the teachers in the new state schools (s. 55) but it had no competence in the area of subjects or standards. Standards and the content of courses were matters for each school, although each had to comply with the Revised Code issued by the Scotch Education Department.[73] However, schools in receipt of government grants were required to be open to inspection, as well as conforming to the Code (ss. 66–7).

The next 40 years saw a few alterations to the system established in 1872, but these are unimportant for the present consideration. However, it became clear that further steps were needed in relation to the schools that remained outwith the state system. Their educational standards often lagged behind those of the board schools, but little could be done. Since the 1872 Act provided for these schools to be transferred to the school boards only by way of gift, there was no real incentive to their managers to make over their responsibilities. Change did not come until 1918.

The Education (Scotland) Act 1918 sought to remedy the defects of the 1872 state system. Retaining the earlier Act as the principal Act, the 1918 Act remodelled responsibilities for education, and consolidated the amendments to it. New local education authorities were created for Aberdeen, Dundee, Glasgow, Edinburgh and Leith,[74] and for each county, and transferred to them the former responsibilities of the school boards (s. 1). Members of each new education authority were elected triennially on the same district basis as for local government, the electors having a single transferable vote (s. 23). The Scotch Education Department, renamed the Scottish Education Department, was to supervise the new authorities and was to regulate departmental grants and teachers' salaries.

Provisions designed better to bring the independent schools into the State system were in s. 18 of the 1918 Act. The new education authorities were bound to accept the transference of independent schools 'upon such terms as to price, rent or other considerations as may be agreed, or may be determined, failing agreement by an arbiter appointed by the Department [sc. of Education] upon the application of either party'. Schools so taken over had to be maintained at the same status and character for at least 10 years. In most cases preservation of character had a religious element, as will be discussed anent the control of education. Indeed s. 18 was largely the outcome of long negotiations between the government and religious denominations, particularly the Roman Catholic hierarchy. But s. 18 was not as mild as it might seem. Coercion was present for, from two years after the date of the Act, no state grants were to be paid to any school remaining independent that might have been transferred to the local authority under s. 18 (s. 18(5)).

After 1918 various Acts and miscellaneous legislation affected the provision of education facilities. Local government in Scotland was reorganised in 1929, and that brought changes in respect of education. The Local Government (Scotland) Act, 1929, vested the former responsibilities of the education authorities in local county or town councils (s. 1). These were discharged through an education committee set up in terms of s. 12(4), in which the majority were councillors. This persisted through subsequent changes in local government and were successively consolidated in the Education (Scotland) Acts of 1946 and 1962. Now the principal ruling statute is the Education (Scotland) Act 1980, as amended by a plethora

---

73 See *supra* at n. 62.
74 These burghs then operated under local Acts separate from the bulk of mainland Scotland which was under the Burgh Police (Scotland) Acts and the Local Government (Scotland) Act 1947. The Local Government (Scotland) Act 1973 applied a unified system.

of later statutes passed by both the Westminster and, following devolution, the Scottish Parliament.[75] The 1980 Act sets the structure for public school education in Scotland, laying duties on local education authorities whose area of jurisdiction corresponds with those of the territorial local authority. Operating under the Local Government (Scotland) Act 1973 as amended, these are responsible for Primary, Secondary and Further Education within their areas.[76] Each authority is advised by an Education Committee,[77] day-to-day matters being dealt with by a local Director of Education and staff. Each authority builds and owns its schools and administers their endowments. The main source of finance is a central government grant from Edinburgh, and only secondarily, the ordinary local rating machinery. Independent and denominational schools still exist, but these have to be registered, controls being possible, including as to the facilities they provide.[78]

Content and control

Broadly, church control over the content of education and the religious proclivities of teachers declines inverse to the growth of state responsibility for educational facilities.

In 1560 the *First Book of Discipline* made it clear that parents were not to have a free say in the education of their children. No father was to 'use his children at his own fantasy . . . but all must be compelled to bring up their children in learning and virtue . . .'.[79] Within the Church-based scholastic system the Kirk was to determine the scope and content of the syllabus and was to be responsible for the training and superintendence of teachers. But, as we have seen, the *First Book* did not achieve its purpose, albeit for reasons other than objection to its educational provisions. Despite this setback the Church was soon able to ensure that its approval was required for the employment of teachers in most schools, whether parochial or otherwise.

The Act 1561 c. 11 was the first statute on Kirk approval of teachers. After narrating that all constitutions so provide, and that it is for the good of both body and soul that children be brought up in the fear of God and in good manners, the Act continues:

> The Three Estates of this present Parliament has statute and ordainit that all scules [schools] both burgh and land, and all universities and colleges be reformit; and that nane be permitted nor admitted to have charge and care thereof in all time coming, nor to instruct the youth privately or openly, but sic

---

75 The 1980 Act implemented recommendations of the Scottish Law Commission Report 54, *Education (Scotland) Bill* (1980). The Education (Scotland) Act, 1981 considerably amended the 1980 Act.
76 The provision of Further Education is optional for an education authority, not a duty: Education (Scotland) Act 1981, s. 1 (2A). See also the Further and Higher Education (Scotland) Act 1992, as amended.
77 An Education Committee has three religious representatives. By s. 124 (2)(b) and (4) of the Local Government (Scotland) Act 1973, as amended most local authorities are required to appoint to their Education Committees a representative of the Church of Scotland, an official from the Roman Catholic Church, and another person interested in religion. In the first two cases the relevant church nominates a candidate for membership. The third is selected having regard to the comparative strengths of denominations in the area. In Orkney, Shetland and the Western Isles, areas that are strongly Protestant and Roman Catholicism weak, there is no requirement to appoint a Roman Catholic, and two persons are selected having regard to the comparative strengths of denominations in the area. See also *infra* following n. 115.
78 See the Self-Governing Schools etc. (Scotland) Act 1989, as amended.
79 *Supra* n. 13.

148   Education

as sall be tryed be [such as shall be tried (sc. approved) by] the superintendents or visitours of the Kirk.

Later statutes, notably the General Assembly Act, 1592, c. 8, reaffirmed the right of the Church to supervise education, and there were attempts to stop Catholic parents from sending children overseas for their education.[80]

In the seventeenth century further Acts of the General Assembly and the Scottish Parliament confirmed the Kirk's jurisdiction over the educators, the peak of this power being reached in the religious settlement of the 1690s. The Act 1690, c.25, required teachers, whether of school or of university, to subscribe the Westminster Confession of Faith exactly as was required of ministers.[81] The justification was that at that period, like ministers, teachers were considered to be public officials, holding office *ad vitam aut culpam*.[82] Three years later the Ministers Act, 1693, c. 38, gave jurisdiction over the qualifications and performance of teachers to local presbyteries, the Act 1696, c. 26, dealing similarly for new parochial schools.

All these Acts were confirmed as part of the Union settlement by the Protestant Religion and Presbyterian Church Act, 1706 c. 6, securing the Presbyterian Church government and incorporated in the Act of Union with England. Thereafter professors, masters, teachers and others holding educational office had to subscribe the Westminster Confession and conform to the Church, and were subject to supervision by the local presbytery.[83] Technically no distinction was made between parochial schools and burgh schools. However, it appears that in practice the Kirk tended to exercise its authority only outwith the larger towns.[84]

As a matter of law, ecclesiastical superintendence of schools remained static throughout the next century, though the literature and records show that supervision was patchy and not always effective.[85] Nonetheless the Parochial Schools (Scotland) Act 1803 provided for church control to continue. As under the earlier legislation, by s. 16 every schoolmaster elected to a post in a parochial school had to be approved by the local Presbytery as to morality and religion in addition to his actual qualifications in the subjects he was to teach. Should the Presbytery for any reason find an appointee unsuitable, the electors had to find an alternate (s. 17). By s. 20 each presbytery was to supervise all schools within its district, and inspect and regulate subjects, hours of teaching and the length of vacations, including in the new parochial schools the Act set up (s. 21).[86] However, presbytery powers to deal with deficiencies in the schoolmaster by censure, suspension and dismissal were restricted to

---

80 The practice was forbidden by the General Assembly of 1578. Cf. Scotland, *supra* n. 38, I, 50. See also the Act 1579 c. 71, which inflicted the pains of barratry on the sons of noblemen and gentlemen who went abroad for their education without Royal permission. There were complaints as to the practice in the Claim of Right, 1689 (1689 c. 28).

81 Erskine 1.5.24. Cf. s. 21 of the Disarming Act 1746 which *inter alia* required all masters and teachers to take 'the oaths required by persons in offices of public trust in Scotland'.

82 Sc. 'during life or good behaviour'. On teachers 'holding office' – a *munus publicum* – see *Malloch* v. *Aberdeen Corporation* [1971] SC (HL) 85, 1971 SLT 245 [1971] 2 All ER 1278; [1973] SC 227. J. Malloch, *The General Teaching Council for Scotland, House of Lords 1971 Court of Session 1973 and subsequently: litigation and politics in Scottish education 1966–1986* (Malloch, 1986).

83 As to university professors see the Blackie case, *supra* n. 22.

84 Argyll III, 9 (Report of Assistant Commissioners). Cf. *Murray* v *Donaldson* (1834) 13 S. 128; *McAlpine* v *Campbell* (1840) 2 D. 481.

85 Scotland, *supra* n. 38, I, 114–30.

86 Dunlop, 474–5.

acting on the complaint of the heritors, the minister or an elder of a parish, not parents. But despite these apparently wide-ranging powers, the 1803 Act did not increase the power of the Church. Indeed, that the authority of the Kirk had to be re-stated reflected a lessening of the effectiveness of its superintendence. Further, the 1803 Act increased the discretion of the heritors in their performance of their responsibilities, altering the balance of power between the clerics and the lay providers of educational facilities.[87]

A schoolmaster therefore had two masters, the heritors and the Kirk, with all the difficulties attendant on such a situation. In some instances this proved too awkward. In others it afforded scope for the increasing secularisation of education to proceed. The attitudes of the Kirk itself were also changing. In 1829 the Education Committee of the Church of Scotland took a step contrary to the ideas of the Reformers. It instructed schoolmasters not to 'press on the Roman Catholic children any instruction to which their parents or their priest might object, as interfering with the principles of their own religion'.[88] In 1832 the same Committee reported to the General Assembly that this step had resulted in the Protestant schools becoming more acceptable to Catholics.[89] Of course, this was part of the general move towards toleration of Roman Catholicism, but it also illustrates the trend towards the removal of religious bias in education.[90]

The 1843 Disruption brought the problems of Church supervision into the open. Many teachers left the established Church. Questions soon arose as to the appointments of schoolmasters and the right of presbytery to try their qualifications. The headmaster of Campbeltown School was deposed by the Presbytery of Cantyre because he had joined the Free Church. He sought to suspend the sentence of deposition and applied for interdict, but the Lord Ordinary held that the position fell under the jurisdiction of the presbytery under the statutes 1693, c. 22, and 1706, c. 6.[91]

The Elgin Academy case, *The Presbytery of Elgin* v *The Magistrates and Town Council of Elgin* (1861) 23 D. 287, became of crucial importance. A grammar school had existed in Elgin at least since 1585. In 1620 a Sang School, later converted into an English school, was established. In 1800 the Elgin schools were united as an academy to serve as the burgh school under the control of the Elgin Town Council. In 1844 and 1849 the Council appointed teachers without referring them for approval by the presbytery, nor requiring them to sign the Confession of Faith and Formula of Worship, omissions which the presbytery frequently and expressly protested. In addition, in 1846 the Town Council effectively breached the presbytery's right to examine the conduct of the school by having the school inspected by state inspectors two days prior to the usual presbytery inspection, and having the school shut and the children on holiday when the presbytery commissioners arrived.

Ultimately in December 1850 the Presbytery of Elgin sought a declarator that the Academy fell within the jurisdiction of the presbytery particularly under the Acts 1633, c. 5, 1690 c. 25, 1693 c. 38, 1706 c. 6, and 43 Geo. III c. 54. They also asked for declarators that the magistrates were bound to appoint as masters in the school only those found qualified by presbytery, that the judicatories of the established church had rights of trial of qualifications, as well as of supervision and of dismissal, and that the masters were under a duty to appear

---

87 Scotland, *supra* n. 38, I, 174–7.
88 Argyll II, xxx.
89 Argyll II, xxx.
90 Cf. the Roman Catholic Emancipation Act, 1829.
91 Judgement was acquiesced in. The case is reported only as a reference in the Note of the Lord Ordinary in *The Presbytery of Elgin* v *The Magistrates and Town Council of Elgin* (1861) 23 D. 287 at 299.

before the Presbytery of Elgin – 'and respectively to acknowledge and profess, and to subscribe the Confession of Faith, as the confession of their faith, and to practise and conform themselves to the worship of the Established Church of Scotland, and to submit themselves to the government and discipline thereof, and never, directly or indirectly, to endeavour the prejudice or subversion of the same . . .'.[92]

The claims of the Presbytery were comprehensive and important. If successful, they meant that the established Church of Scotland had extremely extensive rights of supervision and of interference in the working of almost all educational establishments, even in the face of the opposition of the local authorities. It also meant that teachers unable or unwilling to subscribe the Westminster Confession could not be employed. Indeed matters went even further. All Free Church members could sign the Confession (some with clearer consciences than many established Church members), but the declarators sought would require teachers to conform to the Kirk. Free Church teachers wishing to remain in post would have had to give up their denomination, the whole basis of which was dissent from the constitution of the established church.[93]

It is unnecessary to trace the progress of the case. It took 10 years, with many judgements on questions that arose. In the end, in 1861 the court found in favour of the presbytery, holding that the Academy was a public burgh school, and that by statute the teachers were subject to the jurisdiction, superintendence and control of the presbytery. But the victory was Pyrrhic. The effect was immediate and wide-ranging. The Parochial and Burgh Schools (Scotland) Act 1861 radically transformed the law.[94] For this text its most important provisions relate to the examining of candidates, and subscription of the Confession. In both respects there was great alteration.[95] Section 9 abolished the examination of teachers by presbytery, and provided for four Boards of Examiners of Parochial Schools to be appointed by the four Scottish Universities.[96] The powers of the electors to appoint to teaching posts were not affected, but their appointees had now to be approved by the relevant Board.[97] Section 12 abolished parochial schoolmasters' subscription of the Confession and the Formula of Worship. Instead they had simply to sign a Declaration binding them not to endeavour 'directly or indirectly, to teach or inculcate opinions opposed to the Divine authority of the Holy Scriptures, or to the doctrines agreed upon by the Assembly of Divines at Westminster . . .' and to '. . . faithfully conform thereto in . . . teaching at the . . . school, and . . . not exercise the functions of the said office [i.e. of schoolmaster] to the prejudice or subversion of the Church of Scotland as by law established or the doctrines and privileges thereof'. However burgh schoolmasters were also no longer required to sign the Confession, but, unlike their parochial fellows, were not required to sign the Declaration (s. 22).

---

92 (1861) 23 D. 287 at 288.
93 As to Free Church teachers see N.L. Walker, *Chapters from the History of the Free Church of Scotland* (Edinburgh: Oliphant, Anderson and Ferrier, 1895), 'Schools and Schoolmasters', 113–29.
94 Reference point, *supra* n. 66.
95 *MacCulloch v. Allan (Bothwell)* (1793) Mor. 1471, reversed (1800) 4 Pat. App. Cas. 128, had previously decided that the superintendence of schoolmasters was an ecclesiastical matter not subject to review in the civil courts. See Dunlop, *supra* n. 40, 497–503.
96 At the time Aberdeen, Edinburgh, Glasgow and St Andrews.
97 A link with the Church was retained through s. 9 providing that the four Boards would each consist of six members, three professors from the Arts Faculty and three from the Divinity Faculty of the appropriate university. At this time the professors of Divinity themselves would be church-approved.

In short, the 1861 Act allowed school masters to be appointed who were not members of the Church of Scotland, or even those who did not share its basic beliefs, although in parochial schools they had to promise not to disturb accepted doctrine.[98] Teachers were thus given the freedom of religious opinion that had been effectively given to schoolchildren some 40 years before.[99] Further, Presbytery powers to discipline teachers were restricted. Jurisdiction in cases of immorality or cruelty was transferred to the local sheriff, acting under a libel lodged by the appropriate Presbytery (s. 14). However, 'laicising' was in the wind. The days of the Declaration were numbered.

The trigger was the state assumption of major responsibilities for the provision of schools, as seen above.[100] In addition to reorganising the scholastic system the Education (Scotland) Act, 1872, introduced as a matter of law the so-called 'conscience clause', the right to withdraw from religious instruction, which had been operative since the 1830s in the parochial schools run by the Church of Scotland.[101] The Preamble narrated that custom was to give religious instruction in schools but with a right of withdrawal, and s. 68 of the Act stated: 'Every public school and every school subject to inspection and in receipt of public money . . . shall be open to children of all denominations, and any child may be withdrawn by his parents from any instruction in religious subjects and from any religious observation in any such school; and no child shall in any such school be placed at any disadvantage with respect to the secular instruction given therein by reason of the denomination to which such child or his parents belong, or by reason of his being withdrawn from any instruction in religious subjects . . .' To facilitate that withdrawal, religious observances and instruction in public schools were to take place either at the beginning or end of the school day. The 1872 Act further underlined that shift towards what would now be termed secular education. Parliamentary grants were not to be made for religious instruction (s. 67(2)). By s. 66 the duties of Her Majesty's Inspectorate for Schools were not to extend 'to inquire into any instruction in religious subjects, or to examine any scholar in religious knowledge or in any religious subject or book'.[102] Last, the Act did not re-enact the former Declaration that a teacher would not teach contrary to the beliefs of the Church. A Scottish Education Department certificate of competency was proof that a teacher was qualified to teach, and in its grant the Church had no say.

In practice the 1872 Act was less significant for the Presbyterian churches than for the Roman Catholic denomination. For most Presbyterians formal control over education no longer bulked as important as it had in times past. The state system provided a basically Presbyterian but minimal religious education, though in law the presence of religious education was apparent only by its inclusion in the general powers of the School Boards and by

---

98 Politically the introduction of the Declaration for teachers was eased by a similar Declaration having been introduced for Lay Chairs in the Scottish Universities by ss. 1 and 2 of the Universities (Scotland) Act, 1853: see supra at n. 23. By s. 13 the local Presbytery could complain to the Secretary of State for Scotland about infringements of a teacher's Declaration. If probable cause were shown a Commission of Inquiry might result in the censure, suspension or dismissal of the schoolmaster, but only after a review by the Secretary.
99 See *supra* n. 88.
100 See *supra* at n. 71.
101 See *supra* n. 88. This 'conscience' clause was introduced only in the later stages of the Bill, and carried by the votes of English MPs.
102 This provision, coupled with the severance of church control and the lack of an agreed syllabus had adverse effects on religious education in Scottish schools. See *The Fourth Report on Religious Education* (the Durham Report), (London: SPCK, 1970), 172–5. Later developments partially overcame this: J.J. Robertson, 'The Scottish Solution', 1951 *Year Book of Education*, 336–9, but cf. the Millar Report, *infra* n. 110, 1.4.

the right of parents to withdraw children from religious classes or observances. The number of Presbyterian schools outside the state system shrank, while the number of Roman Catholic independent schools grew.[103] Educational standards diverged as teachers preferred the higher salaries of the state schools. These two problems had to be tackled if there was to be a country-wide system of education.

Discussions between the state authorities and the managers of the voluntary schools took place. These were not confined to the Roman Catholic Church, though as manager of most of the independent schools it had a major part to play. Eventually, following negotiations that involved the Apostolic Visitor, agreement was reached and given effect to in law by the Education (Scotland) Act 1918 as part of a major re-organisation of education.[104]

As far as religious education was concerned, the 1918 Act continued the customary practice of religious instruction in schools with parents having the right to withdraw a child. The custom was narrated in s. 7 and was to continue subject to the conscience clause provided for in the 1872 Act.

Section 18 dealt with the transfer of voluntary or denominational schools to newly constituted education authorities. The authority was to accept the responsibilities for a voluntary school, subject to agreement as to the sale, or lease of the facilities concerned (s. 18(1)). This was an advance from the 1872 Act under which schools might be transferred, but prohibited payments in consideration of the transfer. Churches and voluntary societies were not to be discouraged from transferring a school into the state system by adverse financial effects. Indeed, financial security was both an inducement to transfer, and necessary given the expenditures incurred, particularly by the Roman Catholics, in building schools. It would have been inequitable not to compensate that expense. But the law went further than merely allowing the transfer to occur upon agreement as to terms. Education authorities were bound to accept transfers, and, in the absence of agreement, terms were to be settled by arbitration.

Education authorities were required to hold all transferred schools as public schools of the same character and status as at the date of transfer, and to retain the staff then in post (s. 18(3)).[105] Importantly, provisos to s. 18(3) required that teachers subsequently appointed by the authority had to be approved by the denominational body that used to manage the school; that time allocated for religious instruction (subject to the conscience clause) was not to be reduced from former practice; and that a supervisor of religious instruction appointed by the denominational body had to be given access to the school to give religious instruction. In case of dispute the Scottish Education Department made the final decision (s. 18(4)). Finally, going the other way round s. 18(1) allowed existing schools to be changed into 'special' schools, and for new special schools to be created where necessary at the suggestion of the local education authority, or a church or other relevant body, so long as the Scottish Education Department concurred.

Section 18 therefore created a place for denominational schools within the state system. However, recognising that things would not remain static, provision was made for review. Ten years after a transfer the local education authority might recommend that the

---

103 Table 3 of the *Memorandum with regard to the Provision made for Religious Instruction in the Schools in Scotland*, 1943, Cmnd. 6426, analyses from 1880 by decades and by denomination the numbers of state grant receiving voluntary schools.
104 Murphy, *supra* n. 34, 103; Scotland, *supra* n. 38, II, 44–5; Brother Kenneth, 'The Education (Scotland) Act, 1918, in the Making' (1968) 19 Innes Review, 91–128.
105 Cf. *Norfor* v *Aberdeenshire Education Authority*, 1924 SC 590.

continuance of a particular transferred school was no longer required, or suggest that the religious belief of the parents of children attending the school now indicated that any special conditions ought no longer to apply. If the Scottish Education Department agreed then the special conditions were cancelled, subject if necessary to the payment of further compensation to the previous operators.[106]

In the main the 1918 Act was effective. Many of the remaining voluntary and denominational schools were integrated into the national system. With the standardisation of salaries in the state system teachers were once more willing to work in the formerly independent schools. The precise situation, of course, varied from area to area, and different dioceses of the Roman Catholic and the Episcopal Church had different experiences.

As indicated earlier, local government in Scotland was reorganised in 1929, bringing changes in education. By s. 1 of the Local Government (Scotland) Act, 1929, education became a matter for local councils acting through education committees in which the majority were councillors (s. 12(4)). Special provision was made for the religious interest. Under s. 12(4)(2)(ii) any church or denominational body whose school was transferred under the 1918 Act nominated one representative to the committee. Other churches nominated two further representatives. The voice (or voices) of the churches was thus secured within the secular framework.[107] Another safeguard was that the education committee could not discontinue any customary religious education unless a resolution to that effect had first been approved in a secret ballot by the district's local government electors (s. 31). No such poll was held during the currency of the 1929 Act or thereafter.

Planning in the early 1940s for the post-war period included education. In England this led to the famous 'Butler' Education Act of 1944.[108] Discussion of Scottish education was helped by a Memorandum from the Scottish Education Department outlining how its system had developed.[109] Eventually the Education (Scotland) Act, 1945, consolidated much of the earlier legislation but made minimal change. Section 4 abolished prescription in the 1872 Act that religious instruction be held at either end of the school day and s. 5 allowed boarders at state establishments to attend their own religious instruction and exercises.

In 1946 another broadly consolidating Act tightened the transference of voluntary schools to the state system. Previous provisions as to denominational schools were continued (s. 17(2)) but transfer powers were extended to schools begun after the 1918 Act (ss. 15(1) and 16). Further, following a local public inquiry the Secretary of State could transfer to a local authority with its consent the buildings, endowments and management of a voluntary school where revenue was less than £1,000 per annum and appeared insufficient for its proper running. An innovation was s. 29, expressly providing that in general children were to be educated as their parents wished, a provision clearly apparently at variance with the ideas of the Reformers that no parent should 'use his children at his own fantasy'. However, in practice, with the institution of nation-wide examinations, the element of the parents' wishes was minimal.

---

106 The 1918 Act, s. 18(9), amended by s.1 of the Education (Scotland) Act 1925, allowed the release of a school from denominational status and restraint with the consent of its former managers within the 10-year period.
107 Cf. now *supra* n. 77 and *infra* following n. 115.
108 M. Cruickshank, *Church and State in English Education: 1870 to the Present Day* (London: Macmillan, 1963).
109 *Memorandum with Regard to the Provision Made for Religious Instruction in the Schools in Scotland*, 1943 Cmd. 6426.

The Education (Scotland) Act of 1962, another consolidating statute, repeated occasionally in different terms, but often the exact language of its predecessors. The later 1960s saw further review of religious education. A Committee was asked to review: 'within the existing frame work of the statutory provision governing the obligation to continue religious instruction . . . the current practice of Scottish schools (other than Roman Catholic schools) with regard to moral and religious education'.[110] The terms of reference precluded the examination of the law, so the Committee confined itself to improving that practice. Some recommendations were implemented. These included specialised teachers, alteration in the content of courses and their orientation and the setting aside of one period a week for the subject.[111] The Committee also made suggestions for the mechanics of producing a syllabus. However, the Committee concluded that it did not recommend instituting of examinations in religious studies at 'Ordinary' and 'Higher' levels.[112]

Current arrangements

As indicated above, school education in Scotland is the responsibility of the local authority for the area.[113] The 1980 Education (Scotland) Act, as amended, sets out the structure of public school education in Scotland,[114] and the specific duties of the local education authority within each territorial local authority. Each authority appoints an education committee on which there remains religious representation.[115] In early 2014 the Scottish Parliament was petitioned to abolish this representation on the ground that it gave an unjustified privileged position to religious views. The Scottish government itself responded that it favoured the involvement of religious representatives in education. Nonetheless a Bill to abolish was introduced, but its sponsor dropped it in November 2014 following public consultation.

The principal ruling statute on the content of school education in Scotland is the Education (Scotland) Act 1980, now amended and added to by a plethora of later legislation from both Westminster and, following devolution, the Scottish Parliament.[116] Of these additions the Standards in Scotland's Schools Act, 2000 (2000 asp 6), must be noted. Its s. 2 sets out the general duty of a local authority. Education is to be 'directed to the development of the personality, talents and mental and physical abilities of the child or young person to their fullest potential' (s. 2(1)).[117] 'Due regard', 'so far as reasonably practicable', is to be had to the views of the child or young person 'if there is a wish to express them' in decisions that significantly affect that child or young person, taking account of the child or young person's age and maturity' (s. 2(2)).[118]

---

110 *Moral and Religious Education in Scottish Schools: Report of a Committee Appointed by the Secretary of State for Scotland*, Chairman W.M. Millar (HMSO, 1972).
111 A specialised course in Religious Education with teachers trained in the subject were introduced in the 1970s.
112 This nomenclature of levels in secondary education has been departed from.
113 See *supra* at nn. 76 and 77.
114 In Scotland a public school is one within the state system. The English 'public school' would, in Scotland, be classed as a private school.
115 See *supra* n. 77.
116 Many amendments were made by the Education (Scotland) Act 1981.
117 Direct quotation from Art. 29(1)(a) of the UN Convention on the Rights of the Child. *Supra* n. 1. I am indebted for the point to N. Harris, 'Playing Catch-Up in the Schoolyard? Children and Young People's "Voice" and Education Rights in the UK', 2009 23 *Int. J. of Law, Policy and the Family*, 331.
118 S. 2 has not been the subject of judicial interpretation.

Section 8 retains the provision of the 1872 Act as to religious observance and the prohibition of the use of public monies for religious instruction (as opposed to education). However, many secondary schools have teams of chaplains drawn from local Kirk parishes and other denominations and appointed by the head-teacher. These may conduct school assemblies, and offer some pastoral care for pupils that request it. Chaplains are unpaid. By s. 9 every public school is open to pupils of all denominations, with parents still having the right to withdraw pupils from religious instruction or any religious observance.[119] By s. 10, at the request of their parents, boarders at a public school may attend worship in accordance with the tenets of a particular denomination on Sunday or other days, and receive religious instruction or practice religious observance outside the working hours of the school.[120]

As amended, s. 16 now contains the provision first introduced by the 1918 Act for transferring denominational schools to the state system. Originally designed mainly to cope with Roman Catholic schools, the modern law may be used for any school that has a religious base. The staff of a transferred school are retained and go onto the appropriate point on the state salary scale. A local education authority may establish a new denominational school within the state system, or an existing one be suppressed or converted to non-denominational status under ss. 17 and 22. Additionally by s. 17 of the Standards in Scotland's Schools Act, 2000 asp 6, the management of a self-governing school may be terminated and the school taken over by the local authority. A local authority is now under no duty to provide a denominational school, or to accept the transfer of an existing denominational school into the state system. That said, access to Catholic schools is important for Catholics, and an attempt to redistrict primary schooling in the east of Glasgow was defeated when its effect was to remove a few streets from the catchment area of a Roman Catholic school with a reputation for excellence.[121] As at 2014, 14.4 per cent of the state school system is composed of denominational schools.[122]

Section 21 of the 1980 Act provides for the management of denominational schools within the state system. The appointment of staff sympathetic to the ethos of the school remains important, but this must now interact with the prohibition of discrimination on religious grounds and related questions of employment law.[123] Under s. 21.2A representatives of the relevant church or denominational body have the right to approve the religious belief and character of a teacher whose qualifications have otherwise satisfied the Secretary of State. The Roman Catholic Church is the main beneficiary of this provision. However, the provision may be of limited effect for in some subjects finding qualified Roman Catholic applicants can be difficult.[124] As a result non-Catholics (including atheists) have been appointed to Roman Catholic schools. There have been disputes and media publicity,

---

119 Para 6.16 of the Millar Report of 1972 (*supra* n. 110) states the right of withdrawal right was then little used. I have no data on current practice.
120 In the Highlands and Islands some state schools have boarding accommodation for pupils from remote areas where there is no local school.
121 *Bowie* v *East Renfrewshire Council*, 2010 CSOH 6, 2010 SLT 647.
122 In 2014 there were 2,056 Primary Schools, 364 Secondary Schools and 149 Special Schools in the Scottish state system, a total of 2,569. Of these 366 were Catholic, 1 Jewish and 3 Episcopalian, a total of 370. There were 673,530 pupils. See http://www.scotland.gov.uk/Topics/Education/Schools/FAQs. There were 102 independent schools, as to which see the Scottish Council of Independent Schools, www.scis.org.uk.
123 See Chapter 8, 'Human Rights'.
124 Formerly two of the nine teacher training colleges in Scotland were specifically oriented to Roman Catholic needs, Notre Dame, Glasgow, and Craiglockhart, Edinburgh. Now, teacher training is provided in eight Scottish universities, but without religious orientation.

particularly when the promotion of non-Catholics has been involved, or when church approval for a senior appointment has not been given. Though productive of many newspaper column inches, these have usually been settled. One case has made it to the courts.[125]

Under a 1991 agreement between the local education authority, Glasgow City Council and the local Roman Catholic diocese, the appointment of non-Catholics in Catholic schools was authorised, but certain posts were specifically reserved as requiring diocesan approval. McNab, an atheist, was appointed to teach personal and social education in a Roman Catholic school. Soon afterwards that subject was subsumed into pastoral care. When a promoted post with pastoral responsibilities became vacant, McNab applied but was not called for interview because he was known not to be Catholic. Citing the Employment Equality (Religion or Belief) Regulations 2003 (SI 2003/1660), he alleged discrimination. The authority accepted that by not interviewing him it had discriminated, but argued that being a Catholic was an occupational requirement for the post and allowed under the Regulations. An Employment Tribunal awarded McNab £2,000 in compensation. An appeal held that a proper construction of the Regulations and of Section 21.2A of the 1980 Act did not show that being Roman Catholic was necessarily a genuine occupational requirement for a post in a Roman Catholic school. The drafting of the provisions left it open to the Church to approve the appointment of a non-Catholic teacher if satisfied as to his religious belief (which need not be Roman Catholic) and character. Excluding an applicant from interview on the basis of belief was discriminatory at the point of that decision.[126] The award of compensation to McNab was not disturbed. The Appeal Tribunal also pointed out that the function of 'denominational' schools within the state system was facilitative. The local authority did not and could not have itself a particular ethos to promote, and within its area could support denominational schools that held to divergent and contradictory beliefs.

Educational standards continue to be set by the state and implemented by the local education authority under the 1980 Act and the Standards in Scotland's Schools Act, 2000 asp 6. Monitoring is carried out through inspection under s. 66 of the 1980 Act. When originally enacted its s. 66.2 excluded religious instruction from the duties of school inspectors but s. 16 of the 1981 Act removed that provision. Since 1 July 2011 a 'Scottish Education Quality and Improvement Agency' supervises education in Scotland, bringing together the previous HM Inspectorate of Education and the agency 'Learning and Teaching Scotland' which had been responsible for supporting the curriculum.

Religions now form an element of the 'Curriculum for Excellence', the curriculum at present generally followed in Scottish state schools. Designed to foster knowledge and understanding, skills, capabilities and attributes in each pupil it comprises eight areas: Expressive Arts, Health and Wellbeing, Languages, Mathematics, Religious and Moral Education, Sciences, Social Studies and Technologies. Individual schools determine how best to achieve suitable results from the balance of subjects taught in the school. Pupil choice is allowed as to the areas taken to higher levels. In deciding what is covered as to religion, schools have regard to the communities that they serve. Christianity is usually a major topic, but, within the general curriculum area of 'Religious and Moral Education', students may be introduced to and given a general understanding of, but not instruction in, some or all of Sikhism, Buddhism, Judaism, Hinduism, Islam, as well as Humanism. The levels of understanding expected of the pupils rise throughout the secondary stage of education. The

---

125 *Glasgow City Council* v *McNab* 2007 IRLR 476; [2007] UKEAT 0037_06_1701. Reference point n. 35 *supra*.
126 Interviewing practices have been changed.

structuring of the Religious and Moral Education curriculum area is, however, modified for Roman Catholic schools.[127]

Apart from the public schools, independent private schools exist in Scotland, some with a religious base. In the main they are fee-paying and in matters of secular education are subject to Her Majesty's Inspectorate. They are regulated under Part V of the 1980 Act, as amended, and the Self-Governing Schools etc. (Scotland) Act 1989. Independent schools must be registered by the Scottish Ministers and their approval is subject to a variety of conditions including the education to be offered, the qualifications of the staff, the school buildings and other accommodation and the nature and suitability of the proprietor (s. 94A, 1980 Act, as amended). These schools may include religious instruction as part of their curricula.

Home schooling is competent with the permission of the local education authority under ss. 35–38 of the 1980 Act. The quality of the education is informally monitored to secure that the education provided is efficient. Permission to home-school may be withdrawn if necessary and the child is then required to attend a state school. Clearly in home-schooling a parent may give religious instruction to a child.[128]

Doubtless there will be further discussion in the matter of religion in Scottish schools. Human rights legislation affords an opportunity for challenge, debate and possible amendment of the law.[129]

---

127 Separate documents on 'Principles and Practice' as to religious and moral education for schools and for Roman Catholic schools may be found in the Scottish Education Department website: http://www.educationscotland.gov.uk. A Scottish Catholic Education Service (www.sces.uk.com) was established in 2003 by the Roman Catholic Bishops' Conference of Scotland to implement the policies of the Catholic Education Commission as set by the Bishops.
128 Some charities and businesses provide course materials for home-schooling. These are adapted to the normal school curriculum, and therefore the children may in due course sit the relevant state examinations and gain qualifications for admission to further education or employment.
129 Cf. relevant sections of the Human Rights Act 1998, the Equality Act 2006, the Equality Act 2010, and the (European) Convention for the Protection of Human Rights and Fundamental Freedoms, Rome, 1950, *supra* n. 1. See also Chapter 8.

7 Personal relationships

General

Human rights include the right to marry and found a family.[1] The new concepts of 'rights' notwithstanding, marriage has been part of the law of Scotland as far back as we have knowledge. However, the religious elements that formerly undergirded or were assumed to justify the law have diminished to the point of irrelevance. No area of the interaction of church and state in Scotland has shown more change, and the rate of change has accelerated since the 1970s.

In the past theological dogma moulded the assumptions of the general populace as to what Scottish society would tolerate. However, attitudes to marriage and similar but less formal relationships have changed.[2] Cohabitation now has wider consequences for aliment, support and the division of goods on separation than formerly.[3] Family law has been reshaped. Bigamy, which reflected a common understanding of marriage, has ceased to be a common law crime, and instead has become a statutory offence.[4] The law now affords validity to relationships that would have been anathema in previous centuries – even previous decades. The introduction of same-sex marriage by the Marriage and Civil Partnership (Scotland) Act 2014, asp 5, underlines that traditional Christian theology no longer underpins Scots marriage law. The Marriage (Scotland) Act 1977 has been much amended. A marriage now is constituted in a ceremony conducted by a 'belief body', which is 'an organised group of people . . . the principal object (or one of the principal objects) of which is to uphold or promote philosophical beliefs and which meets regularly for that purpose'.[5] Again the relationships

---

[1] Cf. Schedule 1 to the Human Rights Act 1998, and the Convention for the Protection of Human Rights and Fundamental Freedoms, Rome, 1950, 213 UNTS 222; ETS 5; 1953 UKTS 71, Cmd. 8130, Art. 14. With limited exception the relevant law has been devolved to Scotland under the Scotland Act 1998, s. 30 and Sched. 5. Some matters, including social security and pensions, remain with Westminster. See Sched. 5, Head F.
[2] Cf. J. Mair, 'A Modern Marriage', 2006 10 Edin. L.R. 333.
[3] Family Law (Scotland) Act 1985; Family Law (Scotland) Act 2006, asp 2. See *infra* n. 18.
[4] Marriage and Civil Partnership (Scotland) Act 2014, asp 5, s. 26(3) and Marriage (Scotland) Act 1977, s. 24 (A1–2) inserted by s. 26 of the 2014 Act.
[5] Marriage (Scotland) Act 1977. s. 26(2) as amended by s. 10(4)(a) of the 2014 Act.

of parent and child have been modified. The rights of parents have been equiparated and a marital relationship is no longer crucial in the parental rights of a father.[6]

Marriage

In 1969 a governmental Committee commented that Scots marriage law was deeply embedded in the history and traditions of the social and moral life of the country. For the Kilbrandon Committee the constitution, effects and dissolution of marriage were basic to the structure of a familial society.[7] For many that remains true. However, since 1969 the attitudes of others to marriage and similar relationships have changed.[8] The marriage tie is diminished in its importance, and any theological understanding of the relationship is growing less common.

In fact the interests of a church or a religious or belief body in marriage and those of the state are quite different, and it is time that that be clearly acknowledged. The requirements of each as to the constitution of the relationship should be separately served.

The religious interest in marriage is clear. In traditional Christian theologies marriage is heterosexual and is constituted by the consent of the parties. Some Christian denominations require that consent to marriage be exchanged during a religious ceremonial conducted by clergy.[9] Some do not recognise divorce.[10] Other denominations and religions take different stances.[11] However, whatever their theologies, the interest of all religious/ecclesiastical institutions lies in ensuring that their particular requirements are complied with,[12] although not all may require appropriate belief in their teachings.[13]

The interest of the state in marital relationships and arrangements is secular. It recognises marriage and attaches many consequences to it. Civil law determines the content of the rights and duties of marriage, and how they are recognised, enforced or taken account of in civil society.[14] Marriage can affect pensions, property, social security and benefits, taxation, inheritance and succession and other matters such as consent to medical procedures. It can

---

6 Mair, *supra* n. 2, at 351 opines that there is now little shared understanding of what the legal concept of living together as husband and wife means, and that 'there is much to suggest that it is not a model fit for modern lives'.
7 *Marriage Law of Scotland*, Report by a Committee appointed by the Secretary of State for Scotland, Chairman, Lord Kilbrandon, 1969, Cmnd 4011, para 7.
8 See in *British Social Attitudes, 28* (2011–12 Edition) (London: Sage; National Centre for Social Research, 2012), J. Curtice and R. Ormiston, 'Devolution: On the road to divergence? Trends in public opinion in Scotland and England', 21–36 at 30–36; L. Lee, 'Religion: Losing faith?', 173–84. Cf. *Scotland's Census 2011*, http://www.scotlandscensus.gov.uk; *Churchgoing in the UK* (London: Tearfund, 2007). Cf. J. Mair, 'Public ceremony and private belief: the role of religion in the Scots law of marriage', 2007 Jur. Rev. 280.
9 In Roman Catholicism and its cognates marriage is a sacrament.
10 In Roman Catholicism civil divorce is not possible for those who wish to remain in communion. G. Read, 'The Catholic Tribunal System in the British Isles', 1990–91 2 Ecc LJ 213.
11 For example, the dissolution of a Jewish marriage by the civil authorities is not recognised by some Jewish groups until that dissolution has been subject to their procedures. But see *infra* n. 129 as to compelling the taking of these steps.
12 Parish ministers in Scotland are under no duty to conduct a marriage ceremony. Some ministers have, however, accessed a source of income thereby. Although not allowed to charge a fee, some ministers conducting marriage services are very willing to accept *ex gratia* contributions. (The same applies to burials.) Cf. removal from the authorised list of celebrants if found to be conducting a business of conducting marriages, *infra* n. 65.
13 Atheists, agnostics and others may use traditional ecclesiastical procedures in order to access venues and ceremonials which lend to the occasion and contribute to spectacle in the Wedding Album.
14 Some religions add to these rights and duties, but these additions are not enforceable as a matter of law.

also be relevant in questions of immigration, residence or citizenship.[15] Clear civil procedures have therefore been established for the constitution and termination of marriage,[16] and for the registration of these steps so that the state knows what is going on.

The haphazard development of the law of marriage has confused the interests of theology and the civil authority. In the 1960s the Kilbrandon Committee did consider the introduction of a compulsory civil marriage, with the possibility of separate religious ceremony thereafter, but decided against on grounds of practicality and the avoidance of religious difficulties.[17] That decision should now be reconsidered. There should be a clear and formal separation of the secular and the religious. In addition a different term is required to denote the relationship. A simple civil procedure should be instituted to meet the state's need to know who is in what sort of a relationship with whom (whether a civil partnership or something else). Other ceremonials (including non-Christian forms) could thereafter be conducted as the parties may wish. Solely 'religious' marriages should not be given civil effects. The distinct interests of church and state would thereby be served.

The state also recognises factual quasi-marital relationships in many other forms. Account is taken of relationships that exist without their having been formally instituted or registered, the civil authorities applying rights and duties formerly attributable only in traditional marriage.[18] Even entitlement to reside or remain in the UK may now be determined by 'family' status.[19] The development is not new.[20] Such concerns are not, however, germane to a consideration of church and state, save to note that in Scotland the abolition of former, less formal forms of marriage has meant that many such factual relationships cannot now qualify as legal marriages. 'Habit and repute', an irregular form of marriage that survived the abolition of the two other irregular forms, has recently disappeared.[21] How marriage is constituted and terminated is now wholly determined by the state, precise procedures being required (except in the case of death).

Marriage retains its importance in society. I deal first with the traditional concept, working onwards from there. Marriage confers a known status. The civil rights and duties of the parties to a marriage *inter se* are prescribed by operation of law, and the parties

---

15 See *infra* n. 69.
16 Within Roman Catholicism nullity of marriage is the means of terminating a 'marriage' by holding that it never had occurred. That church procedure is not recognized in Scots law. Catholic 'nullity' is a different concept from that dealt with by the civil courts. See *supra* n. 10, and *infra* n. 120.
17 Kilbrandon Committee, *supra*, n. 7.
18 Family Law (Scotland) Act 1985; Family Law (Scotland) Act 2006, asp 2. Cf. The Scottish Law Commission, *Report on Family Law* (Scot Com. No. 135, 1992), *The Effects of Cohabitation in Private Law*, SLC Discussion Paper No. 86 (1990), and *Family Law: Pre-Consolidation Reforms*, SLC Discussion Paper No. 85 (1990); T. Guthrie and H. Hiram, 'Property and Cohabitation: Understanding the Family Law (Scotland) Act 2006' (2007), 11 Edin. LR., 208–20. *Gow* v *Grant* [2012] UKSC 29, 2013 SC (UKSC) 1, overturning 2011 SC 618.
19 Note the frequent use of the 'right to family life' under the Human Rights Act 1998 as preventing deportation. See also the Immigration Act 2014.
20 Cf. from the 1960s, the definition of 'family' in the Family Allowances Act 1965 s. 3, the National Insurance Act 1965 s. 114 (2)(c) and of the National Insurance (Industrial Injuries) Act 1965 s. 86 (2)(c), together with the concept of 'household' and related arrangements under s. 5 and sch. 2, and ss. 22–4 of the Ministry of Social Security Act 1966, all now replaced. Then (and now), a widow might not cohabit with a man and retain her right to a widow's benefit, mother's allowance or pension, even though there was no formal marriage: National Insurance Act 1965 s. 26.
21 See *infra* at n. 105. Other forms of irregular marriage were abolished in 1939, *infra* n. 95.

can neither validly contract out of nor limit them. 'No conditions can be attached to it. No qualifications can be made on its effect'.[22] Because of its other civil effects the state has restricted how that status is entered into. Marriage in Scotland is now governed by the Marriage (Scotland) Act 1977, as copiously amended.[23] However, before we get there what follows traces the historical roots of the concept of marriage in an application of reformed theology.[24]

Traditional marriage

Although some communities were tolerant of other customs such as 'handfasting',[25] once a formal ecclesiastical structure had been established, Scots marriage law reflected a Christian concept of marriage, first as understood by the Roman Catholic Church, and, following the Reformation in 1560, by the Church of Scotland.

Traditionally a marriage was preceded by a period while the parties were engaged to be married, and that practice remains. Occasionally a result was an action for breach of promise of marriage. This action did not compel the marriage, but could allow recovery of damages for expenses incurred in contemplation of the marriage and for *solatium* (hurt feelings).[26] However, 'breach of promise of marriage' was abolished in 1984, promise of marriage being declared not to be an enforceable obligation.[27]

Scots marriage legislation deals only with its regulation. Marriage itself is not defined in statute law. Marriage is a creature of common law, based on centuries of practice. That said, Chapter XXIV of the Westminster Confession of Faith (1646), 'Of Marriage and Divorce',[28] sets out the principles that for centuries informed the Scots law of marriage.

---

22 Per Lord President Clyde in *Lang* v *Lang*, 1921 SC 44 at 51.
23 Numerous (but not all) amendments to the 1977 Act are in the Marriage (Scotland) Act 2002 asp 8; the Family Law (Scotland) Act 2006 asp 2; the Local Electoral Administration and Registration Services (Scotland) Act 2006 asp 4, and the Marriage and Civil Partnership (Scotland) Act 2014, asp 5.
24 See all the Scottish Institutional writers, Stair, Erskine and Bell, together with Patrick, Lord Fraser, *A Treatise on Husband and Wife according to the Law of Scotland*, 2d ed., 2 vols (Edinburgh: Clark, 1876–78) (first ed. 1846); F.P. Walton, *A Handbook of Husband and Wife according to the law of Scotland*, 3rd ed. (Edinburgh: Green, 1951, previous eds. 1922 and 1893); E.M. Clive, *The Law of Husband and Wife in Scotland*, 4th ed. (Edinburgh: Scot. Univ. Law Inst./ Greens, 1997). The Stair Memorial Encyclopaedia of the Laws of Scotland, now in electronic form, takes recent developments into account.
25 Handfasting was a betrothal usually accompanied by cohabitation for a period prior to marriage. A.E. Anton, '"Handfasting" in Scotland', 1958 37 Scot. Hist. Rev. 89; J. Bartholomew, 'The Highland Clans in the Law of Scotland' (1901), 13 Jur. Rev. 205–13 at 207; Brodie-Innes, *infra* n. 96, at 407; Lovat-Fraser, *infra* n. 100, at 345 n. 1. See also E. Ewen, 'The early modern family', in T.M. Devine and J. Wormald, eds, *The Oxford Handbook of Modern Scottish History* (Oxford: Oxford UP, 2012). On 12 April 1568 Aberdeen Kirk Session imposed a fine on any ecclesiastic present at a handfasting and required the names of the parties to be given in so that banns might be properly called: *Selections from the Records of the Kirk Session, Presbytery and Synod of Aberdeen* (Spalding Club, Aberdeen, 1846), 14.
26 Whether an engagement ring or other gifts between the parties were returnable depended on circumstances. Cf. *Shilliday* v *Smith*, 1998 SC 725, *Thomson* v *Mooney* [2013] CSIH 115, 2014 Fam. LR 15, raising the question of unjustified enrichment.
27 Law Reform (Husband and Wife) (Scotland) Act 1984, s. 1.
28 The Confession was approved by the Scots Parliament on 7 February 1649 (Charles 1, Parl. 2, Sess. 2, Act 16) but this was struck down by the Recissory Act, 1661, c. 46. It was reaffirmed for the state's part by the Confession of Faith Ratification Act 1690 c. 7 (12mo. c. 5).

Notably, its para 1 states that marriage is to be heterosexual and monogamous.[29] In so doing the Confession did not deviate from the Catholic view.[30]

For much of Europe the law of marriage was significantly altered by the Ecumenical Council of the Roman Catholic Church generally known as the Council of Trent, convened in response to the emergence of Protestantism.[31] The decree *de sacramento matrimonii*, adopted in 1563 at its penultimate session, abolished irregular marriage and this passed into the law of those countries that at that time were under papal jurisdiction.[32] The sacrament of marriage was to take place with the participation of a priest in a ceremonial in church. Marriage could not otherwise be constituted. That a valid marriage could be constituted by the consent of the parties alone was rendered impossible. However, the jurisdiction of the Pope in Scotland had been abolished three years earlier by the Papal Jurisdiction Act 1560 c. 2. The Tridentine decisions therefore did not apply in Scotland. For the Scottish Reformers marriage was indeed important, but its constitution was firmly pinned to the consent of the parties. They recognised only two sacraments, baptism and communion. Marriage was not a sacrament, and any intervention of clergy was irrelevant. Marriage might be in regular form in a church, but could also be constituted irregularly by the parties themselves. The result was that for centuries thereafter Scotland had two categories of marriage, regular marriage and irregular marriage, the last traces of the latter having recently been given the quietus.[33]

Regular marriage

Since the abolition of marriage by habit and repute in 2006,[34] legal marriage can now only be 'regular marriage', constituted through compliance with the Marriage (Scotland) Act, 1977.[35] Two forms of regular marriage are effective in Scots law. These are marriage *in facie ecclesiae*, that is, with a religious ceremony (Religious or Belief Marriage) and marriage with a civil ceremony (Civil Marriage). The latter presents no special difficulties, the traditional forms being marginally altered. More difficulty is attendant upon religious marriages due to the patchwork development of the law once account was taken of churches other than the established Kirk.

---

29 'Marriage is to be between one man and one woman: neither is it lawful for any man to have more than one wife, nor for any woman to have more than one husband, at the same time', Westminster Confession of Faith, Ch. XXIV, para 1.
30 The Scots Confession of 1560 does not deal with marriage.
31 The Council of Trent, the nineteenth ecumenical council, marked the start of the Counter-Reformation. Convened in 25 sessions it spread over 18 years in the papacies of Paul III, Julius III and Pius IV (1545–63). Sessions 1–8 were held in Trent, sessions 9–11 in Bologna, and sessions 12–25 again in Trent. The twentieth ecumenical council (Vatican I) was held in 1869–70 and technically did not close until 1960 prior to Vatican II. Trent (Trento) lies in the Adige valley in north Italy. Its name is Latinised as Tridentum, hence the Council's decisions and the form of the Mass which it authorised are known as Tridentine.
32 Ann. 1563: Cc. Trid.: sess. XXIV: Decr. de sacramento matrimonii. Cap.1 Decr. Tametsi, *Enchiridion Symbolorum*, paras 1813–6. Marriage is one of the seven Roman Catholic sacraments.
33 See *infra*, Irregular marriage, n. 95.
34 For transitional arrangements see *infra*, n. 115.
35 Considerable amendments are made by the Marriage and Civil Partnership (Scotland) Act 2014, asp. 5, most of which is now in force. For prior law see 'Obsolete forms of marriage', *infra* n. 95.

Religious or belief marriage

Formerly it might have been proper to title this subsection 'ecclesiastical marriage'. Section 29 of the Registration of Births, Marriages and Deaths (Scotland) Act 1965 referred to marriage solemnised by ministers of 'any Christian denomination', but 'Christian' was undefined and by then marriages were recognised and registered which were conducted by other groups with only an arguable entitlement to use the adjective. The Kilbrandon Committee therefore recommended dropping the adjective subject to the preservation of marriage as monogamous.[36] In its original form the 1977 Marriage (Scotland) Act used the term 'religious marriage' but that has been expanded to 'religious or belief marriage',[37] which allows the Act to encompass a variety of ceremonies including Humanist. However, there is no requirement that the parties should share the particular religious or other belief that is the context of the ceremonial or, indeed, that they should hold any belief at all. The purpose of the ceremony remains formal – making the marriage public. In the seventeenth century Stair (I.4.6) stated: 'The public solemnity is a matter of order, justly introduced by positive law, for the certainty of so important a contract; but not essential to marriage'. Taking up that last clause, it may be noted that the 1977 Act refers to the 'solemnisation' of marriage, indicating that what is important is an exchange of consent within the context of the ceremonial. There is no legal requirement as to a particular form of words. What matters is that the consent of the parties should be clearly signified. Further, there is no requirement that English be used: only that the parties know what they are doing.

Within orthodox Christian theology, marriage is the union for life of one man and one woman to the exclusion of all others. Some might argue from 1 Cor. 6: 16 whether physical connection is necessary to constitute marriage,[38] but the general view was that the exchange of consents sufficed. Thus, in *Leslie* v *Leslie* (1859) 22 D. 993 Lord Deas stated at 1011:

> . . . consent makes marriage. No form or ceremony, civil or religious, no notice before nor publication after, no constitution or cohabitation, no writing, no witnesses even are essential to the constitution of [the contract of marriage].

However, his Lordship has been overtaken. Modern marriage law does now require more than simple consent. Procedures are prescribed and a formal ceremony is required.[39]

Notice of intended marriage

The principle that intended marriages should be publicised goes far back. There is evidence of early Christian churches having procedures through which congregations were made aware of impending marriages.[40] Later, Canon 51 of the Fourth Lateran Council, 1215,[41]

---

36 Kilbrandon Report, *supra* n. 7, para 114. Cf. A.E. Anton, 'The "Christian Marriage" Heresy', 1956 SLT News 201.
37 See *supra* n. 5.
38 Cf. J.D.M. Derrett, *Law in the New Testament* (London: Darton, Longman and Todd, 1970), 'The Teaching of Jesus on Marriage and Divorce', 363–88.
39 Clive, *supra* n. 24, para.05.025; Mair, *supra* n. 8.
40 Tertullian (c. 160–205 AD) *De Pudicitia*, c. 4, 'On Modesty' states 'connections' should be first professed in presence of the Church before they are begun.
41 Canons of the Fourth Lateran Council, 1215, http://www.fordham.edu/halsall/basis/lateran4.asp. Three-hundred-and-fifty years later the Council of Trent repeated the requirement: Ann. 1563: Cc. Trid.: Sess. XXIV: Decr. *de sacramento matrimonii*. Cap.1 Decr. Tametsi; *Enchiridion Symbolorum*, paras 1813–6 at 1816.

164 *Personal relationships*

affirmed that banns of marriage should precede matrimony.[42] Scotland complied.[43] The Scottish Reformers continued the practice, intended marriages being brought to public attention by proclamation in the parish church on two successive Sundays.[44] Anyone knowing any valid reason why the marriage should not occur was invited to bring such to the attention of the officiating minister or the local kirk session. When the civil authorities began to require notice of intention to marry to be given, Church of Scotland banns were accepted as meeting the requirement. Criticised in 1868,[45] it took until 1978, when, consequent upon the civil requirements as to notice imposed by the Marriage (Scotland) Act 1977, with limited exception the Church of Scotland abolished the proclamation of banns.[46]

Now under s. 3 of the Marriage (Scotland) Act 1977 notice of intended marriage, whether a civil marriage or one with some other ceremonial, has to be given to the registrar of the relevant district not more than three months or less than 15 days prior to the date of the intended marriage. The parties must satisfy the registrar that they are free to marry, are over 16 on the day of the marriage,[47] that they understand what they intend and, in the case where a party (or both) is not a British national, that the marriage would be recognised in the state of their nationality. In addition specific evidence of the nationality of each party may now be required.[48] It follows that, while a suitor may surprise with a proposal of marriage, a 'surprise wedding' is impossible.[49] When (or if) the registrar is satisfied that all is in order a Marriage Schedule is issued. This has to be completed as part of the marriage ceremony, and thereafter returned for registration.

Parties

Marriage in Scotland being monogamous, the parties must be free to marry – that is, single.[50] The civil authorities now permit the marriage of persons who in the past would not

---

42 Banns were formal intimation by the minister during a church service that a marriage was to take place at a later date. Prior to the marriage anyone could object to the marriage on a variety of grounds such as the marriage would be bigamous, or the parties were too closely related, or too young.
43 Thus the thirteenth century Synodical Statutes of the Diocese of Aberdeen required a thrice repeated proclamation of banns in the form prescribed by the General Council: SSC, Stat. 66. Cf. Stat. 83; Stat 121; Stat. 155, and Stat. 251.
44 That the calling of banns was a matter *inter sacra* was affirmed by 11 judges to one during the progress of *Hutton v Harper* (1875) 2 R. 893 (1876) 3 R. (HL) 9.
45 The position of banns was criticised in the *Report of the Royal Commission on the Laws of Marriage* in 1868 (1868. Command paper 4059, reprinted 1894 HC 322) and extensively thereafter.
46 GA Act III, 1978, 'Anent the proclamation of Banns'. Banns may still be called if a Scottish resident requires them in order to marry furth of Scotland. Banns remain competent (but not requisite) for Roman Catholic ceremonies under Canon 1093 of the Code of Canon Law.
47 No person domiciled in Scotland may marry if under the age of 16, and a marriage solemnised in Scotland where either party is under that age is void: Marriage (Scotland) Act 1977, s. 3.
48 S. 3.4A-4C of the 1977 Act, inserted by s. 17.2 of the Marriage and Civil Partnership (Scotland) Act 2014, asp 5. Cf. *infra* n. 69.
49 For the parties and celebrant, at least.
50 A polygamous marriage contracted elsewhere may be recognised for social security purposes, and can affect immigration decisions. Polygamy would not be considered a human right: cf. *Reference re Section 293 of the Criminal Code of Canada*, 2011 BCSC 1588. Scots courts can deal as necessary with cases of polygamous marriage: Matrimonial Proceedings (Polygamous Marriages) Act 1972, s. 2.

have been allowed to marry.[51] This not only includes the re-marriage of divorced persons but also the marriage of persons within the degrees of relationship forbidden in Leviticus 18.[52] The current list of 'forbidden degrees' is set out in Sched. 1 to the 1977 Act. In the face of these developments, Church of Scotland practice has been to take no disciplinary action against persons contracting, or ministers officiating at, marriages lawful under statute, and to adopt special provision as to the re-marriage of divorced persons that leaves the matter largely in the hands of the minister concerned.[53] Other denominations and other religions make different provisions within their competences.[54]

Celebrants

Those who may conduct a marriage are subject to the approval of the civil authorities. At first, after the Reformation only ministers of the Kirk could conduct marriage ceremonies valid *ipso facto* in law. Ceremonies conducted by others were clandestine.[55]

According to both the feelings and language of the seventeenth century, any 'minister' not of the Established Church was a layman, and Jesuits and priests were not otherwise distinguished than as representing 'the most objectionable sort of laymen'.[56] It followed that marriages they solemnised were irregular, being vitiated by the lack of qualifications of the celebrant were constituted *per verba de praesenti*, and not as regular marriage.[57] Parties were subject to penalty under the Acts 1661 c. 246 and 1698 c. 6, and used the conviction of that crime to prove the marriage.

Specific statutory provision was eventually made for particular named groups. Quakers and Jews were permitted to use their own forms by s. 8 of the Marriage Notice (Scotland) Act 1878, and general powers to celebrate regular marriages was given to 'priests and ministers not of the Established Church' by s. 2 of the Marriage (Scotland) Act 1834. However, what was meant by the non-established churches was unclear, nor was the category 'priests and ministers' defined. The result was confusion as to the regularity of some marriages. The Registrar General for Scotland took administrative action, accepting for registration marriage

---

51 Marriage of a person divorced for adultery to his or her paramour was prohibited by the Act 1600, c. 29 (repealed by the Statute Law Revision (Scotland) Act 1964) but this bar was avoided through the court not inserting the name of the paramour in the decree. Church law forbad ministers to marry adulterers (GA 1566 Act 3).
52 The Marriage Act 1567 and the Incest Act 1567 c. 14 enacted the Levitical provisions. For the pre-Reformation position see J.D. Scanlan, 'Husband and Wife: Pre-Reformation Canon Law of Marriage of the Officials' Courts', in *Introduction to Scottish Legal History*, Stair Soc. Vol. 20, 1958, 69–81, and *William Hay's Lectures on Marriage*, trans. and ed. J.C. Barry, 1967, Stair Soc. Vol. 24. App. 5 to the Kilbrandon Report (*supra* n. 7) gives a table of the then forbidden degrees of marriage, which they recommended ought to be made statutory, the situation being somewhat labyrinthine. The Marriage Enabling Act 1960 consolidated and extended earlier extensions of the law by the Deceased Wife's Sister Act, 1907, the Deceased Brother's Widow's Marriage Act 1921, and the Marriage (Prohibited Degrees of Relationship) Act 1931. The mid-nineteenth century saw much discussion of the 'forbidden degrees'. Cf. J. Gibson, *The Marriage Affinity Question* (Edinburgh: Free Church, 1854); Lord Salvesen 'The Law of Incest in Scotland', 1941 83 Jur. Rev. 112, 262.
53 GA 1977 Act I, as amended by GA 2004 Act II. The Kirk first took this step by GA 1910 Act XII following the passing of the Deceased Wife's Sister Act of 1907.
54 Cf. on a world-wide basis, N. Doe, *Christian Law: Contemporary Principles* (Cambridge: Cambridge UP, 2013) 254–65.
55 See Clandestine marriage, *infra* at n. 116.
56 *Ballantyne* (1859) 3 Irv. 352 at 370.
57 See Irregular marriage, *infra* at n. 101.

schedules completed by persons he had previously authorised for the purpose. Unfortunately there was no legal basis for his action, though no-one complained. It was therefore useful that the Kilbrandon Committee recommended that a formal register of approved celebrants be established, and this was authorised by the 1977 Marriage (Scotland) Act.[58]

Now the celebrant of a marriage ceremony must be authorised so to act. A 'marriage' conducted by a person who is not properly authorised is not effective in law.[59] Who may act as a celebrant is set out in s. 8 of the Marriage (Scotland) Act 1977. District registrars and their assistants are authorised to conduct weddings (s. 8 (1)(b)), as are ministers of the Church of Scotland (s. 8 (1)(a)(i)), and the holders of a similar status in a recognised religious or belief body (s. 8 (1)(a)(ii)).[60] In addition, named individuals from other bodies may be recognised for the purpose (s. 9).[61] Celebrants of marriages may therefore include Christian ministers and priests as well as celebrants from many other systems of belief, including Muslims, Sikhs, Hindus and Buddhists.[62] Religious associations that eschew 'ministers' or 'priests' (such as Plymouth Brethren) may nominate individual members to be registered as celebrants to solemnise marriages. Authorisation by the Registrar General for Scotland is not automatic on nomination. The Registrar General may require proof of the status of the nominee within the structure of the particular belief system (s. 9). Nominees must be 21 years of age, or older. A nomination may be rejected if the nominating body is not a religious or belief body, or if its marriage ceremony is not of an appropriate form.[63] It may also be rejected if the nominee is not a fit and proper person to solemnise a marriage, or if, in the opinion of the Registrar General, the nominating body has a sufficient number of persons already authorised to act.[64] Approval of a nominee lasts for not more than three years, though it may be renewed, and the territory within which the nominee may act may be limited. In addition under s. 12 a temporary authorisation to conduct a specified marriage or marriages may be granted to an individual, or for a specific period, but still only

---

58 Kilbrandon Committee *supra* n. 7. Previously the courts had struggled with the need to determine whether a celebrant was a 'minister' or a 'minister of religion'. See also *infra* n. 60.
59 Note the assumption that there is a celebrant in addition to the parties. You cannot conduct your own marriage ceremony.
60 Regulations to be made by the Scottish Ministers will list approved denominations and other belief bodies. The current list in the Marriage (Prescription of Religious Bodies) (Scotland) Regulations, 1977, 1977 SI 1670 (S. 121) is partially obsolete as it includes the Congregational Union, a body that no longer exists. The others it lists are the Baptist Union of Scotland, the Episcopal Church in Scotland and other Churches of the Anglican Communion, the Free Church of Scotland, the Free Presbyterian Church of Scotland, the Hebrew Congregation, the Methodist Church in Scotland, the Religious Society of Friends, the Roman Catholic Church, the Salvation Army, the Scottish Unitarian Association and the United Free Church of Scotland.
   By s. 8(1A), inserted by s. 12(2)(b) of the Marriage and Civil Partnership (Scotland) Act 2014, asp 5, no body may be listed unless it so requests and meets the qualifying requirements.
61 Celebrants for same-sex marriages may be registered on the nomination of a religious or belief body only if it so requests and otherwise meets qualifying requirements: s. 8(1C) inserted by s. 12 (2)(b) of the Marriage and Civil Partnership (Scotland) Act 2014.
62 As noted in para 2 of Lord Toulson's judgement in *R (on the application of Hodkin and another) (Appellants) v Registrar General of Births, Deaths and Marriages (Respondent)* [2013] UKSC 77, the Registrar General for Scotland has accepted persons nominated by the Scientology movement as celebrants of marriages in Scotland. In England Scientology had been considered not to be a religion in *R. v Registrar General ex parte Segerdal* [1970] 2 QB 697.
63 The precise wording used in the ceremonies of the nominating body may be asked for: Marriage (Scotland) Act 1977, s. 9 (3).
64 A rejection can be appealed to the Secretary of State. If the ground of rejection is that the nominating body is not a religious or belief body, it may further appeal to the Court of Session: Marriage (Scotland) Act 1977, s. 9 (6).

on proof of status within a recognised belief system. Removal of a nominee from the list of approved celebrants is dealt with by s. 10. The grounds include the request of the nominee or the nominating body, or that the form of ceremony used by the body is no longer of an appropriate form. Alternatively a nominee may be removed if convicted of an offence under the 1977 Act, or has been solemnising marriages as a business for profit or gain, or is not a fit and proper person or (curiously) 'for any other reason'.[65]

Location

A marriage other than a civil marriage can be solemnised anywhere in Scotland, including on board a ship in territorial waters. For many years after its introduction in 1939 civil marriage could take place only in the office of the local registrar. However, since 2002 civil marriage may take place in any location approved by the relevant local authority.[66] Many hotels and other locations, including some ships, have arranged to be so approved.[67]

Form of ceremony

There is no requirement of a particular form of words, or that a marriage ceremony be conducted in English.[68] However, by s. 14 of the 1977 Act, no matter who is solemnising the marriage, the ceremony must include a declaration by the parties, in the presence of each other, the celebrant and two witnesses, that they accept each other as husband and wife, followed by declaration by the celebrant that the parties are husband and wife. That exchange of consent to marriage must be genuine.[69] Where there is a failure of true consent the purported marriage is void.[70]

Forced marriage or deception leading to a marriage is unlawful, the person or persons compelling or arranging the marriage committing a crime.[71] Protection against forced marriage is available for persons fearing such compulsion through court orders under the Forced Marriage (Protection and Jurisdiction) (Scotland) Act 2011, asp 15.[72]

---

65 Reference point, n. 12 *supra*.
66 S. 18A of the Marriage (Scotland) Act 1977 inserted by the Marriage (Scotland) Act, 2002 asp 8, implemented by the Marriage (Approval of Places) (Scotland) Regulations, 2002 SSI 260, as amended by 2006 SSI 573.
67 In the days of irregular marriage (*infra* n. 95) marriages frequently took place in hotels, or other locations. The early issues of the 'Congregational Record' of my church (1870s on) notes marriages celebrated in hotels, cafés, even the minister's manse. A list of locations approved for civil marriage is available from www.gro-scotland.gov.uk, as is the Registrar General's guidance for local authorities.
68 The celebrant may require an interpreter to be present. The interpreter cannot be a party or a witness: Marriage (Scotland) Act 1977, s. 22.
69 There is concern with regard to sham marriages or civil partnerships entered into for immigration, residence or citizenship purposes. Cf. UK Home Office, 'Sham Marriages and Civil Partnerships: Background Information and Proposed Referral and Investigation Scheme', November 2013 and the Immigration Act 2014, Part 4, ss. 48–71. The s. 53 power to extend the referral scheme to Scotland has not yet been exercised. For Scotland see also *supra* n. 48.
70 Marriage (Scotland) Act 1977 s. 20A, inserted by s. 2 of the Family Law (Scotland) Act 2006, asp 2. Such failure includes a party being incapable of understanding the nature of marriage, or of consenting to the marriage or consenting under duress or error, the latter including the other party not being the person the consenter thought he or she was marrying (cf. ? Jacob and Leah, Gen. 29: 16–23).
71 Anti-social Behaviour, Crime and Policing Act 2014, s. 122.
72 Ten orders were issued down to 2014, but as yet there have been no prosecutions for a breach of an order. The Sheriff Court has jurisdiction.

Registration

Since marriage affected rights of property, inheritance and aliment, some form of public record was desirable.[73] At first church records might evidence a marriage. In 1551 the Provincial Council of the Scottish Church required the keeping of parochial registers of baptism and of proclamations of banns of marriage.[74] The General Assembly of 1616 similarly required records to be kept, as did the Assembly of 1639 following the re-establishing of Presbyterianism.[75] However, the clearest ecclesiastical statement of the importance of recording marriages is at the end of the section on the solemnisation of marriage in the Westminster *Directory of Public Worship* of 1644: 'A Register is to be carefully kept where in the names of the parties so married, with time of their marriage are forthwith to be fairly recorded in a book provided for that purpose for the perusal of all whom it may concern'.

However, church records were notoriously erratic, and, apart from that defect, did not contain data on marriages constituted other than in a Kirk ceremony. Matters were therefore considerably improved by the Registration of Births, and Marriages (Scotland) Act 1854, which set up a national system. Records were kept by a local registrar for the district, with duplicates transmitted to the General Register Office in Edinburgh. That system now persists under the Registration of Births, Marriages and Deaths (Scotland) Act, 1965. A completed marriage schedule is registered in terms of ss. 15 or 19 of the Marriage (Scotland) Act 1977. Failure to register a marriage attracts a fine (s. 24). The validity of a registered marriage cannot be questioned with regard to any failure to comply with the provisions of the Act (s. 23A).

Civil marriage

Civil marriage was introduced for Scotland by the Marriage (Scotland) Act 1939. Its justification lay in recognising the wishes of some to marry without religious connotations. It also made it possible for parties whose ecclesiastical community would not recognise their relationship (for example, divorced persons) to marry. This rendered redundant the use of the sheriff's warrant for the registration of irregular marriages constituted by declaration *de praesenti* or by promise *subsequente copula*.[76] Civil marriages are registrable.[77]

The requirements and procedures for civil marriage are now set out in ss. 18–20 of the Marriage (Scotland) Act 1977, as amended. *Mutatis mutandis* they mirror those for religious marriage. Civil marriage is created through the exchange of the consent of the parties in the presence of an authorised district registrar after proper public notice and registration. The location may be anywhere in Scotland, but must not take place in religious premises.[78]

---

73 A. Crowther and A. Cameron, 'Civil Registration; The Law and the Individual in Scotland since 1854', in M.A. Mulhern, ed., *The Law*, Vol. 13 of *Scottish Life and Society: A Compendium of Scottish Ethnology* (Edinburgh: Donald, 2012) 655–71. See also the relevant parts of 'The Scottish Way of Life and Death': http://www.gla.ac.uk/schools/socialpolitical/research/economicsocialhistory/historymedicine/scottishwayofbirthanddeath/
74 SSC Stat 251 (p.142).
75 J.G. Kyd, 'Registration', in M.R. McLarty, ed., *A Source Book of Administrative Law in Scotland* (London: Hodge, 1956), 64 at 66.
76 See *infra* at n. 104. These forms of irregular marriage were abolished by the Marriage (Scotland) Act, 1939.
77 See *supra* at n. 73 ff.
78 Civil Partnership Act 2004, s. 93(3).

The form of words used, any music and readings and poetry incorporated in the ceremony is a matter for the parties. In the past since civil marriage was a non-religious secular procedure religious elements used to be barred. Now, they are permitted so long as they do not involve the participation of the registrar.[79]

Until 2002 civil marriage could take place only in the district office of the relevant local registrar. Now local authorities may approve other sites for the purpose.[80] Locations such as stately homes, castles or hotels may thus be approved as venues for the solemnization of civil marriages.[81] Single-instance approval is also competent, allowing parties to choose whatever venue they wish provided that local authority approval is obtained.[82] Even vessels in Scottish waters may be approved as venues for civil marriage.[83]

Same-sex marriage[84]

The marriage of same-sex couples was introduced by the Marriage and Civil Partnership (Scotland) Act 2014, asp 5.[85] The main innovation is, of course, the marriage of same-sex couples, removing the previous ground of objection,[86] and altering such matters as the 'prohibited degrees of matrimony'.[87] Definitions of 'marriage', 'widow' and 'widower' are inserted in Schedule 1 to the Interpretation and Legislative Reform (Scotland) Act 2010, asp 10, (s. 4(14)). By ss. 8–11 civil partners may marry or convert their partnership into marriage. Other parts of the law relating to civil relationships are amended, including enactments and other documents that may have legal effect or meaning.[88] Section 5(2) adds s. 3A to the Divorce (Scotland) Act 1976 to make it clear 'for the avoidance of doubt' that adultery in a same-sex marriage has the same meaning as within heterosexual marriage. On the other hand s. 5(1), again 'for the avoidance of doubt' provides that the rule that a marriage may be

---

79 General Register Office for Scotland, 'Getting Married in Scotland': http://www.nrscotland.gov.uk/registration/getting-married-in-scotland/marriage-ceremonies-in-scotland
80 The Marriage (Scotland) Act 1977, s. 18A, added by the Marriage (Scotland) Act 2002, asp. 8.
81 There are now several authorised venues in Gretna Green, continuing the tradition of the area. See *infra*, 'Obsolete modes of marriage'.
82 The Marriage (Approval of Places) (Scotland) Regulations 2002, 2002 SSI 260, sets out how that approval can be given. Reg. 11 sets three years as the maximum duration for any one approval, but it may be renewed (Reg. 12).
83 The Marriage (Approval of Places) (Scotland) Amendment Regulations 2006, 2006 SSI 573; Civil Partnership Act 2003, s. 93 (5).
84 Same-sex marriage is not a human right under the European Convention: *Gas and Dubois* v *France*, Judgement, 15 March 2012, ECHR Chamber V, App. No. 25951/07, 2012-II ECHR 245. Notwithstanding, states may enact appropriate legislation.
85 The marriage of same-sex couples entered into in England and Wales is recognised in Scotland: s. 10 and Sch. 2 of the Marriage (Same-Sex Couples) Act 2013, the agreement of the Scottish Parliament being expressed by its Legislative Consent Motion no. 141, Marriage (Same-Sex Couples) Bill (S4M-6924). Consensual homosexual acts in private are decriminalised by s. 80(1) of the Criminal Justice (Scotland) Act 1980, though some homosexual acts remain criminal: Sexual Offences (Scotland) Act 2009, asp 9. As of the end of 2014, 16 countries (and parts of three others) permit same-sex marriages with several others likely to do so.
86 Marriage and Civil Partnership (Scotland) Act 2014, s. 2, removing s. 5(4)(e) of the Marriage (Scotland) Act 1977.
87 Marriage and Civil Partnership (Scotland) Act 2014, s. 1, amending s. 2 of the Marriage (Scotland) Act 1977, and its Schedule 1.
88 Thus the terms widow and widower are extended to apply to the relict of a same-sex marriage (s. 4(10)-(11)) in documents executed after the Act came into effect unless the document specifically provides otherwise (s. 4 (12)).

voidable on grounds of impotence applies only to heterosexual marriage. It is open to belief systems and denominations themselves to elect whether to be registered as allowing their 'celebrants' to conduct same-sex marriage ceremonies.[89]

Of course same-sex marriage runs counter to many religious views. To prevent such views being opened to question under the new regime, s. 19 of the 2014 Act protects freedom of thought, conscience and religion, the right of freedom of expression and any equivalent legal right.

Civil partnership

The Civil Partnership Act 2004, s. 1, introduced civil partnership to UK law. It has later been amended.[90] Part 3 of the Act contains particular provisions that tailor the concept to Scots law. By s. 85 a civil partnership is created by registration under the procedures of ss. 80–100 of the Act. Registration is carried out by district registrars.[91] Eligibility to enter a civil partnership is defined by s. 86 in a list of negatives. A couple is ineligible to register a partnership if not of the same sex, if related in a forbidden degree,[92] if either is under 16, if either is married or already in a civil partnership, if either is incapable of understanding the nature of civil partnership or of validly consenting to its formation. The Act extensively adapts a whole raft of statutory and other law, providing for the parties to a civil partnership access to most of the rights that are available to married couples, including aliment (support), taxation, pensions, occupancy, tenancy and other property rights, rights of succession (s. 131) and rights under policies of assurance (s. 132).[93] By s. 96 it is possible for a couple, one of whom has undergone a gender reassignment under the Gender Recognition Act 2004, to enter a civil partnership immediately after divorce. By s. 128 there can be no 'breach of promise' cases: no rights arise from a promise to enter into a civil partnership, nor any action thereanent in Scotland irrespective of where the promise may have been made.

Civil partnerships are ended by death, presumption of death[94] or by dissolution on grounds analogous to those applicable in divorce (ss. 117–9, 121–2). Nullity is possible (s. 123), as is separation (s. 120).

*

---

89 The Marriage (Scotland) Act 1977, s. 8 was amended in various ways by s. 12 of the 2014 Act. By a new s. 8(1A) the Scottish ministers can prescribe religious or belief bodies whose ceremonies may be recognised for the purpose of marriage. By new s. 8(1B) ministers etc. of a religious belief body may be registered as celebrants if they meet the normal requirements, but by new s. 8(1C), a religious or belief body can be registered for the conduct of same-sex marriage only if it so requests and otherwise meets qualifying requirements. By a new s. 8(1D) there is no duty on a religious body to seek to have a celebrant registered to conduct such marriages. However, the Legal Committee of the Church of Scotland has expressed doubts as to how secure this protection may be in the face of Human Rights anent discrimination: Joint Report of the Theological Forum and the Legal Questions Committee to the Committee on Returns to Overtures, GA Reports, 2015, 23/1.
90 The Marriage and Civil Partnership (Scotland) Act 2014, asp 5, alters some minor details, mainly procedural.
91 In practice registering civil partnerships has been added to the normal duties of district registrars. At the ceremony religious elements may be included, so long as they do not involve the registrar. Cf. *supra* n. 79.
92 The degrees of relationship whether of consanguinity or affinity within which a civil partnership is forbidden are set out in Sch. 10. Relationships of the whole or the half blood are included (s. 86.9).
93 Many amendments made by Sch. 28 to the Act insert the phrase 'or civil partner' into a number of Scottish statutes, for example the Succession (Scotland) Act 1964.
94 Sch. 28, paras 45–6 of the 2004 Act appropriately amended the Presumption of Death (Scotland) Act 1977.

Obsolete modes of marriage: irregular marriage and clandestine marriage

Irregular marriage[95]

For centuries three irregular modes of marriage were available under Scots Law, *matrimonium per verba de praesenti*, by promise *subsequente copula* and marriage by habit and repute.[96] They no longer exist. These modes had existed for centuries throughout Europe,[97] but, as noted above, in 1563 the Council of Trent deprived them of validity.[98] However, being no longer under papal jurisdiction the Tridentine Decree was without effect in Scotland. Irregular marriage continued, the Reformers conceiving of marriage as being primarily theological, and only incidentally civil and in any case not a sacrament.[99] Consent to marriage was effective wherever and however that consent might be given. Constituted by consent alone a religious ceremony was unnecessary for marriage, desirable though it might be.

For centuries irregular marriage was the only recourse for parties wishing to become man and wife in law in Scotland but who could not, did not or would not use the standard forms. Churches would not marry divorced persons, and civil marriage was not possible until 1939. Indeed, despite its name 'irregular marriage' became a regular phenomenon. Because of the legal effects of marriage there were many court cases, often with rights of aliment or inheritance at stake. In due course the emergence of rights to pensions or social security benefits added impetus to court declarators that a marriage existed or had existed.[100] Newspaper reports show many cases were defended, some fiercely, particularly when inheritance was involved.

Matrimonium per verba de praesenti was a verbal exchange of consent to marriage before witnesses.[101] Alternatively a marriage might be constituted by promise *subsequente*

---

95 Reference point, nn. 21, 33, and 67 *supra*.
96 J.W. Brodie-Innes, 'Some Outstanding Differences Between English and Scots Law, 1 The Marriage Law' (1914) 26 Jur. Rev. 396–409. His 'Some Curiosities of International Marriage Law' (1918–19), 13 Ill. LR 183–99, in part traverses the same ground; T.B. Smith, 'Comparative Observations on Scottish and English Consistorial Law in 1952' (1953), 69 ICLQ, 30–45.
97 While they existed they clearly reflected the proposition that all that was required for marriage was the consent of the parties.
98 *Supra* n. 31. There is little trace of Canon Law roots in Scots law. See in *An Introductory Survey of the Sources and Literature of Scots Law*, Stair Society, Vol. 1 (Edinburgh: Stair Society, 1936), D.B. Smith, 'Canon Law', 183–92; and J.C. Gardner, 'The Influence of the Law of Moses', 235–40. Cf. W.G. Miller, 'The Canon Law and Scottish Presbyterianism' (1888) 32 J. of Jurisprudence, 113–27.
99 The seven sacraments of the Roman Catholic Church are baptism, confirmation, holy Eucharist (communion), penance (confession), anointing of the sick (formerly, extreme unction), holy orders and marriage. They are considered necessary for salvation, and as 'signs of grace'. They are effective by their administration. The Scottish Reformers considered the sacraments to consist only of Baptism and Communion.
100 L. Leneman, *Promises, Promises: Marriage Litigation in Scotland, 1698–1830* (Edinburgh: NMS Enterprises, 2003); J.A. Lovat-Fraser, 'Some Points of Difference Between English and Scotch Law' (1894), 10 LQR 340–347.
101 Since at first there was no requirement as to residence or notice, this mode was the basis of 'Gretna Green' marriages. 'Lord Hardwicke's Act' of 1753, 26 Geo. II, c. 33, 'An Act for the Better Preventing of Clandestine Marriage', banned irregular marriages in England and required marriage in England to be celebrated by an Anglican clergyman after the due proclamation of banns or a registrar's licence. Gretna Green, not far over the Border into Scotland on a newly constructed turnpike road, became popular with eloping English couples, as did other Border villages. Another advantage was that eighteenth century Scots law permitted marriage without parental consent at the age of 14 for males and 12 for females. This was raised to 16 for both by the Marriage (Scotland) Act, 1929. By the Marriage (Scotland) Act 1856, 21 days' residence in Scotland was required for a valid *de praesenti* marriage.

172   *Personal relationships*

copula, the marriage being constituted by sexual intercourse on the faith of a prior promise to marry.[102] In either case, if the existence of the marriage was disputed, what had happened had to be proved in court. In the first instance (hopefully) the witnesses could be produced. In the second the existence of the promise required proof, and that proof could be only by the writ or oath of the parties.

In the ordinary case, however, there was an ingenious way of bringing either of these two forms of irregular marriage to the attention of the civil authorities so that it would be recognised in the civil law. The solution lay in the criminal law. Contracting an irregular marriage was a criminal offence, but latterly one without penalty other than the conviction.[103] Accordingly, parties could go to the police, and intimate their offence. Pleading guilty to the offence of contracting an irregular marriage resulted in a criminal conviction. The civil authorities then accepted an extract of that conviction as proof of the marriage and registered the marriage. 'Getting married before the sheriff' therefore became a frequent phenomenon in Scots law, and a tribute to the capacity of the locals to use the law to advantage. Successive annual reports of the Registrar General for Scotland indicate the incidence of the registration of such marriages, though it should be noted that not all 'irregular' marriages went through court procedures, and therefore do not appear in the statistics.[104]

The third form of irregular marriage was 'habit and repute'.[105] Marriage could be presumed if the parties cohabited and it was proved in court that there was a general belief that they were in fact married. Marriage by habit and repute originated with the Scots Act 1503 c. 22, which established a presumption of marriage, allowing a woman reputed as wife to claim terce from the estate of her deceased husband.[106] In its modern form it was not merely a question of establishing the repute of marriage. The parties had to be capable of marriage to each other.[107] Further, a court determination was needed for civil effects to follow.

---

102 On 12 April 1568 Aberdeen Kirk Session ordered the parties to such a marriage to repent before being 'properly' married: *Selections from the Records of the Kirk Session, Presbytery and Synod of Aberdeen* (Spalding Club, Aberdeen, 1846), 14.

103 Irregular marriage was not a crime at common law, *Ballantyne* (1859) 3 Irv 352, but was prohibited by various Acts, for example, 1661 c. 246 and 1698 c. 6. Penalties were abolished by s. 3 of the Marriage (Scotland) Act 1916.

104 Ancestor tracers take note. See Fraser, *supra* n. 24 I, 257. The extract conviction was first made registrable by ss. 47–8 of the Marriage (Scotland) Act 1854. The Marriage (Scotland) Act 1856, s. 2, simplified procedure, allowing registration of irregular marriages by warrant of the Sheriff without formal criminal proceedings. This procedure was abolished by the 1939 Marriage (Scotland) Act along with the *de praesenti* and promise *subsequente copula* forms. 'Habit and repute' always required a determination by a court: see next paras.

105 Reference point, *supra* n. 21.

106 Terce was the right of a widow to a share of the estate of her deceased husband. It was abolished by s. 10(1) of the Succession (Scotland) Act 1964, ss. 8–9 substituting other benefits for a widow. The Canon Law basis was a rescript of Pope Gregory IX, 4.4.1.30: Fraser, *supra* n. 24, I 323; *Dalrymple* (1811) 2 Hag. CR 54. Cf. *Longworth* v *Yelverton* (1862) 1 M. 161; rev. (1864) 2 M. (HL) 49.

107 'The fact to be proved was that the parties themselves did mean and intend to contract the relation of marriage and had truly formed that relation, the indications of which gave rise to the habit and repute. But the belief and understanding of others do not make and constitute the relation of marriage. It is the consent of the parties inferred from and evidenced by the conduct which gives rise to the opinion of others. The most complete proof of habit and repute may often exist in crowded cities, as to persons living together, especially in the lower ranks of life, when nevertheless both knew well that each or one has a spouse living in another place, and when, whatever colour they allow neighbours to assume as to their relation, they never intended to contract, and knew that they could not contract, the relation of marriage'. Per Lord Justice-Clerk Hope in *Lapsley* v *Grierson* (1845) 8 D 34 at 47. See also Fraser, *supra* n. 24, I 322–90; Walton, *supra* n. 24, 29–33. Fraser I at 322–3 thought the facts constituted a pre-contract, converted into marriage by the declarator of the civil court.

Marriage was not truly constituted by habit and repute. Rather the civil authorities presumed a marriage to have occurred, and therefore consequentially applied its civil effects upon proof of a factual situation.[108] An actual exchange of consent to marriage was not proven, but was presumed to have occurred at some former time if a general belief could be demonstrated that the parties, constantly and openly cohabitating together and treating each other as husband and wife, were married.[109] Numerous cases discussed how long a period of cohabitation had to elapse to satisfy the requirement of the law or the public acceptance of the arrangement as a marriage.[110] However, there always had to have been matrimonial intent. Concubinage *simpliciter* did not result in marriage.[111]

Making known the exchange of matrimonial consent would have been advanced had the Reformers abandoned irregular marriages, though perhaps excepting habit and repute as a general means of doing justice in particular circumstances. That said, Scotland now no longer has irregular marriage. As recommended by the Morison Committee,[112] marriage by declaration *de praesenti* and by promise *subsequente copula* were abolished by s. 5 of the Marriage (Scotland) Act 1939.[113] The Committee also recommended that habit and repute should also disappear, but the 1939 Act left that possibility open as a generally useful catch-all provision.[114] It remained available until abolished, subject to transitional arrangements, by s. 3.1 of the Family Law (Scotland) Act 2006.[115]

---

108 A wonderful exhibition of the difficulties to which this concept gave birth is the long-running case of *Longworth* v *Yelverton*, reported in its Scottish aspects as (1862) 1 M. 161, rev. (1864) 2 M (HL) 49. An account of its progress through three jurisdictions is W. Roughead, 'The Law and Mrs Yelverton' (1916), 28 Jur. Rev. 38–67. The inadequate Wikipedia article on the 'Yelverton Case' omits its Scottish element. Cf. http://media.britishnewspaperarchive.co.uk/bna-media.php?id=19&ids=61. See also A.B. Erickson and J.R. McCarthy, 'The Yelverton Case: Civil Legislation and Marriage' (1971), 14 Victorian Stud. 275–91. After losing her case in the House of Lords 'Mrs Yelverton' became a noted author. Cf. www.nps.gov/yose/historyculture/yelverton.htm

109 Fraser, *supra* n. 24, I 391–414; Walton, *supra* n. 24, 34–7. Clive, *supra* n. 24, para 05.025; Cf. C.5.4.9, which established a presumption of marriage. Stair, 1.4.6; 4.45.19 (thirdly): Erskine, 1.6.6: D.I.C. Ashton Cross 'Cohabitation with habit and repute', 1961 Jur. Rev. 21–31. See also *Leslie* v *Leslie* (1859) 22. D 993, particularly Lord Deas at 1011–18; *Campbell* v *Campbell* (1866) 4 M. 876, affd. (1867) 5 M. (HL) 115; *Petrie* v *Petrie*, 1911 SC 360; *Nicol* v *Bell*, 1954 SLT 314; *Low* v *Gorman* 1970 SLT 356; *Doherty or Vosilius* v *Vosilius*, 2000 SCLR 79, 2000 Fam. LR 58; *Ackerman* v *Blackburn et al.* 2000 Fam. LR 35; 2002 SLT 37, 2001 Fam. LR 90; *Weatherill or Sheikh* v *Sheikh*, 2005 Fam. LR 7; *S* v *S* 2006 SLT 471, 2006 Fam. LR 54. *AS* v *CS* [2006] CSOH 55 is unusual as being between living parties. A. Barlow and G. James, 'Regulating Marriage and Cohabitation in 21st Century Britain' (2004) 67 Mod. LR 143–76; W.D.H. Sellar, 'Marriage by cohabitation with habit and repute: review and requiem', in D.L. Carey Miller and D.W. Meyers, eds, *Comparative and Historical Essays in Scots Law: A Tribute to Professor Sir Thomas Smith, QC* (Edinburgh: Butterworths, 1992) 117–36.

110 For example, many of the cases cited n. 109 *supra*, esp. the Opinion of Lord Nimmo Smith in the Outer House proceeding in *Ackerman*.

111 *Cossar* v *Cossar* 1901 4 SLT 44.

112 *Report of the Departmental Committee Appointed to Enquire into the Law of Scotland Relating to the Constitution of Marriage*, Chairman, Lord Morison, 1937, Cmd. 5354.

113 Parties putatively 'married' by such means prior to the 1939 Act coming into force might still prove that their marriage had been so constituted.

114 Again cf. some of the cases *supra* n. 109. Not all were successful.

115 The bulk of the Family Law (Scotland) Act 2006 was brought into force on 4 May 2006 (2006, No. 212). Its s. 3.2 retains the possibility of a declarator of marriage by habit and repute where the cohabitation ended before commencement of the Act, or began before and ended after its commencement, or began before and continues after its commencement. Cohabitation beginning after 4 May 2006 is therefore excluded from the possibility of recognition as marriage by declarator. By ss. 3.3 and 3.4 habit and repute may be invoked where one of the

The corollary of 'habit and repute' used to be a declarator of 'freedom and putting to silence'. That recourse was abolished by s. 42 of the Family Law (Scotland) Act 2006 asp 2.

Clandestine marriage[116]

Since the theory of marriage made the consent of the parties the sole essential to its constitution, it was possible that some might 'marry' with a religious service, but not one conducted by a minister of the Kirk, or one conducted by a Kirk minister but without banns having been called. Such marriages were termed clandestine. A clandestine marriage was a true marriage, but was irregular in mode, being in fact constituted *per verba de praesenti*. Penalties were laid down by the 'Act against clandestine and unlawful marriages', 1661 c. 246, for persons who, 'shall hereafter marry or procure themselves to be married in a clandestine and inorderly way or by Jesuits, priests or any others not authorised by this kirk'. The celebrant was to be banished. The Act 1698 c. 6 added further penalties if the persons so married did not give the civil authorities the names of the celebrant and the witnesses. Technically the marriage was unlawful, but once registration was introduced certification of the marriage ceremony was accepted by the civil authorities and the marriage was duly registered. It is therefore clear that clandestine and irregular marriages might be constituted with a religious ceremony, and they were valid, although there were penalties, and the person celebrating the marriage was not legally qualified so to do.[117]

Dissolution of marriage: divorce

Divorce

The Divorce (Scotland) Act 1976, as amended, is the ruling statute on the ending of marriage during the life of the parties. Before the Reformation, divorce *a vinculo* (from the bonds of marriage) was unknown in Scotland. Separation *a mensa et thoro* (from table and bed) was competent, but this did not cancel the marriage. Rather the various grounds of nullity elaborated by the Catholic Church were used to terminate a 'marriage'.[118] Consistorial jurisdiction was vested in the bishops. Normally, however, the 'dissolution' of marriages formed a proportion of the matériél dealt with by commissary courts, which operated in most of Scotland.[119] In them procedures were more formal.[120]

---

parties is domiciled in Scotland, the other party has died also domiciled in Scotland, they purported to marry outwith the UK, they believed themselves to be validly married, the purported marriage was invalid under its local law, and the party seeking declarator only became aware of this after the death of the other party.
116 Reference point, n. 55, *supra*.
117 Penalties on the parties to, and the celebrant of, an irregular marriage were abolished by the Marriage (Scotland) Act 1916, s. 3. The leading case on these statutes was *HMA* v *Ballantyne* (1859) 3 Irv. 352. See also *HMA* v *Dickson* (1844) 2 Broun 278. Irvine's *Justiciarv Reports*, Vol. 3, Appendix prints the libels and short statements of the proceedings of five prosecutions under these acts. Of these, four (excluding no. IV) narrate the pannel (sc. accused) as having falsely assumed the character of a clergyman, though it is clear, even from the fact that these men maintained records of. the marriages they 'celebrated' and gave 'marriage certificates', that they thought of themselves as acting as ministers.
118 J.D. Scanlan, 'Husband and Wife. Pre-Reformation Canon Law of Marriage of the Officials' Courts', in *Introduction to Scottish Legal History*, Stair Soc. Vol. 20, 1958, 69–81 gives details of the pre-Reformation law. See also *William Hay's Lectures on Marriage*, trans. and ed. J.C. Barry, Stair Soc. Vol. 24, 1967.
119 Fraser, *supra* n. 24, I 1–12.
120 See in *An Introduction to Scottish Legal History*, Stair Society, Vol. 20, Edinburgh, 1958, G. Donaldson, 'The Church Courts', 363–73; J.D. Scanlan, 'Husband and Wife: Pre-Reformation Canon Law of Marriage of the

Divorce *a vinculo* was introduced by the reformed church. Immediately after the 1560 reformation statutes, the old church courts continued to exercise their previous role in family matters despite the abolition of the papal jurisdiction.[121] In 1563 jurisdiction was transferred to the civil commissary courts.[122] Divorce for adultery was contemplated by Head IX of the *First Book of Discipline*, and nominally adultery was made subject to penalty – even death – by the Act 1563 c.10 (c. 74 12mo).[123] The Act 1592 c. 11 (c. 119) stripped an adulterous woman of her rights to dispose of her property to the prejudice of her lawful heirs. Last, the Act 1600 c. 29 (c. 20 12mo) prohibited the marriage of adulterers with the person with whom in the relevant divorce proceedings they had been adjudged to have committed adultery, but the practice soon developed of omitting the name of the 'other party' from the decree.

Immediately after the Reformation the other permissible ground of divorce was desertion. Divorce for desertion (or perhaps its regulation) was introduced by the Act 1573, c. 1, (c. 55, 12mo),[124] though it may be traced to the teaching of the continental reformers, particularly to Calvin.[125] The Kirk has not, however, played any very active part in the development of divorce law since losing its jurisdiction in such matters in 1563. That development has been in the hands of the civil courts and Parliament.

Cruelty and its cognates were introduced by the Divorce (Scotland) Act of 1938, allowing divorce in circumstances that did not fit desertion or adultery.[126] Compared with the interventions of the Church of England, the Kirk was dilatory. The General Assemblies of 1937, 1957 and 1958 discussed divorce law reform, but their deliberations did not have much effect. By contrast the review of the divorce law of England by a group appointed by the Archbishop of Canterbury, *Putting Asunder*, 1966, began the discussion of irretrievable breakdown as a sole ground of divorce that continued through the English Law Commission report *Reform of the Grounds of Divorce: The Field of Choice* (1967, Cmnd. 3123), and eventually resulted in the (English) Divorce Reform Act 1969. The Scottish Law Commission Report *Divorce: The Grounds Considered* (1967, Cmnd. 3256) echoed its English equivalent. The Social and Moral Welfare Board of the Church of Scotland returned to divorce in 1967 and 1968. Presbytery discussion of its 1967 report saw 36 of the home presbyteries accepting irretrievable breakdown as a sole ground of divorce, as did the General Assembly in 1968. The Kirk was not, however, a prime mover in the adoption of 'irretrievable breakdown' as the sole ground of divorce by s. 1 of the Divorce (Scotland) Act, 1976.[127]

Officials' Court', 69–81; R.D. Ireland, 'Husband and Wife: (a) Post-Reformation Canon Law of Marriage of the Commissaries' Courts and (b) 'Modern Common and Statute Law', 82–9; and 'Husband and Wife: Divorce, Nullity of Marriage and Separation', 90–98; Cf. J. Irvine Smith, J. 'The Transition to the Modern Law, 1532–1660' at 25–43.

121 See from n. 120 *supra*, R.D. Ireland, 'Husband and Wife', 90–98; G. Donaldson, 'The Church Courts', 363–73.
122 The Court of Session Act, 1830, s. 33, transferred consistorial jurisdiction to the Court of Session.
123 Church law forbad ministers to adulterers (GA 1566, Act 3).
124 The Act 1573 c. 1 (c.55 12mo) narrated that divorce for desertion had been lawful since August 1560 – the date of the Reformation in Scotland.
125 D.B. Smith, 'A Note on Divorce for Desertion' (1939), 51 Jur. Rev. 254–9. Ch, 24.4 of the Westminster Confession of Faith, 1646, states that desertion or adultery are the only sufficient grounds for divorce.
126 Until the 1938 development judicial separation was the only remedy for such cases.
127 Irretrievable breakdown encompassed the previous separate grounds of divorce, except desertion: Family Law (Scotland) Act 2006 asp. 2, s. 12 (except for proceedings begun before 4 May 2006). Desertion is in effect present through non-cohabitation.

The perception that irretrievable breakdown in the abstract is the ground of divorce, is inaccurate. At least one of four sets of facts has to be established although the court does not place or apportion blame for their occurrence. These are adultery, unreasonable behaviour, separation for one year if the defender is consenting to the divorce and two years' separation without that consent (s. 1(2)).[128] It is competent to move from a judicial separation to divorce (s. 3). In that case divorce may be postponed where a religious marriage is involved, and the applicant is prevented from entering into a religious marriage because of a requirement of the religion involved and the other party could act to remove that difficulty. The court can order the other party so to act.[129]

In 1983 divorce, while remaining possible in the Court of Session, became competent also in the sheriff courts.[130] Of itself that removal from the superior court showed that traditional views were being departed from, and that religion no longer coloured the marital relationship as supremely important and profound. Divorce has been simplified. In addition various historic provisions have disappeared. The pre-Reformation Act 1429 c. 125 requiring pursuers in divorce to swear that their cause was just – the oath of calumny – was abolished by s. 9 of the 1976 Act. Again until abolished by s. 10 of the 1976 Act it was possible for a pursuer in divorce for adultery to cite the paramour and seek damages.[131] The bar to divorce based on collusion between the parties has now disappeared thanks to s. 14 of the Family Law (Scotland) Act 2006 asp. 2.

Taking all these developments together, it is clear that the function of the law of divorce in Scotland is to regulate the ending of marriage in the interest of society in general, not to reflect or implement theological principles.

*

Parent and child

This area of law has undergone much change. I confine what follows to material with religious impact. The 1989 Convention on the Rights of the Child (1989) has some relevance, although it has not been incorporated into UK law.[132]

Traditionally it was for the parents of a child to bring up a child including in matters religious, although as noted in the chapter on Education, the Reformers were anxious that the result should not stray far from their views.[133] The right to decide on the religion was usually

---

128 Desertion was removed from the s. 1(2) list of facts by s. 12 of the Family Law (Scotland) Act 2006.
129 Divorce (Scotland) Act, 1976, s.3A, inserted by s. 15 of the Family Law Act 2006 asp 2. This provision could apply in the refusal of a Jew to obtain a 'divorce', a *get*, from a rabbinical authority. 'Any Hebrew congregation' has been prescribed as being an authority for the purpose of s.3A: The Divorce (Religious Bodies) (Scotland) Regulations 2006, 2006 SSI 253.
130 Sheriff Courts (Scotland) Act 1907 s. 2B, inserted by s. 1 of the Divorce Jurisdiction etc. (Scotland) Act 1983.
131 Conjugal Rights (Scotland) Amendment Act 1861, s. 7.
132 Convention on the Rights of the Child, 1989, 1577 UNTS 3; 1992 UKTS 44, Cm. 1976. The international obligation exists and usually courts endeavour not to run counter to such. However, to be relied on as a matter of law the obligations must be incorporated by domestic legislation: *R (SG and others)* v *Secretary of State for Work and Pensions* [2015] UKSC 16.
133 *First Book of Discipline*, Head V (5) *ad fin* (1560): 'this must be carefully provided, that no father, of what estate and condition that he ever be, use his children at his own fantasy, especially in their youth-head; but all must be compelled to bring up their children in learning and virtue'.

that of the father,[134] unless the child was illegitimate in which case the right was held by the mother. However, illegitimacy has been more or less abolished as a matter of legal consequence.[135] Parental Rights were equalised by s. 10 of the Guardianship Act 1973 (now s. 2 of the Children (Scotland) Act 1995) and relate to any child under 18 (s.2 (7)). The old common law rights and duties were abolished and superseded by 'parental responsibilities' as listed in s. 1(4) of the 1995 Act, which include direction and guidance and the rights listed in s. 2. By s. 3 the mother has same rights. In determining the religion in which a child is to be brought up (at least initially) the views of the child are overlooked. Of course difficulties can emerge when the parents' views as to the appropriate religion differ. Most obviously this can happen when parents' divorce, in which case it is to be hoped that an accommodation can be arrived at.[136] If not the best interests of the child, as seen by the court, are dispositive. The courts are not willing to choose between religions.[137] However, there is a tendency to go with the religion of the parent having custody,[138] though there might be concerns where a religion might imperil physical welfare of the child.[139] Much might depend on assurances given to the court.

---

134 Per Lord. Kyllachy in *Kincaid* v *Quarrier* (1896) 23 R. 676 at 681.
135 Formally illegitimacy was abolished by s. 1 of the Law Reform (Parent and Child) (Scotland) Act 1986, as substituted by s. 21 of the Family Law (Scotland) Act 2006, asp 2. There are no Scottish bastards (in law at any rate) although some of the former incidents of illegitimacy remain in other forms, for example in succession to titles. See *Stair Memorial Encyclopaedia of the Law of Scotland*, Vol. 6, para 690. F.A. Barlow and G. James, 'Regulating Marriage and Cohabitation in 21st century Britain', 2004 67 Mod. L.R. 143.
136 In the past some religious instruction was favoured: *McKay* v *McKay* 1957 SLT (Notes) 17; *McClements* v *McClements*, 1958 SC 286. I do not know what current judicial thinking is on this matter.
137 *McNaught* v *McNaught* 1955 SLT (Sh. Ct.) 9.
138 *M* v *C* 2002 SLT (Sh. Ct.) 82.
139 For example where the religion might disapprove of or avoid medical intervention: see Chapter 8, 12 Medical Practice.

8 Other interactions of religion and law

Education and Personal Relationships have been given separate treatment. The many other interactions of law and religion that affect individuals can be dealt with more summarily.

First, a general observation. In previous centuries the Christian faith as understood mainly through Protestantism undergirded Scottish society and was reflected in Scots law. Of course the Church of Scotland was a major force. As we have seen, slowly other denominations and belief systems gained recognition, affecting and changing expectations. Some of that is clear in history. After the Union of the Parliaments in 1707 Westminster became the UK legislature and modified both UK and Scots law but not always recognising the separate Scots tradition. Whether devolution will change that is unclear. The Christian influence in Scots law is now often inarticulate, but nonetheless real. The principles are there, but only those willing so to do acknowledge their source. Indeed, it is important to note that in many of the topics to which I am coming, 'human rights' is a retrospective classification. Calling for 'human rights' has not always been necessary. The Scots courts were proud that they righted wrongs *ubi ius ibi remedium* – where there is a right a remedy will be given.[1] What is now argued as a human right was often already present in the developing law. Foundations can be well buried.

The move into 'human rights' was not domestic in origin. It came through international law in the train of the Second World War. The UN led the way, followed by other international institutions. In 1945 the Preamble to the Charter of the United Nations reaffirmed a belief in fundamental human rights.[2] The Universal Declaration of Human Rights was adopted by the UN General Assembly in 1948.[3] Its 30 articles inspire. However, it was a Declaration, acknowledgedly not binding law. Binding at the international level came through later conventions, covenants and declarations, notably the International Covenant

---

1 The contrast is with English practice of *ubi remedium ibi ius* – where there is a remedy there is a right.
2 Charter of the United Nations, 1945 1UNTS 1, 1946 UKTS 67, Cmd. 7015. See particularly Arts.1, 55 and 56.
3 'A Universal Declaration of Human Rights', UNGA A/Res. 217 (III) A: Cmd. 7662.

on Economic, Social and Cultural Rights, 1966,[4] the International Covenant on Civil and Political Rights also of 1966,[5] the Declaration on the Elimination of All Forms of Intolerance and of Discrimination Based on Religion or Belief, 1981[6] and the Convention on the Rights of the Child, 1989.[7] The UN continues to emphasise the importance of human rights.[8]

The UN and similar world organisations are not the sole source of international human rights instruments. Within Europe two organisations seek to embed human rights within national legal systems. One is the Council of Europe,[9] parent of the European Convention on Human Rights of 1951,[10] and the European Social Charter, 1961, revised in 1996, replacing its original.[11] The other is the European Union, which has adopted human rights statements and instruments successively throughout its various incarnations, including the European Charter of Fundamental Rights, 2000.[12] There is a move for the European Union to accede to the 1951 European Convention, thus bringing together the major European human rights agencies, but this has had difficulties and is taking time.[13] Notwithstanding, the EU has included various rights within its legislation in the form of Regulations and Directives.[14]

1. Human rights

Historically already present in UK law, human rights were articulated clearly in international instruments adopted in the United Nations and Europe after the Second World War. The UK was to the fore in the drafting of the Council of Europe's European Convention on Human Rights.[15] Subsequently added to by a number of Protocols,[16] the Convention provided for mechanisms to secure their observance in the national laws of its parties. The European

---

4 International Covenant on Economic, Social and Cultural Rights, 1966, UNGA Res. 21/2200 A; 993 UNTS 4; 1977 UKTS 6, Cmnd. 6702; 1967 6 ILM 360 (in force 1976).
5 International Covenant on Civil and Political Rights, 1966, UNGA Res. 21/2200 A; 999 UNTS 171; 1977 UKTS 6, Cmnd. 6702; 1967 6 ILM 368 (in force 1976).
6 Declaration on the Elimination of All Forms of Intolerance and of Discrimination Based on Religion or Belief, 1981, UNGA Res. 36/55; 1982 21 ILM 205.
7 Convention on the Rights of the Child, 1989, UNGA Res. 44/25; 1577 UNTS 3; 1992 UKTS 44, Cm. 1976. Not yet incorporated into UK law: *R (SG and others)* v *Secretary of State for Work and Pensions* [2015] UKSC 16.
8 See the reports, documents and resolutions of the 47 member UN Human Rights Council, created in 2006 by UNGA Res. 60/251: see http://www.ohchr.org.
9 Statute of the Council of Europe, 1949, 1951 87 UNTS 103; 1949 UKTS 51, Cmd. 7778; ETS 1. See http://www.coe.int/. Originally 10 states were members of the Council: in 2015 that had risen to 47.
10 Convention for the Protection of Human Rights and Fundamental Freedoms, Rome, 1950, 1955 UNTS 223; 1953 UKTS 71, Cmd. 8969; ETS 005. Note: the Convention machinery was revised by Protocol 11, *infra* n. 17.
11 European Social Charter, 1965, 529 UNTS 89; 1965 UKTS 36, Cmnd. 2643.
12 Charter of Fundamental Rights of the European Union, 2000, OJ 2000/C 364/01: http://ec.europa.eu/justice/fundamental-rights/charter/index_en.htm, or http://ec.europa.eu/justice/fundamental-rights/charter/index_en.htm
13 Accession may be possible under Art. 6(2) of the basic instrument of European Union. See the Lisbon Treaty amending the fundamental EU treaties, and the relevant Protocol: 2010 UKTS 13, Cm 7901; EC Series 2007 No. 13, Cm 7294; 50 OJ 2007/ 306/1; http://eur-lex.europa.eu/legal-content/EN/TXT/PDF/?uri=OJ:C:2007:306:FULL&from=EN. But see also, Opinion of the Full Court of the European Union, 18 December 2014, on the compatibility of the draft Agreement on [EU] Accession to the European Convention on Human Rights, Opinion 2/13, together with the view of the Advocate General.
14 EU Directives set out required objectives, but how these are implemented within a member state is for that state to determine. Regulations are binding as they are.
15 *Supra* n. 10.
16 To 2014, 16 Protocols have been adopted: not all are in force or adopted by all parties to the Convention.

Commission of Human Rights[17] and a European Court of Human Rights[18] were established under Convention Articles 19–59. When necessary, UK law has been amended to conform to decisions of the Court. But the Convention itself was not incorporated into UK law[19] until the Human Rights Act 1998.[20] This made Arts 2–12 and 14 of the Convention together with Articles 1–3 of its First Protocol part of domestic UK law.[21] The Act also requires UK courts and tribunals to give effect both to these provisions and to determinations made under the Convention procedures (s. 2). The result, perhaps unforeseen by its advocates, has been to open up swathes of UK law to a new scrutiny.[22] It also facilitates innovation. Prior to the Second Reading of a Bill in the Westminster Parliament a minister of the Crown introducing a relevant Bill must make a declaration that the Bill is compatible with the Convention rights, or that while he cannot make such a statement, the government wishes the Bill to proceed (s. 19). Under s. 4 higher courts may determine that an existing legislative provision is incompatible with Convention rights.[23] If so a minister may by order remedy the defect (s. 10). The Act contains one specific safeguard for religious attitudes and belief, but it is both imprecise, not to say woolly, and is restricted to religious organisations.[24] Individuals have no recourse to such protection.

Human Rights in Scotland have an additional facet giving them a protection additional to that of Westminster.[25] Under the Scotland Act 1998 an Act of the Scottish parliament is without legal effect if its provisions are incompatible with rights under the European Convention (s. 29(2)(d)), and the Scottish ministers at Holyrood may not act contrary to the Convention (s. 57(2)). The Acts of Union of 1706 (Scotland) and 1707 (England) are to be construed subject to the 1998 Act (s. 37).

Convention Articles 8–10 are important. Article 8 is the right to privacy. Article 9(1) comprises the rights to freedom of thought, conscience and religion and their manifestation 'in worship, teaching, practice and observance'. By Article 9(2) limitations on the freedom to manifest the s. 9(1) rights are competent if necessary 'in a democratic society in the interests of public safety, for the protection of public order, health or morals, or for the protection of the rights and freedoms of others'. Article 10 is the freedom of expression. Its limitations repeat those of art. 9(2), and add requirements of national security, the prevention of disorder or crime, the protection of reputation, the prevention of the disclosure of information

---

17 The Commission became obsolete in 1996, when the Court was reconstituted as full-time Court. See Convention Protocol 11, Strasbourg 1994, which revised the Convention system's control machinery: 1999 UKTS 33, Cm 4353; ETS 155; 1994 33 ILM 960, with Council explanatory note at 943.
18 Website: www.echr.coe.int
19 International obligations that would change UK domestic law are not given effect in UK law unless incorporated by legislation. However, courts endeavour not to act contrary to UK international obligations: cf. *R v Secretary of State for the Home Department, ex parte Brind*, [1991] AC 696; *Zarkasi v Anindita* [2012] ICR 788.
20 R.J. Reed and J.L. Murdoch, *Human Rights Law in Scotland* (Edinburgh: Bloomsbury Professional, 2011) (new ed. pending). The UK government elected in May 2015 is considering replacing the 1998 Human Rights Act by a British Bill of Rights and restricting – or even ending – recourse to the machineries of the European Court of Human Rights described below. However, the reasoning in cases brought under the prior legislation may still have a degree of persuasive force. It will be interesting to see. But note text at n. 25 *infra*.
21 D. McGoldrick, 'The United Kingdom's Human Rights Act 1998 in theory and practice', 2001 ICLQ 901.
22 The literature is voluminous.
23 A Declaration does not affect the validity of the instant proceedings (s. 4(6)).
24 By s. 13 a court or tribunal determining any question that 'might affect the exercise by a religious organisation (itself or its members collectively) of the Convention right to freedom of thought, conscience and religion' is to 'have particular regard to the importance of that right'.
25 Reference point *supra* n. 20. This may complicate any revision of the Human Rights Act 1998.

Other interactions of religion and law 181

received in confidence or for maintaining the authority and impartiality of the judiciary. Thereafter art. 13 provides that everyone whose Convention rights have been violated has a right to an effective remedy, and art. 14 that enjoyment of the Convention rights are to be 'secured without discrimination on any ground such as sex, race, colour, language, religion, political or other opinion, national or social origin, association with a national minority, property, birth or other status'. These five articles are formidable.

Prior to the 1998 Human Rights Act and influenced *inter alia* by the European Convention, by the tide of international treaties on human rights and by secular 'liberal' opinion, the UK Parliament passed a number of Acts concerning what are now classed as human rights.[26] These included the Equal Pay Act 1970, the Sex Discrimination Act 1975, the Race Relations Act 1976 and the Disability Discrimination Act 1995. Various commissions and tribunals were set up to deal with questions and complaints arising under such legislation, and a good deal of jurisprudence and practice emerged. When the Scottish Parliament was revived, 'equal opportunities' was specified as one of the 'reserved matters' in which Westminster remains the authority.[27] In effect the Scottish Parliament and government are restricted to a hortatory role. This is understandable since one would not wish such matters to vary within major parts of the UK.[28] It follows that the jurisprudence of equality is common to Scotland, England and Wales.

The Equality Act 2006 merged the previously supervisory commissions into a single Commission for Equality and Human Rights. The Commission, functioning in terms of Part 1 (ss. 1–43), is charged with implementing various human rights policies and relevant legislation,[29] including equality and diversity (s. 8), human rights (s. 9). The Commission promotes understanding and practice of good relations between groups and individuals, religion and belief being one of the categories involved (ss. 8–10). Powers to issue codes of practice are given by ss. 14–15, as well as to undertake research (s. 13) and conduct inquiries (s. 16). The Commission, however, does not deal with matters that lie within the competence of the Scottish Parliament (s. 7). Within the Act, Part 2 (ss. 44–80) deals with discrimination on grounds of religion and belief, 'religion' meaning any religion, 'belief' meaning any religion or philosophical belief; and both terms including a lack thereof (s. 44). In brief, s. 45 prohibits discrimination on the grounds of religion including in the provision of goods, facilities and services (s. 46).

Four years later the Equality Act 2010 largely consolidated the basic legislation, while modifying other extant statutory provision. Its Part 2 (ss. 2–12) sets out 'protected characteristics', these including marriage and civil partnership (s. 8), race (s. 9), sex (s. 11) and sexual orientation (s. 12), all matters which could involve religious doctrine, and 'religion or belief' is a category listed as protected by s. 10.[30] Discrimination involving any of the protected

---

26 Reference point *infra* n. 29.
27 'Equal opportunities', including the subject matters of the Equal Pay Act 1970, the Sex Discrimination Act 1975, the Race Relations Act 1976 and the Disability Discrimination Act 1995 are reserved to Westminster by Sched. 5, Head L, para L.2 of the Scotland Act 1998.
28 Only three minor parts of the Act apply to Northern Ireland (s. 217(3)). These relate to offshore work (s. 86), the expiry of an electoral provision as to sex discrimination (s. 105(3)-(4)) and the abolition of the (English) presumption of advancement (s. 199).
29 Specified in s. 33, these include the statutes listed *supra* following n. 26, together with their related Regulations, the Human Rights Act 1998 and parts of the 2006 Act.
30 Protected beliefs have included a belief in democratic socialism (*Olivier* v *Department of Work and Pensions*, ET/1701407/2013) when held with a cogency similar to religious belief, though mere support of a political party might not qualify. A strong commitment to 'left-wing democratic socialist' beliefs could qualify

characteristics is prohibited by ss. 13–25, as is discrimination in a variety of scenarios by much of the rest of the Act. Discrimination may be direct or indirect (ss. 13 and 19). More generally s. 26 deals with harassment, defined as occurring where someone 'engages in unwanted conduct related to a relevant protected characteristic' which 'violates the dignity' of another or creates 'an intimidating, hostile, degrading, humiliating or offensive environment' for that other. For this 'religion or belief' is specified as a relevant protected characteristic (s. 26(5)). Section 27 then protects complainants and others who may be victimised through being made subject to detriment because of their involvement in proceedings under the 2010 Act.

Other human rights obligations developed within the law of the European Union. In particular equality of treatment in employment is required under the European Council Directive 2000/78/EC.[31] In the field of religion or belief that Directive is implemented for the UK by the Employment Equality (Religion or Belief) Regulations 2003 (2003 SI 1660), and the Employment Appeals Tribunal system. The Regulations prohibit discrimination in employment or vocational training on grounds of religion or belief,[32] whether directly (Reg. 3(1)(a)) or indirectly (Reg. 3(1)(b)), by victimisation (Reg. 4) or through harassment (Reg. 5). An employer may contravene the Regulations through the action of an employee albeit without personal knowledge or approval of the discrimination concerned, unless reasonable steps have been taken to prevent such actions (Reg. 22). The Regulations do not apply where being of a particular religion or belief is a genuine and determining occupational requirement, it is proportionate to apply the requirement in the particular case, and either the person to whom the requirement applies does not meet it, or the employer is not satisfied that it has been met, and it is reasonable so to be (Reg. 7).

To explore human rights and religion in the UK would take more than the wordage available to me for this entire book.[33] Accordingly I confine myself here to a sketch, noting certain aspects. Other examples crop up elsewhere in this chapter.

It has been a question how far conscience based on Christian conviction may be recognised within the human rights legislation. The legal ground is now equality. Certainly public officials should not decline to carry out part of their jobs on the basis that it conflicts with conscience.[34] Christian conviction may prevent from being a relationship counsellor involved with adoption by homosexuals on the argument that a full range of service could not be provided.[35] It can be reasonable to require work on a Sunday, even though some on religious grounds believe

---

as a philosophical belief (*General and Municipal and Boilermakers Union* v *Henderson* [2015] UKEAT 0073/14/1303). A strongly held belief in climate change might qualify as a philosophical belief (*Grainger plc* v *Nicholson* [2009] UKEAT 0129/09/0311 [2010] ICR 360). A strong belief in BBC broadcasting values has not qualified as a philosophical belief (*Maistry* v *BBC* [2014] EWCA Civ 1116). Belief in life after death and in spiritualism has qualified (*Greater Manchester Police Authority* v *Power* UKEAT/0434/09/DA: this claim may have failed on other grounds).

31 Council Directive 2000/78/EC, 27 November 2000, OJ L 303, 2,12,2000.
32 S. 77 of the 2006 Equality Act amended Reg. 2 to bring the definitions of religion and belief into congruence with those of that Act.
33 Cf. the 624 pages of J. Dingemans et al, eds, *The Protection for Religious Rights: Law and Practice* (Oxford: Oxford UP, 2013).
34 *Islington Borough Council* v *Ladele* [2010]1 WLR 955 – a registrar unwilling to conduct a civil partnership. An appeal to the European Court of Human Rights failed: Eweida case, third applicant, *infra* n. 45.
35 *Macfarlane* v *Avon Relate Ltd* [2010] EWCA Civ 880; [2010] IRLR 872. An appeal to the European Court of Human Rights failed: Eweida case, fourth applicant, *infra* n. 45. Cf. *McClintock* v *Department of Constitutional Affairs*, 2007 UKEAT/0223/07/CEA, a Justice of the Peace objected to civil partnership and would not place an adoptee with such a couple.

Sundays to be a day of rest.[36] Seventh Day Adventists bee-keepers may be exempt on religious grounds from filing tax returns electronically.[37] However, there is no right to inflict corporal punishment as a manifestation of religious belief as to how to rear children.[38]

Human rights and questions of discrimination become intrusive when a couple running a bed-and-breakfast in their own home refused to accommodate two homosexual men and had to pay damages.[39] Matters might be different when the premises are a hotel,[40] but in one's own home? In both cases the obligation not to discriminate in the provision of services to the public was involved. In both the suppliers were found to have breached that obligation. The former case particularly concerns stalwart Presbyterians in the Highlands of Scotland who engage in the bed and breakfast business.

What of demonstrating one's religious convictions through apparel? There have been cases involving the niqab and similar garb.[41] However, it may be noted that French legislation prohibiting the niqab in public has been found permissible under the European Convention.[42] Religious jewellery has caused other problems.[43]

Much depends on the 'margin of appreciation', available to states under the European Convention in their incorporation of its principles into national law. This is made clear by the Eweida case. British Airways had banned stewardesses from wearing a cross. Eweida, a Coptic Christian, complained that this was discriminatory and infringed the freedom to manifest her religion.[44] The case ultimately went to the European Court of Human Rights, where it was conjoined with three other UK appeals.[45] One of these, the Chaplin case also involved the wearing of a cross, this time by a nurse.[46] Of the four cases the Macfarlane case and the Ladele case were held to lie within the margin of appreciation exercisable by national legal systems.[47] So was the Chaplin case. Chaplin was held to be demonstrating

---

36 *Mba* v *Merton London Borough Council* [2013] EWCA Civ 1562; [2014] 1 WLR 1501: case brought by the employee of a care home that had to function seven days a week.
37 *Blackburn* v *HMRC* [2013] UKFTT 525. The requirement to file electronically was an intrusion of worldliness into their Adventist-principled life.
38 *R (Williamson et al.)* v *Secretary of State for Education and Employment* [2005] UKHL, [2005] 2 AC 246. Cf. *Campbell and Cosans* v *United Kingdom* [1982] 4 EHRR 293 – corporal punishment in Scottish schools ruled unlawful.
39 *Black* v *Wilkinson* [2013] EWCA Civ 820, [2013] 4 All E.R. 1053 – further appeal abandoned.
40 *Hall* v *Bull* [2013] UKSC 73; [2013] 1 All ER 919.
41 *Azmi* v *Kirklees Metropolitan Borough Council* [2007] ICR 1154 – a Muslim teacher should not wear a face-covering veil. *R. (X)* v *Headteachers and Governors of Y School* [2007] EWHC 298; [2007] HRLR 20 – a pupil should not wear a niqab. *R. (Begum)* v *Headteacher and Governors of Denbigh High School* [2004] EWHC 1389; [2004} ELR 374 – a pupil could not insist on a uniform other than one adopted by the school to meet general Muslim sympathies.
42 *SAS* v *France* (2015) 60 EHRR 11. See also *R.* v *Home Secretary* [2014] EWCA Civ 854, where an objection to removal to France based on the French law was rejected.
43 *R (Watkins-Singh et al.)* v *Aberdare Girls High School* [2008] EWHCs 1865; [2008] ELR 561 – wearing a symbol of initiation in Sikhism, the Kara bangle, by a schoolchild permitted. Cf. 'Guidance on the wearing of Sikh articles of faith in the workplace and public places', Equality Commission, 2014. Earlier in *R (Playfoot)* v *Millais School* [2007] EWHC 1698, [2007] HRLR 34, a ban on the wearing by a pupil of a silver ring emblematic of religious belief in chastity until marriage was upheld since the practice was not integral to that belief.
44 *Eweida* v *British Airways Plc* [2009] ICR 303, [2009] IRLR 78; [2010] EWCA Civ 80, [2010] IRLR 322.
45 *Eweida* v *United Kingdom* [2013] IRLR 231; (2013) 57 EHRR 8. Two of the conjoined cases are noted supra nn. 34 and 35.
46 Chaplin had withdrawn her case in the UK on being advised that the decision of the Court of Appeal in the Eweida case meant she had no chance of success.
47 *Supra* nn. 34 and 35.

her beliefs, but considerations of medical security allowed the wearing of jewellery to be forbidden. However, in the Eweida case the Court considered that a fair balance between the public interest and that of the applicant had not been met. It was not necessary that her wish to manifest her belief was a mandatory requirement of that belief system.

It remains to be seen how all such matters will work out in the future. The 'margin of appreciation' in balancing the public interest with that of staunch holders of beliefs is difficult. Some of the early cases have come under criticism as confusing discrimination and freedom of conscience, and there is growing concern as to the effect of a political correctness. The position is not stable.

2. Religious constraints

In the past a number of constraints based on religion were imposed by operation of law. Many of these have disappeared. Thus under successive House of Commons Disqualification Acts, membership of the House was conditioned by the House of Commons (Clergy Disqualification) Act 1801, which barred from membership of the House by clerics of the established churches or of the Roman Catholic Church, although not of other denominations as they developed.[48] The Roman Catholic Emancipation Act 1829, s. 9, preserved the ban on Roman Catholics, although that Act and the Roman Catholic Relief Act 1926 swept away most of the Catholic disabilities. These restrictions were repealed by the House of Commons (Removal of Clergy Disqualification) Act 2001.[49]

Under the Act of Settlement 1701 a person was disqualified from being or becoming the Sovereign if married to or marrying a Roman Catholic.[50] Such a marriage within the UK would be void. Any person in the line of succession might escape the prohibition by relinquishing any right of succession and marrying abroad.[51] That constraint has been abolished by s. 2 of the Succession to the Crown Act 2013,[52] and s. 3 replaces the requirement under the Royal Marriages Act 1772 of the permission of the Sovereign for the valid marriage of the six persons next within the line of succession to the Crown. It is not clear whether the Sovereign might convert to Catholicism without consequences.[53] A corollary of the requirement

---

48 Thus Ian Paisley, the late well-known minister in Northern Ireland was an elected MP.
49 The internal rules of a denomination may prohibit a minister from becoming an MP or a MSP. Roman Catholic rules prohibit a priest from becoming an MP. Such a rule might be challengeable in the civil courts under the Human Rights Act 1998. In the case of the Church of Scotland, such a challenge would be barred by the Church of Scotland Act 1921 and the application of s. 13 of the 1998 Act (cf. *Logan* v *Presbytery of Dumbarton* 1995 SLT 1228). The Church of Scotland rules are in GA Act IV 2001. Roughly speaking, a minister or employee is permitted to take up a part-time elected office if it does not take more than five hours a week. The local presbytery monitors whether office detracts from the ministerial function. Full-time office is not permitted. A minister, deacon or other holding appointment may not be an MP, MSP or MEP. If elected a Church of Scotland minister demits office.
50 Under the Royal Marriages Act 1772 (now repealed by s. 3(4) of the Succession to the Crown Act 2013) the consent of the Sovereign was required for the marriage of someone within a fairly widely defined 'Royal' family. There is an argument that under that Act the Duke of Edinburgh was a bastard, his parents not having had that consent. See *infra* at n. 52.
51 As did Prince Michael of Kent in order to marry the Princess Michael in 1978. Their marriage took place in Vienna.
52 The Act (s. 1) removes the male precedence in succession to the Crown for anyone born after 28 October 2011.
53 The Sovereign is Head of the Church of England. In Scotland when at Balmoral our present Sovereign attends the local church at Crathie. Cf. O. Chadwick, 'The Sacrament at Crathie, 1873', in S.J. Brown and G. Newlands, *Scottish Christianity in the Modern World* (Edinburgh: T&T Clark, 2000).

that the Sovereign be Protestant is that a Roman Catholic cannot act as Regent unless their marriage has been approved.[54]

Turning to other matters, the person who represents the Crown at the General Assembly of the Church of Scotland, the Lord High Commissioner, may not be a Roman Catholic.[55] It used to be the case that a Roman Catholic could not be Lord Chancellor, but this changed in 1974, after which where a Catholic is appointed, his ecclesiastical duties are taken elsewhere for the duration of that tenure of office.[56]

3. Freedom of speech and expression

Blasphemy and heresy

A special aspect of freedom of speech and expression is the protection of theological expression. In practice, blasphemy and heresy are now obsolete as offences. That was not always the case.

To publish or sell works ridiculing or denigrating the Christian religion remains an offence at common law in Scotland, though now unlikely to be prosecuted. The last prosecutions under common law took place in 1843 despite the Scottish Enlightenment.[57] Henry Robinson, a bookseller, was indicted for offering for sale obscene publications and 73 books of an 'impious and blasphemous character'. The diet was deserted *pro loco et tempore* so that more relevant charges could be drawn up.[58] Some months later a Thomas Paterson was indicted for similar offences.[59] Paterson defended himself at length arguing that there was no offence. However, the Lord Justice Clerk observed that the Bible and the Christian religion were part of the law of the land,[60] and Paterson was sentenced to prison for 15 months. The next day Robinson pleaded guilty to two charges and was sentenced to 12 months in prison.[61]

In statute law the Acts 1649 c. 28, 1661 c. 21 and 1695 c. 14 imposed the death penalty on any person who 'not being distracted in his wits, shall rail upon, or curse God, or any of the persons of the blessed Trinity', or on anyone who obstinately continued to deny God or the Trinity. The 1695 Act extended the offence to include denial of the authority of Scripture. Prosecutions were few, and the capital sentence carried out only once.[62] One hundred years later the Doctrine of the Trinity Act 1812, while not altering the criminality of the offence, gave relief from penalty to those who impugned a variety of religious doctrines. The Leasing

---

54 Regency Act 1937, s. 3(2) and the Succession to the Crown Act 2013, s. 3(3) and Sched. para 4.
55 Roman Catholic Emancipation Act 1829, s.12.
56 Lord Chancellor (Tenure of Office and Discharge of Ecclesiastical Functions) Act 1974.
57 How these prosecutions relate to the general religious ferment of the Disruption of 1843 is uncertain.
58 *Henry Robinson* (1843) 1 Broun 590.
59 *Thomas Paterson* (1843) 1 Broun 629. Like Robinson, Paterson, who advertised himself as the 'only atheistic publisher', sold both his own and a variety of books imported from England and the Continent.
60 (1843) 1 Broun 629 at 635–6.
61 *Henry Robinson* (1843) 1 Broun 643. At the end of this report a footnote notes that a Thomas Finlay was convicted in Edinburgh Sheriff court on 6 December 1843 and sentenced to 60 days in prison. There may have been other cases.
62 Hume, I, 560–562. Arnot, *Criminal Trials*, 1785, 322–7, could find only three prosecutions – one person was fined, one outlawed. The one capital sentence was the case of *Aitkenhead* (1696), well dealt with by M.F. Graham, *The Blasphemies of Thomas Aitkenhead: Boundaries of Belief on the Eve of the Enlightenment* (Edinburgh: Edinburgh UP, 2007). The prosecutors and government of the time cannot be immune from criticism, though reflective of the currents of their time. Cf. Arnot (*supra*) 324–7; R. Chambers, II, *Domestic Annals of Scotland* (Edinburgh: Chambers, 1859), 160–166.

Making (Scotland) Act 1825 restricted the punishment for blasphemy to a fine, and, though there were some prosecutions thereafter, the statutory offence soon became obsolete.[63] Spoken blasphemy is not now taken as a crime. An ordinary charge of breach of the peace can be brought, the offence being breaching the peace, not the content of the words used.

Heresy is not the same as blasphemy. It involves holding doctrines different from or contradictory of particular other doctrines. It is not always easy to disentangle the two concepts. It is clear that in Scots practice after the Reformation heresy was not dealt with as such by the civil courts. However, it is also clear that the holding of doctrines divergent from those generally approved could lead to other consequences as the history of the 'Covenanting Times' demonstrates.[64] Now unorthodox religious belief has few civil consequences,[65] though their own canons of orthodoxy remain of concern to churches and other faith groups.

There have been calls for the legal protection of particular religious beliefs by some who consider it blasphemous to criticise or otherwise denigrate what they hold sacred. These have not been acceded to.[66] However, in 1982 the advertising industry has established an independent non-statutory agency, the Advertising Standards Authority, to have competence across all media in the use of advertising.[67] It is not financed by the public purse but by a levy on the members of the industry. The Authority is intended to regulate the content of advertising, sales promotions and direct marketing in the UK. It adopts codes of conduct and makes rulings based on its investigation of complaints, though complaints in relation to broadcasting may be referred to Ofcom, the regulator of broadcasting services as described below.[68] Adjudications by the Authority may be appealed to an independent reviewer. Rulings are published every week, and are carried on its website for at least five years. Complaints have included religious matters. Thus in 2009 Christian groups complained about an advertising campaign posted on the sides of buses and elsewhere in London stating that 'There is probably no God'. The complaint was not upheld. In 2015 buses in some parts of Scotland carried as advertising the suggestion 'Try Praying'.

4. Criminalities

Witchcraft is the sole example of active attempts to sanction a movement directly contradictory to Christianity. Now freed from explicit statutory intervention, its practice may still be subject to questions of public decency. Proscription of witchcraft dates back into Roman

---

63 J.H.A. MacDonald, *The Criminal Law of Scotland*, 5th ed. J. Walker (Edinburgh: Green, 1948), 153; G. Maher, 'Blasphemy in Scots Law', 1977 SLT (Notes) 257. *R.* v *Lemon, R.* v *Gay News* [1979] AC 617, a successful English private prosecution for blasphemy would not have occurred in Scotland. In England blasphemy was not abolished until the Criminal Justice and Immigration Act, 2008 s. 79. Cf. R. Sandberg and N. Doe, 'The Strange Death of Blasphemy', 2008 71 MLR. 971. For history see (English) Law Commission, *Criminal Law: Offences against Religion and Public Worship*, 1985, Law. Comm. No. 145.
64 D.M. Walker, *A Legal History of Scotland*, Vol. III, *The Sixteenth Century* (Edinburgh: Green, 1995) 474–6; H.H. Brown, 'The Old Scots Law of Heresy', 1919, 31 Jur. Rev. 199.
65 An example is that a Regent cannot be a Roman Catholic: Regency Act 1937, s. 3(1)-(2).
66 Cf. reaction in the UK to the 'Mohammed cartoon' as well as the 'Salman Rushdie affair' of the 1980s and thereafter, 'Jerry Springer, The Opera' (*infra* n. 150) and the 'Charlie Hebdo' murders in 2015. The volatility of the adherents of some religions, and their potential recourse to violence, is worrying. G.K. Bhatti's play *Behzt* (Dishonour) in Birmingham in 2004 was cancelled: *Regina (Parminder Singh and another)* v *Chief Constable of the West Midlands Police* [2006] EWCA Civ 1118 [2006] 1 WLR 3374, and the Wikipedia entry for the play.
67 The Advertising Standards Authority: www.asa.org.uk.
68 *Infra* n. 93.

times, but it was only following the Bull of Innocent VIII *Summis desiderentes affectibus* of 9 December 1484 appointing Heinrich Kramer and Jacob Sprenger inquisitors of the phenomenon that coordinated opposition to witchcraft got under way.[69] Prior to the Scottish Reformation there was not the same interest as there was on the Continent, but that changed. Witches were believed in and feared, and steps were taken. The Act 1563 c. 9 gave effect to the injunctions of Ex. 22:18,[70] and James VI, who in 1597 published a book on *Daemonologie*,[71] helped bring Scotland into harmony with Europe.[72] Those days are now past. Prosecutions ceased in the seventeenth century,[73] but the 1563 Act was not repealed until 1935 when the Witchcraft Act prohibited the prosecution of persons for witchcraft, sorcery, enchantment or conjuration and such offences. That ended a sorry chapter of Scottish jurisprudence. Recently Witchcraft and 'Wicca' and similar were accepted as a category of UK belief systems for census purposes,[74] and its associations for trust purposes and for the law of marriage.[75] However, the pretended use of witchcraft and similar arts for fortune telling, the recovery of goods, mediumship and so on for reward, remained offences under the earlier legislation. Such offences are now covered by s. 1 of the Fraudulent Mediums Act, 1951.

There is, of course, a full range of other crimes that may involve religious considerations. In these it is possible for the offence to be 'aggravated' if its commission stems from or is contributed to by religious prejudice whether against an individual or a group.[76] This can come into play in race hatred cases,[77] or may be conjoined to aggravation through prejudice in relation to disability or sexual orientation.[78] Notoriously religious prejudice has played a

---

69 Kramer and Sprenger wrote the *Malleus Maleficarum*, 1487, trans. M. Summers, 1927 (London: Folio Society, 1968; Arrow Books, 1971), the authoritative text of the time on witch-finding. The *Malleus* influenced both catholic and protestant attitudes.
70 J. Goodare, 'The Scottish Witchcraft Act' (2005) 74 Church Hist. 39.
71 James VI and I, *Daemonologie* (Edinburgh: Edinburgh UP, 1966). James may have written to counter the sceptical R. Scot, *The Discoverie of Witchcraft*, 1584, M. Summers, ed. (London, 1930: New York: Dover, 1970). James was theologically literate. Had his second son, Charles, paid attention to the *Basilikon Doron* (many eds), a treatise on living and governing as a Christian which James wrote for his first son Henry who died in 1612, history might have been different.
72 On Witchcraft in Scotland see D.M. Walker (*supra* n. 64), 477–83, with citations to cases in R. Pitcairn, *Ancient Criminal Trials in Scotland, 1488–1730* (3 vols, Edinburgh, 1829–33); C. Larner, *Enemies of God: The Witch-hunt in Scotland* (London: Chatto & Windus, 1981); J. Goodare, *The Scottish Witch-hunt in Context* (Manchester: Manchester UP, 2002); B.P. Levack, *Witch-Hunting in Scotland: Law, Politics and Religion* (London: Routledge, 2007); S. Macdonald, *The Witches of Fife: Witch-hunting in a Scottish Shire, 1560–1710* (East Linton: Tuckwell Press, 2002); L. Normand and G. Roberts, *Witchcraft in Early Modern Scotland: James VI's Demonology and the North Berwick Witches* (Liverpool: Liverpool UP, 2000). While dealing with Criminal Law in his *Institutions of the Law of Scotland* (1684, 5 eds thereafter), George Mackenzie of Rosehaugh, Lord Advocate, wrote extensively on the matter: H.H. Brown, 'Sir George Mackenzie: A Study of Old Scots Crime', 1901, 13 Jur. Rev. 261.
73 The last execution took place in Dornoch in 1727: W.N. Neill, 'The Last Execution for Witchcraft in Scotland, 1722' (sic) (1923) 20 Scot. Hist. Rev. 218; http://www.historylinks.org.uk/Dornoch18.htm
74 See http://www.scotlandscensus.gov.uk/documents/censusresults/release2a/rel2A_Religion_detailed_Scotland.pdf. The census data is very difficult to access!
75 See *supra* Chapter 7, Personal Relationships, 'Marriage', 'Celebrants', following n. 54.
76 Criminal Justice (Scotland) Act 2003, s. 74. See also *Religiously Aggravated Offending in Scotland 2013–14* (Scottish Government, 2014): http://www.scotland.gov.uk/Resource/0045/00452559.pdf
77 Race hatred is dealt with by Part III, ss. 17–29, of the Public Order Act 1986.
78 Offences (Aggravation by Prejudice) (Scotland) Act 2009 asp 8. The Racial and Religious Hatred Act 2006 does not apply in Scotland.

part in the activities of Scottish football fans. There are general controls on football disorder available under ss. 51–69 of the Police, Public Order and Criminal Justice (Scotland) Act 2006, asp 10. Inciting public disorder through stirring up hatred of or against a group, or threatening or offensive behaviour, is proscribed, religion being a potential basis of the conduct (s. 56). Other bases include colour, race, nationality or citizenship, ethnic or national origin, sexual orientation, transgender identity and disability. There has also been later legislation.[79] Parades, including religiously related parades (for example by the (Protestant) Orange Order) are subject to licensing under ss. 62–65 of the Civic Government (Scotland) Act 1982. The holder/organiser of an unlicensed parade, or one that fails to comply with the conditions of a licence, commits a criminal offence (s. 65). In relation to both football and other sports and parades where a child of at least 12 years offends, a parenting order may be made under ss. 4–18 of the Antisocial Behaviour etc. (Scotland) Act 2004, asp 8. If so, the order must as far as practicable avoid conflict with the religious beliefs of the person named (s. 110). Hate crime, whether based on religion or otherwise, remains a matter of concern.[80]

Particular religious factors, occasionally conflated with cultural observances, are recognised as exempting from normal criminal law. Thus the law on slaughter of animals makes provision for Jewish and Muslim practices.[81] Sikhs are exempt from wearing safety helmets on construction sites unless not wearing a turban,[82] or while on a motor-cycle if wearing a turban.[83] As to ceremonial weapons the Criminal Law (Consolidation) (Scotland) Act 1995 s. 47 prohibits the carrying of offensive weapons but without defining the category.[84] However, s. 49 refines the matter, making it criminal to have in a public place and without good reason any blade or article with a sharp point.[85] It is a defence to show that the blade or article is carried for religious reasons (s. 49(5)(b)) or is part of any national costume (s. 49(5)(c)). That would cover a Sikh's ceremonial dagger, or the skean dhu thrust down the sock when wearing highland dress.[86]

Last, in parliamentary or local government elections 'undue influence' constituting a corrupt practice may include threats of 'spiritual injury'.[87] In modern conditions this provision could occasion much discussion.

5. Broadcasting

Broadcasting is a peculiarly effective method of reaching vast numbers. Apart from their international duties as to the use of the radio spectrum, states commonly take a degree of control over broadcasting content but that can collide with freedom of thought and of

---

79 Offensive Behaviour at Football and Threatening Communications (Scotland) Act 2012 asp 1. The behaviour is defined in the same terms as the 2006 Act. The Act is being reviewed as being badly drafted.
80 Cf. the report of a Working Group on Hate Crime (Scottish Executive, 2004): http://www.scotland.gov.uk/Resource/Doc/26350/0025008.pdf and a cross-party report, on religious hatred: http://www.scotland.gov.uk/Publications/2002/12/15892/14531http
81 The Welfare of Animals (Slaughter or Killing) Regulations 1995, 1995 SI 731, Sched. 12. See generally the Slaughter of Animals (Scotland) Act 1980 and the Slaughter of Poultry Act 1967.
82 Employment Act 1989 s. 12; s.13 protects from related racial discrimination.
83 Road Traffic Act 1988, s. 16.
84 *Glancy* v *HM Advocate* 2012 SCL 275; 2012 SCCR 52.
85 Folding pocket-knives with blades under three inches (7.82 cm.) are exempt s. 49(3).
86 Neither excuse applies for aviation flights.
87 Representation of the People Act 1983, s. 15(2)(a).

speech and expression.[88] How religion and religious susceptibilities are treated can vary widely.[89]

The UK distinguishes between the public service provided by the British Broadcasting Corporation (the BBC) and commercial broadcasting services. The BBC is financed by a licence fee paid by all households that have a television receiver,[90] supplemented by the commercial exploitation of its programmes. Commercial broadcasting is financed mainly by advertising. Both use the radio spectrum terrestrially and for direct broadcast by satellite, and both use the Internet. This is subject to state control. By s. 1 of the Wireless Telegraphy Act 1949, it is an offence to broadcast in the UK unless licensed so to do.[91] There is a considerable quantity of legislation as to how broadcasting is organised and its activities regulated.[92] The Office of Communications,[93] established under the Office of Communications Act 2002, the main authority involved, has extensive powers.[94] Virtually all previous supervisory and licensing functions have been transferred to it. Much of the prior legislation otherwise remains on the statute book.[95] In the ultimate, the UK Government retains the power to instruct broadcasters.[96]

Radio, invented in the 1890s, at first served wireless telegraphy. While there was some limited experimental broadcasting in the early 1900s the inventions of the First World War made large-scale broadcasting possible.[97] Because the unalterable laws of

---

88 Cf. the debates of the 1970–80s within UNESCO. Following the 1980 report *Many Voices, One World: Towards a New, More Just, and More Efficient World Information and Communication Order* (UNESCO, 1984; London: Kogan Page, 1988) some UNESCO members, mostly developing countries, called for a 'new information order', in which control over incoming and outgoing communications would preserve states' political, economic and cultural identity. In 1994/5 the US and the UK withdrew from UNESCO citing questions of 'freedom of information' and the 'freedom of the press', returning respectively in 2005 and 1997. Cf. (1984) 23 ILM 220–230 and (1985) 24 ILM 489–90.

89 For a history of UK broadcasting down to its date see A. Briggs, *The History of Broadcasting in the United Kingdom*, 3 vols, London: Oxford UP: Vol. 1, *The Birth of Broadcasting* (1961); Vol. 2. *The Golden Age of Wireless* (1965); Vol. 3, *The War of Words* (1970). See also R.H. Coase, *British Broadcasting: A Study in Monopoly* (London: Cass, 1950; Routledge, 2013). For the US see E. Barnouw, *A History of Broadcasting in the United States*, 3 vols, New York: Oxford UP: Vol. 1. *A Tower in Babel: A History of Broadcasting in the United States to 1933* (1966); Vol. 2, *The Golden Web: A History of Broadcasting in the United States from 1933 to 1953* (1968); Vol. 3, *The Image Empire: A History of Broadcasting in the United States from 1953* (1970). For other countries see E.M. Barendt, *Broadcasting Law: A Comparative Study* (Oxford: Clarendon Press, 1993).

90 Technically the licence applies to the receiving equipment not the property where it is installed. Licensing was initially instituted by an Agreement between the BBC and the Post Office as licensing authority, and currently is authorised by ss. 365 and 402 of the Communications Act 2003. The fee is set by the Department of Culture, Media and Sport.

91 Radio transmission was first subjected to licensing by the Wireless and Telegraphs Act 1904.

92 This includes satellite broadcasting. F. Lyall and P.B. Larsen, *Space Law: A Treatise* (Farnham, UK: Ashgate, 2009) 256–69. Cf. Press TV, *infra* n. 94.

93 Website: www.ofcom.org.uk

94 Under the Communications Act 2003 and the Wireless Telegraphy Act 2006 Ofcom has powers to grant or revoke broadcasting licences, to issue instructions and to fine offending broadcasters. In January 2012, Ofcom revoked the license of Press TV (based in Teheran) to transmit to the UK using the Sky TV facilities; revocation published 20/01/12 on the website, stakeholders.ofcom.org.uk

95 The main extant legislation comprises the Broadcasting Acts 1981, 1990, and 1996, together with the Cable and Broadcasting Act 1984.

96 Broadcasting Act 1981. *R v Secretary of State for the Home Department, ex parte Brind* [1991] AC 696, where the power was challenged unsuccessfully.

97 There is nothing like war for spurring technological development.

190   *Other interactions of religion and law*

physics made (and make) international rules necessary if harmful interference between radio users was to be avoided, these were soon agreed, and, though massively expanded, still exist.[98]

Each sovereign state organises broadcasting and telecommunication services within its jurisdiction as it decides.[99] Until commercial television began in 1955, in the UK broadcasting was in the hands of a monopoly, the British Broadcasting Corporation, the BBC. How it dealt with religion has affected how religion is now dealt with in both public service and commercial broadcasting. I first summarise the institutions.

The British Broadcasting Corporation

A British Broadcasting Company, formed in 1922 by a consortium of wireless apparatus manufacturers, was licensed to operate eight transmitters.[100] However, its financial arrangements were extensively criticised.[101] At the time UK telegraph and telephone services were state monopolies run by the Post Office.[102] A Departmental Committee, the Sykes Committee, set up to review how UK broadcasting should be organised, favoured the public control of broadcasting, but not under the aegis of the Company.[103] Among those giving evidence was the then Managing Director of the British Broadcasting Company, one J.C.W. Reith, the son of a minister of the United Free Church of Scotland, and later to become Lord Reith of Stonehaven.[104] He suggested that a single controlling authority was essential in order to have a uniform national policy. He also was concerned that broadcasting should be a public service, though given his then position he could not propose the transfer of the Company's operating interests. These ideas came to play a great part in public discussion and helped form the views of the next Departmental Committee on Broadcasting, the Crawford Committee of 1925. This recommended that 'the broadcasting service should be conducted by a public corporation acting as Trustee for the national interest, and that its status and duties should correspond with those of a public service'.[105] The British Broadcasting Corporation, the BBC, established on that basis by Royal Charter, began operation on 1 January 1927,

---

98   Radio-telegraphic Convention, Final Protocol and Regulations, Berlin, 1906, 1909 UKTS 8, Cd. 4559; http://earlyradiohistory.us/1906conv.htm. For later international regulation see F. Lyall, *International Communications: The International Telecommunication Union and the Universal Postal Union* (Farnham UK: Ashgate, 2011).

99   See the Preamble to the Constitution of the International Telecommunication Union, 1825 UNTS 331; 1996 UKTS 24, Cm. 3145.

100 The Wireless Broadcasting Licence, 1922, Cmd. 1822.

101 Operational costs were to be defrayed by the profits of the individual manufacturing companies, and from receiving one-half of the fees for reception licences. No reception licences were to be issued for foreign radio sets in order to provide a market for the more expensive British manufactured receivers. It was argued that it was incongruous thus to protect manufacturers' profits.

102 The Telegraph Acts 1868–69 and the Telephone Transfer Act 1911.

103 *Report of the Broadcasting Committee, 1923*, 1923 Cmd. 1951.

104 Reith, Director General of the BBC 1926–38, was an interesting if flawed man. His Presbyterian background certainly affected his rule in the BBC. 'Reithian' now denotes a style of management, probity, commitment to public service, and (probably) impatience with others who do not share these characteristics. See Reith's *Into the Wind* (London: Hodder, 1949); A. Boyle, *Only the Wind Will Listen* (London: Hutchinson, 1972); I. McIntyre, *The Expense of Glory: Life of John Reith* (London: HarperCollins, 1995); M. Leishman, *Reith of the BBC: My Father* (Edinburgh: St Andrew Press, 2008).

105 *Report of the Broadcasting Committee, 1925*, 1926, Cmd. 2599, para 20(a). See also *A Public BBC*, First Report of the Committee on Culture, Media and Sport, 2004–05 (HC 82 I-II) paras 224–37.

under licence from the Postmaster-General, with Reith as its Director General.[106] The Charter and Licence (later replaced by an Agreement between the BBC and the relevant Secretary of State) have been renewed eight times with minor variation, occasionally after examination by a departmental committee or a Royal Commission. Of these the major inquiries were the Ullswater Committee of 1935,[107] the Beveridge Committee of 1949–51,[108] the Pilkington Committee of 1960[109] and the Annan Committee of 1976–77,[110] the last two being concerned with broadcasting in general, not just the BBC. The most recent parliamentary committee on broadcasting reported in 2004.[111]

The current BBC Charter[112] and related Agreement[113] date from 2006 and run to 31 December 2016.[114] The Charter sets out the constitution of the BBC, providing for the BBC Trust[115] and a separate Executive Board. Articles 4–5 state the duty of the BBC to 'inform, educate and entertain', and the 'Public Purposes' of the BBC. Reith would approve. The 12-member Trust is the guardian of the public interest.[116] It sets the strategic direction of the Corporation and thereafter has a supervisory role. The Executive Board delivers the broadcasting services. The Charter does not specifically mention religion, but Clause 9 of the Agreement provides that the BBC Trust is to have regard to the importance of reflecting the 'nations, regions and communities' of the UK (Art. 9(1)) and to the 'importance of reflecting different religions and other beliefs' (Art. 9(2)(a)). Under s. 170 of the Broadcasting Act 1996 the BBC has adopted a 'Fairness Code', and compliance with which remains a duty under the Agreement (Cl. 45).

Commercial broadcasting

Commercial broadcasting within the UK is now supervised by the Office of Communications, which has assumed the duties of a number of previous regulatory authorities.[117]

In the UK commercial broadcasting began with television, not radio. The Television Act 1954 permitted commercial television services regulated by an Independent Television Authority to be provided. Such services are now mostly provided by private companies, their major source of financing being advertising. Commercial enterprises bid for franchises

---

106 The 1926 Charter and Licence are appendices B and C to the *Report of the Broadcasting Committee, 1935*, 1936, Cmd. 5091.
107 *Report of the Broadcasting Committee. 1935*, 1936 Cmd. 5091.
108 *Report of the Committee on Broadcasting, 1949*, 1951 Cmd. 8116.
109 *Report of the Committee on Broadcasting, 1960*, 1962 Cmnd. 1753, with Evidence, 1962 Cmnd. 1819, 1819-I.
110 *Report of the Committee on the Future of Broadcasting*, 1977, Cmnd. 6753.
111 *A Public BBC*, First Report of the Committee on Culture, Media and Sport, 2004–05, Report and Evidence (HC 82 I-II).
112 *Broadcasting: Copy Royal Charter for the Continuance of the British Broadcasting Corporation*, 2006, Cm 6925.
113 *Broadcasting: An Agreement Between Her Majesty's Secretary for Culture, Media and Sport and the British Broadcasting Corporation*, 2006, Cm 6872.
114 Debate as to the future of the BBC has begun.
115 This 'trust' is legally unusual. Art. 12 of the Charter states: 'The word "trust" is used in the name of the BBC Trust in a colloquial sense, to suggest a body which discharges a public trust as guardian of the public interest. The word is not used in its technical legal sense, and it is not intended to imply that the members of the Trust are to be treated as trustees of property or to be subject to the law relating to trusts or trustees'.
116 There are 10 ordinary members of the Trust, a Chairman and a Vice-Chairman. One ordinary member is designated for each of England, Scotland, Wales and Northern Ireland (Arts 13–14).
117 *Supra* n. 94.

192 *Other interactions of religion and law*

to provide television services within particular areas for specified periods.[118] Later bidding rounds do not always renew these franchises. In addition Channel 4 is a hybrid with a remit to provide public service television.[119] Originally set up under ss. 10–13 of the Broadcasting Act 1981, and now operating under ss. 23–27 of the Broadcasting Act 1990 and ss. 199–203 of the Communications Act 2003, Channel 4 is an independent statutory corporation without share-holders.[120] It operates on a not-for-profit basis, reinvesting its revenues in its activities. Financed by advertising revenue and sponsorship it receives no government funding.

Commercial broadcasting by radio within UK territory was introduced following a lengthy defiance by would-be broadcasters. From the 1960s broadcasts to the UK were transmitted from ships and other off-shore structures outwith the UK territorial jurisdiction, and therefore not subject to UK legislation.[121] Often known as 'pirate radio', the programming, usually of 'rock' and similar music, was in stark contrast to that of BBC radio.[122] Eventually government recognised the impossibility of coping with the 'pirates' and that regulation would be preferable. The Sound Broadcasting Act 1972 therefore allowed independent companies to be licensed to provide on-shore commercial radio broadcasting.[123] This is now dealt with under the Broadcasting Act 1990.

Apart from licensed broadcasters, a number of unlicensed radio stations, some of which broadcast religious programming, are also active. *Ex natura* these are not subject to control, though Ofcom has significant powers to suppress such stations, including search and the seizure of equipment.[124]

Religion in broadcasting

Religion in UK broadcasting has developed from an early reflection of mainstream Christianity to a more inclusive attitude. Many faiths now have their tenets and festivities included in modern programming, even atheism and agnosticism. The current arrangements are in the hands of Ofcom and the BBC. Of the two Ofcom is now the more important.[125]

Ofcom was created to bring together and modernise the broadcasting standards that had been developed by three previous regulators, the Independent Television Commission for

---

118 Bids are assessed on a variety of rounds, including intended programming. The company ITN (Independent Television News) mainly provides news services to the other commercial broadcasters, though it can produce other programming, for example documentaries or dramas.
119 Communications Act 2003, s. 265(3). This includes experiment and innovation, providing for a culturally diverse society, contributing to educative interests and being distinctive.
120 Broadcasting Act 1990, s. 23 and Sch. 3.
121 Long before this 'Radio Luxembourg' had been transmitting to the UK from its base, well outside UK control.
122 The Marine, etc., Broadcasting (Offences) Act 1967, gave legal effect to the European Agreement for the Prevention of Broadcasts transmitted from Stations outside National Territories, Strasbourg, 1962, 1968 UKTS 1, Cmnd. 3497, a united European attempt to quash such stations. See now Part 5 of the Wireless Telegraphy Act 2006.
123 The bulk of the stations so licensed provide service in a locality. The national providers are few.
124 Wireless Telegraphy Act 2006, ss. 97–104. Providing material for unlicensed broadcasts is a criminal offence (s. 85).
125 In 2014 to facilitate its carrying out of its functions Ofcom entered into a Memorandum of Understanding with the British Board of Film Classification (BBFC) (the authority with regard to videos under the Video Recordings Act 1984) and the Authority for Television on Demand (ATVOD) which in 2010 had been designated by Ofcom as co-regulator for On Demand Programme Services. The parties are committed to working together, though the arrangement is not legally binding.

commercial television, the Radio Authority for commercial radio, and the Broadcasting Standards Commission, which had dealt with taste and decency, fairness and privacy. Now under ss. 319–28 of the Communications Act 2003 Ofcom publishes codes on 'standards objectives' for broadcast content, with which broadcasters must comply, but with limited exception for the BBC.[126] In setting standards Ofcom has to take into account international obligations as well as domestic concerns (s. 319(7)).[127] Areas covered are listed in s. 319(2). Section 319(2)(e) identifies religion as one of these, the objective being that 'the proper degree of responsibility is exercised with respect to the content of programmes which are religious programmes'. However, the treatment of religion has a further refinement. By s. 319(6) Ofcom standard requirements for religious programmes must 'contain provisions designed to secure' that the programmes 'do not involve (a) any improper exploitation of any susceptibilities of the audience for such a programme; or (b) any abusive treatment of the religious views and beliefs of those belonging to a particular religion or religious denomination'.

For two years after its inception Ofcom operated on the basis of a Code developed by one of its predecessors, the Independent Television Commission.[128] Its Section Seven (Religion) provided:

> 7.1 General requirements
> Section 6(1)(d) of the Broadcasting Act 1990 requires 'due responsibility' to be exercised with respect to the content of religious programmes. In particular such programmes must not involve: any improper exploitation of any susceptibilities of those watching the programmes; or any abusive treatment of the religious views and beliefs of those belonging to a particular religion or religious denomination.
>
> 7.2 Every attempt must be made to ensure that the belief and practice of religious groups are not misrepresented, and that programmes about religion are accurate and fair. Programmes and follow-up material to programmes must not denigrate others' beliefs.
>
> Religious belief and practice are central to many people's lives and capable of evoking strong passions and emotions. The United Kingdom contains communities with different faiths and cultures, with religious sensitivities particular to each. To avoid unintentional offence, all broadcasters should be aware of these sensitivities. Licensees may find it helpful to take advice from a group which is representative of the main religious traditions within their audience.
>
> 7.3 In general, religious programmes on Channels 3, 4 and 5 should reflect the worship, thought and action of the mainstream religious traditions present in the United Kingdom, recognising that these are mainly, though not exclusively, Christian. Religious programmes provided for a particular region or locality should take account of the religious make-up of the area served.

---

126 Notwithstanding these exceptions, by Clauses 91–95 of the Agreement (*supra* n. 113), the BBC is required to cooperate with Ofcom (Cl. 91) including as to religious programming (Cl. 46(2)(a)(iii)), may be required to take remedial action (Cl. 93), and could be fined by Ofcom for a breach of standards (Cl. 94).

127 The Preamble to the section of the current Broadcasting Code, to which we are coming, cites as relevant Arts 9, 10 and 14 of the European Convention on Human Rights, 1951, ETS 5, 1953 UKTS 71, Cmd. 8969, respectively the right to freedom of thought, conscience and religion, to freedom of expression and the right to enjoy the rights and freedoms of the Convention without discrimination.

128 See Ofcom website: http://stakeholders.ofcom.org.uk/broadcasting/broadcast-codes/legacy/itc-programme-code/

7.4 The identity of religious bodies featured in programmes must be clear to the viewer, where practicable in sound and vision.

7.5 Programmes may not include appeals for money by organisations whose aims are wholly or mainly religious, unless the conditions set out under Section 6 of this Code are met.

7.6 Religious programmes may quite properly be used to propound, propagate and proclaim religious belief but neither programmes nor follow-up material may be used to denigrate the beliefs of other people. Religious programmes on non-specialist channels may not be designed for the purpose of recruiting viewers to any particular religious faith or denomination.

A programme designed for the purpose of recruiting viewers is one which includes a message or challenge directed specifically at viewers rather than, for example, at a congregation or other group appearing in the programme. A 'specialist' service is a religious channel licensed under Schedule 2 Part II paragraph 2 of the Broadcasting Act 1990.

7.7 It is quite proper for a religious body or member of it positively to advocate the merits of a particular religious belief, or view of life. But religious programmes must not persuade or influence viewers by preying on their fears.

7.8 Except in the context of a legitimate investigation, religious programmes may not contain claims by or about living people or groups, suggesting that they have special powers or abilities, which are incapable of being substantiated.

7.9 Where published material, such as a book, tape, video or information pack, is clearly related to a programme, and a useful addition to it, the conditions set out in Section 8.1 of this Code apply. Offers of follow-up material must make it clear that no further contact will be made except at the instigation of the viewer. Licensees must satisfy themselves that follow-up material is responsible in tone and content.

On-air announcements permitted by Section 8.1 may offer free publications to viewers, but may not contain any other free offer.

Section Seven concluded by cross-referring to other sections of the Code for guidance on achieving due impartiality when political issues are included in religious programming.

In contrast, when Ofcom issued its own Broadcasting Code in 2005 it was terse as to religious broadcasting. That characteristic and its terms have persisted through the later versions.[129] Section Four of the 2013 Broadcasting Code begins by outlining the principles to be applied in religious programming. These, drawing on s. 319 of the 2003 Act, are that broadcasters shall exercise responsibility, and that there should be no improper exploitation of the susceptibilities of an audience, or abusive treatment of religious views and beliefs of those who belong to a particular religion or denomination. Thereafter it sets out Rules and definitions:

Rules:

4.1 Broadcasters must exercise the proper degree of responsibility with respect to the content of programmes which are religious programmes.

---

129 Broadcasting Codes were issued by Ofcom in 2005, 2008, 2009, 2100 (two), and 2011 and 2013.

Meaning of a 'religious programme':

A religious programme is a programme which deals with matters of religion as the central subject, or as a significant part, of the programme.

4.2 The religious views and beliefs of those belonging to a particular religion or religious denomination must not be subject to abusive treatment.

4.3 Where a religion or religious denomination is the subject, or one of the subjects, of a religious programme, then the identity of the religion and/or denomination must be clear to the audience.

4.4 Religious programmes must not seek to promote religious views or beliefs by stealth.

4.5 Religious programmes on television services must not seek recruits. This does not apply to specialist religious television services. Religious programmes on radio services may seek recruits.

Meaning of 'seek recruits':

Seek recruits means directly appealing to audience members to join a religion or religious denomination.

4.6 Religious programmes must not improperly exploit any susceptibilities of the audience.[130]

4.7 Religious programmes that contain claims that a living person (or group) has special powers or abilities must treat such claims with due objectivity and must not broadcast such claims when significant numbers of children may be expected to be watching (in the case of television), or when children are particularly likely to be listening (in the case of radio).

Such is the current outcome of debate and concern as to religion in broadcasting that has taken place throughout the history of the medium. The contrast between this treatment of religion and the pre-Ofcom Code is significant. Matters religious are no longer subject to scrutiny and control to the extent of earlier years. The change may be categorised as improvement or not depending on personal views. Assumptions of the primacy of Christianity had vanished even before Ofcom took over. Now clearly many streams of religion can now flow through the broadcast media. Getting there has taken time, and reflects societal mutation.

The creation of the British Broadcasting Corporation in 1926 did not alter how Reith had dealt with religious broadcasting within the Broadcasting Company. An early Company broadcast was a religious address on Christmas Eve 1922, and in the following months with the active co-operation of Randall Davidson, then Archbishop of Canterbury, Reith brought into being as the first of the national advisory committees that still advise the BBC, the Central Religious Advisory Committee (CRAC). This, composed of leaders of the major denominations, was taken over by the BBC as one of its advisory committees established under Clause 9 of the 1926 Charter. The Committee was solely advisory, and soon was aided by equivalent local committees throughout the country.

Slowly more religious broadcasts were introduced, Asa Briggs identifying three major stages as being present in the years 1927 to 1933.[131] A daily religious service was begun, then on Sundays religious broadcasting increased, and lastly a generalised differentiation between Sunday broadcasts and the rest of the week became apparent. The range of

---

130 I omit cross-reference to other parts of the Code that deal with charity or funding appeals.
131 Briggs, *supra* n. 89, I 229.

religious opinion and its reflection in a public service came to be queried. The Central Religious Advisory Committee suggested an equitable distribution of religious opinion, but only within the parameters of 'mainstream Christianity', a bias criticised in the 1930s.[132]

In 1933 the BBC appointed a religious director and this aided development throughout the 1930s, by the end of which religious broadcasting was a secure area within the BBC. Not only were more religious services broadcast, but a series of remarkable radio plays were commissioned, of which the most famous was Dorothy Sayers' cycle 'The Man Born to be King' of 1942.[133] However, pressure for the secularisation of Sunday broadcasting began. In 1935 the Ullswater Committee suggested that Sunday programmes could be a little lighter and popular in character, in at least one of the BBC services.[134] Because of the War and routine extensions of the BBC Charter during it, broadcasting was not formally reviewed until the Beveridge Committee of 1949–51. During the War religious broadcasting had been developed to some extent as a propaganda tool.[135] Questions emerged as to whether the increased political and military concern emergent in religious broadcasts with regard to foreign events might spill over into domestic social matters. It was decided it should not, and this was embodied in what is known as the 'Concordat' of August 1941 under which ministers of religion might only expound the moral and religious principles and criteria on which political decisions ought to be taken. Criticisms and suggestions of detail and of policy decisions were not within their purview. This was accepted by CRAC and enforced through the vetting of scripts.[136]

Neither the Beveridge Committee of 1949–51,[137] nor the Pilkington Committee of 1960[138] recommended major structural change in the BBC. However, the former did recommend that the object of religious broadcasting should not be to seek converts to one particular church but to maintain the elements common to all religious bodies. Even so, the Committee wrote of maintaining that common element 'as against those who deny spiritual values', which is somewhat different.[139] However, the Pilkington Committee operated in a different environment, commercial television having begun under the Television Act 1954. There had been concern that commercial broadcasting would allow religious groups to buy advertising, so constraints were built into the 1954 Act. Under Sch. 2 religious advertising was forbidden – a provision carried over into later versions of the legislation. By s. 8 commercial television broadcasters were bound to comply with the recommendations of a religious advisory committee, similar to CRAC,[140] and religious broadcasts including of services had to be approved centrally by the Independent Television Authority.[141] However, as to religious broadcasting the Pilkington Committee accepted the propositions then current in the BBC.[142] Broadcasters were not required to be neutral, should reflect mainstream

---

132 M. Dinwiddie, *Religion by Radio* (London: Allen & Unwin, 1968), 33–8, 78–80.
133 D.L. Sayers, *The Man Born to be King* (London: Harper, 1943; Gollancz, 1969).
134 *Report of the Broadcasting Committee. 1935*, 1936 Cmd. 5091, para. 100.
135 On a different line, C.S. Lewis delivered three series of 'Broadcast Talks', later to form the basis of his *Mere Christianity* (many eds).
136 Briggs, *supra* n. 89, II 622–3.
137 *Supra* n. 108.
138 *Supra* n. 109.
139 Beveridge Committee, *supra* n. 108, Rec. 60, but cf. its Report para 252.
140 By this time CRAC had been extended to include members from other religions.
141 D. Lloyd, 'Some Comments on the British Television Act, 1954' (1958) 23 Law & Contemporary Problems, 165–74.
142 Pilkington Committee, *supra* n. 109. The Committee referred to the BBC *Handbook* of 1960.

Christian tradition, should show the significant relationship between the Christian faith and the modern world and should seek to reach those on the fringe, or quite outside the organised life of the churches. Within these constraints, broadcast religion should not be a vehicle for any one group, though this was not to dilute programming beyond utility. Explicit doctrinal exposition was allowable, but not undue emphasis on difference or the disparagement of other faiths.[143]

By the time of the Annan Committee of 1977 things had moved on. While the 1960 objectives were still thought of as a rough working guide, they needed revision. General guidelines had been worked out between the BBC and the Independent Broadcasting Authority, the latter being by then the supervisor of commercial broadcasting. These were:

1 To seek to reflect the worship, thought and action of the principal religious traditions represented in Britain, recognising that these traditions are mainly, though not exclusively Christian;
2 To seek to present to viewers and listeners those beliefs, ideas, issues and experiences in the contemporary world which are evidently related to a religious interpretation or dimension of life;
3 To seek also to meet the religious interest, concerns and needs of those on the fringe of, or outside, the organised life of the Churches.

The Committee recognised that this was a fundamental departure from previous objectives, abandoning the 'mainstream' concept that had been tied to varieties of Christianity. However, it accepted that that was what religious broadcasting departments had been doing for some time. Notwithstanding, the Committee thought that the Christian denominations should retain a primary place in religious broadcasting.[144]

By the time of the Broadcasting Act 1990 things had changed again. The Independent Television Commission Broadcasting Code recognised the importance for many of religious belief.[145] Christianity was noted as the mainstream religious tradition in the UK, but room was to be made for other religions. Their role was recognised in Sec. 7.2, of the Code, and, sensitivity to the potential audience was called for, particularly in local broadcasting. These matters are now dealt with by Sec. 4 of the 2013 Ofcom Broadcasting Code.[146] I have already noted its terseness. It provides scope for many religions (and many strands within them), to be given exposure within the broadcasting media.

In the past there were suggestions that religious broadcasting should not have special status within the broadcasting organisations, and that religion could be subsumed within the general category of 'talks'.[147] That does seem to have had some effect within commercial organisations, but not within the 'public service' broadcaster. The BBC retains a religious broadcasting department, whose head, interestingly, is currently (2015) a Moslem. The 2004 broadcasting review was firmly of the view that that religion should not be shunted into a digital ghetto, and, that with some funding and more imagination, it could attract greater success than hitherto.[148] To a degree the current arrangements reflected that. The review

---

143 Pilkington Committee, *supra* n. 109, para 288.
144 Annan Committee, *supra* n. 110, para 20.
145 *Supra* n. 128.
146 *Supra*, following n. 129.
147 Annan Committee, *supra* n. 110, para 20.18. In 1980 I thought this should be tried. I have changed my view.
148 *A public BBC*, *supra* n. 111, para 73 and Recommendation 8.

did note the importance of 'signposting programmes that might cause offence to certain viewers',[149] but considered that the possibility of causing religious offence should not prevent broadcasts.[150]

Whether religions and religious movements should be able to purchase advertising slots in the commercial broadcast media has exercised many. The short answer is that they now can, but subject to Ofcom control.[151] In 2004 Ofcom entered into arrangements under which broadcast advertising is dealt with by the Broadcast Committee of Advertising Practice (which sets the standards for content), and the Advertising Standards Authority (Broadcast). The former has adopted the UK Code of Broadcast Advertising – the BCAP Code – with which advertisers are expected to comply.[152] The latter, a subdivision of the Advertising Standards Authority deals with complaints. These arrangements were renewed for a further 10 years in 2014.[153]

Finally, within local radio and satellite broadcasting, various organisations are able to provide religious programming, many exclusively so and confined to one point of view. Balance is not required.

6. Oaths

The oath is found in all European legal systems. Scotland is no exception. Based originally upon the expectation of contravention resulting in condign religious penalty, an oath goes beyond (though shading into) a solemn undertaking. An oath has many purposes. The oath or solemn vow undergirds duties to obey, to serve, to act faithfully in the exercise of an office. In civil or criminal proceedings the oath guarantees truth. The vitality of oaths in a theologically pluralistic society is remarkable, indicating a fondness for tradition, maybe a degree of superstition, and, for some, continuing religious belief. But over the centuries there has been change.

Oaths may be promissory in respect of the execution of functions, or serve within judicial procedures.

The Promissory Oaths Act 1868, as amended, now regulates that category of oaths. In the past its religious content and the religious convictions of those taking it made promissory oaths an important tool of government. They were used to protect the interests of the established Kirk.[154] They were used to exclude from public position and to guarantee the

---

149 *A public BBC*, supra n. 111, para 186 and Recommendation 33.
150 Cf. the attempts in 2005–07 to stop the presentation both in theatres and on the BBC of 'Jerry Springer: the Opera'. See the Wikipedia entry for the Opera and *R (On the application of Green)* v *City of Westminster Magistrates Court* [2007] EWHC 2785, [2008] HRLR 12. Cf. also supra n. 66.
151 The arrangements are set out in an Ofcom statement, *infra* n. 153. See also the *Memorandum of Understanding between Office of Communications ('Ofcom') and the Advertising Standards Authority (Broadcast) Limited ('ASA(B)') and the Broadcast Committee of Advertising Practice Limited ('BCAP') and the Broadcast Advertising Standards Board of Finance Limited ('BASBOF')*, Ofcom, October 2014 These arrangements comply with the EU Audiovisual Media Services Directive, 2010/13/EU. The designation in July 2010 of the Advertising Standards Authority as co-regulator with Ofcom for video on demand was confirmed in December 2014. See *Regulation of Advertising in Video on Demand Services*, Ofcom, December 2014.
152 The standards are regularly reviewed. Chapter 15 of the BCAP Code deals with 'Faith, Religion and Equivalent Systems of Belief': http://www.cap.org.uk/Advertising-Codes/Broadcast.aspx
153 Ofcom Statement: *Renewal of the Co-regulatory Arrangements for Broadcast Advertising*, 4 November 2014. See also *supra* nn. 125 and 151.
154 Cf. the oaths required of Episcopalian minister by ss. 2 and 4 of the Scottish Episcopalians Relief Act, 1792. I. Guild, 'Synodical Government in the Scottish Episcopal Church', 1996 Ecc L.J. 493.

trustworthiness of the holders of public office.[155] Scotland had its own Test Acts.[156] Statutes attempted to ensure that persons in positions of responsibility would properly discharge their duties to the sovereign of the day,[157] such as the Unlawful Societies Act 1799, passed at the height of the wars connected with the French Revolution, which prohibited oaths to subvert the existing polity.[158] These efforts are no longer made, and the promissory oath is largely ceremonial.[159] However, failure timeously to take a required oath results in either vacation of or disqualification from office.[160]

There are major exceptions to my generalisations. A slew of oaths remain of constitutional importance. These include the Sovereign's Oath prescribed by the Protestant Religion and Presbyterian Church Act 1706, c. 6, undertaking to protect the Church of Scotland, the Coronation Oath Act 1567, c. 8 (amended by the Union legislation and later practice) and the Oaths taken by a Regent under s. 4(1), and the Schedule to the Regency Act 1937. What may happen when there next is a demise of the Crown is uncertain. Another set of important constitutional oaths are the oaths of allegiance taken by Westminster MPs and members of the House of Lords,[161] and by the Members of the Scottish Parliament, the Scottish Ministers and the Scottish Government under s. 84 of the Scotland Act, 1998.[162]

Oaths are important in the administration of justice and the conduct of civil and criminal affairs. They have been revised and simplified, but previous examples, now defunct, indicate the weight that used to be placed upon their religious content. The oath of calumny had long roots in continental jurisprudence.[163] To prevent false allegations and calumnious suits, parties had to swear that the facts alleged were just and true.[164] There were oaths of verity, of

---

155 See *supra* Chapters 2–5, and 6 Education. The question of the 'Burgess Oath' fractured many elements of the Secession movement of the eighteenth century.
156 Religion and the Test, 1681 c. 6 (repealed 1690 cc.7 and 58) and 1685 c.13 (repealed 1690 c. 58), was to be taken by anyone in a position of public trust. The equivalents for England including the Corporation Act 1661, and the Test Acts 1673 and 1678, were intended to restrict the holding of public office to members of the Church of England. These were all repealed by the Sacramental Test Act 1828, and the Roman Catholic Relief Act 1829.
157 The Jacobite Rising of 1715 occasioned the Church Patronage (Scotland) Act 1718, which required Episcopalian ministers to pray for George I and his family at all services, and to abjure the 'Old Pretender', James, son of James VII, who had been deposed in the 'Glorious Revolution' of 1688.
158 The 1799 Act was not repealed until the Criminal Law Act 1967.
159 The Statute Law Revision Act 1883 repealed many acts that required promissory oaths to be taken prior to the assumption of a public office. As to layers of history behind ceremony cf. W. McBryde, 'The two Presidents: reflections on the Installation of a Lord Justice Clerk', 2013 SLT 15.
160 Promissory Oaths Act 1868, s. 7.
161 Parliamentary Oaths Act, 1866, s. 1. These are regulated by the Standing Orders of each House. Elected MPs who do not take the required oath or affirm cannot take their seat but remains eligible for parliamentary allowances – as in the case of members of Sinn Fein elected for Northern Ireland constituencies. Cf. *infra* n. 179 and related text.
162 The original 'Scottish Executive' was renamed the 'Scottish Government' by s. 12(2)(a) of the Scotland Act 2012. Members of the Welsh Assembly take an oath or affirm allegiance under the Government of Wales Act, 2006, s. 23, as Welsh may ministers on appointment (s. 55). Members of the Northern Ireland Assembly and ministers are not so required.
163 Act 1429 c.16, c. 125 12mo. Its history is traced in *Paul* v *Laing* (1855) 17 D. 604. See also *Paterson* v *Kilgour* (1865) 3 M. 1119.
164 Latterly this oath was required only in divorce actions: Court of Session Act 1830, s. 36, repealed by s. 10(1) and Sch. to the Civil Evidence (Scotland) Act, 1988.

200 *Other interactions of religion and law*

credulity and the oath on reference.[165] In each, one party could require the other on oath to state or deny the truth of an assertion as to fact. The appeal to the conscience of a party was final as to the fact involved, though its implications might require interpretation. Various obligations might be proved only by writ or oath of the debtor.[166] However, proof by oath in civil proceedings was abolished by s. 11(2) of the Requirements of Writing Act 1995.[167] That said, it remains interesting that in Scotland a person holding a conscientious objection to participation in abortion and other medical areas can establish this by a statement made on oath.[168]

Most current non-promissory oaths are found in the administration of justice and judicial proceedings. A creditor claiming in a bankruptcy proceeding presents an oath of credit.[169] Jurors in civil[170] or in criminal cases[171] swear that they will truly find the facts remitted to them. A witness swears to tell the truth, the whole truth and nothing but the truth. The omission of the words 'the whole truth' from the oath is impermissible and does not excuse a witness.[172]

Oaths remain important. Last century Green's *Encyclopedia of the Laws of Scotland* suggested that: 'It is found that a witness giving his testimony on oath will tell the truth

---

165 See Lord Moncreiff in *Pattison* v. *Robertson* (1846) 9 D. 226 at 229 – 'It has been a fixed rule of the law of Scotland for centuries that a party, pursuer or defender, even after all other methods of discussion or evidence have failed, may say to his adversary before the Court, though I cannot produce evidence to shew the truth, I appeal it to your own oath, and to your conscience as a Christian man'. Cases include *Jamieson* v *White*, 1992 Lexis; *Keanie* v *Keanie*, 1940 SC 549; *Pollock* v *Whiteford*, 1936 SC 402; *Muir* v *City of Glasgow Bank* (1879) 6 R. (HL) 21; *Mein* v *Towers* (1829) 7 S. 902; *Adams* v *Maclachlan* (1847) 9 D. 560; *Longworth* v *Yelverton* (1867) 5 M. (HL) 144 at 145–6; cf. earlier Opinion of Lord Deas therein (1865) 3 M. 645 at 671 and Lord Young in *Paterson* v *Paterson* (1897) 25 R. 144 at 152; *M'Kie* v *Wilson* 1951 SLT 40; *Ianucci* v *Rippa* 1972 SLT (Sh. Ct.) 13; on the oath see Baron David Hume's *Lectures, 1786–1822*, Vol. V (ed. GCH. Paton, 1957, Stair Soc. Vol. 18), 315–30. The oath on reference might be required at any time prior to the extraction of a final decree: *Longworth* v *Yelverton* (1865) 3 M. 645, aff'd (1867) 5 M. (HL) 144. Only matters provable by parole evidence could be proved by oath. Obligations restricted to proof by writ could not: *Perdikou* v *Pattinson* 1958 SLT 153.
166 That the writ did not have to be probative of the debtor diminished the use of the oath: *Paterson* v *Paterson* (1897) 25 R. 144; *Smith's Trustees* v *Smith*, 1911 SC 653; Stair IV.44.5.
167 J.M. Thomson, 'Promises and the requirements of writing', 1997 SLT 284; cf. W.W. McBryde, 'Promises in Scots law', 1993 ICLQ 48.
168 See *infra*, 12 Medical Practice; Abortion Act 1967, ss. 4(1) and (3). In *Greater Glasgow Health Board (Appellant)* v *Doogan and another (Respondents) (Scotland)* [2014] UKSC 68 at para 10 *ad fin*. Lady Hale noted that s. 4(3) was included to meet the then requirement of corroboration in Scots civil cases and that that requirement had subsequently been abolished (by s. 1 of the Civil Evidence (Scotland) Act 1988). Cf. Scot Law Comm., *Proposals for Reform of the Law of Evidence Relating to Corroboration*, 1967, SLC Rep. No. 4.
169 Bankruptcy (Scotland) Act, 1985, s. 11; Bankruptcy (Scotland) Regulations 1985, 1985 SI 1925 (S. 147), Reg. 5, and Sch. Form 2. Cf. *Clydesdale Bank* v *Grantly* 2000 SCLR 771.
170 Jury Trials (Scotland) Act 1815, s. 3l: 'Oath to be administered to the jury. The clerk of the jury court, before proceeding to the said trial, shall administer to the jury the following oath; videlicet, 'You swear by God, and as you shall answer to God at the great Day of Judgment, that you shall well and truly try (as the case may be), these issues, or this issue, and a true verdict give according to the evidence'.
171 *Regiam Maiestatem*, I.12 (ed. Lord Cooper, Stair Soc. Vol. 11, 1947): Act 1436 c. 2, c. 138 12mo: Baron Hume, *Commentaries on the Law of Scotland Respecting Crimes*, II, 316.
172 In *M'Laughlin* v *Douglas and Kidston* (1863) 4 Irv. 273, a Roman Catholic clergyman persuaded the judge to omit the 'whole truth' from the oath, and appealed, unsuccessfully, against imprisonment for contempt when he refused to answer some questions: cf. L.J-G. McNeill at 286. The questions did not infringe the confessional.

Other interactions of religion and law 201

more exactly than if he were making a statement without such sanction'.[173] An early writer on Evidence was of the view that: 'The practice [of oath taking] is founded on the well known fact, that perjury is rare compared with false or coloured statements made without the sanction of an oath'.[174] But is that now the case? It is more than 50 years since a Sheriff observed, *obiter*, that 'in the not too distant past, the certainty of perpetual condemnation to condign darkness (or worse) in perpetuity, was, to large numbers, an assured consequence of all swearing, and so provided a real and strong deterring sanction. It is questionable whether such considerations loom so large in the realm of modern thought'.[175]

The Statutory Declarations Act 1835 considerably reduced the occasions on which oaths had to be taken in the conduct of official and important business. Their replacement by declaration procedures opened up many professions to persons previously unable for reasons of conscience to engage in them. Now for many official purposes outside the courts a statutory declaration asserting the truth or accuracy of a statement suffices.[176]

It would appear logical that an oath may be taken only by those holding a religious belief, and this used to be strictly enforced. However, it was not necessary that that belief be Christian.[177] Section 1 of the Oaths Act 1838 enacted that an oath binds provided that it is administered in the form that the person taking the oath declares is binding upon him. The Court does not enquire into the nationality or faith of any person, but will employ such formality as is required if the matter is brought to its attention and the formalities can be conveniently used. If special formalities are not reasonably practicable, then also by s. 1 the Court may require the individual to affirm under the procedures developed in the nineteenth century.

The move towards today's general permission of affirmation as an alternative to the oath was slow. The (English) Quakers Oaths Act 1695 was the first step. Parallel legislation for Scotland did not come until the Justiciary Courts Act 1828, and that only in criminal proceedings. The Affirmations (Scotland) Act 1855 extended affirmation in civil proceedings to all whose religious belief precluded them from taking an oath and this was extended to criminal proceedings by the Oaths Relief in Criminal Proceedings (Scotland) Act 1863. Two years later the Affirmations (Scotland) Act 1865 consolidated the prior law. However, at this stage the right to affirm was predicated upon holding a religious belief that barred the taking of oaths (sc. under a construction of Matt. 5: 34–37, and James 5: 15). It was not available to those for whom other grounds of conscience made swearing impossible. Thus, although it might be argued that atheism or agnosticism is a form of religious belief, atheists and agnostics were excluded from the procedure. A person without belief in God could not properly guarantee the truth of his statements by reference to anything.

Affirmation, and therefore access to public offices for which an oath was required, became available to atheists and agnostics in 1888. This is attributable largely to Charles

---

173 Viscount Dunedin, et al., eds, *Encyclopaedia of the Laws of Scotland*, 3rd ed. (Edinburgh: W. Green & Son, 1926–52) s.v. Witness, para. 1432.
174 W.G. Dickson, *Law of Evidence in Scotland*, 2nd ed. (Edinburgh: Bell & Bradfute, 1864), Vol. 2, 959.
175 Sheriff- Substitute Dickson in *Cuthbertson v Patterson*, 1968 SLT (Sh. Ct.) 21.
176 'False statutory declarations and other false statements without oath': False Oaths (Scotland) Act 1933, s. 2, and s. 3, 'False declarations &c. to obtain registration &c. for carrying on a vocation'. Cf. the statutory declaration on an Income Tax return.
177 A. Alison, *Practice of the Criminal Law in Scotland* (Edinburgh: Blackwood, 1833), 437. 'All persons who believe in God and a future state are admissible, of whatever creed or religion they may be'. Alison continued that the form of the oath depends upon the form of the belief held. 'But whatever the form of the swearing, the nature of the oath is everywhere the same; it is an appeal to Heaven, calling upon God to witness what is said and invoking his vengeance if it is false'.

Bradlaugh and his associates. Using the analogy of affirmation on ground of conscience, then statutorily available to Quakers and Moravians,[178] Bradlaugh, elected MP for Northampton in 1880, sought to take his seat in Parliament, offering to affirm allegiance but without taking the parliamentary oath. A series of cases on the privileges and powers of the House of Commons ensued.[179] The Oaths Act 1888 resulted, under which atheists, and those who by reason of their religious belief object to the taking of oaths, may make a solemn affirmation in prescribed terms (s. 2).

The Oaths Act 1978 consolidated the law. It permits the Scottish form of swearing with an uplifted hand throughout the UK (s. 3). By s. 4(1) an oath binds a person if it is administered in the form which he declares is binding on him. By s. 4(2) the validity of an oath is not vitiated by an absence of religious belief. Section 5 permits affirmation instead of an oath. Section 6 prescribes its form, and stipulates for the 'omission of any words of imprecation or calling to witness'. Naturally perjury after oath or affirmation is a criminal offence, and that is backed up by the False Oaths (Scotland) Act 1933 (consolidating the law relating to false swearing in specified instances), and ss. 44-46 of the Criminal Law (Consolidation) Scotland) Act 1995, though false swearing and perjury had been criminal offences in Scotland for many years.[180]

The balance between the religious and ceremonial aspects of an oath is now a matter for the individual. In most cases a major function of the solemnities is to emphasise the importance of the occasion or proceedings. Thus the oath of allegiance required of persons acquiring British nationality is justified by the civic importance of the transaction.[181] In some instances the immediate sanction for breach of oath or affirmation is forfeiture or disqualification from office,[182] or prosecution for perjury. It may be a question, however, whether the religious oath should continue as the norm in judicial proceedings. Those of belief could choose that mode. Belief should not be depreciated by its assumption.

7. Sunday observance

The Scottish Sunday has gathered many tales, but in most of Scotland the strict sabbatarianism of last centuries has been departed from. This has occurred as a social change, old Scots Acts on the profanation of the Sabbath simply going out of use prior to being formally repealed. Unlike the position in England, major legislative initiative has been unnecessary.[183] This section is concerned with general rules of or for society. Discrimination against an individual who wishes to observe Sunday for religious reasons is considered elsewhere.[184]

---

178 Quaker and Moravian Affirmation Acts of 1833 and 1838. These, as a matter of religious doctrine, held the swearing oaths unlawful. The word of a Christian was enough.
179 *Clarke* v *Bradlaugh* (1881) 7 QBD 38; *Bradlaugh* v *Clarke* (1883) 8 App. Cas. 354; *Bradlaugh* v *Gossett* (1884) 12 QBD 271.
180 Perjury is not civilly actionable as such, though following a conviction consequential loss might be recovered
181 British Nationality Act 1981, s. 42, and Sch. 5, as substituted by the Nationality, Immigration and Asylum Act, 2002, Sch. 1, together with the British Nationality (General) Regulations 2003, 2003 SI 548, Reg. 6 and Sch. 3. Cf. *Secure Borders, Safe Havens: Integration with Diversity in Modern Britain*, 2002 Cm 5387, which preceded the 2002 Act.
182 *Supra* n. 160.
183 Cf. the debates in England surrounding the Sunday Trading Act 1994 and its predecessors, particularly the Shops Act 1950.
184 See *supra* n. 36, and *infra* n. 239.

History

The observance of certain days as set apart from the ordinary is a practice of great antiquity.[185] The original basis of such practices was religious, whether as discipline or duty. However, for many the 'holy day' has been transmuted to the holiday, a rather different concept, and broadened beyond religion. The Bank Holiday introduced by the Bank Holidays Act, 1871,[186] has metastised, and the 'holidays' clause is now an integral part of most full-time employment contracts.[187] In short, holidays are considered a necessary social institution, perhaps even a human right.[188]

In post-Reformation Scotland the Christian Sunday was afforded special status. Christmas and Easter and other holy days were not,[189] but it was unthinkable that there should not be law on Sunday observance. Christendom had possessed such laws for many centuries and it would have been surprising had Scotland not followed the pattern.

Sunday observance laws may manifest the power of the Christian church, or more charitably, reflect a belief as to holy days found in many societies. Both elements are certainly present, but either is too facile an explanation for a difficult topic. The seven-day cycle antedates Christianity, and may not be solely the result of Jewish practice based on the account of the Creation in the first chapters of Genesis.[190] The seven-day cycle seems to be in some way 'natural'.[191] If a seven-day week is the norm, why should Sunday be the special day? At this point the Christian reference is definite. A day of rest on Saturday was already common in the eastern Roman Empire, and, of course, the rule in the Holy Land. Christianity therefore entered upon a known practice, but converted it to mark the resurrection of Jesus on the first day of the week. However, initially Sunday was not observed as a day of rest because Christianity was to an extent a religion of the poor and slaves who had to work.[192] Then later, when Christianity was proscribed, there was little point in indicating one's religion to the authorities by refusing to work like everyone else.[193] It is therefore not surprising that the first references to Sunday (always as the Lord's

---

185 Exodus 20: 8–11.
186 Now s. 1 and Sch. 1 of the Banking and Financial Dealings Act 1971.
187 See now the Employment Protection (Consolidation) Act 1978, and s. 1(4)(d)(i) of the Employment Rights Act 1996.
188 *Supra* n. 36, *infra* nn. 239, 248, 249.
189 The *First Book of Discipline* Head I.3 condemns various practices including feast days such as Christmas and Epiphany (Easter) as not being commanded in Scripture. The 'obstinate maintainers and teachers of such abominations ought not to escape the punishment of the civil magistrate'. The Easter Act 1928 prescribing that Easter should be the first Sunday after the second Saturday in April (that is, between 9 and 15 April) remains unimplemented in the absence of the agreement of all churches, including the Orthodox churches, which operate to a different calendar.
190 W. Rordorf, trans. A.A.K. Graham, *Sunday: The History of the Day of Rest and Worship in the Earliest Centuries of the Christian Church* (London: SCM Press, 1968), 9–38, quotes or refers to most of the basic material. In the French Revolution as part of a general revision of time-keeping a year was set as 12 months, divided into three 10-day weeks of 10-hour days, each hour being numerically denoted from one to 10 and divided into 100 minutes. Additional days were inserted as necessary to maintain congruence with the solar cycle. The French Revolutionary Calendar lasted from late 1793 to 1805. It was revived very briefly in 1871 by the Paris Commune.
191 The number seven has magical significance for many, and may be linked to the lunar cycle.
192 See the extensive references to slaves and the common people in Paul's letters (for example, Philemon, I Cor. 7: 21–4) though Paul was also acquainted with the superior orders (Acts 17:4).
193 A.M. Sherwin-White, 'The Early Persecutions and Roman Law Again' (1952) 3 *J. Theo. Stud.* 199–213; G.E.M. de Ste. Croix, 'Why were the Early Christians Persecuted' (1963) 26 Past and Present, 5–38. P.R.

Day, or the first day of the week) make it plain that the Church met early to worship, and then treated the day like any other.[194] Tertullian's reference to business affairs being deferred on Sunday may indicate that by that time Sunday had developed into a day of rest for Christians, but this is not entirely clear.[195] The context goes on to refer in similar terms to the whole of Pentecost, and may indicate that partial rest rather than total rest was Christian practice. The first legal rules on the matter are explicit. By a Mandate of 3 March 321 AD Constantine laid down that, with the exception of farmers, 'All judges and urban peoples and artisans of all crafts should rest on the venerable day of the Sun'.[196] It is unnecessary to consider whether this was unambiguously a Christian piece of legislation.[197] It was adopted as such by Constantine's successors, and is the starting point of a long series of laws anent Sunday observance, the principal Roman versions of which are to be found in the *Codex Theodosianus* of AD 438, mainly in Title 2.8. From then on rules as to Sunday observance were normal. In mediaeval times they were largely sanctioned through ecclesiastical penalties, but with the development of effective civil authority Sunday observance laws came into vogue.

In Europe Sunday observance was concomitant with the influence of the Roman Catholic Church and its Protestant analogues. Attempts at international agreement on such matters were not unknown in Victorian times.[198] Elsewhere Sunday laws have come under judicial scrutiny. Thus in 1961 *McGowan* v *Maryland*[199] the US Supreme Court held that the Maryland Sunday Closing Laws did not contravene the First Amendment (which prohibits an establishment of religion) because their purpose was the protection of public health through assuring a common day of rest, and not the coercion of a particular religious view. Warren CJ wrote: 'Moreover it is common knowledge that the first day of the week has come to have special significance as a day of rest in this country. People of all religion and of no religion regard Sunday as a time for family activity, for visiting friends and relatives, for late-sleeping, for passive and active entertainments, for dining out and the like . . . Sunday is a day apart from all others. The cause is irrelevant; the fact exists. It would seem unrealistic for enforcement purposes and perhaps detrimental to the general welfare to require a state to choose a common day-of-rest other than that which most persons would select of their own accord'.[200] This view is not unchallenged, but it serves.[201]

Coleman-Norton, *Roman State and Christian Church: A Collection of Legal Documents to ad* 55 (London: SPCK, 1966), App. on Persecutions.
194 Acts 16: 13; 20: 10. Justin (ob. AD 165) *Apologia* 1. 67, the earliest specific reference in Christian writing to the Lord's Day as Sunday, and the *Epistle of Barnabas*, 15 ad. fin., are not evidence of rest on the Lord's Day.
195 Tertullian (c. AD 220), *De Oratione*, 23.
196 CJ 3.12.2: Coleman-Norton, *supra* n. 193, doc. no. 34.
197 There may be a Mithraic element or of the cult of Sol Invictus in the Constantine mandate, especially since the name used is not 'the Lord's day' but the 'day of the Sun', and Constantine is known to have venerated Sunday. For another three years his coinage was stamped 'Soli Invicto'. See A.A. Vasiliev, *History of the Byzantine Empire, 324–1453* (Madison: U. Wisconsin Press, 1952) 49 ff; A. Alföldi, trans. H. Mattingly, *The Conversion of Constantine and Pagan Rome* (Oxford: Clarendon Press, 1949, 1969) 48, 54 ff; Rordorf, *supra* n. 190, 162–6; Coleman-Norton, *supra* n. 193, 83–4; G.H. Halsberghe, *The Cult of Sol Invictus* (Leiden: Brill, 1972).
198 Cf. Minutes of the International Conference on Sunday Rest, Paris, 24–27 September, 1889, HC Sess. Papers, 1890–91, Vol. LXXXIII, 277, C. 6215.
199 *McGowan* v *State of Maryland* (1961) 366 US 420, 6 L Ed 2d 393.
200 366 US 420 at 451–2; 6 L Ed 2d 393 at 414.
201 Cf. the dissent by Justice Douglas (366 US 420 at 561–81) who saw such argument as a naive way to avoid the question of the establishment of religion clause in the US Constitution.

What of modern Europe? The European Court of Justice has held that at least in such matters as the opening of shops so long as European Union law is complied with, national law can determine what restrictions, if any, to impose, either nationally or regionally.[202]

Scotland

As in other matters, the views of the Roman Catholic Church and that of the Reformers coincided. The first formal Sunday legislation in Scotland was the Act 1503 c. 28 (c. 83 12mo) 'Anent faris haldin apon halidais or within kirkis or kirk yardis' which, as is obvious from its title, extended beyond questions of Sunday. Despite ecclesiastical exhortation, the Act and its successors seem to have been ineffective. In 1551, just before the Scottish Reformation, the Scottish Council of the Roman Catholic Church found it necessary to repeat that abuses of Sunday were not to be tolerated,[203] and this was backed by further parliamentary enactment. By the Act 1551 c. 8 (c. 17 12mo), those who disturbed Sunday worship were to be fined.

The Reformers were clear that Sunday should be free of work, and that all should come to church to hear the sermon. '. . . Sunday must be straitly kept, both before and after noon in all towns'.[204] In following years 15 statutes were directed to various aspects of the problems of securing Sunday observance, including the Act 1690 c. 7 ratifying the Westminster Confession of Faith.[205] Chapter XXI.8 of the Confession affirmed that the Sabbath was to be kept holy, with not only rest from work being stipulated for, but also rest from 'words, and thoughts about . . . worldly employments and recreations . . .'.[206]

After the Union the Scottish Episcopalians Act, 1711, s. 8, confirmed the pre-reformation legislation, a provision which, curiously, remains in force albeit the 'Sunday' statutes themselves have gone.[207] In practice, application of the old Scots Acts became erratic.[208] In his *Commentaries* Hume noted that only one prosecution occurred during the eighteenth century, and in that instance the diet had been deserted.[209] As a result the jurisprudence

---

202 *Stoke-on-Trent City Council* v *B & Q plc* [1993] 1 CMLR 426.
203 *Statutes of the Scottish Church, 1225–1559*, D. Patrick, ed. (1907), 54 Scottish History Society, 138.
204 The *First Book of Discipline*, Head IX. 3. The *Second Book of Discipline* does not deal with such matters.
205 As noted in the title 'Time', *Stair Memorial Encyclopaedia of the Laws of Scotland*, Vol. 22, para. 817 n. 13, these were the Sunday Acts 1579 (c 8; 12mo c 20), 1594 (c 8; 12mo c 201) and 1661 (c 281; 12mo c 18); Market-days Act 1592 (c 17; 12mo c 124); Markets on Sundays Act 1592 (c 6; 12mo c 163); Justices of the Peace Act 1661 (c 338; 12mo c 38); Markets Act 1663 (c 42; 12mo c 19); Profaneness Acts 1672 (c 58; 12mo c 22), 1690 (c 55; 12mo c 25), 1693 (c 64; 12mo c 40), 1695 (c 16; 12mo c 13), 1696 (c 31; 12mo c 31) and 1700 (c 12; 12mo c 11); Confession of Faith Ratification Act 1690 (c 7; 12mo c 5); and the Scottish Episcopalians Act 1711 (c 10). See also the Report from a Committee of the General Assembly of the Church of Scotland on the Sabbath Observance (Scotland) Bill, 1834, 1834, HC 405; I.U.P., British Parliamentary Papers, *Sunday Observance*, Vol. 2, 9–11. The 1834 Bill would have increased penalties on Sunday working, but would have removed penalties for non-attendance at church.
206 The Scots Confession of 1560 is silent as to Sunday.
207 Scottish Episcopalians Act 1711, s. 8: 'Provided always and it is the true Intent and Meaning of this Act That all the Laws made against Prophaness and Immorality and for the frequenting of Divine Services on the Lords Day commonly called Sunday shall be still in force and executed against all Persons that offend against the said Laws or shall not resort either to some Church or to some Congregation or Assembly of religious Worship allowed and permitted by this Act'.
208 Cf. the reports of various select committees and commissions for England collected in three volumes on 'Sunday Observance' in the Irish University Press series of British Parliamentary Papers.
209 D. Hume, *Commentaries on the Law of Scotland Respecting Crimes*, 4th ed. (Edinburgh: Bell & Bradfute, 1800; rep. Law Soc. Scot., 1986), I, 563.

regarding Sunday was not fully developed. For example, the defence of necessity in immunising acts that otherwise might be construed as profanation of the Sabbath was rarely raised, and then to no satisfactory conclusion. At first instance *Phillips* v *Innes* (1835) 13 s. 778 held it lawful for an apprentice barber to bind himself to work on Sunday, provided that his work was necessitous. On appeal the Inner House considered that the work of barbers on a Sunday was indeed a necessary work, being required to ensure that men were suitably and respectably shorn for attendance at church. The House of Lords did not share that view, feeling that shaving and haircutting ought to be completed before the onset of the Sabbath.[210] On the other hand *Wilson* v *Simson* (1844) 6 D. 1256 held it reasonable that an employer should require an employee who had already been to church to work on Sunday so that others could go to church. Such reasoning indicates the triviality of the question of profanation in the early part of the nineteenth century. However, later in that century Sunday observance in Scotland became of acute concern to many and the positions and arguments then deployed still have their adherents.[211]

One area of dispute was the running of Sunday trains between Edinburgh and Glasgow.[212] A North British Railway Company Sunday service begun in 1843 was vehemently opposed and withdrawn in 1845.[213] Sunday observance continued to be a matter of debate.[214] J.A. Hussey's Bampton Lectures of 1860 marked a further turning point.[215] Though Hessey's reasoning was criticised,[216] the controversy renewed in a different aspect, secular rather than religious influences becoming increasingly present. There was much debate in courts of the churches, in the newspapers and by way of book and pamphlet.[217] In 1865 an influential cleric, Norman MacLeod, made a crucial, not to say inflammatory, intervention. During a debate in the Presbytery of Glasgow on the re-introduction of Sunday trains, MacLeod alleged that strict sabbatarianism had been imported into Scotland through Puritan influence.[218] The immediate cause of the debate, Sunday trains, was forgotten as dispute became general and acrimonious. Was observance of the Sabbath itself a 'creation ordinance'?

---

210 (1837) 2 Shaw and McL. 465. The Shops Act 1950 s. 67 prohibited hairdressers or barbers from working on Sundays in Scotland. This quaint remnant of Sunday laws was repealed by the Deregulation and Contracting Out Act, 1994, s. 24(b).
211 Notably the Free Church of Scotland and the Lord's Day Observance Society: http://www.dayonescotland.org/
212 England saw similar argument. In Anthony Walpole's *Barchester Towers* (1857) Mrs Proudie and Mr Slope rail against Sunday trains.
213 Cf. Hugh Millar, 'A Vision of the Railroad', The Witness, 4 March 1843, quoted Fleming I, 5. See also n. 218 *infra*. Sunday trains were not the only subjects of attack. Proposals to open the Edinburgh Botanic Gardens on Sundays in 1863 were opposed by 36000, 14000 being in favour.
214 For example, R. Cox, *Sabbath Laws and Sabbath Duties* (Edinburgh: Maclachlan & Stewart, 1853).
215 J.A. Hessey, *Sunday. Its Origin, History and Present Obligations* (London: Cassell, 1860). Cf. Fleming I, 212.
216 For example, J. Gilfillan, *The Sabbath Viewed in the Light of Reason, Revelation and History, with Sketches of its Literature* (Edinburgh: Elliot & Maclaren, 1861).
217 For example, F.D. Maurice, *The Commandments Considered as Instruments of National Reformation* (London: Macmillan, 1866); J. MacGregor, *The Sabbath Question: Historical, Scriptural and Practical* (Edinburgh: Free Church, 1866). See also R.D. Brackenridge, 'The Sabbath War of 1865–66' (1969) XVI RSCHS 23–34. R. Cox, *Literature on the Sabbath Question*, 2 vols (Edinburgh: Maclachlan & Stewart; London: Simpkin Marshall, 1865), provides a wide-ranging and well-annotated bibliography to its date.
218 'The Lord's Day: Substance of a Speech delivered at a meeting of the Presbytery of Glasgow on Thursday, 16th November 1865', by Norman MacLeod 1865. Pamphlet attacks on the speech include, G. Macaulay, 'The Lord's Law and Day: a review of Dr Macleod's speech', 1866; J. Gibson, 'The Decalogue in the Old Testament Dispensation' and 'The Sabbath', both 1865. A humorous comment on the whole matter is D. Macrae, 'Trial of Dr. Norman Macleod for the murder of Mr. Moses' Law', 1866. Cf. n. 213 *supra*.

Other interactions of religion and law 207

Naturally, given the furore, the status of the early Scots Acts came up. Were they still of any effect? They were not. Their penal clauses had vanished. *Bute* v *More* (1870) 9 M. 186, and its successor *Nicol* v *M'Neil* (1877) 14 R. (J.) 47, both decided that in acting under summary procedures the authorities had sought the wrong remedy. As Lord M'Laren later stated: '[I]n the case of *Bute* v *More* no precedent could be found for a conviction under these Acts and neither the ingenuity of counsel nor the experience of the judges composing the court was able to find any form of process under which a person might be penalised for contravention of [the Sabbath observance] statutes. Therefore it is not saying too much when I conclude that these statutes are not likely to be again enforced'.[219] Two years later the Statute Law Revision (Scotland) Act 1906 did away with many parts of the old Acts.

Matters were further clarified when in *Brown* v *Magistrates of Edinburgh*, 1931 SLT 456, Lord Mackay was asked to interdict the Magistrates from licensing Sunday cinema performances in contravention of the Sunday laws. The Magistrates argued that these laws were in desuetude. This was to be inferred from several factors; that the laws had reference to 'quaint punishments' (sc. the jougs[220] and stocks), that the public opinion of Scotland no longer required their enforcement, that they had not been enforced within living memory, that band performances in public parks on Sunday were allowed, as were Sunday concerts and once a year charity cinema performances. The bona-fide traveller provisions under the then liquor licensing law[221] and Sunday golf were also brought up in argument. Most tellingly perhaps, the point was put that the Acts compelling church attendance were no longer observed. As to that point the pursuer's counsel expressly conceded that parts of the Acts against profanation and for encouraging of church attendance were probably in desuetude.

Brown's action failed. First, he was held to have no right to a declarator as to the magistrates' powers in advance of their being exercised. Second, the Acts on which he based his case did not prohibit cinema performances. However, in the course of his Opinion Lord Mackay considered the argument that the Sunday Acts were in desuetude.[222] He carefully noted that disuse is not to be equated with desuetude. Adopting the reasoning of Erskine,[223] he held it 'clear in law that desuetude requires for its operation a very considerable period, not merely of neglect, but of contrary usage of such a character as practically to infer such completely established habit of the community as to set up a counter law or establish a

---

219 *Middleton* v *Tough* (1904) SC (J.) 32 at 38.
220 An iron collar fastened by a chain to a wall. Offenders would be so detained for a period, usually of hours.
221 As to the 'bona fide' traveller, see *infra* n. 258.
222 As narrated by Lord Mackay these Acts were: 1503, c.83 (c.28); 1579, c.70 (c.8); 1592, c.124 (c.17); 1593, c.163 (c.6); 1594, c.201 (c.8); 1661, c.18 (c.281); 1661, c.38 (c.338); 1663, c.19 (c.43); 1672, c.22 (c.58); 1690, c.5 (c.7); 1693, c.40 (c.64); 1696, c.31 (c.31); and 1701, c.11 (1700, c.12) – the figures in brackets giving the chapter number in the Record edition. A tabular analysis of the principal Acts is in the Report from a Committee of the General Assembly of the Church of Scotland on the Sabbath Observance (Scotland) Bill, 1834, 1834 HC 405; I.U.P., British Parliamentary Papers, *Sunday Observance*, Vol. 2, 9–11. See also above, n. 205.
223 For Erskine it was perfectly proper to interpret law by statute. '[H]ence also, as a posterior statute may repeal or derogate from a prior statute, so a posterior custom may repeal or derogate from a prior statute even though that prior statute may contain a clause forbidding all usages that might tend to weaken it; for the contrary immemorial custom sufficiently presumes the will of the community to alter the law in all its clauses, and particularly in that which was intended to secure it against alteration; and this presumed will of the people operates as strongly as their express declaration. No statute can, however, be repealed by mere non-usage or neglect of the law, though for the greatest length of time; for non-usage is but a negative which cannot constitute custom – there must be some positive act that may discover the intention of the community to repeal it': Erskine, I.1.45.

quasi-repeal'.²²⁴ In the absence of proof to the contrary, legislation left by revisers on the statute book was not to be considered to be in desuetude. In *Brown* Lord Mackay was not willing to allow the case to go to proof as 'it would not be to the public advantage to allow a proof at large of these averments'.²²⁵ On the other hand he expressly made the point as arguing against desuetude, that the existence of *Bute* and of *Nicol* meant that there had 'been at least two prosecutions under the Acts which only fell, as they did fall, upon technical questions of the competency of process'.²²⁶

Brown left doubts about the remnants of the Sunday statutes. Uncertainty lingered on. In 1948 the fifth edition of the then authoritative MacDonald's *Criminal Law* briefly mentioned one or two unreported examples, though these were really cases of breach of the peace.²²⁷ The solution has been the regular pruning of the statute book when legislation considered to be 'spent, obsolete and unnecessary' is repealed. As noted earlier, a 1906 Act had repealed some parts of the Sunday observance Acts. The bulk of the remainder was given its quietus by the Statute Law Revision (Scotland) Acts of 1964 and the Statute Law (Repeals) Act 1989. There now remains only the section of the Westminster Confession that relates to the keeping of Sunday, Chapter XXI.8 being part of statute law by the Confession of Faith Ratification Act 1690, c. 7. A current major text, Gordon's *Criminal Law*, does not deal with Sabbath breaking at all.²²⁸

So much for sabbath-breaking. However, Sunday has other aspects. Under the older law Sunday was for many legal purposes a *dies non*, a principle expressed in the maxim *dies dominicus non est juridicus*, which still has some application. Arrestments and poindings executed on a Sunday are void.²²⁹ On the other hand criminal warrants may be granted and executed on Sundays, and arrest without warrant is, of course, competent.²³⁰ In civil actions citation on a Sunday is probably incompetent.²³¹ This point was reserved in *McNiven* v *Glasgow Corporation*, 1920 SC 584, which decided that in a civil action, where a period of limitation is operative and that period expires on a Sunday, service must take place prior to that date. Citation on the day after is incompetent. Similarly, in dealing with Bills of Exchange, Erskine III. 2, 33 noted that if a Sunday were the last day of grace on a note, protest for non-payment must be taken by the creditor on the Saturday preceding. Section l of the Sunday Observance Act 1833 still provides that meetings companies and corporations to elect officers due to be held on a Sunday are to be held on the Saturday preceding or Monday following.

---

224 *Brown* v *Magistrates of Edinburgh*, 1931 SLT 456 at 458.
225 *Brown* v *Magistrates of Edinburgh*, 1931 SLT 456 at 460.
226 1931 SLT 456 at 460.
227 J.H.A. Macdonald, *A Practical Treatise on the Criminal Law of Scotland* (Edinburgh: Green, 1948), 153.
228 G. Gordon, *The Criminal Law of Scotland* (Edinburgh: Green, 1967, 1978, 1992, 2000, 2005).
229 Stair III.1, 37: IV.47, 26.
230 *Cameron* v *HMA*, noted 14 *Green's Encyclopaedia of the Laws of Scotland* (3rd ed.), 265.
231 W.J. Dobie, *Law and Practice of the Sheriff Courts in Scotland* (Edinburgh: Hodge, 1948), 126; *Oliphant* v *Douglas* (1633) Mor. 15002; Stair III.1, 37; III. 3, 11; IV. 47, 27. Holyrood Abbey and the ground round the royal palace served as a sanctuary for debtors until imprisonment for civil debt was abolished in 1880. On occasion there could be more than 6,000 residents who by reason of the *dies dominicus* rule could safely emerge on Sundays. One minister used to ride every Sunday down to his charge in the Borders, preach and return to the sanctuary that evening. Creditors employed many stratagems to trap debtors into staying outwith the sanctuary bounds into Monday so that they could be seized or served with court summonses. See P. Halkerston, *History, Law and Privileges of the Palace and Sanctuary of Holyrood House* (Edinburgh: Macfarlane and Stewart, 1831).

However, the *dies dominicus* principle is not always applicable. Specific statutory provision is made for a number of instances where it is considered that citation and execution of warrants and actions ought to be allowed. A distinction is made between public and private acts in the application of the idea that Sunday is a *dies non*. Valid marriages may be entered into, though such marriages are unusual.[232] Contracts entered into on a Sunday are not void.[233] Further, in *Elliot* v *Faulke and Shute* (1844) 6 D. 411 a bill of exchange dated on a Sunday in London and accepted in Edinburgh on a lawful day was held valid. Though the date looked to was that of the acceptance, yet the Lord Ordinary observed that: 'It is very wrong, certainly, to transact business on a Sunday, but, if so done, is not null. *Fieri non debet, sed factum valet*, nor was it ever held otherwise'.[234]

Modern times

The trend towards a Sunday in which more activities are treated as normal than was the case in former generations may be said to be general throughout most of Scotland, with the exception of those areas in which the Free and Free Presbyterian Churches have their main concentrations.[235] Thus, in 1967 the beginning of a Sunday ferry service to Skye was the subject of protest by the majority of the non-established churches in Skye. In 1971 there was pressure in that island for the tourist authorities to publish separate lists of those willing to take bed-and-breakfast clients throughout the week, and of those who would not take such guests on the Sabbath. In 1989 the Western Island Council adopted a byelaw prohibiting the use of a pier to ship goods or vehicles on a Sunday. This was held *ultra vires* of the Council as it was directed towards Sunday observance, not to the technical operation of the pier.[236] Such matters are likely to persist.[237] An argument might be made that local custom or deference to conscience could justify local rules, as contemplated by the European Union in the case of shop opening.[238] Finally, however, it should be noted

---

232 Stair II. 4, 60. Cf. J.K. Cameron, ed., *The First Book of Discipline* (Edinburgh: St Andrew Press, 1972), Head IX, 'Concerning the Policie of the Kirk': the section 'On Marriage' (191–9 at 195–6) states in church on Sunday before the sermon as being most expedient for a marriage, and this was general practice for some decades. See the footnotes to the section. By the time of the Westminster *Directory of Worship*, 1644, it was advised that marriage be not celebrated on a Sunday, Sunday 'not being the ordinary time of marriage'.
233 Erskine III.1.10.
234 (1844) 6 D. 411–2. The Inner House adhered.
235 Cf. J.L. MacLeod, *The Second Disruption: The Free Church in Victorian Scotland and the Origins of the Free Presbyterian Church* (East Linton: Tuckwell, 2000), 31–5.
236 *Western Isles Islands Council* v *Caledonian MacBrayne Ltd*, 1990 SLT (Sh. Ct.) 97.
237 In December 2011 the Free Church (Continuing) Presbytery of Skye deplored a dance arranged for a Sunday in January 2012: http://www.hebrides-news.com/sabbath-breaking_dance_in_skye_271211.html. Because of local opposition Sunday ferries to Lewis and Harris in the Hebrides began only in 2006. Tarbert (on Presbyterian Harris) was the last port to accept such sailing, a service to it from Uig (Skye) beginning in October 2011: http://www.hebrides-news.com/harris-sunday-ferry-231011.html. Continuation of Sunday services to Harris from summer 2012 was to depend on financial considerations: http://www.hebrides-news.com/sunday-ferry-16312.html. On the inauguration of the Sunday ferry to Harris (Uig in Skye to Tarbert) on 1 July 2012, the local Free Church presbytery wrote to the ferry operator, Caledonian MacBrayne, calling on it to desist and to repent of its sins. Air services to Stornoway (Lewis) on Sundays began in 2002. On objections in April 2012 to an unattended vending machine operating in a Lewis garage on Sunday see http://www.pressandjournal.co.uk/Article.aspx/2721309 or http://www.thescottishsun.co.uk/scotsol/homepage/news/4245966/Isles-fury-over-dispenser-selling-food-on-Sundays.html
238 See *supra* at n. 202.

that it can be reasonable to require people to work on a Sunday, even though they believe Sundays to be a day of rest.[239]

Particular examples

Sunday figures in some areas of law. They may have begun as much for religious as other reasons, but in most the religious element has faded.

Fish and game[240]

Fishing on Sundays, a well-known way of profaning the Sabbath even today, was forbidden by the Act 1661, c. 28l.[241] Over the years, conservation came to be the justification for the prohibition rather than religious observance, and in *Middleton* v *Tough* (1908), 15 SLT 991, the then statutory law imposing a weekly close time for salmon was held imperative, taking precedence over legislation on Sabbath observance. The present law is the Salmon and Freshwater Fisheries (Consolidation) (Scotland) Act 2003, asp 15, s. 13(2), prohibiting fishing for or taking salmon on Sunday.[242] The general legislation as to fishing in Scotland is now clearly secular.[243]

The grouse shooting season opens on 12 August, 'the Glorious Twelfth'. Should 'the Twelfth' fall on a Sunday, traditionally the season opens one day later. There is extensive legislation as to the protection of animals and birds, but Sunday does not figure in it.[244] However, by tradition not law, game is not shot or otherwise taken on a Sunday.[245]

Labour

The using of 'handy labour' and working on the Sabbath was expressly prohibited by the Act 1579 c. 8 (c. 3), later bolstered by the Act 1661 c. 28l. The field is now occupied by a variety of later statutes too numerous to deal with here. When introduced the Factories Acts regulated the bulk of the cases that the earlier statutes might have dealt with, but almost throughout their currency prohibited Sunday working only by women and young persons.[246] Such was part of the general mass of legislation on social matters that began during Victoria's reign, and it is fairly certain that, although there was some religious basis for legislation

---

239 *Mba* v *Merton London Borough Council* [2013] EWCA Civ 1562; [2014] 1 WLR 1501. The case was brought by the employee of a care home that necessarily functioned seven days a week.
240 S.S. Robinson, *The Law of Game, Salmon and Freshwater Fishing in Scotland* (Edinburgh: Butterworths, 1990).
241 Sunday fishing was deemed a cause of the Aberdeen earthquake of 1608; *Selections from the Records of the Kirk Session. Presbytery and Synod of Aberdeen* (Edinburgh: Spalding Club, 1896), 64 (Kirk Session, 13 November 1608).
242 Salmon includes sea-trout, s. 69(1).
243 See also the Aquaculture and Fisheries (Scotland) Act 2007, asp 12.
244 C.T. Reid, *Nature Conservation Law* (Edinburgh: Greens, 2009). Major legislation includes the Wildlife and Countryside Act 1981, and the Wildlife and Natural Environment (Scotland) Act 2011, asp 6. Cf. F. Lyall, 'Law and the Environment', in M. Mulhern, ed., *The Law* – Vol. 13 of *Scottish Life and Society: A Compendium of Scottish Ethnology* (Edinburgh: Donald, 2012), 459–78.
245 Taking or killing deer at night is unlawful, unless the deer is causing serious damage: Deer (Scotland) Act 1996, s. 18.
246 Cf. Factories Acts Extensions Act, 1867, s. 7. Its most recent manifestation, s. 93 of the Factories Act 1961, was repealed by the Employment Act 1989.

at that time, there were also important social considerations that led to its introduction. Religious considerations seem now to be no more, and there are no legal bars to Sunday working in Scotland. However, in 2001 that position allowed the retail firm Argos to dismiss employees in Scotland who refused to work Sunday shifts. This caused outrage. Section 1 of the Sunday Working (Scotland) Act 2003 therefore extended to Scotland relevant provisions of the Employment Rights Act 1996, giving employees in shops and betting shops the right to refuse to work on Sundays.[247] How well-used this right is, is unknown.[248] On the other hand it should again be noted that 'human rights' notwithstanding it can be reasonable to require work on a Sunday, even though the worker believes Sunday to be a day of rest.[249]

Trading

For the avoidance of doubt: Scotland has no laws about Sunday trading. The Sunday Trading Act 1994 applies only to England (s. 9(4)).

Gaming and betting[250]

Gaming or playing (perhaps only in the time of the sermon) was prohibited under the Act 1579, c. 8 (c. 3). Under Scots criminal law it was an offence to keep a common gaming house.[251] The Suppression of Betting Houses Act, 1853 which made betting shops unlawful in England, was extended to Scotland in 1874,[252] and in later years other statutes were passed, aiming at suppressing gaming and betting.[253] Eventually the tide turned, and the provisions as to Sunday gaming and betting have now all gone. First the Racecourse Betting Act, 1928, allowed totalisator betting. The Betting and Lotteries Act 1934 went further, permitting on track gambling and regulating bookmaking activities. At that stage account was still taken of religion, s. 1 (1)(b) prohibiting betting by way of bookmaking or totalisator 'on any Good Friday, Christmas Day or Sunday'. Following a Royal Commission, the Betting and Gaming Act 1960 revised the law on off-course betting and gaming.[254] Licensed betting shops were required to shut on Good Friday, Christmas Day and Sundays (s. 5 and Sch. 2). This remained the position when betting and gaming law was revisited in 1963,[255] until in 1994 the Sunday prohibition was removed.[256] Controlling gaming clubs under the 1963 Act proved problematic.[257] The Gaming Act 1968 therefore introduced licensed casinos. It

---

247 The 2003 Act is a rare example of a successful Private Member's Bill becoming law.
248 The Sunday provisions of the 1996 Act apply only to shops and betting shops.
249 *Mba* v *Merton London Borough Council* [2013] EWCA Civ 1562; [2014] 1 WLR 1501, *supra* nn. 36, 239, 249. Belief in Sunday observance may not trump the need to provide a seven day care service. The case was brought by the employee of a care home that necessarily functioned seven days a week.
250 R. McKenzie, 'Betting, gaming and lotteries', Stair Memorial Encyclopedia reissue.
251 MacDonald, *supra* n. 227, 154; *Greenhuff* (1838) 2 Swinton 128.
252 The Suppression of Betting Houses (Amendment) Act, 1874. *Henretty* (1885) 5 Coup. 703.
253 For example, the Burgh Police (Scotland) Act 1892, s. 393. The Kirk pressed for stiff legislation. See W.P. Paterson and D. Watson, eds, *Social Evils and Problems*, Church of Scotland Commission on the War (Edinburgh: Blackwood, 1918); Fleming II, 185.
254 *Royal Commission on Betting and Gambling, 1949–51*, 1951, Cmd. 8190.
255 Betting, Gaming and Lotteries Act, 1963, s.10 and Rule 1 of Sch. 4, Rule 1.
256 Deregulating and Contracting Out Act, 1994, s. 20.
257 See *Rex* v *Commissioner of Police for the Metropolis, ex parte Blackburn* [1968] 2 QB 118. For budgetary reasons the Commissioner had instructed that the law should not be rigorously enforced.

prohibited gaming between 2 a.m. and 19.30 p.m. on any Sunday in premises so licensed in Scotland (s. 18(2)), and that remained the rule for just under 40 years. The comprehensive replacement of gambling legislation by the Gambling Act 2005 makes no mention of Sunday, or of any requirement as to the closure of premises in deference to religious considerations.

Licensed premises[258]

Passing to a tavern or alehouse on Sundays (perhaps only in the time of sermon or prayers) was specifically prohibited by the Act 1579, c. 8 (c. 3), and would also have been struck at by the more general acts against the profanation of the Sabbath.[259] The development of the law in this area has, however, been conditioned by general concepts of temperance and the suppression of drunkenness rather than by the more precise question of profanation of the Sabbath. A licensing system for the selling and provision of intoxicating liquor was foreshadowed by the Alehouse Act 1756 and was begun under the Licence (Duty) Act of 1808. The present system of licensing certificates was introduced by the Sale of Liquor Act 1828 (the Home-Drummond Act). The licensee had to comply with certain formalities and 'not keep open House or permit or suffer any drinking or tippling in any part of the premises thereto belonging, during the Hours of Divine Service on Sundays, or other days set aside for Public Worship, by lawful authority'. The 1853 Public Houses (Scotland) Act went further, limiting the supply and public consumption of alcohol to the six ordinary days of the week.

Originally one function of the legislation was to secure a distribution of inns and hostelries along the main commercial routes.[260] Some of the early Acts therefore required that licensed premises be a stated number of miles apart. It is therefore not surprising to find the famous institution of the bona-fide traveller in early currency. He is first found in the negative in s. 22 of the Public Houses Acts Amendment Act 1862, which made it an offence to induce a licensee to supply liquor on a Sunday outwith the hours permitted in the licence. That the traveller was included is not stated in the section but is found in the side-note. The bona-fide Sunday traveller who by that status could be served alcohol became a well-known phenomenon (or disguise) around whose person and qualification much case law and humour developed.

In the latter nineteenth century the churches became very concerned about temperance, and were active in a variety of ways, most notably through the Temperance Societies. It was thought that the introduction of the Veto Poll under the 1913 Temperance (Scotland) Act might have an effect on the whole question of temperance, but in the aftermath of the First World War this proved not to be the case.[261] However, in areas rendered 'dry' following a veto poll, there was no sale or public consumption of alcohol at all, let alone on the Sabbath.[262]

The 1959 Licensing (Scotland) Act consolidation of the licensing statutes retained veto polls under Part VIII, and the bona-fide traveller under s. 147. However the Licensing

---

258 Reference point, n. 221 *supra*.
259 The Acts 1661 c. 281, 1672 c. 58, and 1690 c. 7.
260 *Royal Commission on Licensing (Scotland) 1931*, 1931 Cmd. 3894, evidence of J. Keith, Q.C., at para 216.
261 The 1913 Act was based on the *Minority Report* of the *Royal Commission on Liquor Licensing Laws, Final Report*, 1899 C.9379, at pp. 270–279; Fleming II, 181–4.
262 Veto polls were abolished by the Licensing (Scotland) Act 1976 s. 131, though existing 'dry' areas could continue until the local licensing authority determined otherwise. I am unaware of any dry areas remaining.

(Scotland) Act 1962 revised the whole question of permitted hours. The bona-fide traveller provisions disappeared and it is unlikely that they will be resuscitated.[263] Standard permitted hours (12.30 pm and 2.30 pm, and 6.30 pm and 10 pm) were set for the Sunday operation of licensed premises, registered clubs and licensed canteens throughout Scotland (s. 4). Public houses were, however, not included in the permissions as to Sunday opening.

In 1970–73 a major investigation of liquor licensing law on both sides of the Border was undertaken.[264] The Scottish Committee suggested longer opening hours generally and opening hours for public houses on Sunday to commence after 12.30 p.m. to avoid the time of normal Sunday services. The Licensing (Scotland) Act 1976, currently the principal Act on the matter, incorporated these modifications while retaining the 1962 hours for other licensed premises. Subsequent amendments have not disturbed the Sunday provisions. Under the Licensing (Scotland) Act 2005 asp 16, the general rule is that the sale of alcohol is permitted only under licence. Its s. 4 contains a statement of the objectives of licensing system. These do not include Sunday observance.

Conclusion

The future of Sunday as a special day, protected by law as a day of rest for religious reasons, is uncertain. Sunday has been assimilated to the general holiday, a weekly day of rest (on which double time for work may be payable) without reference to its religious origin. The keen interest and controversy over Sunday observance of earlier years has largely disappeared. Society does not actively seek the preservation of the older practices. This is in marked contrast with the events of last century, but seems to be in harmony with the trend of organised religion. Church attendance statistics indicate that a diminishing proportion of the population attach a religious significance to Sunday, and, once Sunday is seen simply as a recreational day, it is difficult to retain the practices and prohibitions of an era when social feeling was stronger. Controversy has, in the main, been muted, reflecting and being reflected by less militant attitude on the part of many of the denominations in Scotland. Along with other churches the Church of Scotland was fully consulted for its interest before the 1964 Statute Law Revision (Scotland) Act deleted the bulk of the old Scots Sunday legislation. Its assent to the proposed repeals, taken with later Reports of the then Committee on Church and Nation, indicate that that Kirk at least no longer seeks to maintain Sunday observance in the old form through the use of the secular arm. That said, as indicated at the start of this section, it does seem that the seven day week corresponds to something innate in man, for its prevalence is not otherwise to be explained. It is convenient that in general, save for services of necessity, that one particular day be the usual day of rest. In Scotland it remains Sunday.

8. Social welfare

Outside the burghs, the Church of Scotland parish was an important unit of local government well into Victorian times and beyond.[265] For almost three centuries after the Reformation the heritors of parishes *quoad omnia* (and church collections) throughout Scotland were

---

263 The 1962 Act gave effect to the Guest Committee, *Scottish Licensing Law. First Report*, 1960, Cmnd. 1217.
264 *Report of the Departmental Committee on Scottish Licensing Law* (The Clayson Committee), 1973 Cmnd. 5354; *Report of the Departmental Committee on Liquor Licensing*, Chairman Lord Erroll, 1972 Cmnd. 5154.
265 W.G. Black, *Scottish Parochial Law other than Ecclesiastical* (Edinburgh: Green, 1893). See also *supra* Chapter 2 following n. 52.

the major source of poor relief, administered by kirk sessions until the Poor Law (Scotland) Act 1845 established parochial boards for the purpose and authorised assessments to be levied on the owners and occupiers of parish lands and properties to finance their work.[266] The emergence of welfare state in the early twentieth century, starting with such as the Old Age Pensions Act 1908 and the National Insurance Act 1911, decreased the need for action by the Kirk and other denominations and the institution of National Health Services for England and Scotland in 1946/7 took over the area of health, nationalising existing hospitals and bringing the medical professions into the system.[267] Now obligations of charitable relief are still recognised by churches, but social welfare in many of its developed forms is generally seen as the responsibility of the state. That said, various denominations and religious bodies still provide social welfare, including hospices and care centres, retirement homes, de-toxification units and the like. Roman Catholic adoption societies have run into trouble since they are unwilling to provide adoption services to same-sex couples.

9. Charities

Charitable activities often have religious roots, although these may not always be clearly articulated. An association for charitable purposes is constituted as a trust or a company limited by guarantee in order to provide a clear framework for its activities, and giving legal personality in order to own or lease property, operate bank accounts, employ personnel and so on. In Scotland the establishment of a trust is a simple matter: anyone may declare that they hold property in trust for a specified purpose. However, such a trust or company may wish to gain charitable status for tax purposes, with a consequent increase in revenue. With such status, charities may receive donations from tax-payers and recover from the state the income tax already been paid by the donor on the money so given. To qualify for charitable status a 'charity' must now be entered in the Scottish Charities Register, established under the Charities and Trustee Investment (Scotland) Act 2005 asp. 10. This requires that the trust should be for the public benefit. Most charities intent on 'good works' have little difficulty in meeting that requirement. Religion was different.

Religious organisations may engage in secular charitable activities. There is clear justification in granting them charitable status in law for those purposes. They may also serve a cultural function as social groupings. However, many denominations and religious groups have come financially to rely on the state granting them charitable status for their religious activities. In the twentieth century therefore there is an inversion between church and state in such matters. Churches used to finance their religious functions and their secular charitable activities out of their own income. Now many are dependent on what amounts to state subvention in order to carry out their fundamental function – the dissemination of their particular religious beliefs. This should be stopped. Secular charity by religious bodies should continue to receive financial aid through 'Gift Aid', but not for the employment of ministers and others, or the maintenance of buildings for ecclesiastic purposes unless the building has

---

266 Black, *supra* n. 265, 74–153; T. Ferguson, 'The Poor; Welfare and Social Services', in M.R. McLarty, ed., *A Source Book and History of Administrative Law in Scotland* (Edinburgh: Hodge, 1956), 177–93. Parish boards dealt with welfare until replaced by County Councils; Black, at 154–87. Cf. M. Steven, *Parish Life in Eighteenth-Century Scotland* (Dalkeith: Scottish Cultural Press, 1995), 'Poor Relief', 81–90.

267 National Health Service Act 1946; National Health Service (Scotland) Act 1947. See also W. Beveridge, *Social Insurance and Allied Services*, 1942, Cmd. 6404. The National Health Services have undergone many subsequent changes.

architectural or 'landscape' merit. That would usefully test the reality of the religious convictions of congregations or other supporters. There are too many stories of unscrupulous ministries.

In Scotland it took time before 'trusts for the advancement of religion' were afforded charitable status for tax purposes. In 1888 a Scottish case held that religious purposes were not charitable under the then taxation statutes.[268] It was not until a 1953 Scottish appeal to the House of Lords held that, while the taxation statutes are UK statutes, they are framed on the basis of English law and its definitions.[269] That meant that 'trusts for the advancement of religion', long recognised in England, could have charitable status in law in Scotland.[270] The remit of the special section of the then Inland Revenue (tax authorities) in Scotland that dealt with charities was widened to cover trusts for the advancement of religion, and to process claims.[271]

In 1990 the Law Reform (Miscellaneous Provisions) (Scotland) Act put charities in Scotland on a new basis, and established new mechanisms for their regulation. Small trusts could continue to qualify for charitable status and were subject to central supervision, but larger bodies were treated differently. By s. 3 a category of 'designated religious bodies' was established.[272]

Following particular cases of abuse,[273] charity law was reconsidered in both England[274] and Scotland.[275] The Charities and Trustee Investment (Scotland) Act 2005, asp 10, set up an Office of Scottish Charity Regulator (OSCR) (s. 1), the Scottish Charity Register (s. 3) and procedures for registration (ss. 4–6).[276] Although there was pressure to omit 'the advancement of religion' as a charitable purpose it has been retained (s. 7(2)(c)) and the promotion of religious or racial harmony has been included (s. 7(2)(k)). The Regulator must be satisfied both that the purposes of an applicant body lie only within the list in s. 7(2) (s. 7(1)(a)), and that they provide public benefit, whether in Scotland or elsewhere (s. 7(1)(b)). What constitutes 'public benefit' is loosely indicated in s. 8. No particular purpose is presumed to be of public benefit (s. 8(1)). Regard is had to any gain or benefit to members

---

268 *Baird's Trustee* v *Lord Advocate* (1888) 15 R. 682.
269 *Inland Revenue Commissioners* v *Glasgow Police Athletic Association*, 1963 SC (HL) 13.
270 *Commissioners for Special Purposes of Income Tax* v *Pemsel* 1891 AC 531, esp. per Lord Macnaughten at 583. English Charity law goes back to the Charitable Uses Act, 1601, and many cases thereafter.
271 C.R. Barker ed., *Charity Law in Scotland* (Edinburgh: Green, 1995); D.G. Cracknell, *Cracknell on Charities* (London: Financial Times Law and Tax, 1996); J. Warburton and D. Morris, eds, *Tudor on Charities* (London: Sweet & Maxwell, 1995).
272 In 2001, 10 religious bodies were so designated, covering five Christian denominations.
273 There had been instances where the organisers of recognised charities took huge salaries and/or expenses, leaving little for the ostensible beneficiaries.
274 'Private Action, Public Benefit', a Report by the Strategy Unit (Strategy Unit, September, 2002); with the Government's response, 'Charities and Not-for-Profits: A Modern Legal Framework' (Home Office, July 2003). English charity law, which is similar to that of Scotland outlined below, is operated through the Charity Commission, now under the Charities Acts 2006 and 2011 and other legislation. See C. Alexander, *Charity Governance* (London: Jordan, 2014); P. Luxton and J. Hill, *The Law of Charities* (Oxford: Oxford UP, 2001) (new ed. 2015).
275 *CharityScotland; The Report of the Scottish Charity Law Review Commission*, Chair, J. McFadden (Edinburgh: Scottish Executive, 2001: P. Spicker et al., 'Consultation on the Review of Scottish Charity Law: Analysis of the Responses' (Edinburgh: Scottish Executive, 2002).
276 The Office is known as OSCR (usually pronounced Oscar): http://www.oscr.org.uk/. For its initial years see 'Protecting charitable status – A report on individual charity reviews, 2006–2011' (Edinburgh: OSCR, 2012). This indicates that in 2012 there were more than 23,000 registered charities in Scotland.

of the applicant body and/or to the public, together with any dis-benefit to the public. In the latter instance, where only a section of the public is benefited, regard is had to any condition attaching to participation (including any charge or fee) that is unduly restrictive (s. 8(2)(a)-(b)). Registered charities submit annual reports and accounts (ss. 44–48), and are supervised in their activities (ss. 28–37). However, s. 65 of the Act retains the provision of s. 3 of the 1990 Act, allowing a religious body with charitable status to be designated by the OSCR as suitable for lighter supervision. This can occur where the body has the advancement of religion as its principal purpose, regular public worship as its principal activity, has been established in Scotland for at least 10 years, has a membership of at least 3,000 resident in Scotland who are at least 16 years of age, has an internal organisation having supervisory and disciplinary functions and has clear requirements as to the keeping and auditing of accounts. The only change from the 1990 Law Reform Act is that while its s. 3 required the body to have the promotion of a religious objective as its principal purpose, by s. 65(1)(a) its principal purpose must now be the advancement of religion, whatever that means.

Chapter 7 (ss. 49–64) of the Charities and Trustee Investment (Scotland) Act 2005 asp 10 provides for a new form of charitable association, the Scottish Charitable Incorporated Organisation, the SCIO.[277] This goes some way to meet some of the needs discussed by the Scottish Law Commission in 2009.[278] The new invention allows a charity to be incorporated but supervised and regulated only by the Office of Scottish Charity Regulator. Other incorporated charities report to and are regulated by both the Office and by the Registrar of Companies under the Company Law legislation. An existing charitable trust or company may apply to convert into a SCIO. As an incorporated body, a SCIO has legal personality and transacts its business itself, not through trustees. For most purposes that means that its members do not incur personal liability, which may be an advantage. A SCIO must have a constitution, at least two members, have its principal office in Scotland and act for charitable purposes. Its existence depends on entry on the Charity Register. It cannot convert to another form, and can cease only through dissolution on removal from the Register. Like the trustees of any charitable trust, members of a SCIO must act in its best interests. It is too soon as yet to determine how useful the SCIO is for religious charities or other religious bodies such as congregations.

10. Public duties

British law recognises 'conscience' in a variety of ways, but for specific purposes only, and is slow to permit conscience to exempt an individual from a duty that attaches to other members of the community.[279]

---

277 The Scottish Charitable Incorporated Organisations Regulations 2011, SSI 2011 No. 44; The Scottish Charitable Incorporated Organisations (Removal from the Register and Dissolution) Regulations 2011, SSI No. 237; The Scottish Charitable Incorporated Organisations (Removal from the Register and Dissolution) Amendment Regulations 2013, SSI No. 362. See also 'SCIOs: A Guide. Guidance on the Scottish Charitable Incorporated Organisation for charities and their advisers' (Edinburgh Office of the Scottish Charity Regulator, 2011).

278 Cf. Scottish Law Commission: *Report on Unincorporated Associations*, 2009 (SLC No. 217); *Discussion Paper on Unincorporated Associations*, 2008 (SLC Discussion Paper No 140); *Discussion Paper on Supplementary and Miscellaneous Issues relating to Trust Law*, 2011 (SLC Discussion Paper No.148). The 2009 Report contained a draft Bill which would have introduced a 'Scottish Association with Limited Personality' (SALP), which associations might choose to adopt.

279 F. Lyall, 'Conscience and the Law', in *Conscientious Objection in the EC Countries, Proceedings of a Meeting of the European Consortium for Church-State Relations, Brussels-Leuven, 1990* (Milan: Giuffre Editore, 1992), 165–80.

In the UK there is no legal duty to vote so questions of conscience do not arise. Census returns are required under the Census Act 1920. Failure to provide information when required to provide it invites a fine. There is no general provision for conscience in the census legislation. However, when a question as to religion was inserted in the 2000 census form, refusing or neglecting to provide that information was exempted from penalty.[280] The Population (Statistics) legislation also imposes duties to provide information, failure being sanctioned by a fine.[281] Withholding tax on grounds of conscience (for example not to pay one's 'share' of funding nuclear weapons) is unlawful.[282] The morality of a tax is a matter for Parliament alone.[283] Conscience is recognised in some medical areas.[284] Were the death penalty for murder reintroduced, doubtless a 'conscience clause' would be necessary, though to whom it might effeir is moot.[285]

The only public duty for which conscientious grounds may provide an exemption is that of juror. In Scotland this is covered by the Law Reform (Miscellaneous Provisions) (Scotland) Act 1980 ss.1–3.[286] By Schedule 1 various persons are ineligible, disqualified or excusable as of right from jury service, this last (Group E) including persons in holy orders, regular ministers of any religious denomination and vowed members of any religious order living in a monastery, convent or religious community. Someone called for jury service may be excused if 'there is good reason why he should be excused from attending' to serve as a juror (s. 1(5)). The court itself may also excuse a potential juror on unspecified grounds (s. 1(6)). There are no cases on this clause. Failure to serve on a civil or criminal jury is an offence for which a fine may be imposed. In an English case the High Court commented that 'membership of a religious sect or movement cannot be regarded as a passport to excusal from jury service'.[287] The court emphasised the importance of jury service as performing a 'vital role in the administration of justice in the criminal courts. Doubtless many members of the public find that a jury summons involves difficulty and inconvenience. Serving on a jury is an onerous task: many forms of public service are. But without juries the system of justice would collapse. Performance of jury service is an important obligation of every citizen'.[288] I expect Scottish courts would take a similar line. Attendance at a court or other

---

[280] Census Act 1920, Sch. Para 5A, inserted by s. 1 of the Census Amendment (Scotland) Act 2000, asp. 3, s. 1, and for England by the Census Amendment Act 2000, s.1. These amendments do not apply in Northern Ireland. In the 2001 census some 390,000 gave their religion as 'Jedi'. As a result 'Jedi Knight' was included in the 2011 census as a religious class, just below Shintoism and just above Atheist. In England and Wales 176,632 and in Scotland 14,052 gave their religion as Jedi. See the 2011 Census results: http://www.scotlandscensus.gov.uk/ and www.ons.gov.uk.

[281] Population (Statistics) Acts 1930 and 1960, and the Statistics and Registration Service Act 2007.

[282] *Cheney* v *Conn* [1968] 1 All ER 779. Recourse to the mechanisms of the European Convention on Human Rights has also been ineffective: *C* v *The United Kingdom* (1983) 37 D.R. 142, Application no. 10358/83.

[283] *Mohr* v *Henry*, 1992 S.L.T. 285 – an attempt to argue the morality of the then new (and since abolished) community charge, the 'Poll Tax'.

[284] See *infra*, 12 Medical Practice.

[285] The Murder (Abolition of Death Penalty) Act, 1965.

[286] Jury service in England is regulated by the Juries Act 1974, as amended, and Practice Direction of the High Court.

[287] *R* v *Crown Court at Guildford ex parte Siderfin* [1990] 2 QB 683 at 691; [1989] 3 All ER 73. Mrs Siderfin, a member of the Plymouth Brethren, claimed that jury service was contrary to her religious beliefs. The matter was returned to the lower court for further consideration.

[288] Ibid.

public proceeding may be adjusted to take account of a party's religious convictions, but this is at the court's discretion. There is no right to demand a change of date.[289]

11. Military service

When the Military Service Act 1916 introduced compulsory military service for the first time in the UK, account was immediately taken of questions of conscience.[290] Statutory exemption was given to men 'in holy orders or regular ministers of any religious denomination' (s. 2(1)). For others a local tribunal could exempt from service on various grounds including 'a conscientious objection to the undertaking of combatant service' (s. 2(1)(d)). Exemption might extend only as to combatant service, and the individual could be required to perform other work necessary for the war effort. Sanctions, other than societal disapproval (the 'White Feather'), were minor.[291] The 1916 Act was repealed in 1920. The National Service (Armed Forces) Act 1939, with similar provisions, was enacted on the day that the UK declared war on Germany. The National Service Act of 1948 consolidated legislation enacted during the war.[292] The expiry of the National Service Act (Duration) Order 1953 ended compulsory military service for those becoming 18 after 1 January 1959 and those whose call-up had for a variety of reasons been deferred.[293]

While conscription existed it caused much debate and some court cases. First World War local tribunals caused concern as their grant or withholding of exemption could lack consistency.[294] During the Second World War and later, tribunals were staffed by experienced men and legally qualified chairmen.[295] For the ordinary individual, exemption from military service on ground of conscience depended on satisfying a tribunal as to the genuine nature of the conscientious objection. Care was taken to recognise genuineness.[296] An appeal lay to a special appellate tribunal or on grounds of law to the courts. The applicant might be ordered to serve but only for non-combatant duties. Alternatively the tribunal could order the individual to perform specified civil work for the period of national service plus 60 days.[297] The individual did not have the right to choose or offer a substitute service, although (anecdotally) informal arrangements might be made. Penalties under the 1948 Act were

---

289 *Ostreicher* v *Secretary of State for the Environment* [1978] 3 All ER 82 – a Jewess objector asked too late to have the date of a public inquiry hearing altered.
290 There were two Military Service Acts in 1916, January and May. The second removed an exemption from conscription of married men: cf. Deut. 20:7; 24:5.
291 The Representation of the People Act 1918 s. 9(2) disqualified a conscientious objector from voting in elections for five years unless he could prove he had been doing work of national importance, a penalty not abolished until the Representation of the People Act, 1949.
292 The National Service Act 1941 conscripted unmarried women aged 20–30.
293 The National Service Act (Duration) Order 1953, 1953 SI 1771, had extended the life of the conscription clauses of the 1948 Act. Cf. Hansard 1953 154 HL Deb. 408–63 and 520 HC Deb. 1573–651 where the reasons for conscription were explored.
294 J.W. Graham, *Conscription and Conscience: A History* (London: Allen & Unwin, 1922); J.M. Rae, *Conscience and Politics: The British Government and the Conscientious Objector to Military Service, 1916–1919* (London: Oxford UP, 1970); D. Boulton, *Objection Overruled* (London: Macgibbon and Kee, 1967).
295 D. Hayes, *Challenge of Conscience: The Story of the Conscientious Objectors of 1939–1949* (London: Allen & Unwin, 1949); R. Barker, *Conscience, Government, and War: Conscientious Objection in Great Britain, 1939–45* (London: Routledge, 1982).
296 The Australian National Service Acts, 1951–53 were more accommodating of conscience.
297 Some occupations, for example mining, engineering, ship building or the maritime service gave automatic exemption.

more severe than under the 1916 Act. Non-compliance with the order of a tribunal could result in up to two years' imprisonment after trial on indictment and/or a fine, or up to one year after summary trial and/or a fine.[298]

What 'a regular minister of any religious denomination' under the 1948 Act and its predecessors meant gave rise to a number of cases involving Jehovah's Witnesses. These decided a 'minister' had to be formally set apart spiritually from other members of the group and have a duty to minister and to preach.[299] The doctrine that all adult male Witnesses were 'ministers' did not meet the criteria. A similar result was arrived at as to the Christian (Plymouth) Brethren who do not ordain ministers, though some members are recognised as preachers.[300] A student minister, not yet ordained, was not a regular minister.[301] Other difficulties were encountered over whether a group was a 'religious denomination', the cases tending to require numerical strength,[302] and a shared religious belief.[303]

Outside wartime, tribunals tended not severely to penalise a claim of conscience so long as it was genuine and not merely an attempt to escape duty. In wartime few had their claim accepted, and were punished if they proved intransigent.[304]

That military service personnel are now volunteers largely eliminates the question of conscience. However, the possibility remains of a change of conscience during service and there are procedures to deal with that.[305] The normal procedures for leaving service in advance of contract may be invoked, or the objector released from further service. Alternatively personnel can apply to an Advisory Committee that reports to the Secretary of State for Defence.[306] To seek to persuade military personnel to take advantage of these procedures can be an offence.[307]

Finally, while reported cases and known practice tended to require a religious rather than an ethical basis for the claim of conscience, the legislation used language that might have allowed consideration of an ethical objection. We may be going down that route. The Gulf Crisis of the early1990s, Iraq and Afghanistan, required the recall of members of the Reserve Forces (who remain subject to call-up for a period of years following upon regular volunteer service), and members of the Territorial Army (an auxiliary part-time force). Some so recalled are rumoured to have raised questions of exemption on the basis that, while they would defend the UK, they did not approve of UK involvement in the military preparations for similar wars. There is no formal evidence whether such considerations may have led to release from service.

12. Medical practice

Religion and law can interact in a variety of ways in medical practice, often involving either the recognition of conscience or its overruling.

---

298 National Service Act 1948, s. 19.
299 *Guy* v *Mackenna*, 1917 JC 59; *Saltmarsh* v *Adair*, 1942 JC 58; *Walsh* v *Lord Advocate*, 1956 SC (HL) 126.
300 *Montgomerie* v *Mackenna* 1918 JC 55.
301 *Marshall* v *Haig* 1918 JC 47.
302 *Kick* v *Donne* (1917) 33 TLR 325 – a group of 50 in only one village was considered insufficient to constitute a denomination.
303 *Hawkes* v *Moxey* (1917) 25 Cox CC 689 – Mormons held to be a denomination; *Bratt* v *Auty* (1917) 26 Cox CC 67 – a Friendly Society involved in good works held not to be a denomination.
304 See *supra* nn. 294 and 295.
305 An opportunity to deal with this in the Armed Forces Act 2011 was not taken. See the unofficial website, Forceswatch: http://forceswatch.net/sites/default/files/ForcesWatch_briefing_conscientious_objection.pdf
306 Hansard 1970 807 HC Deb. (WA) 423.
307 *R.* v *Arrowsmith* [1975] QB 678; cf. *Arrowsmith* v *The United Kingdom* (1975) 19 DR 5, Application no. 7050/75.

Treatment

Adult patients in possession of their faculties may lawfully consent to or refuse medical treatment even if refusal will terminate life in the near or further future.[308] Thus Jehovah's Witnesses have died following refusing blood transfusions.[309] Doctors cannot omit a lawful procedure or operation because of personal beliefs,[310] nor are nurses immune from dismissal on grounds of failure to obey instructions because they have a conscientious objection to the treatment concerned.[311] Medical secretaries cannot refuse to type a letter that deals with a treatment of which they disapprove.[312] Children with sufficient understanding may themselves consent to medical treatment.[313] What is in the best interests of the child is the overruling principle. The views of a parent or parents are not dispositive.[314] A failure of parents to summon medical attention for a sick child based on their own religious belief is criminal,[315] unless the belief is such that the child's need was not appreciated.[316] In appropriate cases the court will make an order to permit medical intervention. In Scotland a court may give consent in the child's interest or the local authority may assume parental rights under Part II of the Social Work (Scotland) Act 1968, and give consent.[317] Alternatively the person having care and control of a child but without parental rights may give consent.[318]

Nursing homes or hospitals run by religious groups may, for theological or doctrinal reasons, take a view different from orthodox medical practice. Registered Christian Science Nursing Homes used to be required to have their practices thus indicated in their names.[319] Now appropriate intimation can be a condition imposed on a registered care home by the current supervisory body for such establishments.[320]

---

308 Cf. *infra* at n. 335, Termination of Treatment and Right to Die.
309 Occasional newspaper reports. The Royal College of Surgeons of England has a *Code of Practice for The Surgical Management of Jehovah's Witnesses* (London: RCSE, 2002). I believe its recommendations are implemented in Scotland.
310 *R v Bourne* [1939] 1 KB 687.
311 *Owen v Coventry Health Association*, 30 August 1986, Official Transcript – 1983 WL 914546 – objection to electro-convulsive therapy.
312 *Janaway v Salford Health Authority* [1989] 1 AC 537.
313 Age of Legal Capacity (Scotland) Act s. 2(4) with the Children (Scotland) Act 1995, s. 90.
314 *In Re A (Children) (Conjoined Twins: Surgical Separation)* [2001] Fam. 147. On 'best interests' see also *Law Hospital NHS Trust v Lord Advocate*, 1996 SC 301, *infra* n. 336; cf. *Airedale National Health Service Trust v Bland* [1993] AC 789.
315 *R v Senior* [1899] 1 QB 283; *R v Sheppard* [1981] AC 394. Senior, a member of the 'Peculiar People' sect had not sought medical help for a sick child as that would show insufficient trust in God and the power of prayer. In *Sheppard* the jury had not been instructed to consider whether the child needed aid, and the accused had either not appreciated how ill the child was or had wilfully neglected him.
316 Inference from *Downes* (1875) 1 QBD 25, and comment in *R v Sheppard* [1981] AC 394.
317 In England a court gives consent. *M Children's Hospital NHS Foundation Trust, Applicant, and Mr and Mrs Y* [2014] EWHC 2651 (Fam).
318 Children (Scotland) Act 1995, s. 5. The person giving consent must not know that the parent would decide otherwise.
319 Cf. Registered Homes Act 1984, c.23, s. 37, now repealed.
320 'Social Care and Social Work Improvement Scotland', operating under ss. 59–60 of the Public Services Reform (Scotland) Act, 2010, asp. 8. A body corporate (s. 44 and Sch. 11) it is unpronounceably denoted as SCSWIS (!) throughout the Act.

Abortion

In Scotland abortion is a crime at common law. However, after the Second World War a practice emerged, particularly in Aberdeen, under which an abortion carried out in a hospital for medical reasons was not prosecuted.[321] In England abortion was a criminal act, although on occasion a jury might not convict.[322] However, for both jurisdictions previous law has been amended by the Abortion Act 1967.[323] A foetus of under 24 weeks may be aborted by a registered medical practitioner if two registered medical practitioners are of the opinion that the physical or mental health of the pregnant woman, or of the existing children of her family, would be seriously injured, or that the woman's life would be at risk if the pregnancy continues, or that there is a substantial risk that the child, if born, would be severely handicapped.[324] The decision to terminate is one for the medical practitioners.[325] The father cannot intervene.[326]

Section 4 (1) of the Abortion Act 1967 is the best-known provision as to conscience in UK medical law. Whether a person has a conscientious objection to abortion is not supposed to be a consideration in appointments to medical posts with gynaecological responsibilities. Under s. 4(1) medical personnel have the right on grounds of conscience not to participate in an abortion unless the operation is necessary to save life or to prevent grave permanent injury to physical or mental health (s. 4(2)). Persons claiming an exemption must establish that they hold that conscientious objection (s. 4(1)).[327] In Scotland this may be by a statement made on oath (s. 4(3)). The exemption applies only to personnel actually participating in the treatment ending a pregnancy.[328]

Human fertilisation, embryology and experiment

In vitro fertilisation, sperm donation and surrogate motherhood happen.[329] Section 38 of the Human Fertilisation and Embryology Act 1990 provides a 'conscience clause' for persons

---

321 D. Baird 'Induced abortion: epidemiological aspects' (1975), 1 *J. Medical Ethics* 122. In Scotland criminal prosecution is normally a matter for the Crown. Private prosecutions are rare, but may occur either with the consent of the Lord Advocate, or by permission of the High Court of Justiciary provided the private prosecutor has an interest sufficient to justify the proceeding. See *X* v *Sweeney* 1982 JC 70.
322 *R* v *Bourne* [1939] 1 KB 687. A doctor carried out an abortion on a 14-year-old who had been violently raped by five soldiers.
323 The Act provides 'an exhaustive statement of the circumstances in which treatment for the termination of a pregnancy may be carried out lawfully', per Lord Diplock in *Royal College of Nursing* v *Department of Health and Social Security* [1981] AC 800 at 826 D.
324 Abortion Act 1967, s. 1(1), as amended by the Human Fertilisation and Embryology Act 1990, s. 37. Abortion law is to be transferred to the Scottish Parliament in the further devolution of powers following the referendum of 2014.
325 *Paton* v *British Pregnancy Advisory Service Trustees* [1979] QB 296, an English case likely to be followed in Scotland. An appeal to the European Commission on Human Rights, on the ground of the father's 'right to family life' failed: *Paton* v *United Kingdom*, App. No. 8416/78; (1981) 3 EHRR 408.
326 *Kelly* v *Kelly* 1999 SC 285 – the unanimous Opinion of three judges. An abortion is not an actionable wrong done to the foetus. A foetus is not a legal person. No-one can intervene. Cf. *Paton, supra* n. 325.
327 Although s. 4(1) was enacted with a view to Roman Catholic doctrine, a conscientious objection need not be based on religious grounds. An atheist may conscientiously object to abortion.
328 *Greater Glasgow Health Board (Appellant)* v *Doogan and another (Respondents) (Scotland)* [2014] UKSC 68, a unanimous judgement reversing *Doogan and Wood, Petitioners* [2013] CSIH 36 (also a unanimous opinion), which reversed [2012] CSOH 32.
329 Commercial surrogacy is unlawful: Surrogacy Arrangements Act 1985, as amended. The regulation of assisted reproduction is reserved to the Westminster Parliament: Scotland Act 1998, Sched. 5.

otherwise under a duty to participate in any activity governed by the Act.[330] The ground of 'conscience' is not restricted to a religious base, but must be shown to exist by the person claiming it (s. 38(2)). In Scotland a statement made on oath meets this requirement (s. 38(3)). I am unaware of published practice as to how well the claim of conscience under the Act works.

Transplants

Various pieces of legislation permit the use of human tissue for transplantation or for educational purposes.[331] Supervision of such matters now rests with the Scottish ministers under the Human Tissue (Scotland) Act 2006, asp 4.[332] In *inter vivos* transplants or tissue culling for education or research is a matter for the donor. Consent to post-mortem transplants, if needed,[333] may be given pre-mortem verbally or in writing by the donor or post-mortem by various persons including relatives (ss. 6–7). However, others may not give post-mortem consent if the deceased's known views to the contrary are clear (s. 7(4)).

Cultural procedures

The Female Genital Mutilation (Scotland) Act 2005 asp 8 prohibits the practice. Infant circumcision is lawful.[334] Circumcision thereafter may also occur as a normal medical procedure.

Termination of treatment and right to die

In Scotland adults in command of their faculties may refuse medical treatment, including treatment of a potentially fatal medical condition.[335]

In *Law Hospital NHS Trust* v *Lord Advocate*, 1996 SC 301, the Trust sought guidance and permission for the withdrawal of treatment from someone in a persistent vegetative state.[336] In exercise of its *parens patriae* jurisdiction the Inner House of the Court of Session set out conditions and a procedure to be adopted, but being a civil court restricted its decision to civil consequences.[337] However, thereafter the Lord Advocate issued a statement that where a termination of treatment was executed by medical practitioners and compliant with procedures set out by a court, there would be no criminal prosecution.[338]

---

330 The Act establishes the Human Fertilisation and Embryology Authority to supervise and regulate the matters contained in its title, including scientific experiments on human foetal tissue. See also *In the matter of the Human Fertilisation and Embryology Act 2008* [2015] EWHC 2602 (Fam).
331 Human Organs Transplants Act, 1989; Human Tissue Act, 1961. Cf. Human Reproductive Cloning Act 2001; Human Tissue (Scotland) Act 2006, asp 4. See also the Human Organ Transplants Act 1989: Transitional and Savings Provision Order, 2006, SSI 2006 No. 420, and relative Regulations at 1996 SSI 399 and 2006 SSI 390.
332 See also *supra* n. 331.
333 A Procurator-fiscal (the local Crown prosecutor) may authorise the taking of materials for post-mortem examination (s. 5).
334 Some clinics advertise their services, usually for Brit Mila, the traditional Jewish ceremony.
335 Treatments may be painful, cause bad reactions and have distressing side effects. A patient may wish not to undergo such for possible limited gain. Cf. the Purdy death, *infra* n. 339.
336 The case is similar to the English *Airedale NHS Trust* v *Bland* [1993] AC 789.
337 Permission to withdraw treatment was later given in *Law Hospital NHS Trust* v *Lord Advocate (No. 2)*, 1996 SLT 869.
338 Printed at 1996 SLT 867 – the end of the SLT report of the first *Law Hospital* case. A private prosecution would not occur: *supra* n. 321.

What of assisted suicide? Following the availability of suicide in Switzerland and elsewhere the question has arisen whether people of full capacity should be allowed to end their lives with medical assistance. That would run counter to much religious belief. In England s. 2 of the Suicide Act 1961, which penalises helping procure a death under these circumstances, has given rise to a number of difficult cases.[339] That Act does not apply in Scotland. In such cases the Crown might decide not to prosecute, and there have been no private prosecutions.[340]

In 2013 an Assisted Suicide (Scotland) Bill was introduced in the Scottish Parliament, but in May 2013 failed on a free vote of 82 to 36.[341] Under the Bill persons would have been able to request assistance to end their lives if they considered that their quality of life unacceptable due to a terminal or life-threatening condition, or a progressive condition that was either terminal or life-threatening. Procedures were to be set to authorise a suicide and to ensure that suicide was not undertaken lightly. Euthanasia was forbidden. The act terminating life had to be the person's own deliberate act, but assisting that suicide would have attracted no civil or criminal liability.[342] Assisted suicide is likely to remain contentious.

Burial or cremation

To complete the picture:

The Scottish Reformers made little of burial.[343] Now a 'good send-off', often with secular music,[344] is a regular occurrence. Parishioners used to have burial rights within the parish graveyard.[345] Most cemeteries are now run by private companies or local authorities, not the

---

339 *R (Pretty)* v *Director of Public Prosecutions* [2002] 1 AC 800, departed from by *R (Purdy)* v *Director of Public Prosecutions* [2009] UKHL 45, [2010] 1 AC 345; *R on the Application of Nicklinson and another* v *Ministry of Justice: R* v *Department of Public Prosecutions* [2014] UKSC 38. After the Purdy case and in accordance with judicial comment, the (English) Director of Public Prosecutions issued guidelines as to the prosecution (or otherwise) of persons accompanying a person intending suicide abroad. Debby Purdy, a sufferer from multiple sclerosis starved herself to death (December 2014). Her condition deteriorated but lack of finance made travel abroad impossible. Nicklinson, paralysed by a stroke, died of a heart attack in August 2012 but his family was permitted to continue the case. On 23 June 2015 in *Nicklinson and Lamb* v *UK* the ECHR held inadmissable appeals to that court against the UK decisions refusing to permit assisted suicide: ECHR (Fourth Section) Appl. Nos 2478/15 and 1787/15.

340 After *Purdy* the Lord Advocate issued a statement that, because assisted suicide is not a crime in Scotland, no guidance as to possible prosecution is required. This reasoning lies behind the dismissal of the *Petition of Gordon Ross* [2015] CSOH 123. Cf. C.G. Stephen, 'From Pretty to Purdy: suicide and assistance from across the border', 2008 SLT 267; F. Stark, 'Necessity and policy in *R (Nicklinson and others)* v *Ministry of Justice*, 2014 Edin. LR 103. On private prosecutions in Scotland see *supra* n. 321.

341 The Bill was introduced by Margo Macdonald, MSP, who had Parkinson's disease. She died in 2014. The Health and Sports Committee criticised it as potentially normalising and endorsing suicide, provoking negative societal attitudes and judgements about disability, but made no recommendation as the Bill was on a free vote. The Bill fell on 27 May 2015. Cf. the Assisted Dying Bill, introduced for England in the House of Lords in 2014.

342 In Canada the Supreme Court has held unlawful a ban on a similar procedure: *Carter et al.* v *Canada (Attorney General)* 2015 SCC 5.

343 'Concerning Burial of the Dead' in 'The Directory for the Publick Worship of God', adopted by the Westminster Assembly 1645, approved by the General Assembly (Edinburgh 3 February 1645, Sess. 10) and the Scottish Parliament (Charles 1, Parl. 3, Sess. 5), 1645. A burial was to be very simple, without eulogy or protracted ceremonial.

344 The interestingly defiant 'My Way' by Frank Sinatra remains popular at cremations. 'Always Look on the Bright Side of Life' from the Monty Python film, *The Life of Brian*, also has a following.

345 All residents of the parish were eligible. The right was not in perpetuity, and amounted to a 'right of decomposition', after which the lair might be re-used: J.M. Duncan, *Parochial Ecclesiastical Law of Scotland* (Edinburgh:

Kirk.³⁴⁶ The owner of a lair has enforceable rights.³⁴⁷ Next of kin or executors are not bound by the wishes of the deceased as to the disposal of a body.³⁴⁸ Prior to burial a corpse may be stolen.³⁴⁹ Unlawful interference with a grave, 'violation of sepulchers', is a crime.³⁵⁰ Cremation used to be unthinkable, but in Victorian times pressure for its introduction, particularly in England, increased.³⁵¹ Much land was being swallowed by graveyards, and parish cemeteries were filling up.³⁵² Cremation facilities are regulated under the Cremation Act 1902.³⁵³ Ceremonies are optional.³⁵⁴ In neither burial nor cremation is it required that a minister of religion should conduct the ceremonial, although the Church of Scotland considers that, as part of its self-declared duty to bring the ordinances of religion to the whole of Scotland, a parish minister should, if available, in the last resort conduct the funeral of a parish resident.

Bell & Bradfute, 1869) 255, 262; W.G. Black, *Parochial Ecclesiastical Law of Scotland* (Edinburgh: Green, 1888) 67–70 (2d ed. 1891, 75–80). Now only families may use previously utilised lairs. Sepulture within a church was generally illegal, except in ancient family lairs: W.G. Black and G.R. Robertson, *Parochial Ecclesiastical Law of Scotland*, 4th ed. (Edinburgh: Hodge, 1928) 233.

346 Some modern cemeteries have portions set aside for Moslem burials. New cemeteries in forests and other open ground are planned.

347 *M'Bean* v *Young* (1859) 21 D. 314; but cf. *Wright* v *Wright* (1881) 9 R. 15.

348 Next of kin take precedence in the arranging and location of a funeral unless the deceased has indicated otherwise: *C* v *M*, 2014 SLT (Sh. Ct.) 109. Cf. *C* v *Advocate General for Scotland*, 2012 SLT 103.

349 Per Lord Moncrieff, *Dewar* v *HM Advocate*, 1945 JC 5 at 14. In England body parts may be stolen from their custodians if they have been removed for dissection or preservation for teaching or exhibition purposes: *R* v *Kelly*, *R* v *Lindsay* [1999] QB 621; cf. *Dobson* v *North Tyneside Health Authority* [1996] 4 All ER 474, a case concerning a brain.

350 *HM Advocate* v *Soutar* (1882) 5 Coup. 65; *HM Advocate* v *Coutts* (1899) 3 Adam 50. Disinterment may be permitted in case of error, *Paterson, Petitioner* 2000 SC 574, or to permit relocation of a corpse, *McIntosh, Petitioner* (1894) 2 SLT 206.

351 See the narration of the origin of cremation in England by Cranston J. in the *Ghai* case (*infra* n. 354) [2011] QB 591 at 627F-629E.

352 Former restrictions in the Cremation Regulations have been abolished. A curiosity is that where a local authority is dealing with a corpse, as occasionally it will have to, it may not cremate the body if there is evidence that cremation would have been against the beliefs of the deceased: Social Work (Scotland) Act, 1968, s. 28(1). Presumably circumcision might indicate that the deceased abhorred cremation.

353 The Burial and Cremation (Scotland) Bill, introduced October 2015 will consolidate existing legislation. Crematoria must be certified: Cremation Act 1952. To avoid the concealment of crime through destruction of evidence, a medical certificate by the deceased's doctor or the post-mortem pathologist, or the consent of the local Procurator-fiscal is required: Cremation, Scotland, Regulations 1935, No. 247/S.9, Reg. 8. The unauthorised recycling of coffin lids from cremations is theft: *Dewar* v *HM Advocate*, 1945 JC 5.

354 Scotland has no open-air crematoria, and cremation outwith registered premises would be a criminal offence. However, in 2010 the English Court of Appeal held that the cremation of a Hindu within a structure open to the air was lawful: *R (on the Application of Ghai)* v *Newcastle City Council* [2011] QB 591. The final decision turned on the right of manifestation of belief. Scotland may follow.

9 Conclusion

This chapter is mis-titled, but deliberately. It has been 35 years since my last book-length venture into these waters. Much has changed. And there are no indications that change has ceased. There is no conclusion to the process, but some points can be made.

Constitutionally, there has been the revival of the Scottish Parliament and the devolution to it of legislative competence over many topics. The Scotland Act 1998 is an intriguing piece of legislation.[1] Rather than devolving named areas, it reserved to the Westminster Parliament a list, with all other matters passing to the government and Parliament at Holyrood. Now many Scottish concerns no longer have to wait for a slot in the Westminster legislative timetable. We have also had the 2014 referendum on independence. Independence was convincingly defeated, but the matter seems not to have gone away. However, I note that the Scottish Government's white paper, *Scotland's Future*, published as part of the referendum proceedings, indicated that there would be no change to the legal status of any religion or of Scotland's churches and that the protections for human rights would continue.[2]

The arrangements for the established Church of Scotland create an 'establishment' that is minimal compared with that of the Church of England. There are no endowments or lands inherited from previous centuries, nor an assured voice in either Parliament. Suffice it to say that the Kirk still has a role in state ceremonies, and is recognised in statute by the Church of Scotland Act 1921.[3] Only its own members are now subject to its processes. The Kirk has adapted its procedures so as not to fall foul of developments in the civil law. It has implemented the requirements of the Disability Discrimination Act 1995 as to access to its sites. It has changed its disciplinary procedures so as to separate inquiry, prosecution and decision. It has enshrined non-discrimination in its selection and employment requirements. Harassment and victimisation are proscribed. It might have done all of these otherwise. However, that a few of these developments happened after it failed in its attempt to have its courts not

---

1 The 1998 Act has been added to by the Scotland Act 2012, and a further devolution of powers is pending.
2 *Scotland's Future: Your Guide to an Independent Scotland* (Edinburgh: Scottish Government, 2013) paras 590 and 608.
3 C. Munro, 'Does Scotland have an established church?', 1997 Ecc LJ 639; R. King Murray, 'The Constitutional Position of the Church of Scotland', 1958 PL 155.

fall into the category 'public authority' under the Human Rights Act 1998 may explain some of them. Thereafter the *Percy* case opened up the area of 'minister' for scrutiny, holding in the final decision that being a 'minister' did not necessarily exclude civil tribunals from considering an appropriate case. The Kirk cannot always rely on the Church of Scotland Act 1921 and plead that a matter is for the church alone. *Percy* and later English cases have shown that 'who is a minister' and what that label infers is now not clear – muddled, indeed. Is religious 'ministry' an office, or should this area be re-thought for the purposes of the civil law, removing the potential conflict between office and employment? Many employments have aspects of 'office', but are subject to ordinary law. As a matter of civil law, being 'employed by God' is no longer an adequate concept, no matter how religious institutions may view the situation. If there is a status of 'minister of religion', entry to that status should be clarified. Churches, and groups claiming to be churches, could be left to think of the matter however they might wish, but the civil law could be clear. Indeed, in *Percy* Lady Hale found it difficult to discern any difference between the duties of clergy appointed to minister to spiritual needs, of doctors ministering to bodily needs and judges administering the law.[4]

That said, subsequent to *Percy* no Scottish cases have involved the Church of Scotland. It remains to be seen whether any will arise from the 2015 decisions as to homosexuals in ministry. Will there be more fall-out, and if so, might questions of property arise? Further, apart from that area it is clear there are fissures within the Kirk. Evangelicals take a more traditional theological view than (it appears) the majority. The Kirk's adoption of a 'mixed economy' in the matter of sex has underlined the difficulty. At the end of Chapter I suggest means to secure a reasonable and peaceful withdrawal for those unable to go along with 2015 developments, or for those who in the future may come to consider the Kirk to have departed from its traditional identity and beliefs.

Recent surveys show that in the UK religious belief is a minority interest. Scotland is not an exception. Since World War II the Church of Scotland has seen its membership collapse and its influence wane.[5] The re-establishment of the Scottish Parliament has diminished a Kirk whose General Assembly was often previously referred to as the Voice of Scotland. The Kirk is no longer an expression of national identity. It has lost relevance on the UK and domestic stage, and to some extent has been replaced by an emergent Scottish nationalism that is not necessarily linked to a drive for independence. The new Scottish Parliament has afforded no special place to the Kirk, though its ministers among others may be invited to participate in the 'Pause for Thought' at the start of proceedings.

In law, non-established Christian denominations and other faith groups are voluntary associations, as are the institutional structures of those other religions that have come to Scotland. These operate under their own several constitutions. Trustees usually hold their

---

4 *Percy v Church of Scotland Board of National Mission* [2005] UKHL 73, [2006] 2 AC 28, 2006 SC (HL) 1 Para 151 *ad fin*.
5 Eighty years ago J. Buchan and G. Adam Smith, *The Kirk in Scotland, 1560–1929* (London: Hodder and Stoughton, 1930) published to mark the union of 1929 noted the Church's lessening influence and status. The decline forecast in J.N. Wolfe and M. Pickford, *The Church of Scotland: An Economic Survey* (London: Chapman, 1980), has proved accurate in terms of finance, membership and age-profile. The upkeep of churches, built cheaply by the Free Church following the Disruption and carried into the 1929 reunion has proved a burden, and the decline in membership has affected income. Cf. A. Herron, *Kirk by Divine Right: Church and State, Peaceful Coexistence* (Edinburgh: St Andrew Press, 1985). Most denominations have declined: S. Bruce, *Scottish Gods: Religion in Modern Scotland, 1900–2012* (Edinburgh: Edinburgh UP, 2014). The Roman Catholic Church is considering closing some churches and uniting parishes.

property although newer arrangements are now available. The terms of any trust will be enforced. So long as they do not transgress the provisions of their constitutions, and observe natural justice, these associations are unlikely to trouble the civil courts.[6]

Areas of church-state relations have seen differing degrees of mutation. Marriage and divorce are now completely controlled by the state. While marriage may still be constituted in a religious (or belief) ceremonial, civil marriage exists, and the introduction of same-sex marriage departs from former theologies. The requirement of the exchange of consent by the parties was earlier a fundamental, but its continuance is unrelated to religious doctrine. Marriage is now constituted only through compliance with the requirements and procedures set by the state. It would be better completely to separate these from other ceremonial. Divorce is civil alone: whether a religious group recognises divorce is a matter for it, and divorce has civil effect only if obtained through the civil procedures. Education is mainly secular, avoiding some of the problems across the Border, though making particular provision for Roman Catholicism. Most schools have chaplains, as do all universities where many faiths and traditions are now represented. Freedom of speech in universities has the potential for problems with moves to bar extremist speakers. In a different area charities and charitable status should be re-examined. Secular charitable activity by religious organisations should continue to be supported. However, the dissemination of religious belief should be the financial responsibility of those of religious conviction, unassisted by state subvention.

The new factor in the interaction of religion and law has been the incorporation of major portions of international human rights agreements and the making directly relevant the decisions of their tribunals by the Human Rights Act 1998. But the transmutation of worthy principle into formal legal obligation carries major problems. Legislative articulation requires, first, precision as to what the words used mean and, second, enforcement mechanisms. Encouragement to be good becomes the requirement of conduct that is compliant with the terminology. Proper conduct is induced but leaves the heart and conscience unaffected. The protection of minorities can segue into an ability to compel, disturbing as minority beliefs and an intolerant secularism are transmuted into over-riding law. The hortatory becomes coercive. Political correctness stifles, manipulates and bullies.

Whether UK Human Rights law is operating successfully is open to question. Many cases have turned on technicalities, much depending on whether discrimination is direct or indirect and on the definition of a 'protected characteristic'. The area is muddled. The Equality and Human Rights Commission in its various incarnations may have been unduly zealous in supporting complainants. Indeed, I have heard it suggested that, given the legislative proscription of harassment, perhaps Commission personnel could be accused of that offence. Agendas may have been pushed. Reported cases and administrative actions are of concern to those who subscribe to the traditional Christian ethos as conditioning the society in which we live. As I write, the Equalities Commission published a report on the outcome of its call for evidence on how the current system is working.[7] It contains examples of what might be considered to be absurdities ascribable to people trying to avoid trouble with the human rights enforcement mechanisms. The former Chairman of the Commission has suggested that the law may have got it wrong in relation to race. Preventing the expression

---

6 Dispute within non-Christian religious a faith associations has not yet resulted in legal action in Scotland. Cf. in England the Sikh temple case *Shergill* v *Khaira* [2014] UKSC 33.
7 M.K. Beninger, et al., *Religion or Belief in the Workplace and Service Delivery. Findings from a Call for Evidence* (Equality and Human Rights Commission, March 2015).

of prejudice may not be the best way.⁸ The same may apply to religion. The religious should not be silenced by fear or by the tyranny of the stewards of political correctness. Diversity and the manifestation of diversity should be allowed. The normal rules as to civil disturbance provide sufficient back-up if necessary. The expression of religious belief and conviction verbally and otherwise should not be penalised unless or until it significantly transgresses public order. Engineering should be eschewed.

What is needed is the reconsideration and re-balancing of human rights and matters religious. Whether the intention of government to modify or replace the Human Rights Act by a UK Bill of Rights will do this, remains to be seen. In the meantime Lady Hale, Vice-President of the UK Supreme Court, has noted the problem.⁹ The Council of Europe recently adopted a Resolution on the matter.¹⁰ Its para 6.2 calls for reasonable accommodation within the principle of indirect discrimination to respect freedom of religion (6.2.1), and the upholding of freedom of conscience within the workplace while also protecting against discrimination (6.2.2). Para 6.4 calls on member states to 'uphold the fundamental right to freedom of expression by ensuring national legislation does not unduly limit religiously motivated speech'.

I hope a reasonable accommodation will be found between competing interests and convictions, no matter how strongly held. That will require restraint on the part of those holding strong views of whatever religious hue (or none) who come into a position of authority. Profound conviction or dogmatism combined with office can tempt to action, but it does not confer immunity from seeking the general good through argument and discussion rather than by fiat.¹¹

---

8 T. Phillips, documentary Channel 4, 19 March 2015: 'Things We Won't Say about Race That Are True'. Cf. his article, *Daily Mail*, 16 March 2015, http://www.dailymail.co.uk/news/article-2996235/At-man-dares-tell-truth-race-Ex-race-tsar-says-silencing-debate-devastating-harm-Britain.html

9 Lady Hale, 'The Conflict of Equalities' July 2013, https://www.supremecourt.uk/docs/speech-130710.pdf; 'Religion and Sexual Orientation: The clash of equality rights', March 2014: https://www.supremecourt.uk/docs/speech-140307.pdf; 'Freedom of Religion and Belief', June 2014: https://www.supremecourt.uk/docs/speech-140613.pdf. But note her 'Secular Judges and Christian Law' 2015 17 Ecc LJ 170.

10 Council of Europe Assembly Res. 2036, 29–01–2015, 'Tackling intolerance and discrimination in Europe with a special focus on Christians'. See also Council of Europe PACE Res. 2076 (2015) and Recommendation 2080 (2015). Cf. P. Edge and L. Vickers, *Review of Equality and Human Rights Law Relating to Religion or Belief*, EHRC Research Report 97, 2015, Ch 5 'A duty of reasonable accommodation'.

11 Cf. M.M. Cuomo, 'Religious Belief and Public Morality: A Catholic Governor's Perspective' (1984–85), 1 Notre Dame J.L. Ethics and Pub. Policy 13.

Index

Abbey of Deer 11
Aberdeen, Presbytery of 95–6
Abortion Act 1967 221
Act for Setling the Quiet and Peace of the Church, 1693 11
Acts of the Scottish Parliament *see* under years below
Act of Security, 1707 138–43
Act of Settlement 1701 184
Acts of Supremacy 16–17
Act of Union, 1706 (Scotland) 180
Act of Union, 1707 (England) 180
Act to facilitate the foundation and endowment of additional schools in Scotland (1838) 143
Adultery 14, 169–70, 175–6
Advertising 186, 191, 196–8
Advertising Standards Authority 186, 198
Affirmations (Scotland) Acts 201
Agnosticism 201–2
Aitchison, Lord, 77–9, 90, 98, 112–13, 116–8
Alehouse Act 1756 212
Allan v *Macrae* (1791) 106
Alverstone, Lord 126
Anderson, J. 66
Angus, Presbytery of 80–3
Annan Committee 1976–77 191, 197
Anti-Burghers 106
Anti-Catholic statutes of 1560 5
Anti-discrimination legislation 81–5
Antisocial Behaviour etc. (Scotland) Act 2004 188
Ardmillan, Lord 116–17
Argyll Commissions 144–5
Arminian theologies 71, 125
Articles Declaratory of the Constitution of the Church of Scotland in Matters Spiritual (1921) 69–99

Asher, A. 66–7
Assisted Suicide (Scotland) Bill 2013 223
Associate Congregation 106, 121
Associated Presbyterian Churches 102
Associate Presbytery 21, 101, 106
Associate Synod 48, 106–8
Association, non-established churches 133
Atheism 87, 155–6, 159, 185, 192, 201–2, 217, 221
Auchinloss v *Black* (1793) 108, 114
Auchterarder cases 29, 32–40, 49–55, 115
Augustine: 'Two Cities' 2
'Auld Licht' controversy 106, 120
Austin, J. 20; *The Province of Jurisprudence Determined* 56
Authorities, ecclesiastical and secular 2, 15

Baird Trust Reorganisation Act 2005 131
Ballantyne v *Presbytery of Wigtown* (1936) 77–80, 84, 90–1
Bampton Lectures 1860 (Hussey) 206
Bank Holidays Act 1871 203
Bannantyne v *Lord Overtoun* (1904) 92
Bannantyne v *Overtoun* (1902) 106, 124
Bannatyne and Others v *Lord Overtoun and Others* (1904) 123
Banns of marriage 164, 168
Baptism 162
Baptist churches 103
Barrier Act 1690 2, 67, 74, 94–6
Basilikon Doron 15
Basis and Plan of Union 69, 72–3, 127
Bastards (Scottish) 177
BBC (British Broadcasting Corporation) 189–91, 195–8
BCAP Code (UK Code of Broadcast Advertising) 198

Beaton, D. 6
Beaton, J. 6, 103
Begg, J. 70
Belhaven, Lord 54
Belief bodies 158–9
Belief marriage 163–8
Betting and Gaming Act 1960 211
Beveridge Committee 1949–51 191, 195–6
Biblical criticism 87
Bigamy 158
Black Acts 1584 15
Blackie, J. 138
Blasphemy 185–6
Blessing services 95
Board of Education 145
Board of National Mission 81
Board of Examiners of Parochial Schools 150
Bona-fide travellers 212–13
Bonomy, Lord 130
Books, heretical 12
Book of Common Worship (English) 109
Boyle, Lord 40, 50, 60, 105
Bradlaugh, C. 201–2
Braxfield, Lord 108, 114
Breach of promise of marriage 161
Brentnall v *Free Presbyterian Church of Scotland* (1986) 107, 115, 118
Bribery Act 2010 85
Bridge v *South Portland Street Synagogue* (1907) 107
Briggs, A. 195–6
British Broadcasting Corporation (BBC) 189–91, 195–8
British Railways Board v *Pickin* (1974) 93
Broadcasting 188–98
Broadcasting Acts 191–2, 197
Broadcast Advertising Code (BCAP Code) 198
Broadcasting Code (2005) 193–5, (2013) 197
Broadcast Committee of Advertising Practice 198
Broadcasting 'Concordat' (1941) 196
Broadcasting 'Fairness Code' 191
Broadcasting franchises 191–2
Broadcasting Standards Commission 193
Brougham, H. Lord 35–7, 54, 115, 142–5
Brown v *Magistrates of Edinburgh,* (1931) 207–8
Bryce, J. 27, 40–1
Bryson v *Wilson* (1752) 105–6
Buchanan, R. 28–9, 40, 54
Buchan v *Brodie* 1984 (unreported) 77–9
Buddhism 104
Burgess Oath 21, 101, 105–6
Burgher Seceders 120
Burial 223–4
Burnett v *St. Andrew's Episcopal Church* (1888) 131–2

Bute v *More* (1870) 207–8
'Butler' Education Act 1944 (England) 153
Butter, T. 38

Call, the 26–8, 32–5
Calvinism 66, 71, 126–7
Cameronians 21, 101
Cameron, Lord 82
Campbell, J. 37–8, 52–3
Campbell, R. Vary 67
Campbelltown case (1837) 121
Campbell v *Presbytery of Kintyre* (1843) 50
Campbeltown School 149
Cantyre, Presbytery of 149
Caplan, Lord 82
Cardross cases 106–7, 110–11, 114–16
Cassie v *The General Assembly of the Church of Scotland* (1878) 65
Catechism 12–13, 16, 140
Catholic Church, *see* Roman Catholic Church
Celebrant, marriage 165–7
Celtic Christianity 4
Census 187, 217
Census Act 1920 217
Central Religious Advisory Committee (CRAC) 195–6
Ceremonies, marriage 158–71
Chalmers, T. 23, 26–8, 35, 43–4, 48
Chapel Act 1834, 29–31
Chapel Act cases 23, 29–31, 46–52, 55–7, 63
Chapels of ease 29–31
Chaplin case 183–4
Charities 214–16, 227
Charities and Trustee Investment (Scotland) Act 2005 215–16
Charity Register 216
Charles I 16
Charles II 16–17
Children: medical treatment of 220; rights of 176–7
Christian faith, human rights and 178, 182–4
Christian Science Nursing Homes 220
Church Act 1567 c. 6 9–10
Churches (Scotland) Act 1905 18, 67, 71, 74, 97, 128, 139
Church and Nation, Committee on 213
Church Jurisdiction Acts 10–15
Church Missionary Society 25
Church of Christ 18, 26
Church of God 5
Church of Jesus Christ of Latter Day Saints 104
Church of Scotland 2, 5–21, 225–8; Declaratory Articles and 69–99; Disruption of 21–68, 75, 101–2, 123, 143–4; education and 134–57; outside establishment and 100–33; personal relationships and 158–77

Church of Scotland Act 1921 69–99, 133, 225–6
Church of Scotland Courts Act 1863 63–4
Church of Scotland General Trustees 76, 92–3, 97
Church of Scotland (Property and Endowments) Act 1925 70, 76
Church Patronage in Scotland, Select Committee on 1833–4 53–4
Church Patronage (Scotland) Acts 20, 64, 77
Church Patronage (Scotland) Act 1711 25
Circumcision 222
Civic Government (Scotland) Act 1982 188
Civil law 23, 33–4, 83–5, 96, 159–60
Civil marriage 162, 168–9, 227
Civil Partnership 158, 170
Civil Partnership Act 2004 170
Claim of Right 1689 10, 17,
Claim of Right 1843 38, 46, 55–6
Clandestine marriage 174
Clapham Sect 26
Clark, T. 38–9
Clark v *Stirling* (1839) 38–9, 50
Clelland, J. 48
Cockburn, Lord 31, 59
Codex Theodosianus 204
Cohabitation 158
Columba 4
Commentaries on the Law of Scotland Respecting Crimes (Hume) 205
Commercial broadcasting 189–92
Communications Act 2003 193
Communion 162
Company Law legislation 216
Concessions 7
Concordat of Leith 1572 11
Concubinage 172
Confession of Faith 9, 16, 67, 103, 138, 149–50
Confession of Faith Ratification Acts 7–8, 18–19, 25, 91, 208
Congregational Union 103, 122–3
Conscience clauses 150–2, 216–18, 221–2
Conscription 218–19
Consent, in marriage 163
Constable, A. 66–7
Constantine, Mandate of 3 March 321 AD 204
'Constitution of the Church of Scotland', Bill to declare 70
Consuetude 73
Convention of Estates 7
Cooke, A. 39–40
Cook, G. 30
Cooper, Lord 93
Coronation Oath Act 1567 10, 199
Cottenham, Lord 35
Council of Europe 179–80, 228
Council of Trent (1545–63) 162, 171
Counter-Reformation 5

Couper v *Burns* (1850) 122
Court of Teinds 29, 48–9, 63
Covenanters 15–19
CRAC (Central Religious Advisory Committee) 195–6
Craigdallie v *Aikman* (1805) 120–3, 127–8
Craigie v *Marshall* (1850) 121–2
Craig v *Anderson and the Presbytery of Deer* (1893) 66
Creedal formulation 96–7
Cremation 223–4
Cremation Act 1902 224
Criminalities 186–8
Criminal Law (Consolidation) (Scotland) Act 1995 188, 202
Criminal Law of Scotland, The (Gordon) 208
Cruelty, divorce for 175
Cruickshank v *Gordon* (1843) 40, 45, 51–2
Culsalmond case 45–6, 51–2
Cuninghame, Lord 60–1
Cuninghame v *Presbytery of Irvine* (1843) 47–51
Cunningham, J. 44
Curriculum for Excellence 156
Curriehill, Lord 117
Cursing and Beating of Parents, Act 1661 15
Cy près schemes 131–3

Daemonologie (James VI and I) 187
Darwin, C.: *Origin of Species* 87
Davey, Lord 126
Davidson, R. 195
Daviot case 39–40, 50
Deas, Lord 110, 114–17, 163
Declaratory Act 1833 27
Declaratory Acts 126–7
Declaratory Articles 69–99
Denominational schools 139–40
Desertion, divorce for 175
Dies dominicus non est juridicus 208–9
Dies non 14, 208–9
Diocese of Southwark v *Coker* (1998) 81
Directory of Public Worship 16, 168
Disability Discrimination Act 1995 84–5, 181
Discrimination legislation 81–5, 178–83
Disestablishment 67–70
Disruption cases 50–62, 75
Disruption of the Church of Scotland 21–68, 75, 101–2, 123, 143–4
Dissenters 143
Divine Right of Kings 15–16
Divorce 159, 165, 170, 174–6, 227
Divorce *a vinculo* 174–5
Divorce (Scotland) Acts 169–70, 174–5
Divorce: The Grounds Considered (Scottish Law Commission) 175
Divorce Reform Act (England) 1969 175
Doctrine of the Trinity Act 1812 185

232 Index

Dominican Order 135
Douglas, J. 8
Drummond v *Farquhar* (1809) 106
Drummond Young, Lord 130–1
Dunbar v *Presbytery of Abernethy* (1889) 66
Dunbar v *Presbytery of Auchterarder* (1849) 58–9
Dunbar v *Skinner* (1849) 105, 109–10, 116
Dunbar v *Stoddart* (1849) 58
Dunkeld, Presbytery of 38–9
Dunlichity 39–40
Dunlop, A. 44
Dunn v *Brunton* (1801) 120
Dunpark, Lord 118

Earl of Kinnoull and Rev. R. Young v *Presbytery of Auchterarder* (1838) 32, 50
Earl of Kinnoull and Rev. R. Young v *Rev. John Ferguson and others* (1841) 32, 36–7
Earl of Kinnoull and Rev. R. Young v *Rev. John Ferguson and others* (1843) 32, 38
Earl of Kinnoull v *Ferguson* (1841) 51
Earl of Kinnoull v *Ferguson* (1843) 51–2
Ecclesiastical cases 34, 111–12
Ecclesiastical marriage 163
Ecumenical Council of the Roman Catholic Church (1545–63) (Council of Trent) 162, 171
Ecumenism 5
Edinburgh, Presbytery of 20, 105
Edinburgh Sheriff Court 129
Education 30, 134–57, 227
Education Act 1944 (England) 153
Education Bill (England) 1820 143–5
Education Commission, England 145–6
Education Committee, Church of Scotland 149
Education of the Lower Orders in the Metropolis, Commission on 1816 142
Education of the Poor, Commission on 1817–9 142–3
Education (Scotland) Acts 145–7, 152–7
Educational Endowments, Commission on 1818 143
Edwards v *Begbie* (1850) 116
Edwards v *Cruickshank* (1840) 40–5, 51
Edwards v *Leith* (1843) 40, 45
Eldon, Lord 120, 123, 127
Electoral reform 1832 22
Elgin Academy case 149–50
Elimination of All Forms of Intolerance and of Discrimination Based on Religion or Belief, Declaration on 1981 179
Elizabeth I 1, 7
Elliot v *Faulke and Shute* (1844) 209
Embryology 221–2
Employment Appeals Tribunal 81, 182

Employment Equality (Religion or Belief) Regulations 2003 156, 182
Employment Rights Act 1996 119, 211
Employment Tribunals 81–3, 119, 156
Endowments 8–11, 63, 70–1, 76
Engagement to marry 161
Engels, F. 87
English, teaching of 140–1
Episcopacy 2, 12, 15–20, 105–7
Episcopal Church 63, 102, 132, 145
Episcopalian Church 105
Equality Acts 181–2
Equality and Human Rights Commission 181 226–8
Equal opportunities 181
Equal Pay Act 1970 181
Equal Treatment Directive 82
Erastianism 2, 16, 22, 30, 64, 71
Erskine, Ebenezer 21, 48, 207–8
Estates of the Kingdom of Scotland 17
European Charter of Fundamental Rights 2000 179
European Convention on Human Rights 1951 179–82
European Council Directive 2000/78/EC 182
European Court of Human Rights 180, 183–4
European Court of Justice 205
European Social Charter 1961 179
European Union 179, 182, 209
European Union Equal Treatment Directive 82
Euthanasia 223
Evangelicals 23–7, 35, 48, 55–7
Eweida case 183
Exchequer Estimates 1832 14

Facilities, educational 140–7
Factories Acts 210
'Fairness Code' 191
False Oaths (Scotland) Act 1933 202
Family Law (Scotland) Act 2006 173, 176
Fathers, rights of 159
Female Genital Mutilation (Scotland) Act 2005 222
Ferguson Bequest Fund v *The Congregational Union* (1899) 122–3
1503 Acts 172, 205
1551 Acts 14
1560 Acts 7–8, 91, 162
1561 Acts 147–8
1563 Acts 14, 175
1567 Acts 9–15, 199
1572 Acts 11–12
1579 Acts 13–15, 210–12
1581 Acts 14
1587 Acts 11–12
1587 Annexation Act 11
1592 Acts 11–15, 148, 175

Findhorn Community 104
Finlay, R.B. 70, 86
First Book of Discipline 1560 8–11, 24–5, 136–40, 147, 175
First Covenant December 1557 7
Fish and game, Sunday observance and 210
Forbes v *Eden* (1865) 107, 112
Forbidden degrees of matrimony 165
Forced Marriage etc. (Protection and Jurisdiction) (Scotland) Act 2011 167
Form of Church Government 16
Formula of Worship 149–50
Fornication Act 1567 14
1429 Acts 176
1496 Acts 135
Fourth Lateran Council, 1215 163–4
Franchises, broadcasting 191–2
Fraudulent Mediums Act 1951 187
Free Church College 129
Free Church (Continuing) v *Free Church* (2005) 107–8
Free Church Declaratory Act (1892) 87–8, 125
Free Church Model Trust Deed 124
Free Church of Scotland 21–2, 56, 63–71, 87–8, 97, 101–2, 106–8, 119, 123–31, 138
Free Church of Scotland (Continuing) v *General Assembly of the Free Church of Scotland* (2005) 129
Freedom of speech and expression 185–6, 227
Free Presbyterian Church of Scotland 102, 118–19, 129
French Alliance 6–7
French Revolution 143, 199
Fullerton, J. 43, 60, 109–10, 116
Fundamentals of the faith 87–8

Gaelic, abolition in schools 140–1
Gaelic Schools Society 144
Galbraith v *Smith* (1837) 121
Gambling Act 2005 212
Gaming Act 1968 211–12
Garioch, Presbytery of 45–6
Gender Recognition Act 2004 170
General Assemblies 15–16
General Assembly 1832 27; 1833 27; 1834 23; 1838 34–5; 1839 41–2
General Assembly Act 1592 15
General Assembly Act V, 1799 57
General Assembly Act 17, 1889 66–7
General Assembly Act III, 1910 67
General Assembly Act I, 2015 96–7
General Assembly of the General Baptist Churches and Evans v *Taylor* (1841) 106
General Associated Synod 101
General Statutes of the Provincial Council of the Prelates and Clergy of the Realm of Scotland 6
Geneva Catechism 136

Genital mutilation 222
Gift Aid 214–15
Gillespie, T. 21
Gillies, Lord 47
Glasgow City Council v *McNab* (2007) 156
Glasgow, Presbytery of 206
Grammar schools 135
Grants in aid 143
Great Charter of the Church, The 1592 15
Greenshields v *Magistrates of Edinburgh* (1710) 19–20, 102, 105
Grieve, Lord 119
Guardianship Act 1973 177

Habit and repute, marriage by 171–4
Haldane, R., Viscount 86, 94–6
Hale, Lady 82–3, 226–8
Halsbury, Lord 126–7
Hamilton, P. 6
Hamilton, Presbytery of 46–7
Handfasting 161
Hate crime 188
Hendry settlement (Strathbogie) 41, 45
Heresy 185–6
Heritors 26, 29, 140–2
Heterosexual marriage 159, 162
Higher Criticism 87
Hinduism 104
HM Inspectorate of Education 156
Hobbes, T.: *Leviathan* (1651) 20
Hoffman, Lord 82
Holyrood Parliament 1, 92–3, 180, 225
Home-Drummond Act (Sale of Liquor Act) 1828 212
Home schooling 157
Homosexuality 88–9, 95–7, 226; *see also* same-sex marriage
Hope, C. 34–6
Hope, J. 28–33, 39, 49, 53–4, 58–60, 80, 115–16, 121–2
Hospitals 13, 220
House of Commons Disqualification Acts 184–5
Human Fertilisation and Embryology Act 1990 221–2
Human rights 77, 158–9, 178–83, 211
Human Rights Act 1998 84–5, 180, 226–8
Human Tissue (Scotland) Act 2006 222
Hume, D.: *Commentaries on the Law of Scotland Respecting Crimes* 205
Hussey, J.: Bampton Lectures 1860 206
Huxley, T.H. 87

Idolatry 7
Illegitimacy 177
Impotence 170
Incest Act 1567 c. 15 14–15
Independent Television Authority 191

234 Index

Independent Television Commission 192–4
Independent Television Commission Broadcasting Code 197
Inglis, J., Lord President 62, 65
Inland Revenue 84, 215
Innes, A.T. 100
Innocent VIII 187
Interim Acts 28
International Covenant on Civil and Political Rights, 1966 179
International Covenant on Economic, Social and Cultural Rights, 1966 178–9
International law 134, 178–81
Interpretation and Legislative Reform (Scotland) Act 2010 169
Inverkeithing parish 21
Inverness, Presbytery of 39–40
In vitro fertilisation 221–2
Irregular marriage 171–4
Irvine, Presbytery of 48
Islam 104
Iure devoluto 32, 64–6
Ivory, Lord 47, 61

James, Lord 126
James VI and I 1, 14–15; *Basilikon Doron* 15; *Daemonologie* 187
James VII and II 10, 17
Jeffrey, F. 28
Jehovah's Witnesses 104, 219–20
Jews 104, 165, 188
Johnston, C. 70, 94
Judicial review 79
Jurisdiction 104, 109–11, 117
Jury service 217–18
Justiciary Courts Act 1828 201

Kessen, A. 38–9
Kilbrandon Committee (1969) 159–60, 163, 166
Kincairney, L. 107
Kirkintilloch case 121–2
Kirkmabeck parish 77
Knox, J. 6–8
Kramer, H. 187

Labour, Sunday observance and 210–11
Ladele case 183
Laicising 150
Lang v *Presbytery of Irvine* (1864) 61, 116–17
Law Hospital NHS Trust v *Lord Advocate* (1996) 222
Law Reform Act 1990 216
Law Reform (Miscellaneous Provisions) (Scotland) Acts 215–17
Learning and Teaching Scotland 156
Leasing Making (Scotland) Act 1825 185–6
Lecture schools 135

Legislative freedom 70–1
Leo XIII 103
Leslie v *Leslie* (1859) 163
Lethendy case 38–9, 50–3
Leviathan (1651) (Hobbes) 20
Leviticus 14, 165
Lex, Rex (1644) (Rutherford) 16
Liberty of opinion 67, 87–91, 96
Licence (Duty) Act 1808 212
Licensing (Scotland) Acts 212–13
Livingston, A. 46–7
Livingstone (1841) 46–7, 51
Local Government (Scotland) Acts 146–7, 153
Location of marriages 167–8
Lockhart v *Cumming* (1851) 63
Lockhart v *Presbytery of Deer* (1851) 60–1
Logan v *Presbytery of Dumbarton* (1995) 77, 79–80
Longer Catechism, The 16
Low, Lord 125–6
Luther, M.: *Ninety-five Theses* 5
Lyell, C.: *Principles of Geology* 87

MacAlister and Others v *Young and Another* (1904) 123–4
Macaulay, T. Lord 25
MacCormick v *Lord Advocate* (1953) 92–3
MacDonald, A. 119
MacDonald, J.: *A Practical Treatise on the Criminal Law of Scotland* 208
MacDonald v *Free Presbyterian Church* (2010) 115, 119
Macfarlane case 182–3
MacFarlane, D. 27
MacIntosh v *Rose* (1839) 39–40, 50
Mackay, Lord 78–9, 84, 91, 207–8
MacKay v. *MacLeod* (1952) 129
MacKenzie, Lord 47
MacLeod, N. 206
Macleod v *Clacher* (1993) 132
MacMillan v *The General Assembly of the Free Church of Scotland,* (1859) 110
MacMillan v *The General Assembly of the Free Church of Scotland and Beith and Others* (1861) 110–11
MacMillan v *The General Assembly of the Free Church of Scotland and Beith and Others* (1862) 111
MacMillan v *The Free Church of Scotland* (1862) 117
MacMillan v *The General Assembly of the Free Church of Scotland* (1864) 106–7
MacMillan v *The Free Church of Scotland* (1864) 107, 111
Malleus Maleficarum (1487) 187
'The Man Born to be King' (Sayers) 195
Mandate of 3 March 321 AD (Constantine) 204

Marbury v *Madison* (1803) 93
Margin of appreciation 183–4
Marischal College 138
Marischal, Earl 11
Marnoch (Strathbogie) cases 40–5, 50–7
Marriage 158–69, 184, 227
Marriage and Civil Partnership (Scotland) Act 2014 158, 169–70
Marriage *in facie ecclesiae* 162
Marriage Notice (Scotland) Act 1878 165
Marriage (Scotland) Acts 158–69, 173
Marx, K. 87
Mary II of England 17
Mary of Guise 6–7
Mary, Queen of Scots 6–9
Mass 7–9
Matrimonium per verba de praesenti 165, 168, 171–4
Maule, Fox 55
McDonald v *Burns,* (1940) 112–13, 116
McFarlane v *Presbytery of Coupar* (1879) 65–6
McGonagle v *Glasgow Unitarian Church* (1955) 107
McGowan v *Maryland* (1961) 204
McIver, A. 130
McNab v *Glasgow City Council* (2007) 140, 156
McNiven v *Glasgow Corporation* (1920) 208
Meadowbank, Lord 121
Mearns, D. 28
Medical practice 219–24
Medwyn, Lord 53, 59–60
Melville, A. 18; *The Second Book of Discipline* 12, 15, 21, 24–5, 137
Memorial of Protest GA Act IX, 1715 25
Methodist Church 100, 103
Middleton v *Anderson* (1842) 45–6, 51
Middleton v *Tough* (1908) 210
Military service 218–19
Ministers: election of 77; retirement of 83–4; sphere of 63; suspension of 64
Ministers Act 1693 18, 66–7, 148
'Mixed economy' 96–7, 226
M'Laren, Lord 207
Moderates 21–3, 27–30, 35, 44, 54, 57, 138
Moncreiff, J. 28, 59–62, 65, 108, 114, 122
Monogamy 162–4
Mora, taciturnity and delay 84, 119
Moravians 202
Morison Committee (1937) 173
Mormons 104
Mummery, J. 81–2
Murray, C. 85, 96
Murray, J. 36–7, 43
Muslims 188

National Church Association 91
National Covenant 1638 16–17

National Establishment of Religion 125
National Health Services 214
National Insurance Act 1911 214
National Service Act 1948 218–19
National Service Act (Duration) Order 1953 218
National Service (Armed Forces) Act 1939 218
Negative Confession 1581 15
Negative obedience 52
'New Age' groups 104
'New Light' controversy 106, 120
New Parishes (Scotland) Act 1844 63
Nicol v *M'Neil* (1877) 207–8
Nietzsche, F. 87
Nigerian independent churches 104
Ninety-five Theses (Luther) 5
Ninian 4
Non-Christian faiths 104, 226–7
Nonconformists 143
Non-established denominations 100–33, 219, 226–7
North British Railway Company 206
Notice of marriage 163–4
Nullity of marriage 170, 174
Nursing homes 220

Oath of calumny 199
Oaths 198–202
Oaths Acts 201–2
Oaths Relief in Criminal Proceedings (Scotland) Act 1863 201
Obedience 52
Ofcom 186, 192–8
Office of Communications 189, 191
Office of Scottish Charity Regulator (OSCR) 215–16
Old Age Pensions Act 1908 214
Old Catholic Church 102–3
Old Deer parish 66
Oliver v *Skerret,* (1896) 113
Original principles 71, 85, 120–3
Original Secession Church 132
Origin of Species (Darwin) 87
Orthodox Church 102
Osborne, Lord 80, 130–1
Osborne v *Southern Reformed Presbytery* (1831) 108
OSCR (Office of Scottish Charity Regulator) 215–16
Outside establishment 100–33

Paisley Abbey 64–5
Panel on Doctrine 90
Papacy 9
Papal Bull: *Summis desiderentes affectibus* 1484 187; *Ex Apostolatus Apice,* 1878 103
Papal Jurisdiction Act 1560 7, 91, 162

236 *Index*

Parades, licensing of 188
Parens patriae jurisdiction 222
Parents, rights of 159, 176–7, 220
Parishes 4–5
Parmoor, Lord 86
Parochial and Burgh Schools (Scotland) Act 1861 150–1
Parochial Schools (Scotland) Act 1803 142, 148–9
Parricide Act 1594 15
Paterson, T. 185
Paterson v *Presbytery of Dunbar* (1861) 61
Paton, Lady 129–30
Patronage 15, 18–21, 33, 51–4, 60, 103; abolition of 25, 64, 67; defined 24; Veto Act and 23–8
Patronage Act 1690 25
Patronage Act 1711 32–7
Peel, R. 55
Penal law 14
Pentecostal churches 103
Percy v *Board of National Mission of the Church of Scotland* (2002) 226
Percy v *Church of Scotland Board of National Mission* (2005) 63, 77, 80–3, 85
Personal relationships 158–77
Perth, riot of 1559 7
Phillips v *Innes* (1835) 206
Pilkington Committee 1960 191, 196–7
Pirate radio 192
Pitman, Lord 78
Plymouth Brethren 104, 219
Police, Public Order and Criminal Justice (Scotland) Act 2006 188
Political correctness 227–8
Poor Law 30, 46
Poor Law (Scotland) Act 1845 214
Poor relief 13, 30, 39, 52, 143, 214
Popery 7, 18
Population (Statistics) legislation 217
Positive obedience 52
Post-Disruption period 57–68
Powers of the Church with regard to the Confession, Committee on 1901 67
Practical Treatise on the Criminal Law of Scotland, A (MacDonald) 208
Preamble for Ordination of ministers and elders 90
Preamble to the Charter of the United Nations 178
Predestination 126–7
Prelacy 17–18
Pre-Reformation Scotland 4–5
Presbyterian Church, education and 151–3
Presbyterianism 2, 5, 12, 15–20, 69–74, 101–2, 168

Presbytery of Elgin v *The Magistrates and Town Council of Elgin* (1861) 149–50
Presbytery of Lews v *Fraser* (1874) 62–3
Presbytery of Relief (Relief Church) 21, 101, 121–3, 131–2
Presbytery of Strathbogie (1842) 40–5
Presbytery of Strathbogie and Rev. J. Cruickshank and Others, Suspenders (1839) 40–5, 50–2
President of the Methodist Conference v *Preston (alt. Moore)* (2013) 83
Principles of Geology 1833–8 (Lyell) 87
Pringle Trust, Petitioners (1946) 132
Privy Council 8–11
Privy Council Committee on Education for Scotland 145
Privy Council decree 1616 140
Promise *subsequente copula* 168, 171–3
Promissory Oaths Act 1868 198–9
Property rights 24–6, 70–1, 76, 119–33
Protestantism 178
Protestant Religion and Presbyterian Church Act 1706 2, 19, 91–2, 148, 199
Protestants 6–8, 100
Province of Jurisprudence Determined, The (Austin) 56
Public benefit 215–16
Public disorder 188
Public duties 216–18
Public Houses (Scotland) Act 1853 212
Public Houses Acts Amendment Act 1862 212
Public service broadcasting 189–91
Puritan influence 206
Putting Asunder, 1966 175

'Quaint punishments' 207
Quakers 103, 165, 202
Quakers Oaths Act 1695 201
Qualifications 11, 24, 27–8, 33–5, 36
Quasi-marital relationships 160
Quoad civilia 122
Quoad omnia 29–30, 63, 143, 213–4
Quoad sacra 47–50, 122

Racecourse Betting Act 1928 211
Race Relations Act 1976 181
Radcliff, H. 118
Radio 189–98
Radio Authority 193
Raikes, R. 25
Rankine, J. 66–7
Recissory Act 1661 16, 25
'Reel of Bogie' 44
Reform Acts (1832) 22, 53, 56
Reformation, in Scotland 5–21, 103, 135–7
Reformed Presbyterian Church of Scotland 122

Reformers 72, 88–9, 137, 140, 162, 171, 176–7, 205, 223–4
Reform of the Grounds of Divorce: The Field of Choice 175
Regency Act 1937 91–2, 199
Registrar General for Scotland 166, 172
Registrar of Companies 216
Registration of Births, and Marriages (Scotland) Act 1854 168
Registration of Births, Marriages and Deaths (Scotland) Act 1965 163, 168
Regular marriage 162–70
Reith, John, Lord 190–1, 195
Relationships, personal 158–77
Relief Church ('Presbytery of Relief') 21, 101, 121–3, 131–2
Religion: broadcasting and 191–8; constraints on 184–5; human rights legislation and 182–4, 226–7
Religious marriage 163–8
Religious prejudice 187–8
Religious schools 139–40
Remarriage 165
Representation (Scotland) Act (1832) 22, 53
Requirements of Writing Act 1995 200
Reserved matters 1, 181
Reserve Forces 219
Restoration of the monarchy 1660 16, 25
Restoration of the Roman Catholic hierarchy in Scotland 1878 103
Revised Code, education (1860) 143
Revolution 1688 17
Revolution Settlement 18
Right to die 222–3
Rights of the Child, Convention on (1989) 176, 179
Robertson, Lord 112, 126
Robinson, H. 185
Rodger, A. Lord 81
Roman Catholic Church 5–12, 100–3, 113, 135, 145–6, 151–6, 184–5, 205, 227
Roman Catholic Emancipation Act 1829 184
Roman Catholic Relief Act 1926 184
Ross, Lord 118
Row, J. 8
Royal Commission on Education in Scotland 1864–7 144
Royal Marriages Act 1772 184
Royal supremacy 16–17
Rutherford, S.: *Lex, Rex* (1644) 16

Sabbatarianism 202
Sabbath breaking 208
Sacraments 162
Sale of Liquor Act (Home-Drummond) 1828 212

Salmon and Freshwater Fisheries (Consolidation) (Scotland) Act 2003 210
SALP (Scottish Association with Limited Personality) 133
Salvation Army 103
Salvesen, Lord 107
Same-sex marriage 96, 158, 169–70, 227
Sang Schools 135, 149
Sasine Register 128
Sayers, D.: 'The Man Born to be King' 195
School boards 145–6, 151–2
Schools 139–40; *see also* Education
Scientology 104
SCIO (Scottish Charitable Incorporated Organisation) 133, 216
Scotch Education Department 145
Scotland Act 1998 1, 134, 180, 199, 225
Scotland's Future 2013 225
Scots Acts 20, 172, 205–7
Scots Confession 5–11, 15–16
Scottish Association with Limited Personality (SALP) 133
Scottish Benefices Act 1843 54–8
Scottish Charitable Incorporated Organisation (SCIO) 133, 216
Scottish Charities Register 214–5
Scottish Commissioners (Union negotiations) 19
Scottish Council of the Roman Catholic Church 205
Scottish Education Department 146, 152–3
Scottish Education Quality and Improvement Agency 156
Scottish Episcopal Church 102, 109–10
Scottish Episcopalians Act (the Toleration Act) 1710 102, 105–6
Scottish Episcopalians Act 1711 20, 25, 109, 205
Scottish Independence 225
Scottish Law Commission 216; *Divorce: The Grounds Considered* 175
Scottish Parliament 1, 7–9, 16, 181, 225–6
Scottish Society for the Propagation of Christian Knowledge 144
'Scottish solution' in education 139–40
Scottish Sunday 14, 202–13
Scotus, John Duns 6
Seceders 21, 120–1
Secession Church 105–6
Secessions 25, 48
Second Book of Discipline (Melville) 12, 15, 21, 24–5, 137
Secularism 2–3, 227
Self-Governing Schools etc. (Scotland) Act 1989 157
Separation 26, 170, 174–6
Separation *a mensa et thoro* 174
Seven-day cycle 203

1705 Acts 19
1706 Act of Security 19, 92
1706 Acts 19, 48, 63, 91–2, 148, 180, 199
1746 Acts 102
1748 Acts 102
Sex Discrimination Act 1975 81–2, 181
Sexual morality 14–15
Shand, Lord 126
Sharpe v *Worcester Diocesan Board of Finance Ltd* (2013–5) 83
Shorter Catechism, The 16
Sikhs 188
Single sovereign theory 20–1
1600 Acts 175
1633 Acts 140–1
1646 Acts 141
1649 Acts 25
1661 Acts 15–16, 25, 165, 210
1669 Acts 16–17
1690 Acts 17–20, 25, 148, 205, 208
1696 Acts 141
1698 Acts 165
Skerret and Murchison v *Scottish Football Union* (1896) 107
Skerret v *Oliver* (1896) 107, 112
Skinner, W. 109–10
Smith, Moderator of the General Assembly of the Free Church of Scotland, et al. v *Morrison, et al.* (2009) 75, 85, 88, 129–30; (2011) 75, 85, 88, 108, 129–31
Smith v *Galbraith* (1843) 114
Social and Moral Welfare Board of the Church of Scotland 175
Social welfare 13–14, 213–14
Social Work (Scotland) Act 1968 220
Society of Friends, Meetings 103
Society for the Propagation of Christian Knowledge 25–6
Solatium 161
Solemnisation of marriage 163
Solemn League and Covenant 1644 15, 17
Sound Broadcasting Act 1972 192
Sovereign's Oath 199
Sovereignty 16
Sperm donation 221–2
Spiritual injury 188
Spiritualist churches 104
Spottiswoode, J. 8
Sprenger, J. 187
Standards in Scotland's Schools Act 2000 154–6
State control, independence from 71–2, 75
Statute 1567/1579 9–10
Statute Law (Repeals) Act 1989 208
Statute Law Revision (Scotland) Acts 14, 207–8
Statute Law Revision (Scotland) Act 1964 213
Statute Law Revision (Scotland) Bill 1963 91

Statutory Declarations Act 1835 201
Stewarton case 47–55, 63
Stewart v *Presbytery of Paisley* (1878) 64–5
Stipends 76, 84
Stoddart, W. 58
St Paul's Chapel, Aberdeen 109–10
Strathbogie (Marnoch) cases 40–5, 50–7
Strath Free Church, *Strath/Sleat* 130–1
Sturrock, P. 58–62
Sturrock v *Greig* (1849) 58–62, 115–16
Substance of the Faith 87–91
Succession to the Crown Act 2013 184
Suicide Act 1961 223
Sumptuary laws 14
Sunday Closing Laws (Maryland) 204
Sunday observance 202–13
Sunday Observance Act 1833 208
Sunday Schools 25
Sunday Trading Act 1994 211
Sunday trains 206
Sunday Working (Scotland) Act 2003 211
Suppression of Betting Houses Act 1853 211
Supremacy 16–17, 22, 60
Surrogate motherhood 221–2
Sykes Committee (Broadcasting) 1923 190
Synod of Whitby 664 AD 4

Teinds 10–11, 29, 76
Television Act 1954 191–2, 196
Temperance 212–13
Temperance (Scotland) Act 1913 212
Temperance Societies 212
'The Ten Years' Conflict' 22, 46, 52, 123
Termination of medical treatment 222–3
Territorial Army 219
Tertullian 204
Test Acts 199
Theological Commission 2009–11 95–6
Theological Commission on Same-sex Relationships and the Ministry, Report (2013) 88
Third party property 122
Thirds of benefices 9
Thomson v *Anderson* (1887) 132
Thurso case 122
Titles of Religious Congregations Act 1850 106
Toleration Act 1710 102, 105–6
Trading, Sunday observance and 211
Traditional marriage 160–1
Transplants 222
Trayner, Lord 125–6
Treaty of Edinburgh 1559 7
Treaty of Union 1707 2, 19, 48, 74, 90, 92, 94
Tribunals 218–19
Tridentine Decree *de sacramento matrimonii* 1563 162, 171

Trust purposes 131–3
Trusts 215
Tübingen School 66
'Two Cities' (Augustine) 2

Uist, Lord 130–1
Ullswater Committee 1935 191, 195
Undue influence 188
Unincorporated voluntary associations 100–33
Union negotiations 18–20, 69–71
'Union of the Crowns' 1
Union of the Parliaments 1707 1–2, 14–15, 141, 178
United College of St Leonard's and St Salvator's 138
United Free Church Act I 1906 71–3
United Free Church Declaratory Act anent the Spiritual Independence of the Church 1906 Act I 127–8
United Free Church of Scotland 21, 68–74, 97, 101–2, 106, 123–31
United Kingdom 15, 179–84, 226–7
United Nations 178–81
United Original Seceders 133
United Presbyterian Church 21, 68–71, 101, 106–7, 123–31
United Reformed Church 100
United Secession Church 21, 121–3
United States Supreme Court 93, 204
Universal Declaration of Human Rights 1948 178–81
Universities 137–9; *see also* Education
Universities (Scotland) Acts 138–9
University of Aberdeen 14, 137–8
University of Edinburgh 137
University of Glasgow 14, 137–8
University of St Andrews 6, 14, 137–8
Unlawful Societies Act 1799 199
Unreasonable behaviour, divorce and 176

Veto Act (1834) 23–31
Veto Act cases 32–46, 50–2, 55–8
Veto Poll 212

Violation of sepulchers 224
Voluntaries 26, 71, 123

Wallace v *The Ferguson Bequest Fund* (1879) 122
Warren, E. 204
Welfare 13–14, 213–14
Wellwood, Lord 66
Welsh, D. 56
Wesleys 25
Western Island Council 209
Westminster Assembly 1643–53 16
Westminster Confession of Faith 16–18, 21, 63, 66–9, 73–4, 87–94, 101, 125–6, 138, 148–50, 161–2, 205, 208
Westminster Parliament 1–2, 16, 20, 92–3, 225
West v *Secretary of State for Scotland* (1992) 80
Whitfield, G. 25
Wicca 187
Widowhood 169
Widow's Fund 46
Wight v *Presbytery of Dunkeld* (1970) 61–2
Wigtownshire 77
Wilberforce, W. 26
William III of England 17–19
Willock, J. 8
Wilson v *Jobson* (1771) 106
Wilson v *Presbytery of Stranraer,* (1842) 47, 51
Wilson v *Simson* (1844) 206
Winram, J. 8
Wireless Telegraphy Act 1949 189
Wishart, G. 6
Witchcraft 186–7
Witchcraft Act 187
Women, divorce and 175
Wood, Lord 52

Young, Lord 65–6, 125–7
Young, R. 32–8, 51
Young v *MacAlister* (1902) 124
Yule Vacance Act 1711 20